IMAGES
of America

Floyd Ingraham's Springwater
A Finger Lakes Hamlet

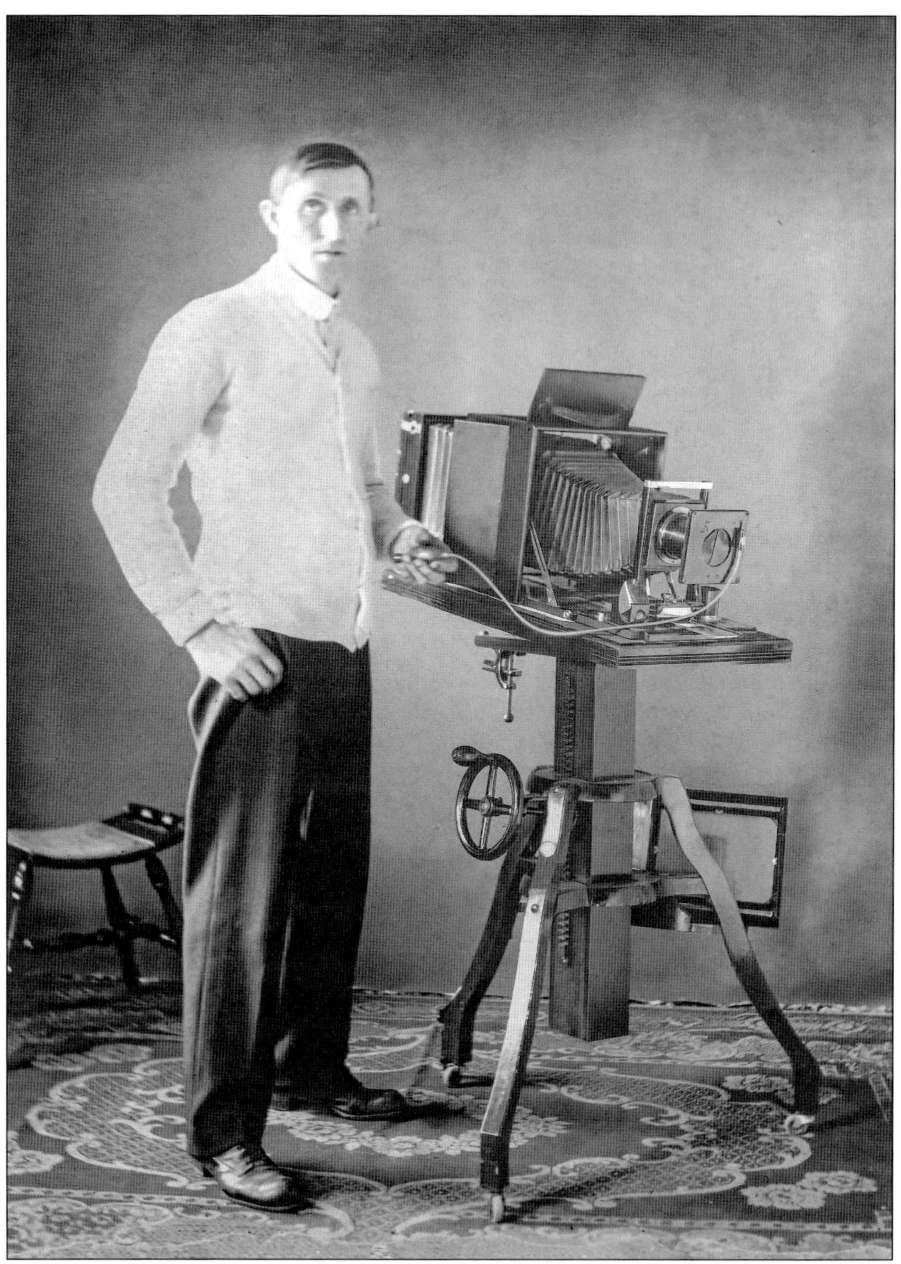

Photographer Floyd Ingraham took this self-portrait in his home studio in Springwater, New York. The camera is believed to be an early-1900s Long Focus Wide Angle Wizard studio camera made by the Manhattan Optical Company. Hundreds of Ingraham's glass negatives and photographs have survived. Some are featured in this book. (Courtesy of Ron and Sharon Ingraham.)

On the Cover: The songs would have been lively around the campfire at this 1908 Canadice Lake campsite. The edge of a cot and a table with an oil lamp can be seen inside the tent. At far left is Floyd Ingraham with his banjo. Next to him is Veda McClellan with what appears to be Floyd's fiddle. Seated to the right of Veda is Gertrude Ford with a guitar. At far right is Gertrude's brother Leon. (Courtesy of Paul Holbrook.)

IMAGES
of America

Floyd Ingraham's Springwater
A Finger Lakes Hamlet

Julie Jeffery Manwarren
Photograph Contributions by Paul Holbrook

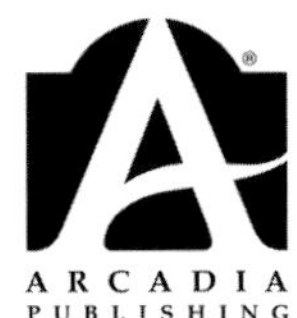

ISBN 978-1-4671-0689-4

Published by Arcadia Publishing
Charleston, South Carolina

Printed in the United States of America

Library of Congress Control Number: 2021935305

For all general information, please contact Arcadia Publishing:
Telephone 843-853-2070
Fax 843-853-0044
E-mail sales@arcadiapublishing.com
For customer service and orders:
Toll-Free 1-888-313-2665

Visit us on the Internet at www.arcadiapublishing.com

To the Ingraham family and the memory of Floyd Ingraham, whose gift and photographic legacy have preserved Springwater and its people as he knew it.

Contents

Acknowledgments

This book was born out of a partnership and friendship with Paul Holbrook. I am deeply grateful for his contributions, attention to detail, and guidance. His work in the preservation of early-20th-century photography is invaluable.

Thank you to Ron and Sharon Ingraham for their contributions to this book along with the kindness and hospitality they showed on my many visits to Springwater.

I am also greatly indebted to Carol King, her writing class, and the writing friends I have made over the years. To Bob Gelik, Josette Abruzzini, Sarah Phillips, Liz Baumeister, and so many others—you have made me a better writer. Thank you to my friends and family. I am so thankful for your love, support, and prayers as I tackled this project in a pandemic. Thank you to my father, John T. Jeffery, and to Valerie Manwarren for hours of help.

Paul and I would both like to thank our spouses, Jeannette Holbrook and Phil Manwarren, and our children, for their love and support. You allowed us the time and space to pursue this project, and we are so grateful.

Thank you to the Springwater–Webster Crossing Historical Society for research assistance and photographic contributions. Thank you specifically to Donna Walker, Douglas Morgan, Joyce O'Neil, Rick Osiecki, and Mark and Linda Hopkins for help and contributions to this book and the kindness and hospitality you have shown. Thank you to Amie Alden and Holly Walton of the Livingston County Historian's Office, members of the Wayland Historical Society, Lore DiSalvo, Jane Schryver, Pam Lansky, Michel Knight, and others for research help and contributions.

Unless otherwise noted, all photographs are believed to have been taken by Floyd Ingraham and appear courtesy of Paul Holbrook as part of his private collection.

INTRODUCTION

In the first two years of the 20th century, an amateur photographer picked up his camera to take pictures of the people and places he knew and loved. In the two decades that followed, Floyd Ingraham took hundreds of images in and around his hometown of Springwater, New York. In doing so, he preserved forever a people and a place representative of small, rural communities in the early 1900s.

Ingraham's glass negatives were stored in an old shed and remained there for decades until they were sold in the 1970s. When the collection resurfaced in 2019, Paul Holbrook purchased hundreds of the Ingraham glass plates on eBay. A collector and restorer of vintage negatives, Holbrook removed 100 years of dirt and damage to return the images to their original appearance. Holbrook reached out to Julie Manwarren, a writer and historical researcher, and they began a project that developed into this book.

Ingraham's hometown and lifetime residence, the small agricultural village of Springwater, along with the communities of the western Finger Lakes region provided the setting for his pictorial legacy. The township of Springwater is in Livingston County, south of Hemlock and Canadice Lakes, on New York State Routes 15 and 15A.

The first mapping of western New York and the Finger Lakes was done by the French. Jesuits traveled the area with fur traders during the mid-1600s, recording lakes, streams, and inlets and detailing the number of longhouses of the Haudenosaunee. The Native American Seneca people hunted, fished, and inhabited the land around the western Finger Lakes up until the late 18th century. In 1779, many were driven out by Gen. John Sullivan and relocated to reservations.

Seth Knowles is recognized as being the first non-native settler in the area now known as the town of Springwater. Knowles had come from Massachusetts to Pittstown (now Livonia), New York, in 1805. In 1806, he, his son Jared, and brother-in-law Peter Welsh followed an old Native American trail over Bald Hill to the Hemlock Valley. He cleared land and built a log cabin about a mile from the head of Hemlock Lake. Knowles left to retrieve his family, later transporting them and their possessions on a sleigh across the ice of Hemlock Lake. Other early settlers were Eber Watkins, Joshua Herrick, Adam Miller, and Hosea Grover. Grover built the first store in the village of Springwater. Samuel Story built the first frame house and sawmill in the area. In the first half of the 19th century, Springwater grew to include a blacksmith shop, distillery, numerous mills, churches, and schools. Descendants of these first settlers still live in the area today.

The first school was a log cabin built in 1810–1811 on the corner of what is currently Kellogg Road and Main Street. The school was torn down in 1815 by John Wiley, who built a house on the site, later the location of the Higgins residence. A new one-room schoolhouse was constructed in 1813–1814 close to the current intersection of Routes 15 and 15A, known as the four corners. This schoolhouse was the site of the first town meeting and election of officers in 1817. The oldest church in Springwater was the Congregational Church, organized on February 10, 1821, with 12 members.

On April 17, 1816, the New York state legislature passed an act that became effective in April 1817 to create the township of Springwater from parts of the towns of Naples and Sparta. Originally part of Ontario County, Springwater later became part of Livingston County when that county was formed in 1821. John Roberts, an early settler, suggested the name "Springwater." According to Orson Walbridge in his book *An Early History of the Town of Springwater, Livingston County, NY*, Roberts did so because he had "never before seen a place where the springs were so numerous." The fresh and abundant water supply continues to benefit the people of Springwater to this day.

A fire in 1883 destroyed the community records kept at the town hall. The loss of the records inspired Walbridge to write and publish his history. This resource preserved many of the facts of Springwater's early history and chronicled its early settlement. Walbridge's work includes stories of Native American inhabitants in the area, local wildlife, and how the first residents interacted with the land and the lakes around them. His history gives a backdrop to Floyd Ingraham's Springwater.

Ingraham's ancestors settled in Springwater by the mid-1800s. From the last half of the 19th century to the early part of the 20th century, the people of Springwater saw the arrival of the railroad, automobiles, and advances in agriculture and industry. They welcomed electricity, telephone lines, and indoor plumbing into their homes. Springwater grew and became a thriving community. Hemlock and Canadice Lakes drew visitors to the area. Roads and highways provided infrastructure and opened connections between the small hamlets and villages that surrounded the lakes.

Born and raised in Springwater, Floyd Ingraham entered adulthood in a town that boasted a population of more than 2,000. He chronicled his time and place in hundreds of photographs before he died at the age of 38 in 1920. In the first decade after his death, the town continued to grow. The Cannon Miller Radio Factory, Miller Fishing Lures, and the nearby Gunlocke Chair Factory provided jobs after World War I.

After an outbreak of waterborne illness, the city of Rochester, New York, began using Hemlock and Canadice Lakes in 1876 as a source of clean water for its growing population. As the city purchased land around the lakes to protect water quality, cottages and other buildings were torn down or moved beginning in 1895. Future development was prohibited. Without the tourism industry provided by the lakes, growth in nearby communities slowed. A benefit is that much has been preserved. Some houses and buildings remain from Floyd Ingraham's day. The preservation of land and lake acreage has maintained a natural habitat for wildlife and created enjoyable places to hike or kayak for nature lovers. In 2010, the state purchased the lakes and surrounding land from the City of Rochester to create the 6,849-acre Hemlock-Canadice State Forest.

Descendants of Floyd Ingraham and the individuals in his pictures are still residing in Springwater and nearby Finger Lakes communities. The spirit of Floyd Ingraham's Springwater lives on. Hardworking and resilient, the people of New York's Finger Lakes region value their present way of life as much as they do their rich history.

Floyd Ingraham's photographs have survived for over a century. Discovering clues in the images, tracing available history, and gathering evidence from the Ingraham family and members of the Springwater–Webster Crossing Historical Society has led to the identification of many of the people and places in Ingraham's photographs. The stories behind the images can now be told.

One

THE PHOTOGRAPHER

Floyd George Ingraham was born October 14, 1881, in Springwater. He was the son of Marchus and Nettie (Ford) Ingraham.

Ingraham began photographing the people and scenes of Springwater by the turn of the 20th century. One of Ingraham's earliest identified images is of his brother Otto around 1900. He took a picture of local doctor Hubert Knickerbocker in 1901, and news of his photography business was published in the *Cohocton Valley Times and Index* in 1902. Ingraham's images of the people and scenes of Springwater were taken in the two decades that followed.

Ingraham was a jack-of-all-trades. He was a farmer, stone mason, interior painter, plasterer, and wall paperer. He married Anna Cork in 1909, and the couple had one son, Kenneth.

Ingraham owned a Reko folding box camera and an early 20th century Wizard studio camera. He also purchased the contents of a photography studio in 1915. Even though glass plate negatives were not cheap at the time, hundreds of Ingraham's have survived and been restored. In them he captured the beautiful landscape of his community. A patchwork of farmland rolled and rose beneath Ingraham like a rumpled quilt as he stood with his camera high above the hamlet on Springwater's hills.

Ingraham's scenic views are easily recognizable, as many became real-photo postcards. His wonderful pictorial record of his hometown has preserved the historical connection of homes and businesses still standing in Springwater and surrounding communities.

Family and individual portraits were taken outdoors and in his home studio. His stool and wicker chairs are recognizable in many of those portraits, and his subjects often held a copy of *Studio Light* magazine, a Kodak publication.

Ingraham died on January 22, 1920, after surgery for a burst appendix. He is buried in Mount Vernon Evergreen Cemetery in Springwater. He left behind his wife, Anna; son Kenneth; and a rich photographic legacy. This remains a timeless gift to the town of Springwater and the Finger Lakes region.

While he was not the only Springwater photographer in his day, Ingraham truly captured the spirit of the region and its people. His photographs offer a view of daily life in the early 20th century and preserved a time and place typical of small agricultural communities across America.

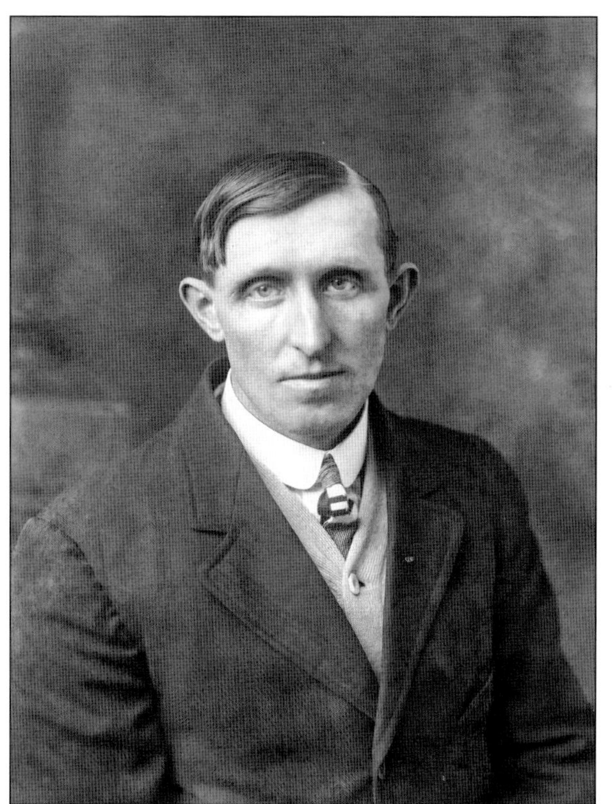

Floyd George Ingraham was born on October 14, 1881, in Springwater. The oldest son of Marchus and Nettie (Ford) Ingraham, Floyd learned masonry and wallpapering from his father. He began taking pictures sometime around the turn of the 20th century, continuing until his death in 1920.

The Ingraham home on Main Street in Springwater was built before 1872. In 1892, Marchus Ingraham purchased the house once owned by Dr. Arnold Gray. The property included fields on the hill behind it. At far left is a woman believed to be Amanda Ingraham, Marchus's mother. Others are, from left to right, Floyd, Otto, Nettie, and Marchus Ingraham. The house remains standing where Kellogg Road meets Main Street. The photographer for this image is unidentified. (Courtesy of Ron and Sharon Ingraham.)

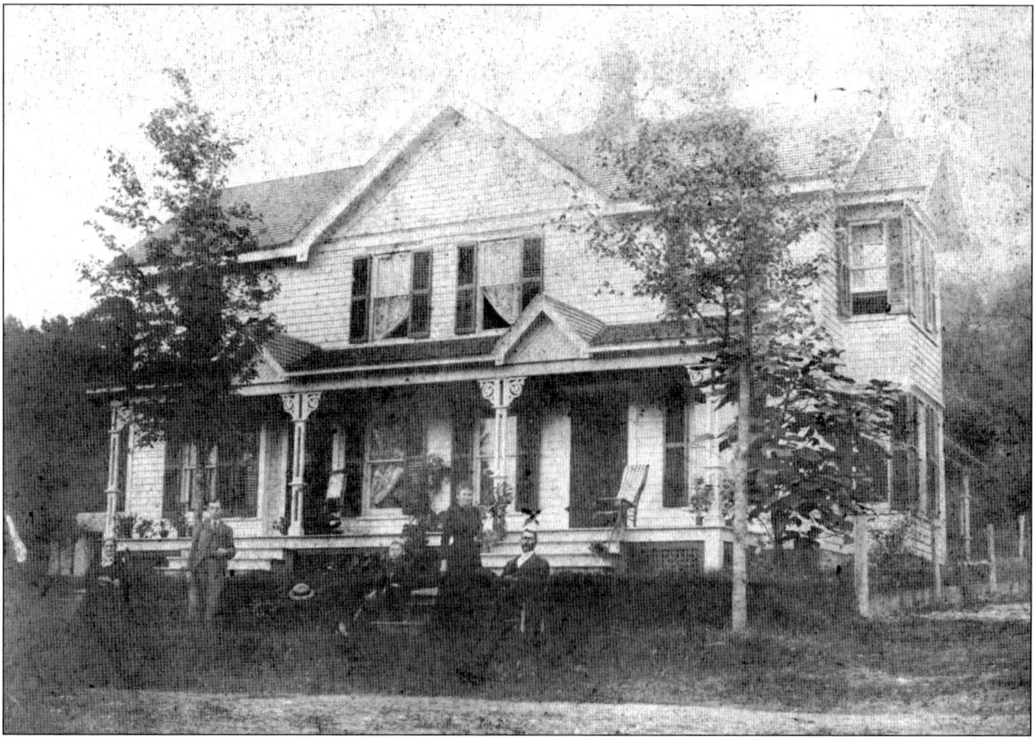

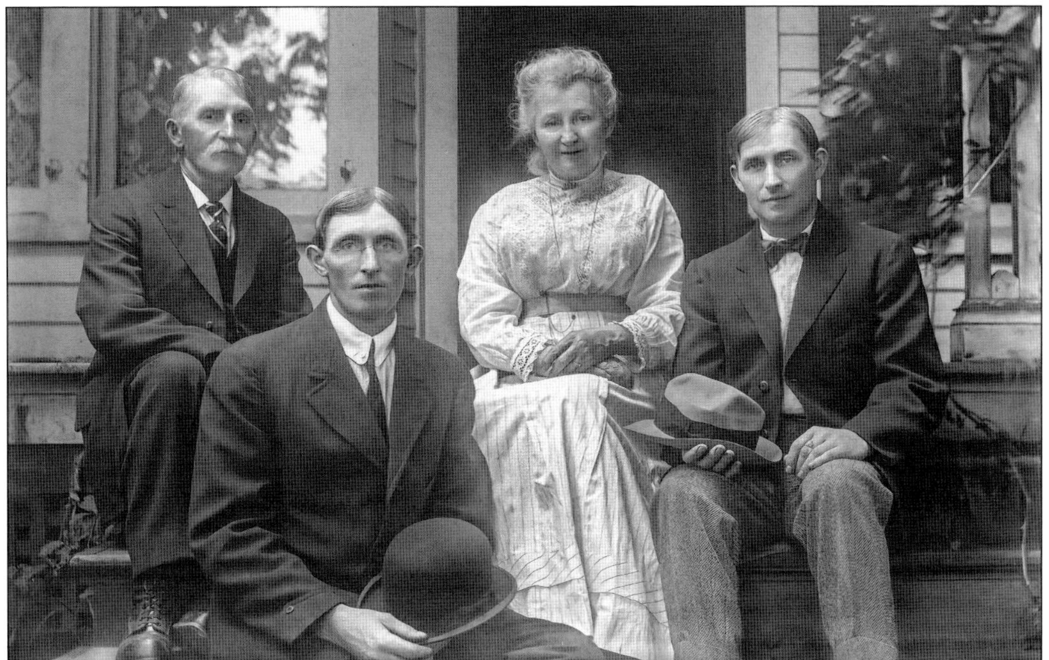

Nettie and Marchus Ingraham are seated on the porch of their home with their sons Floyd (left) and Otto. The Ingraham family also had a farm in Springwater and worked as masons, building chimneys, walls, and foundations in their community. Marchus Ingraham and Annette "Nettie" Ford were married in Springwater in 1877. Marchus was the son of Hiram and Amanda (Jackman) Ingraham. Nettie was the daughter of John and Louisa (Lyon) Ford.

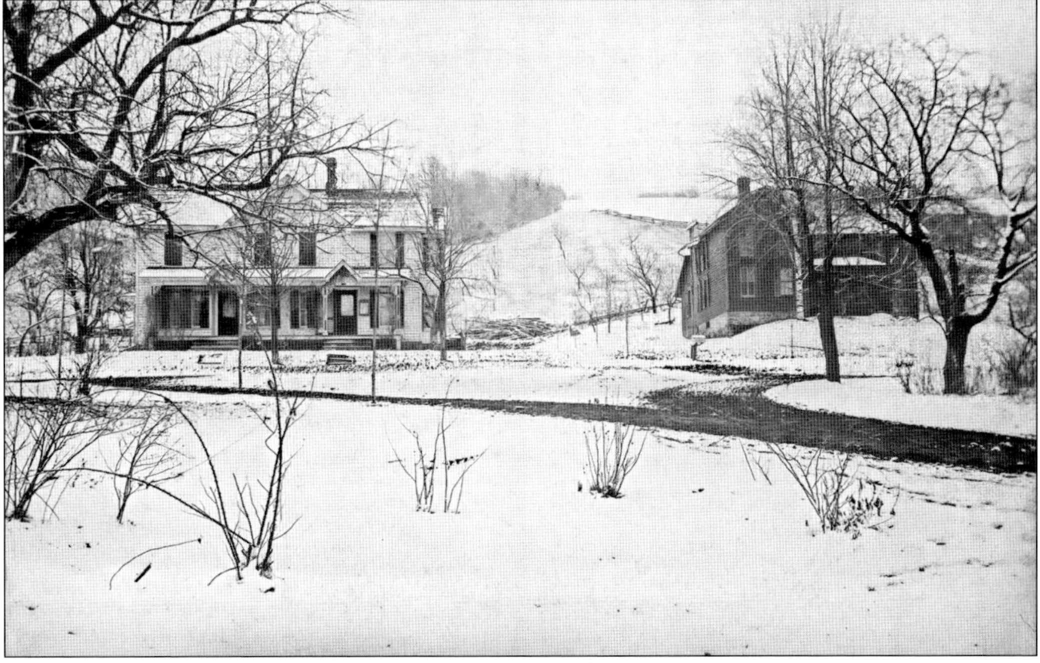

This view of the Ingraham home also shows a house on the right that would later become the home of Kenneth Ingraham, Floyd's son. Kenneth lived there with his wife, Margaret, until his death.

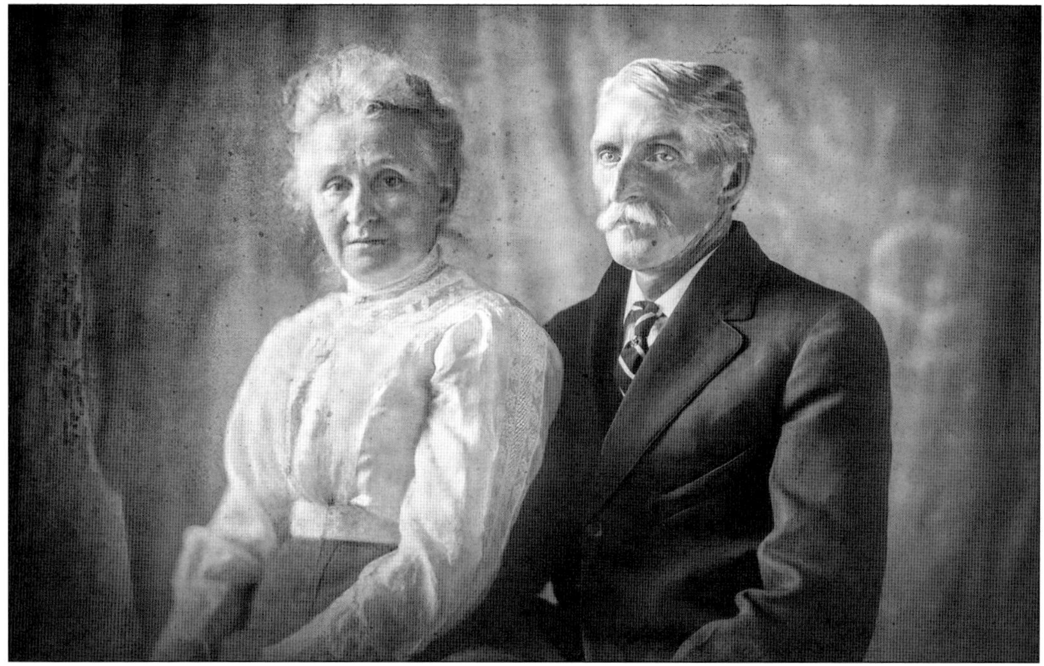

Marchus and Nettie (Ford) Ingraham's community activity included membership in several volunteer organizations. They served as president and vice president, respectively, of the Springwater National Protective Legion. Marchus was a member of the Independent Order of Odd Fellows (IOOF), and Nettie was a member of the Daughters of Rebekah, a unit of IOOF. The Ingrahams were members of the Advent church in Springwater.

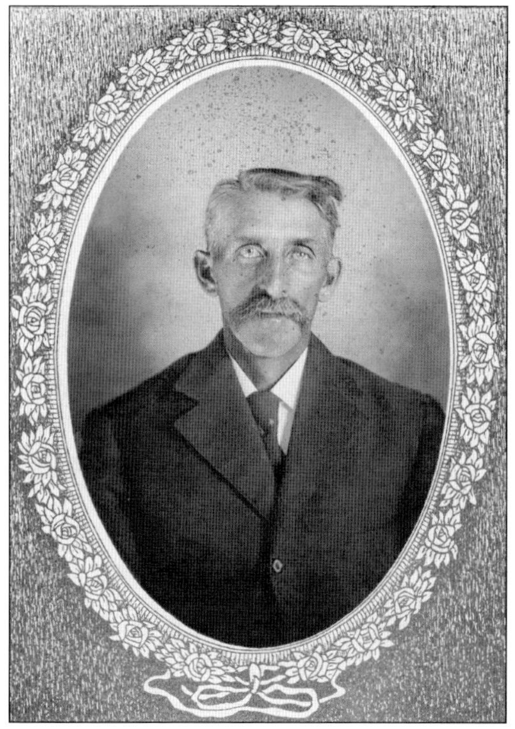

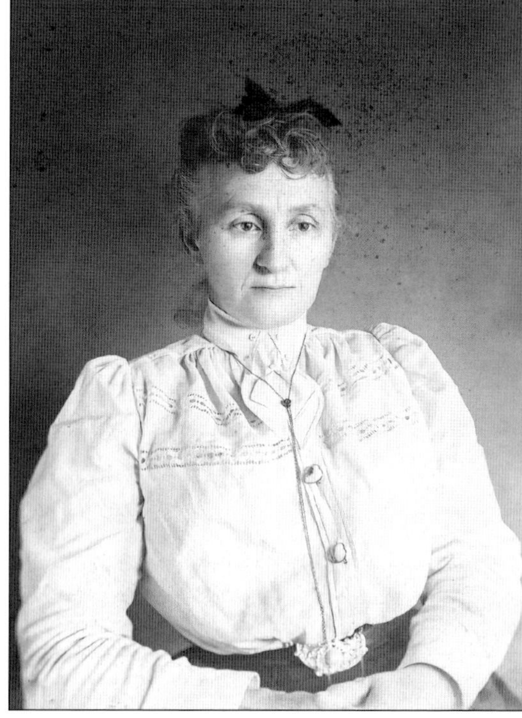

Floyd Ingraham's mother, Nettie Ford, was born in April 1856 to John and Louisa (Lyon) Ford in Springwater. She was close to her only brother, Melvin Ford. Nettie was active in the Advent church and in her volunteer work with the Daughters of Rebekah and the Springwater National Protective Legion. She suffered a series of strokes later in life. She died in 1931 and is buried in Mount Vernon Evergreen Cemetery. (Courtesy of Ron and Sharon Ingraham.)

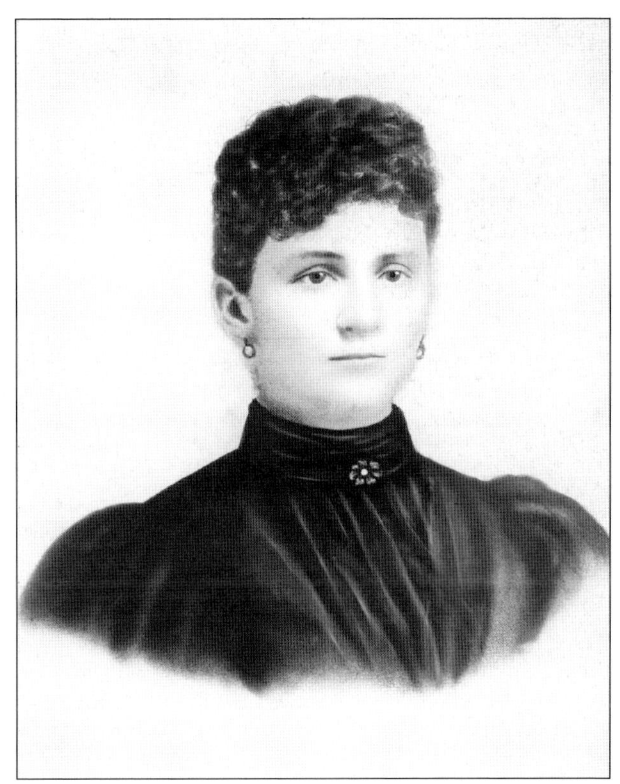

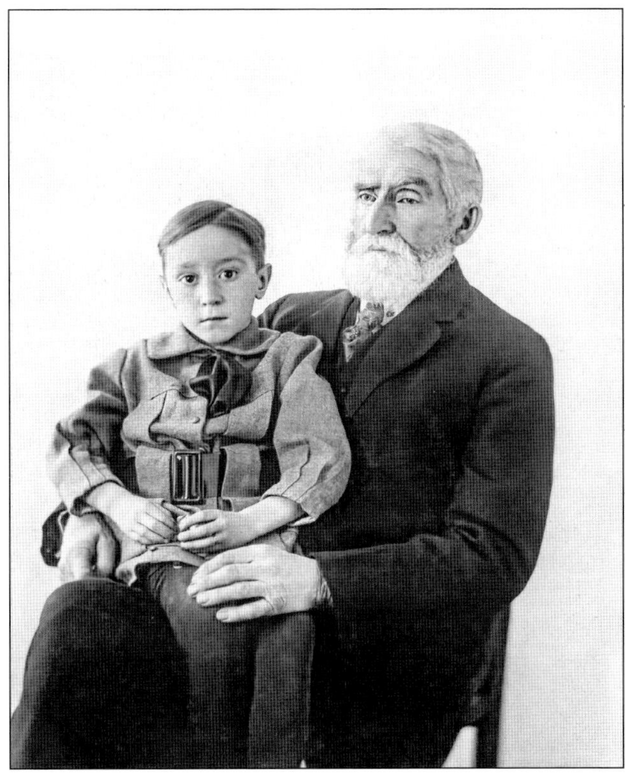

Floyd's father, Marchus Ingraham, is seen here with his grandson Kenneth Ingraham. Marchus was born to Hiram and Amanda (Jackman) Ingraham on August 8, 1855, in Springwater. They moved to Canadice when Marchus was a child. He returned to Springwater as an adult. He worked as a farmer, beekeeper, stone mason, carpenter, and rural mail carrier. Marchus was one of three original mail carriers when the postal route was first established in Springwater in 1903. He died in 1942 and is buried in Mount Vernon Evergreen Cemetery. (Courtesy of Ron and Sharon Ingraham.)

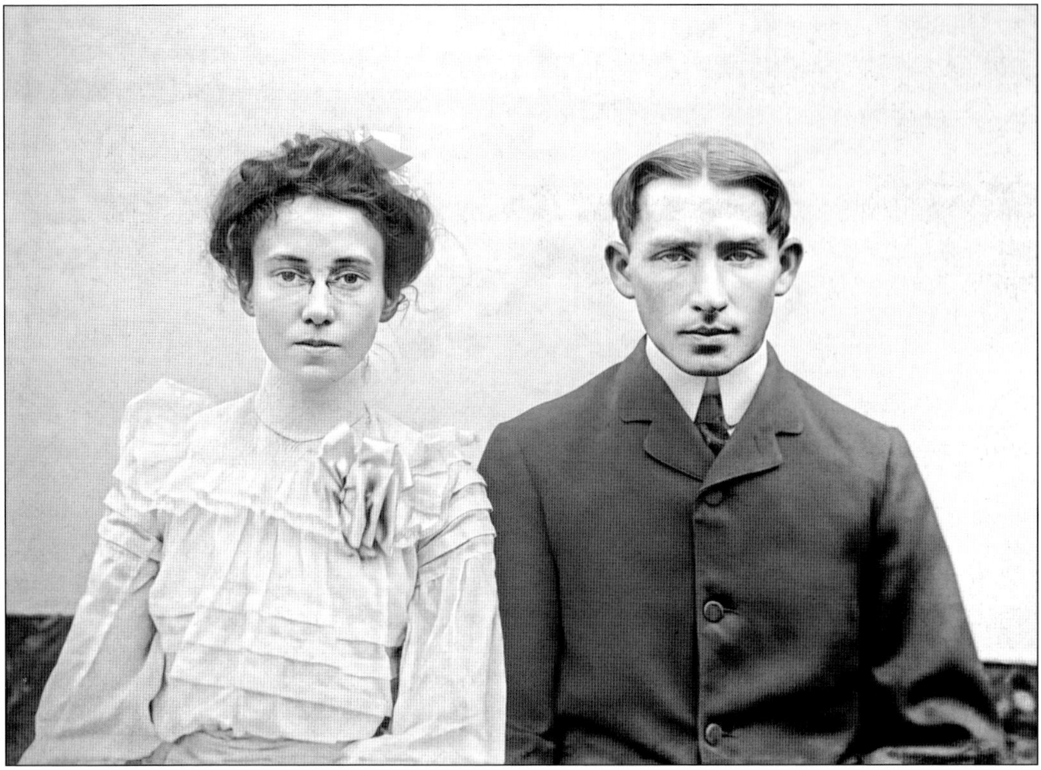

Floyd Ingraham's only sibling, Otto Hiram Ingraham, married Blanche Batterson on August 13, 1903. The couple had one son, Carl Otto Ingraham, and resided in Wayland, New York. They moved to Buffalo, New York, where Otto worked as a chauffeur. After Floyd's death in 1920, they returned to Springwater.

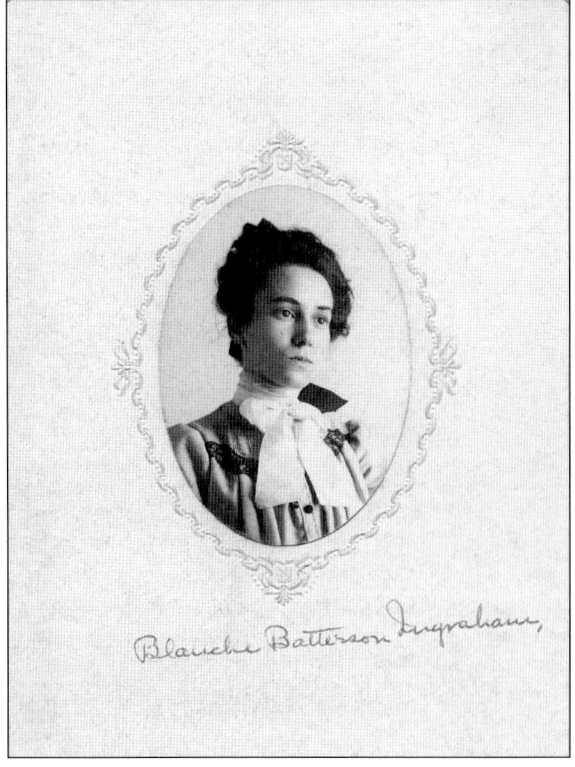

Blanche (Batterson) Ingraham was born on September 5, 1884, to Arthur and Margaret (Long) Batterson. She had two brothers and one sister and grew up in Springwater. Her mother died in 1900 when Blanche was 16 years old. Blanche lost her only son, Carl, in 1907. After Otto's death in 1922 left her a widow at the age of 37, she returned to Buffalo, where she managed a boardinghouse. (Courtesy of Ron and Sharon Ingraham.)

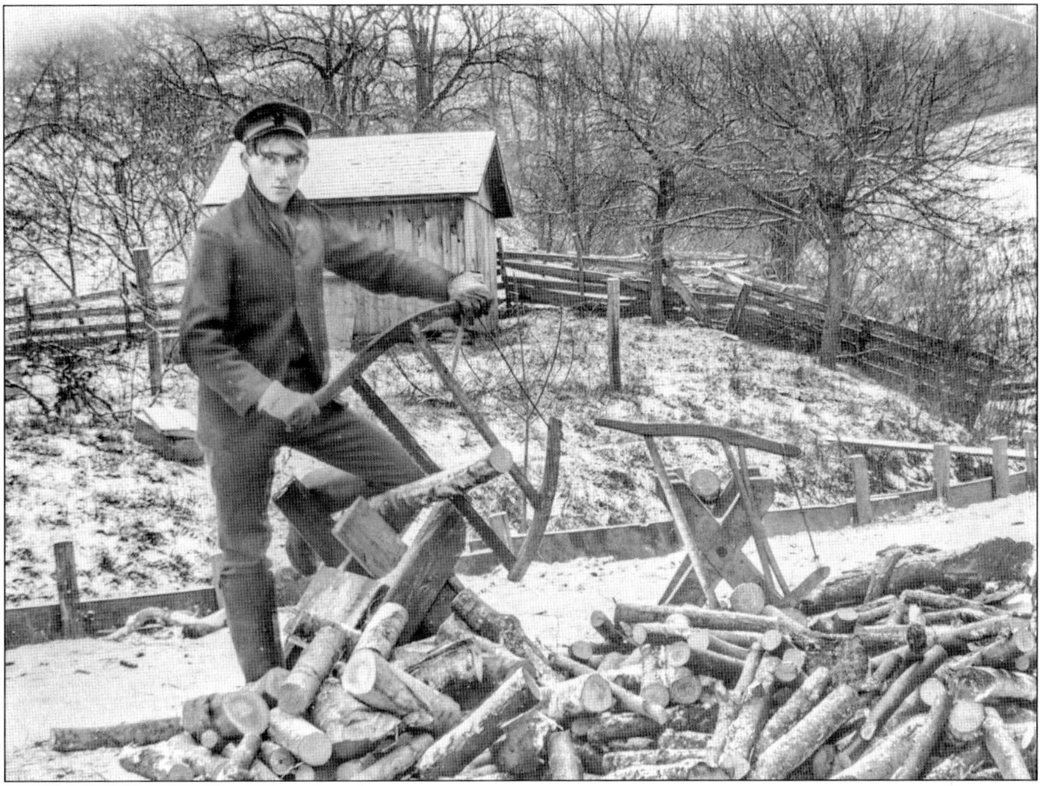

Otto Hiram Ingraham was born on April 11, 1883, to Marchus and Nettie Ingraham. He worked on the family farm, then for J.M. Miller of Wayland. Later, he worked as a chauffeur for a wealthy Buffalo family, the Pierce Arrow Auto Company, and finally for the Cannon Miller Radio Factory in Springwater. This photograph of Otto at the wood pile is believed to be one of Floyd Ingraham's earliest photographs, taken around 1900. (Courtesy of Ron and Sharon Ingraham.)

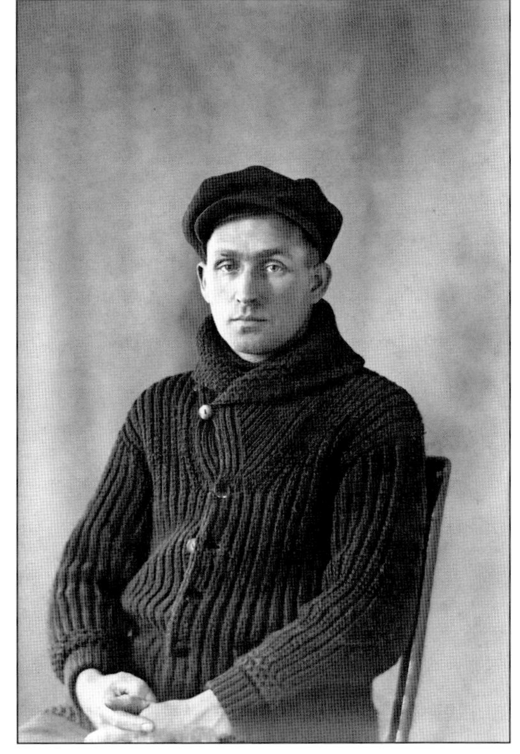

Otto Ingraham, the only brother of Floyd Ingraham, died on April 26, 1922, at the age of 39. While operating a large press machine at the Cannon Miller Radio Factory in Springwater, he lost the first finger of his right hand. He died a week later from a blood infection at the hospital in Dansville, New York. He is buried in Mount Vernon Evergreen Cemetery.

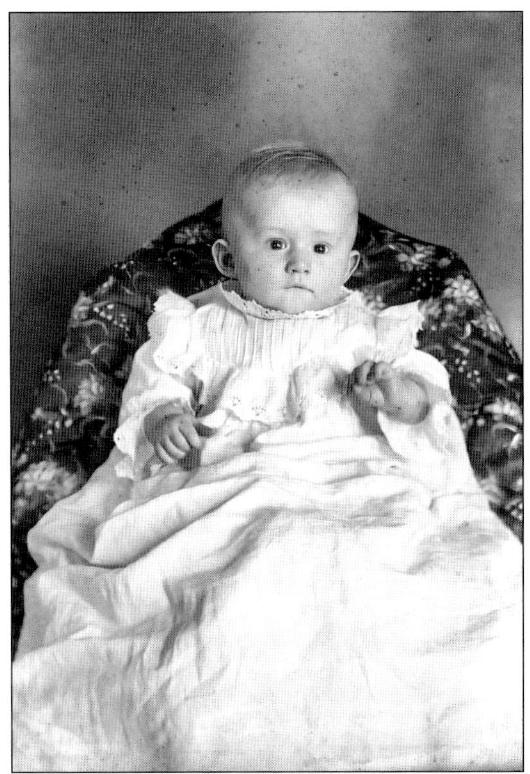

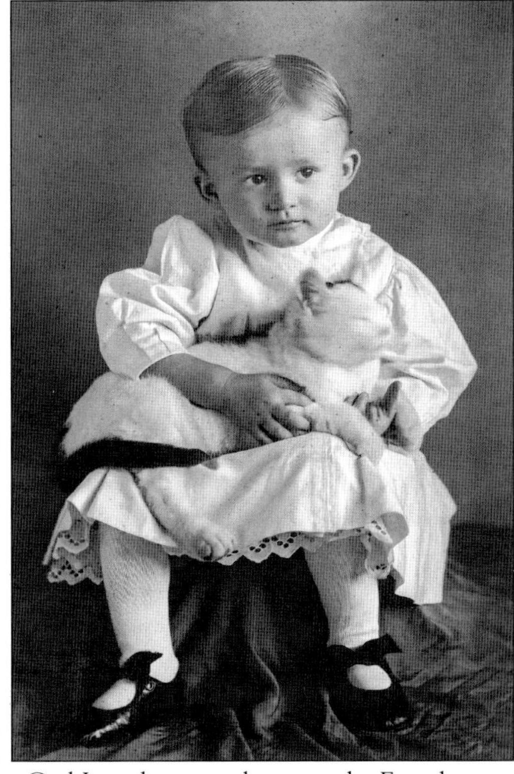

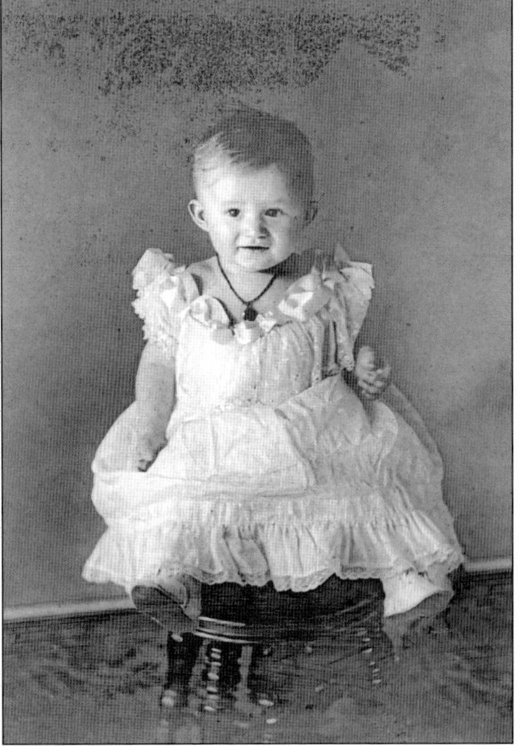

Carl Ingraham was born on the Fourth of July in 1904. The only son of Otto and Blanche Ingraham, Carl was the first grandson of Marchus and Nettie (Ford) Ingraham. Floyd Ingraham produced many photographs of his nephew from birth to age three. Babies, even boys, wore dresses for the first couple years of their life until they were out of diapers. Then little boys wore breeches, which were knee-length trousers.

Carl Ingraham died on October 27, 1907, at age three of what his obituary referred to as "enteritis," which is a gastrointestinal virus. He was only sick for a few days. Watched over by his parents and grandparents, everything medically available at the time was done to save the toddler's life. He is pictured here with his mother, Blanche (Batterson) Ingraham.

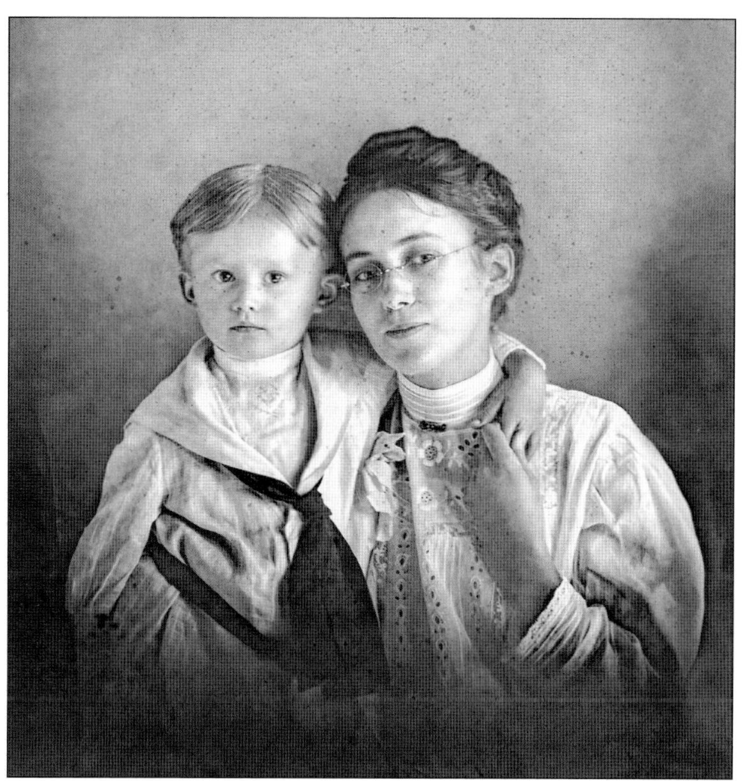

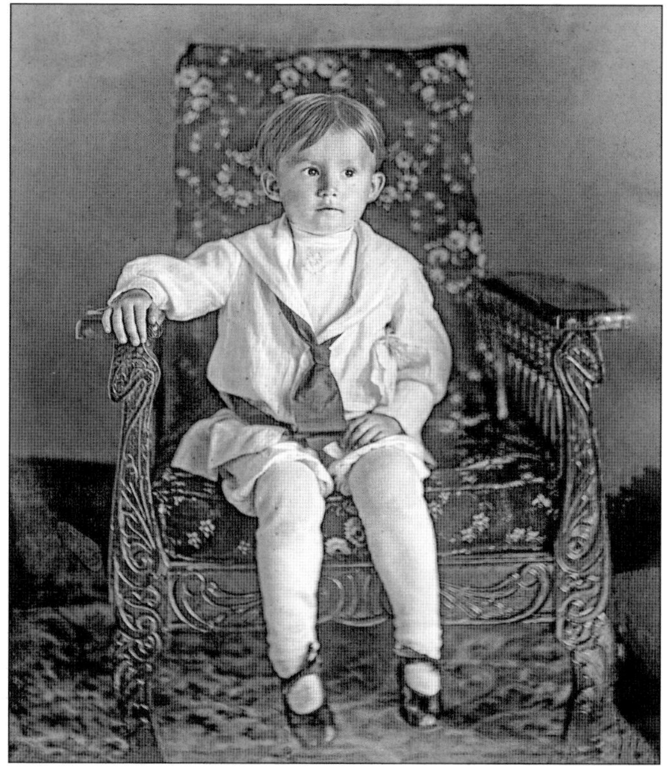

Carl Ingraham's obituary in the *Cohocton Daily Times* read, "Little Carl was an unusually bright child and was beloved by everyone who knew him. His parents and grandparents to whom he was bound by the tenderest ties, have the sincere sympathy of this community in their sad bereavement." Carl Ingraham was buried in Mount Vernon Evergreen Cemetery.

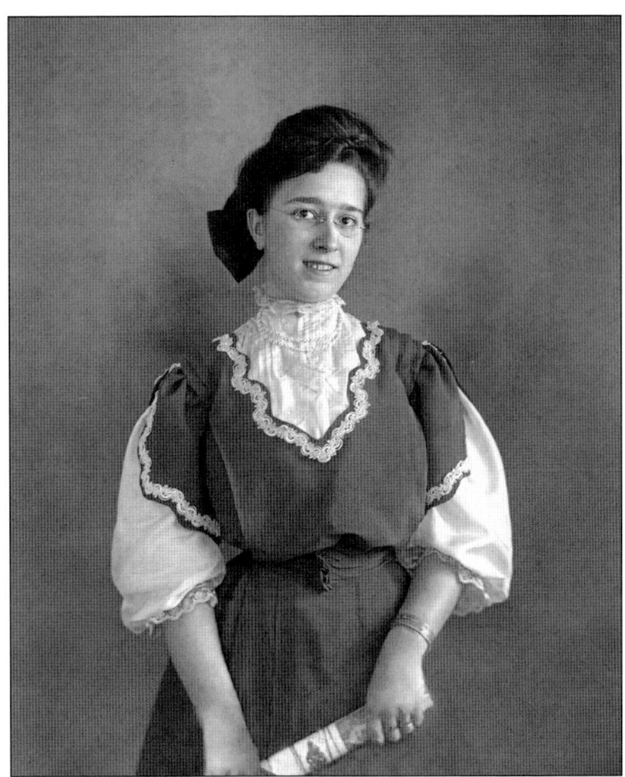

Anna Elisabeth Cork was born in Cohocton, New York, on January 22, 1891, to Joseph and Luthera (Loveland) Cork. By 1900, the family had moved to Springwater, where Anna attended the Union School. The first report of Anna and Floyd Ingraham knowing each other is in 1904 when Anna visited his family. This photograph was taken in 1907, when Anna was 16.

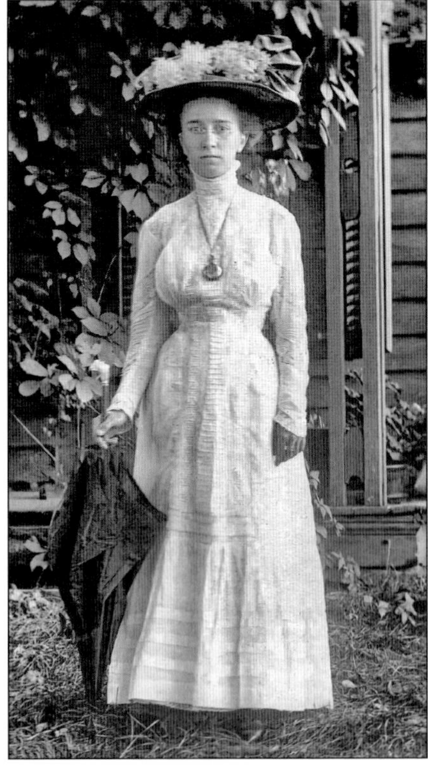

The daughter of Joseph and Luthera (Loveland) Cork, Anna lost her parents before the age of 23. She made her own clothing, including her wedding dress, which she is pictured in here. Floyd Ingraham and Anna Cork were married by Rev. Walter Dailey on September 1, 1909, at the home of Anna's parents, Joseph and Luthera Cork. They lived with the Corks during the early years of their marriage. Later, they moved into Ingraham's parents' home on Main Street in Springwater. Anna would go on to outlive everyone she knew and loved in her youth. She died on July 16, 1981, at the age of 90. She is buried in Evergreen Cemetery on Reynolds Gull Road in Springwater. (Courtesy of Ron and Sharon Ingraham.)

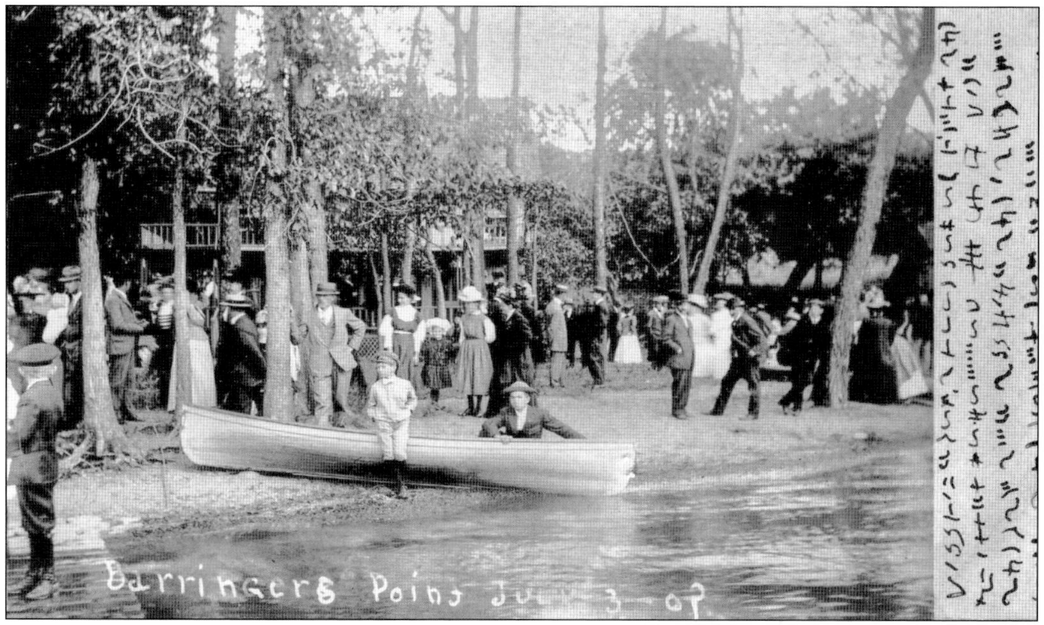

By 1901, Floyd Ingraham was taking pictures of local residents and scenic views that he sold as real-photo postcards, like the one seen here of the Advent church picnic at Barringer Point on Canadice Lake. Ingraham was established as a first-class photographer by 1902. He hosted exhibits and sold his work locally. He purchased a studio from H. Skinner of Wayland in 1915. He charged $1 to $2 for pictures and $1 for a dozen postcards. (Courtesy of Ron and Sharon Ingraham.)

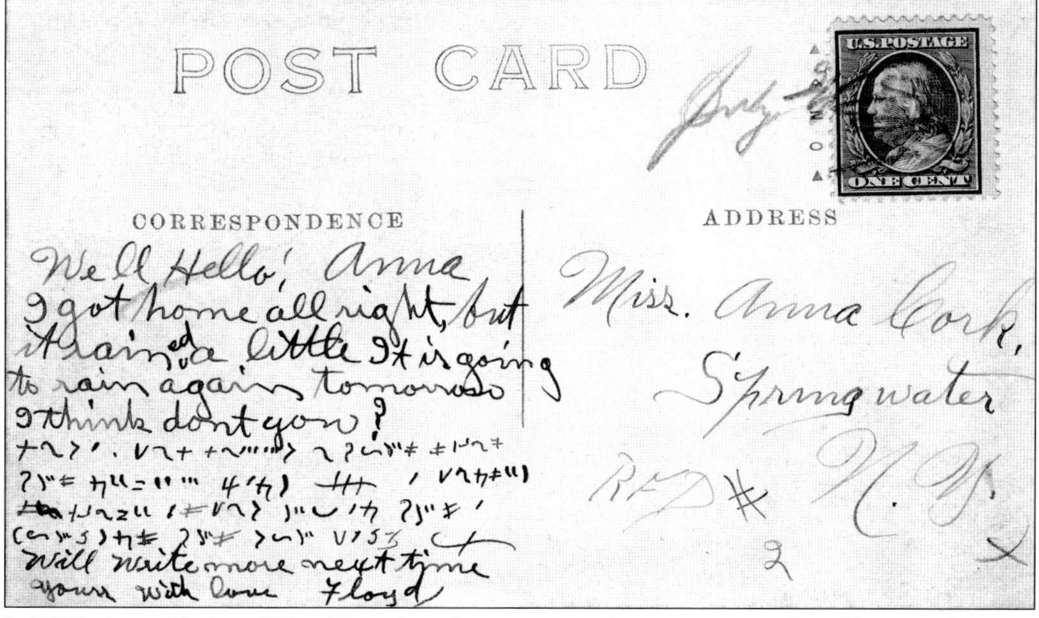
POST CARD

U.S. POSTAGE
ONE CENT

CORRESPONDENCE

Well Hello! Anna
I got home all right, but
it rained a little It is going
to rain again tomorrow
I think don't you?

Will write more next time
yours with love Floyd

ADDRESS

Miss. Anna Cork,
Springwater
N.Y.
RFD # 2

In 1908, Anna Cork and Floyd Ingraham began to spend more time together. She was a frequent guest in the Ingraham home. During their courtship, they called on friends and family, attended dances and house parties, and enjoyed time at the lakes. Ingraham sent her some of his picture postcards during their courtship, as seen here and above. His message included shorthand that has yet to be deciphered. (Courtesy of Ron and Sharon Ingraham.)

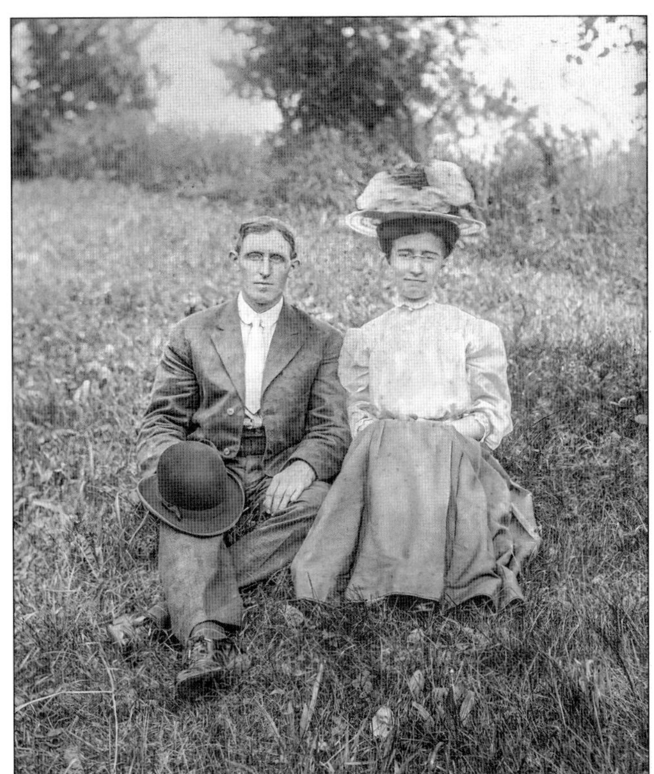

Anna and Floyd Ingraham's married life also consisted of much work. Many days were filled with harvesting what was grown on the Cork and Ingraham farms. They grew beans, potatoes, tomatoes, and a variety of vegetables. The family had a large berry patch and fruit trees. Anna canned and pickled fruit and vegetables to last the winter. When Floyd was not taking pictures or up on the thrasher harvesting in the fields of Springwater, he was working as a hired hand in the community.

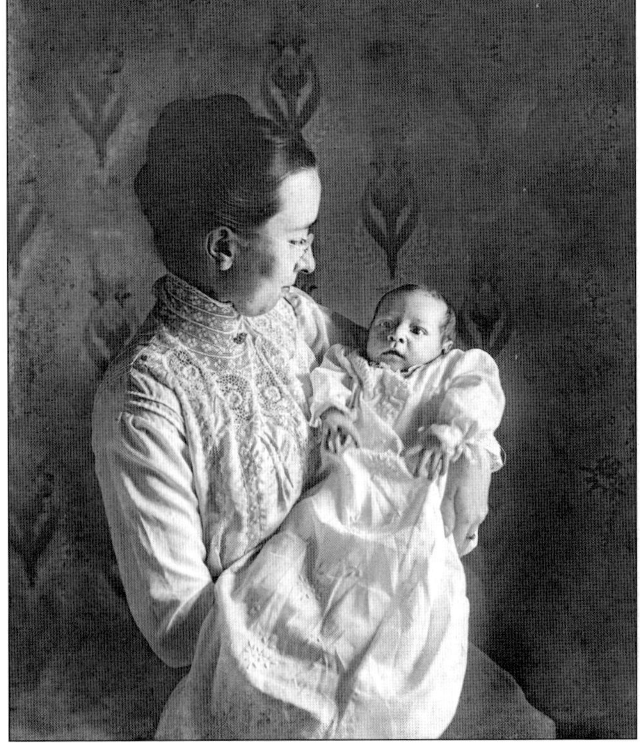

This picture, taken on November 23, 1913, is believed to be the first photograph of Kenneth Marchus Ingraham, born on October 26, 1913. Anna was sick for much of her pregnancy and was attended by a midwife and doctor for the birth. Kenneth was born just four months after Anna's mother, Luthera (Loveland) Cork, passed away. Anna's father, Joseph Cork, had died the year before.

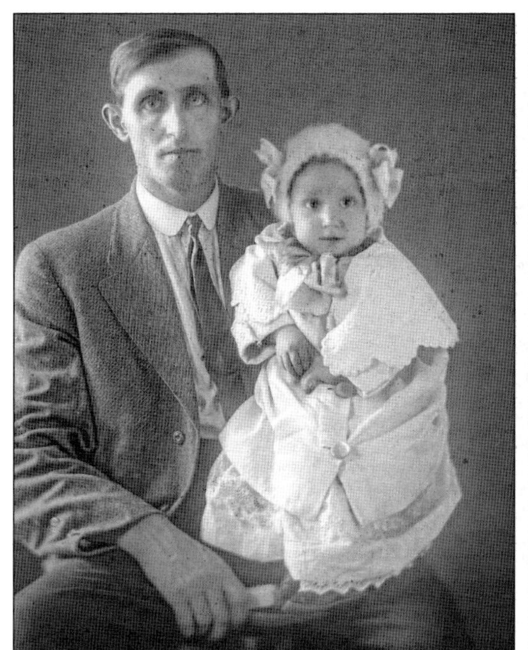

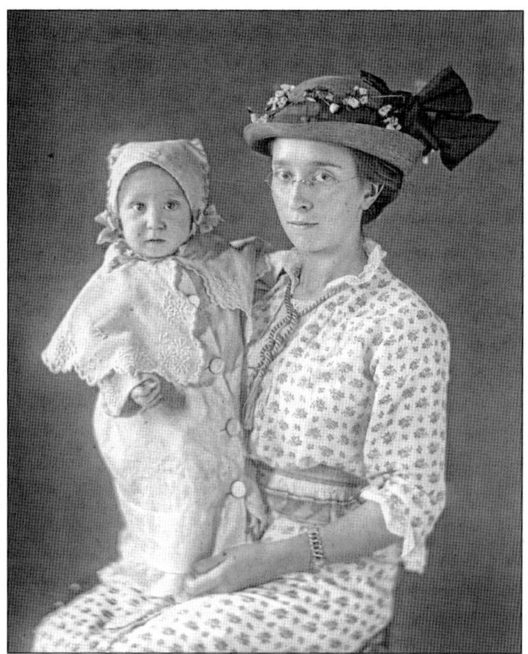

Kenneth Marchus Ingraham was the only child of Floyd and Anna Ingraham and the only grandchild of Marchus and Nettie Ingraham to survive to adulthood. Kenneth was a favorite subject of his father, who is pictured here in their earliest-known portrait together. Kenneth, like his father, resided in Springwater and became an active and respected member of the community.

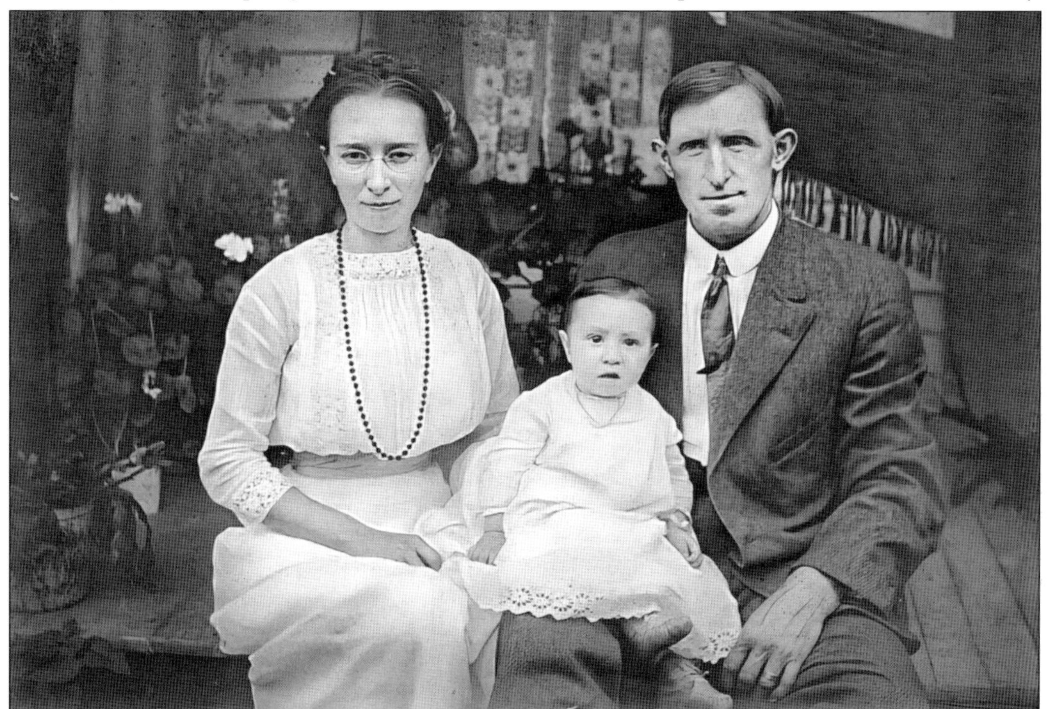

Anna, Kenneth, and Floyd Ingraham are shown here in one of their few family portraits. (Courtesy of Douglas Morgan.)

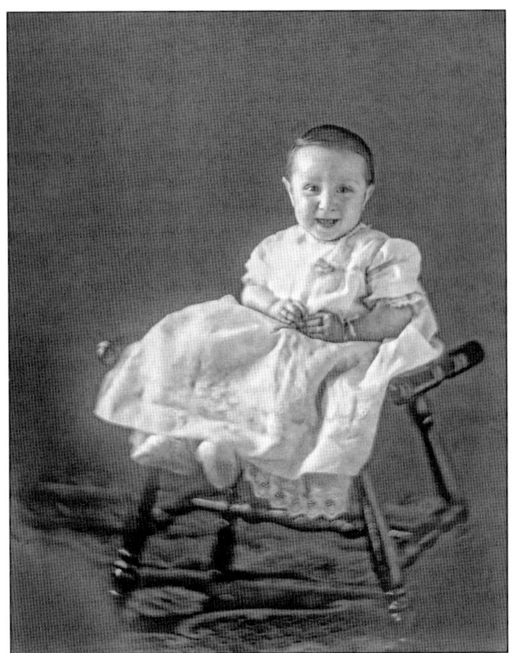

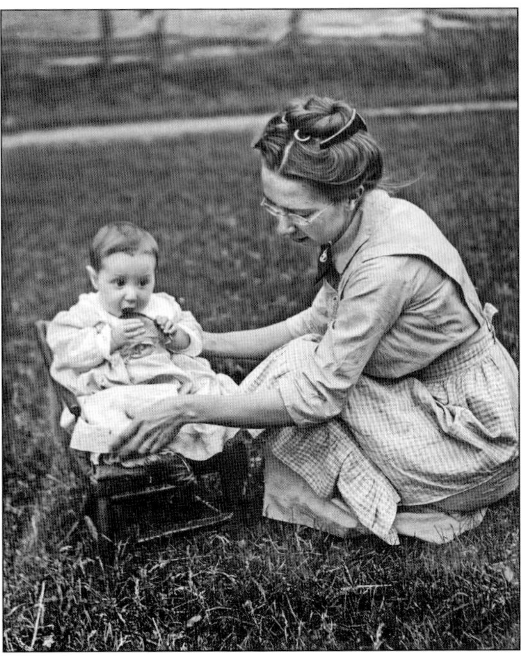

Like other little boys of the early 20th century, Kenneth Ingraham wore dresses until he was breached (out of diapers). His hair was left to grow long as a young child, and curls were common for baby boys. He is seen below on a late-19th-century or early-20th-century painted wooden rocking horse.

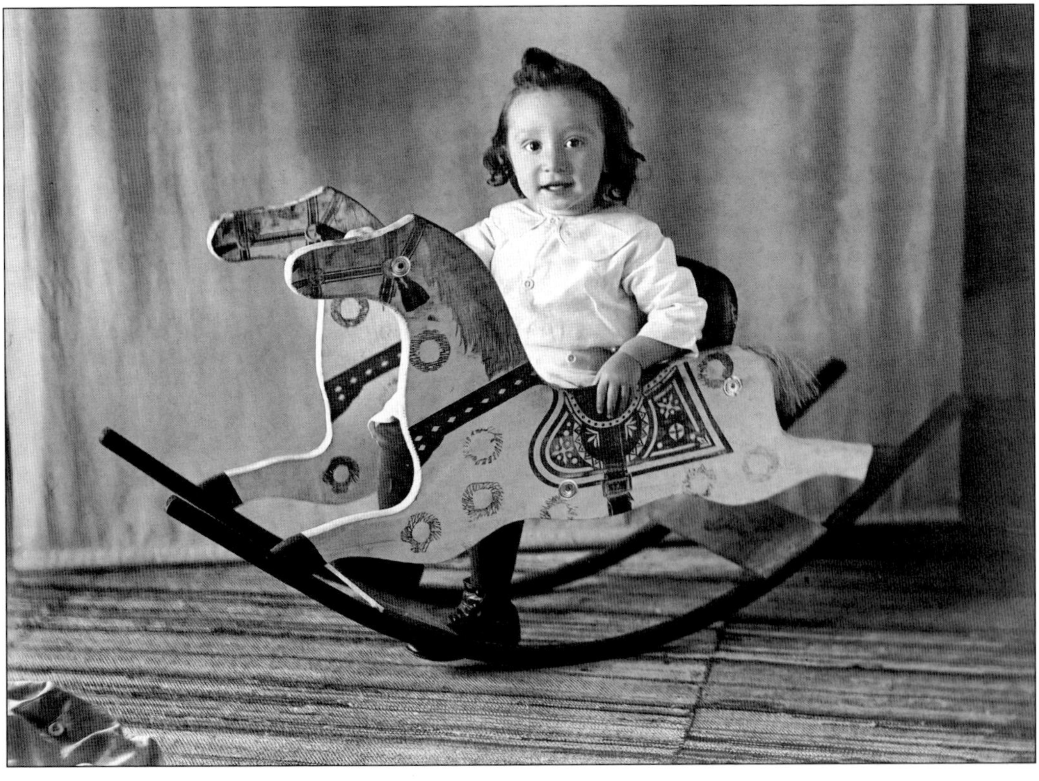

Children spent their days alongside their parents, and beginning at a young age were expected to help with household chores and work on the farm. Anna Ingraham made most of Kenneth's childhood clothing. He attended Springwater schools.

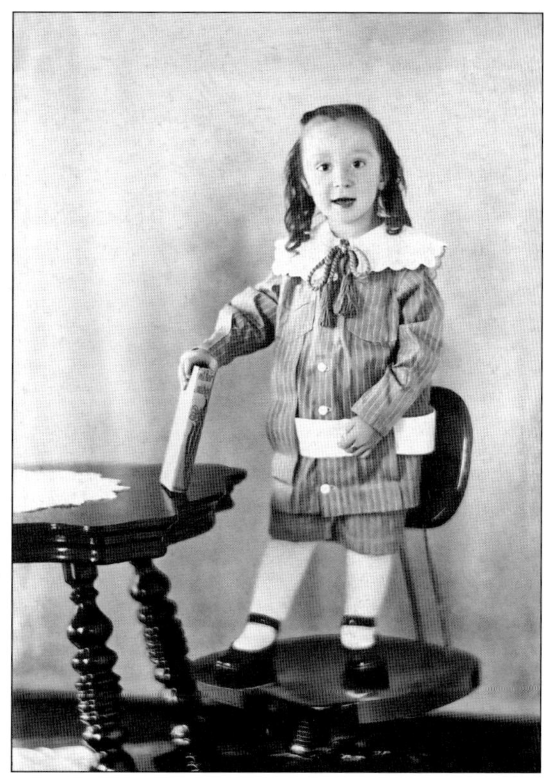

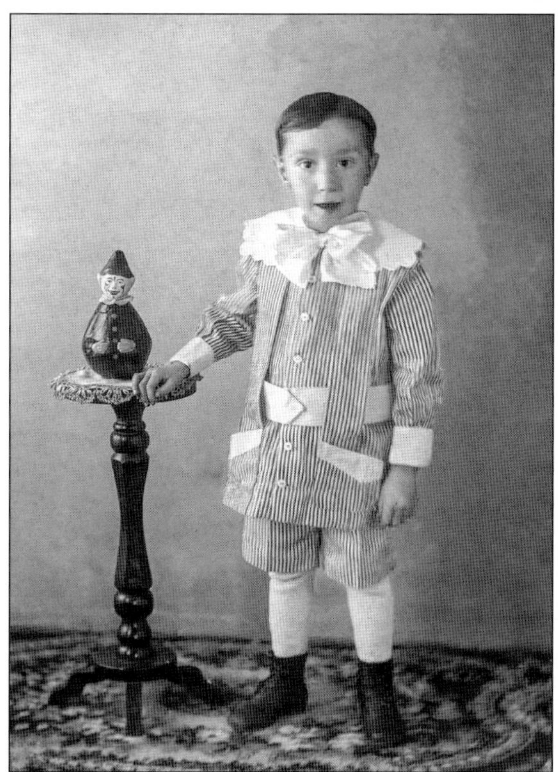

Kenneth Ingraham is pictured here at age four. As an adult, he delivered papers and milk, and installed wallpaper like his father. He also ran a gas station in Springwater and worked at Gunlocke Chair Factory. He was a member of Springwater Methodist Church and the IOOF. He married Margaret Vivien Connors on March 6, 1936, and had three children. Kenneth and Margaret were married 38 years when Kenneth died on January 14, 1975. He is buried in Mount Vernon Evergreen Cemetery.

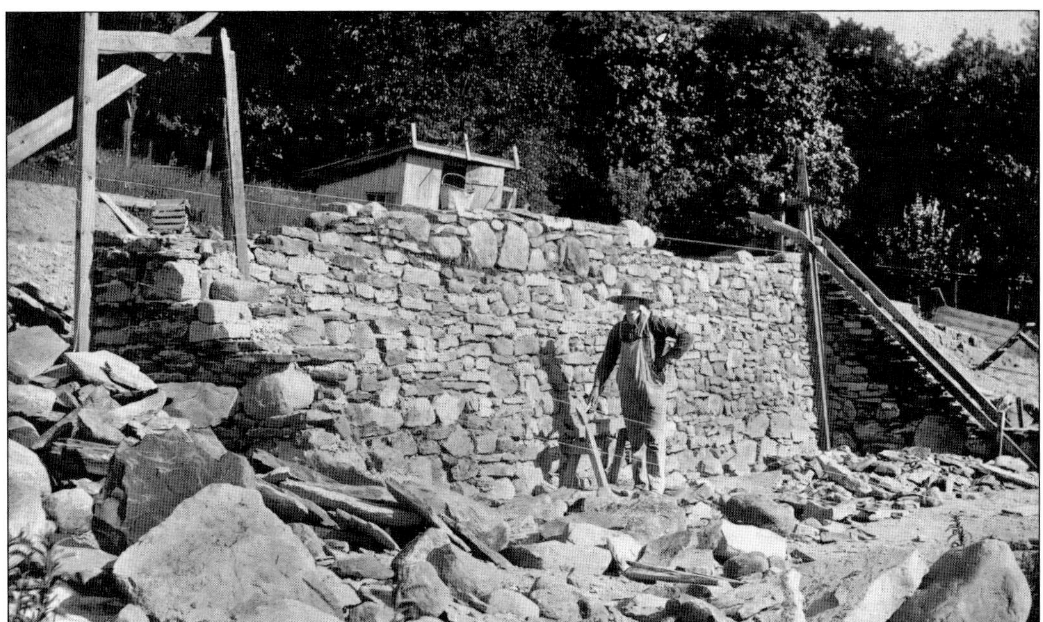

When Floyd Ingraham was not taking pictures or working in the fields during harvest, many other opportunities for work were available. He did stone masonry and odd jobs, including wallpapering, painting, plastering, bicycle repair, and cement work. He installed some of the first cement sidewalks in Springwater. This image shows Ingraham working on a barn at Milton Kuhn's farm on Old Bald Hill Road. Ingraham charged $3 for a full day of masonry work. He built many chimneys, walls, and foundations that still stand today. (Courtesy of Ron and Sharon Ingraham.)

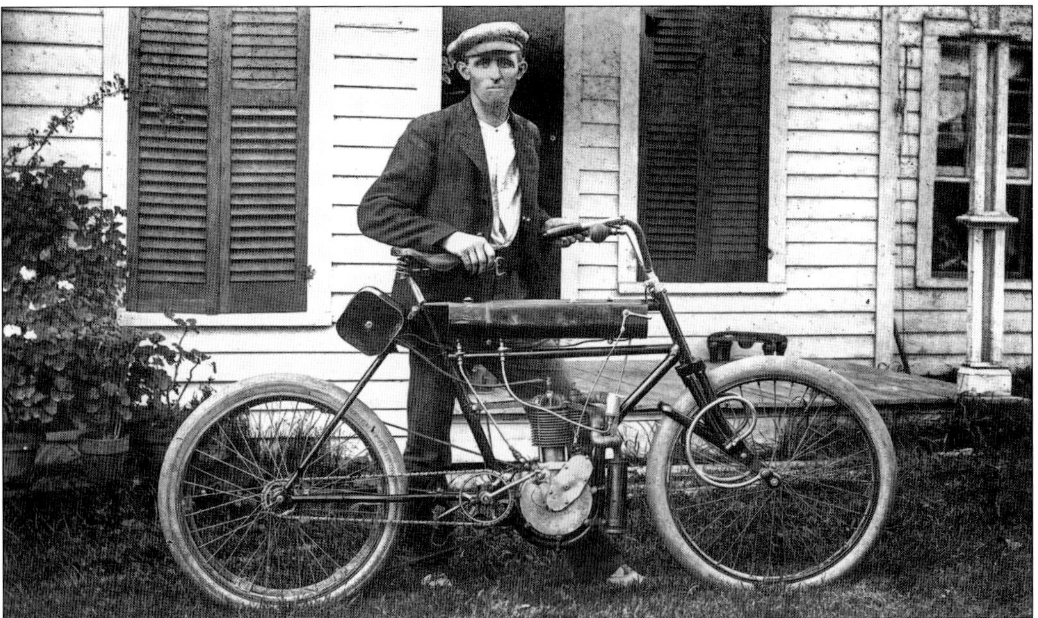

Floyd Ingraham owned a bicycle and machine repair shop in 1905. He purchased this Curtiss motorcycle in June 1906 from Burdette Johnson. Ingraham was a member of the IOOF, the Knights of the Maccabees, the Springwater Grange, the Springwater chapter of the National Protective Legion, and the Advent church. (Courtesy of Ron and Sharon Ingraham.)

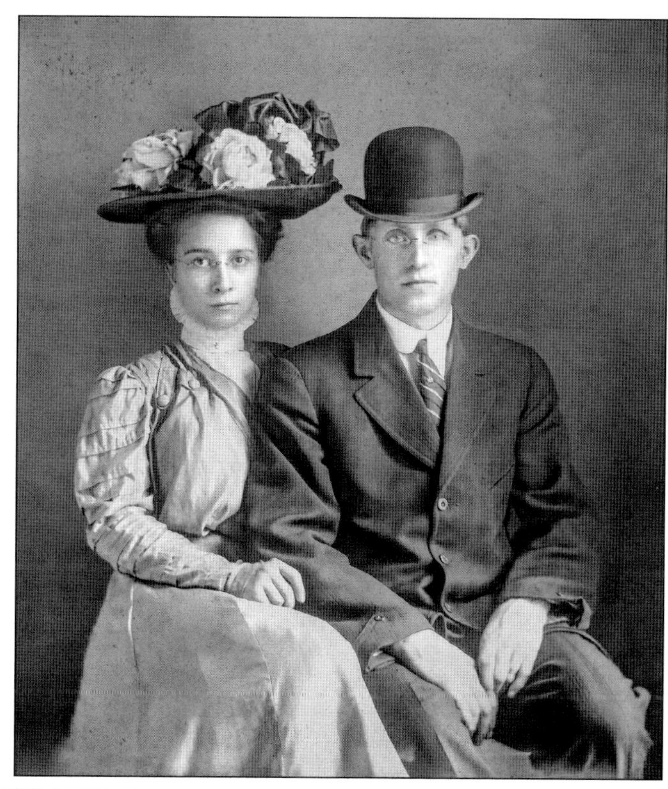

Anna (Cork) Ingraham loved hats and made her own clothing. Pictures of her reveal the latest fashions of the early 20th century. Katherine Hendershott's millinery shop in Springwater provided hats for the women of Springwater from the late 1800s to 1920. It is possible that Anna is wearing one of Hendershott's creations here.

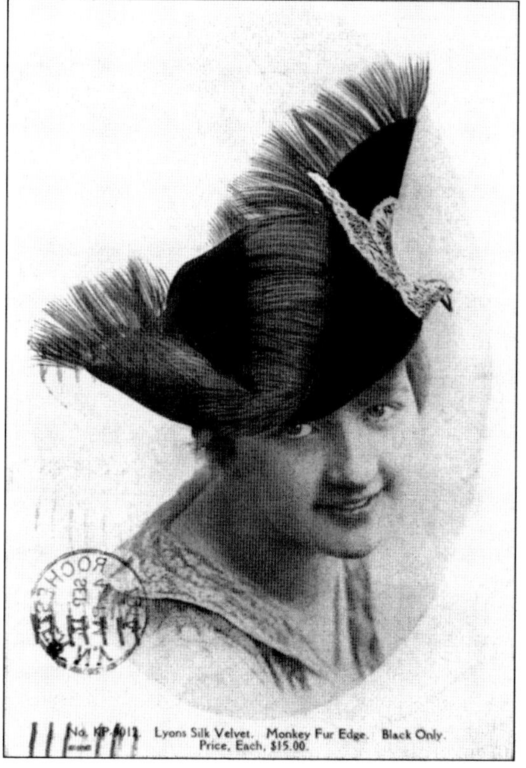

Katherine "Kate" Hendershott was born to John D. and Lydia (Grover) Hendershott of Springwater. She learned how to make hats and operated a millinery business in Springwater. Her shop was in the family residence on Main Street near the Shannon Building, across the street from the Empire Hotel. Hendershott traveled back and forth between Rochester and Springwater, bringing the latest fashions to the ladies of the Finger Lakes. In 1920, she found work with the Sibley, Lindsday, and Corr Company of Rochester. She died in 1945 and is buried in Mount Vernon Evergreen Cemetery. (Courtesy of Springwater–Webster Crossing Historical Society.)

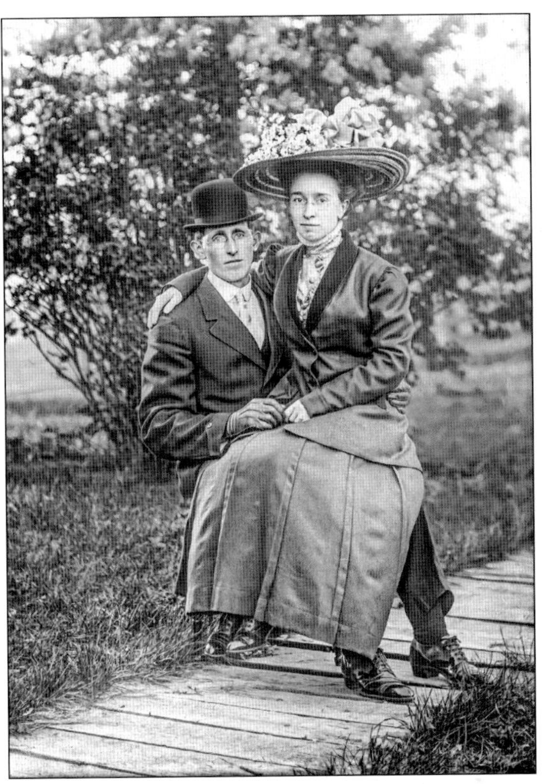

Floyd and Anna (Cork) Ingraham were actively involved in their community. They attended church and community events and were members of several volunteer organizations. They often called on friends or welcomed guests into their home. Anna was visiting a friend on January 19, 1920, when she was called home. Floyd, who was not feeling well, had worsened. He died three days later.

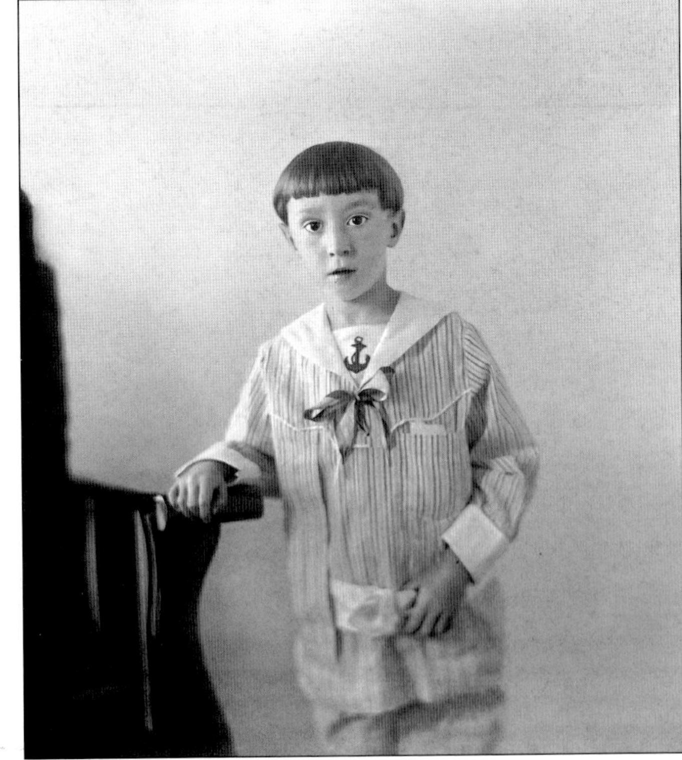

This is the last known picture of Kenneth Ingraham taken by his father, Floyd, in December 1919 before Floyd's death on January 22, 1920. Kenneth was six when his father passed away suddenly. His mother Anna said of her son in the days following Floyd's death, "Kenneth was very brave."

Floyd Ingraham became ill on January 16, 1920. Three days later, due to his acute pain, a doctor was called to the home. Ingraham was diagnosed with a burst appendix. Due to a previous snowstorm, the people of the town came to clear drifts away for their beloved friend, and a team and sleigh were commissioned to rush him to the closest hospital, in Dansville, 12 miles away. He survived surgery but died two days later on January 22, 1920, at age 38.

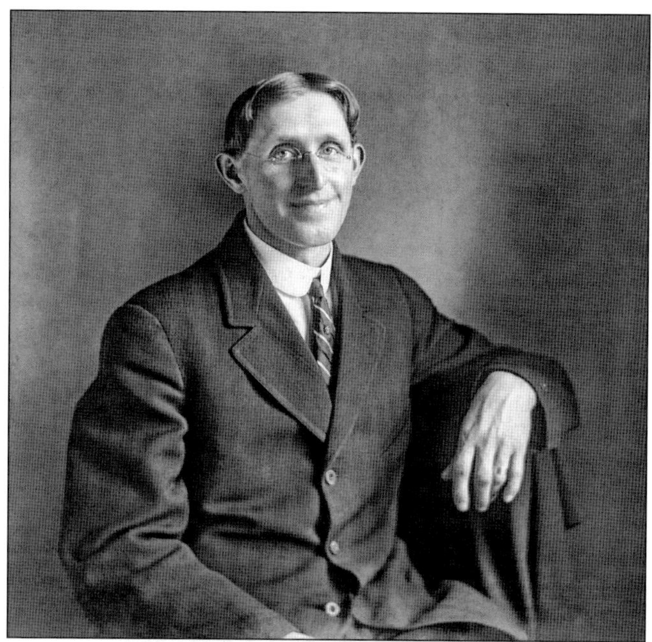

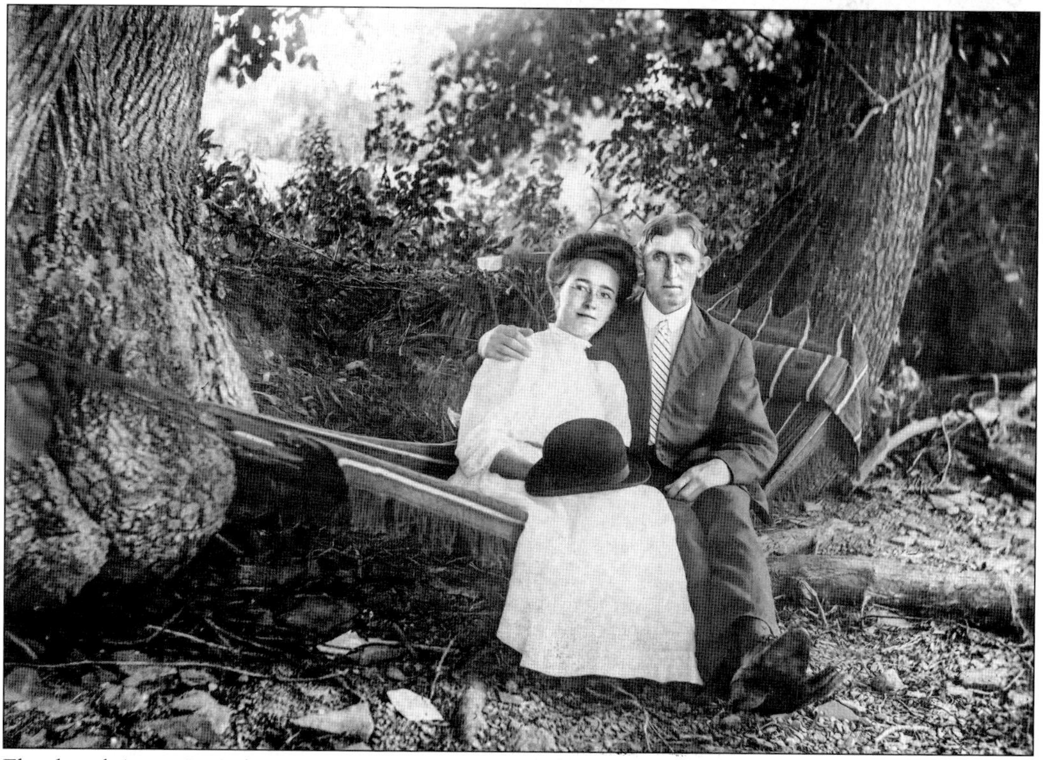

Floyd and Anna Ingraham were married for 10 years when he suddenly passed away. As a result, Anna was widowed at age 29 with a six-year-old son, Kenneth. She stayed in the home and cared for Floyd's parents until their deaths. Anna went to work at the Cannon Miller Radio Factory in Springwater. In 1931, she married Floyd Caskey. Anna and Kenneth kept Floyd Ingraham's photographs and glass negatives as long as they lived.

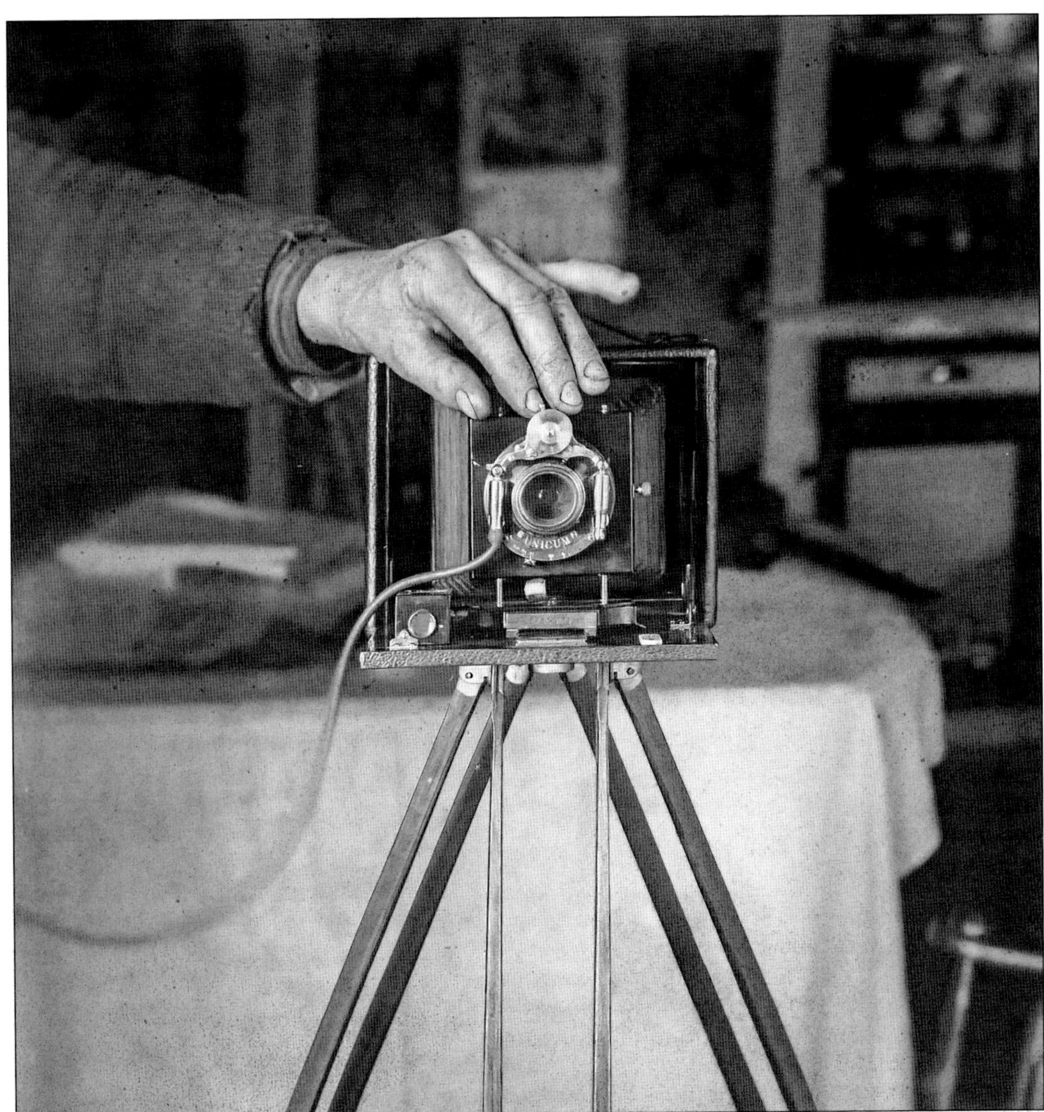

Currently there are hundreds of known Floyd Ingraham photographs. Glass negatives matching proofs owned by the Ingraham family, prints with Ingraham's handwriting, a photographer's stamp, or known props and clues in the pictures themselves identify the images as Ingraham's. This Reko camera was made by the Rochester Optical Company. Its wooden body could store three plateholders for dry glass plates. The Bausch and Lomb lens seen here had a Unicum two-blade shutter. The circular dial on top allowed for a speed of 1/100 of a second. It was one of the best shutters of its time. Unlike the large studio camera Ingraham owned, this camera would have been easily carried anywhere on Springwater's hills. Gelatin dry glass plates were inserted into wooden holders and placed inside the camera. Ingraham used the mechanics of the camera to capture light and process the latent image onto the plate. Early photographers also had to be chemists. The glass negative would be placed in developing solution. The paper for printing, such as a postcard, was placed under the negative in a frame in a traditional darkroom. The image was transferred to the print, and the print would then be dried and ready to distribute to customers. Ingraham's photographic legacy has historical importance for the town and people of Springwater, preserving a glimpse of early-20th-century life.

Two

Springwater and Its Neighbors

Springwater, a small town in the Genesee River Valley, was typical of other small communities at the turn of the 20th century. Its Main Street ran through the center of town and was the hub of business and community life. A patchwork of over 32,000 acres of farmland and forest spread out in all directions from the center of town.

During Ingraham's life, there were numerous small schoolhouses scattered throughout the township. Many of the early one-room schoolhouses built in the 1800s and early 1900s still stand. Several small country churches were frequented by Springwater residents. The bells of Springwater's Advent church and the Methodist church rang throughout the valley on Sunday mornings, or to wail out a fire warning. Clara (Mack) Bennet wrote in her article "Church Still Serves," published in *Thoughts by a Country Woman*, that on one occasion, the ending of World War I, those same bells "rang, and rang, on the evening of November 11, 1918, as if they would, by their very strength, bind the world in lasting peace."

Beautiful homes were built in Springwater and the surrounding Finger Lakes communities in the late 19th and early 20th century. Various styles of architecture—Colonial Revival, Greek Revival, and Victorian Queen Anne—can be seen in Finger Lakes homes photographed by Ingraham. Many remain. Though some have suffered the ravages of time, all of their spindles, towers, roof lines, and doorways stand as testaments to the craftsmanship and beauty of another era.

Ingraham's photographs taken in neighboring towns add to the historical record of a bygone era. Each Finger Lakes hamlet and village had its own significance and struggles. Their relationship to each other and the lakes has changed over time, but glimpses of what Ingraham saw 100 years ago remain.

The agricultural landscape of the Finger Lakes in the early 20th century was preserved forever by Floyd Ingraham. His Springwater and nearby communities were places of heights and valleys, beautiful lakes, and neighborly people. They were home to hardworking families and a peaceful, simple way of life. The beautiful scenes in Ingraham's photographs reflect a region that was cleared for farmland. Now grown over, much of it has returned to forest. But anyone who climbs high enough and can see far enough might catch a glimpse of the Springwater Ingraham knew and loved.

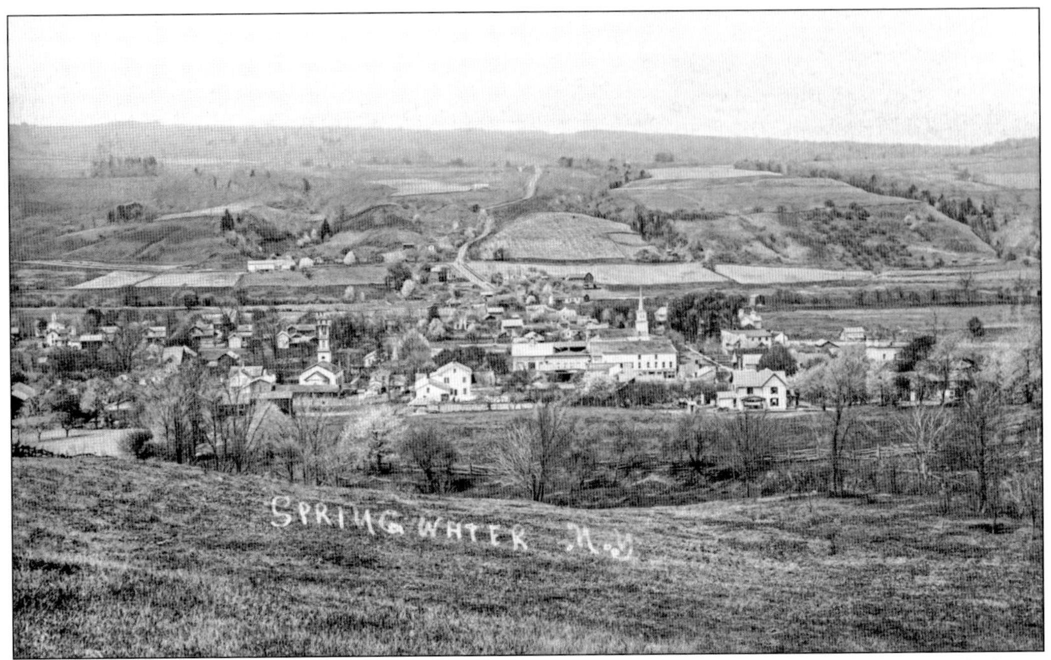

This photograph is one of many scenic views Floyd Ingraham took to print as a real-photo postcard. His postcards averaged 5¢ each. Springwater's Advent church with its prominent steeple is recognizable on Mill Street. The Methodist church can also be seen. School No. 2 on School Street, a white building with a bell tower, is at far left. It was replaced in 1912. Mill Street, also known as New York State Route 15, rises in the distance.

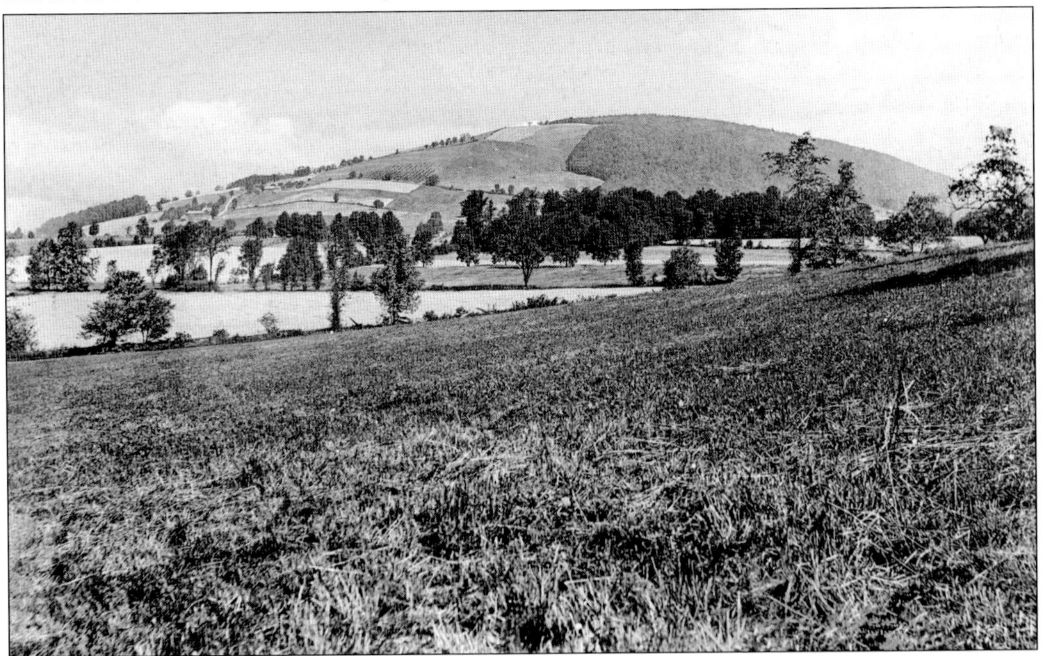

Bald Hill is a landmark in Springwater. Here, it is viewed from Johnson Hill Road. The first settlers came over this hill to Springwater in the early 1800s. It was named Bald Hill by early settlers due to its bald appearance from signal fires set by Native Americans.

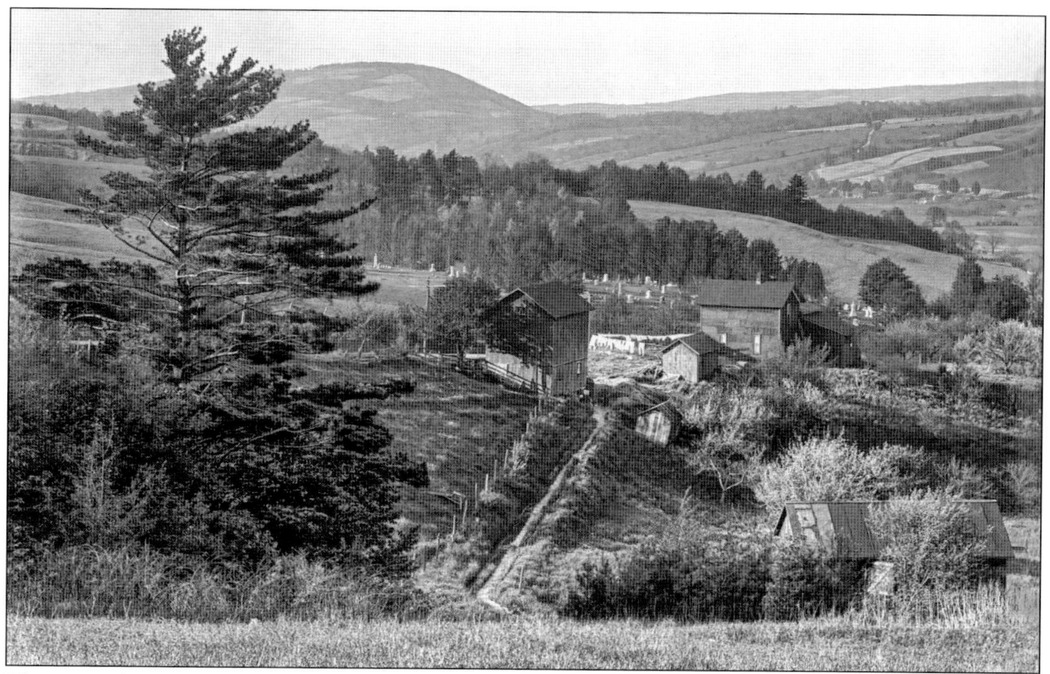

This view from Springwater's West Hill looks north with Bald Hill in the distance. Mount Vernon Evergreen Cemetery can be seen beyond a barn and residence with clothes drying on the line. This view is no longer possible as the area is now overgrown with trees, such as the tall evergreen at left.

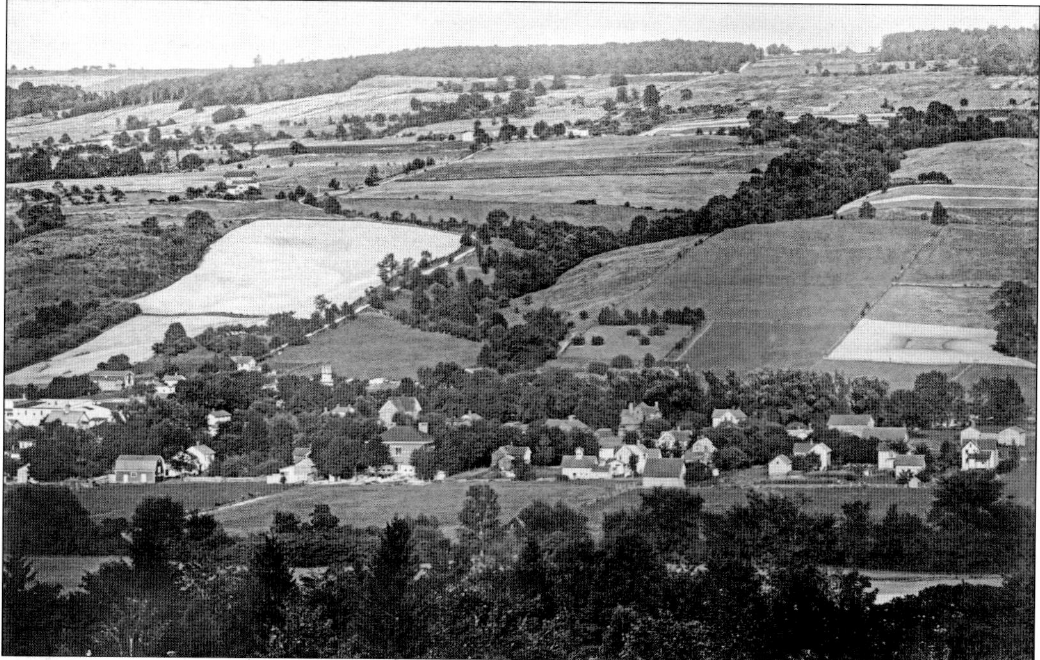

Taken above Kellogg Road and Mount Vernon Evergreen Cemetery, this view of Springwater shows a patchwork of farmland on the area's hills. Houses and barns along School Street and Main Street (now New York State Route 15A) can be seen. This eastward view reveals a glimpse of East Avenue and Canadice Road in the distance.

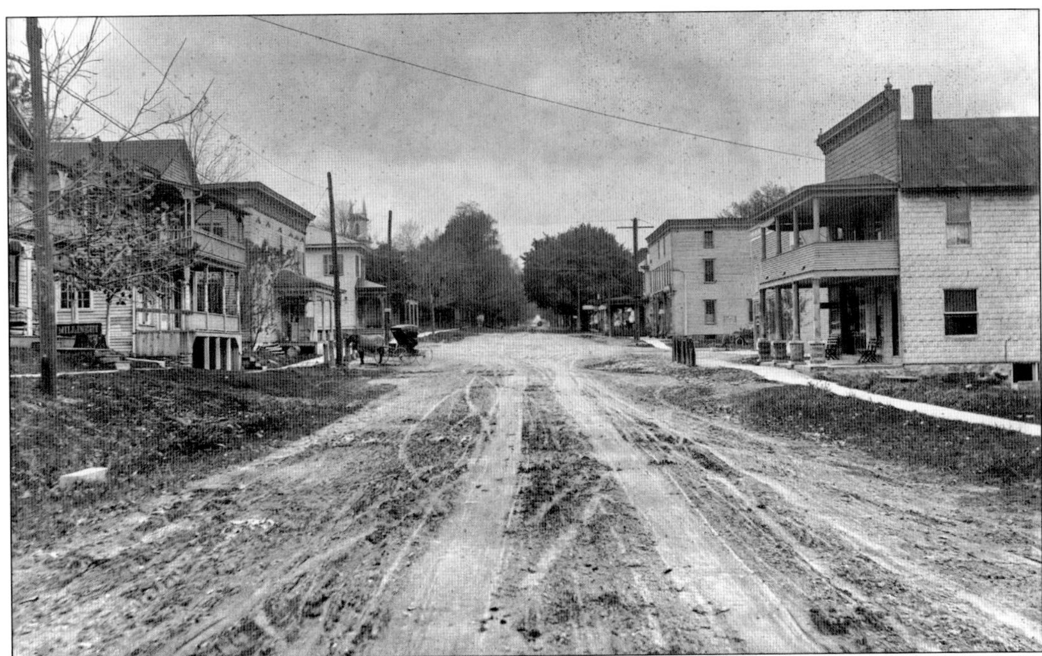

This view of Springwater's Main Street faces south. Some of the buildings seen here are still standing. Businesses are visible at the four corners, where East Avenue and Mill Street meet Main Street. In the early 1900s, they included a hotel, stores, automobile sales, and a funeral director. The building with the balcony on the right became the Red and White Store.

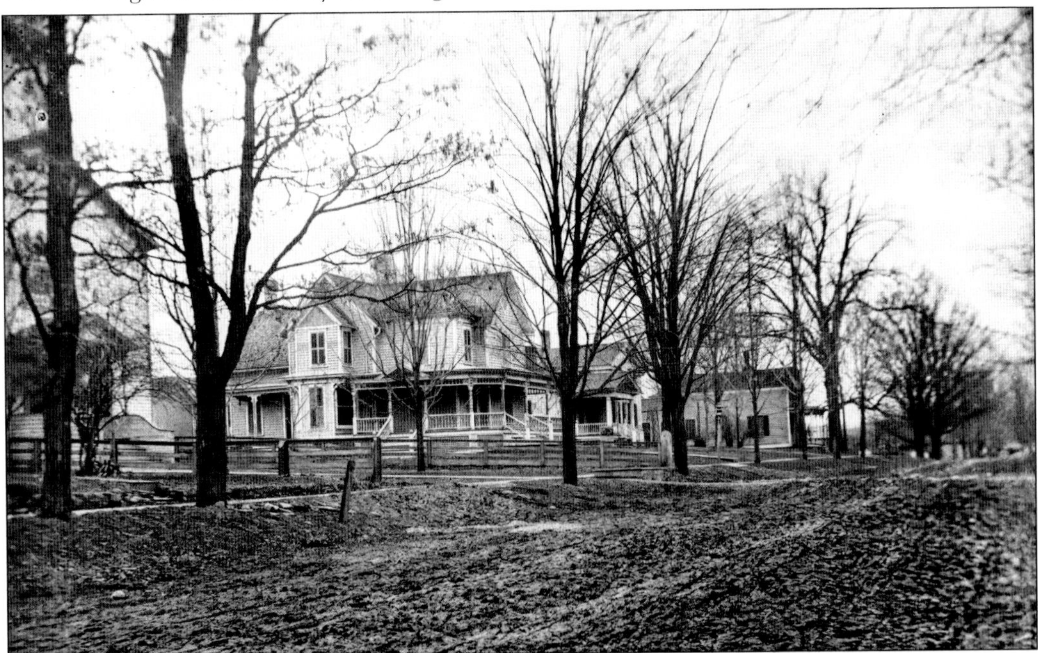

The two houses shown just south of the Methodist church on Springwater's Main Street are still standing. The house in the foreground was home to Dr. F.W. Host in 1902. The wraparound porch has been greatly reduced, but it has survived for more than 100 years along with its neighbor on the right—the boyhood home of Charles Mack, first husband of Clara (Seward Mack) Bennett.

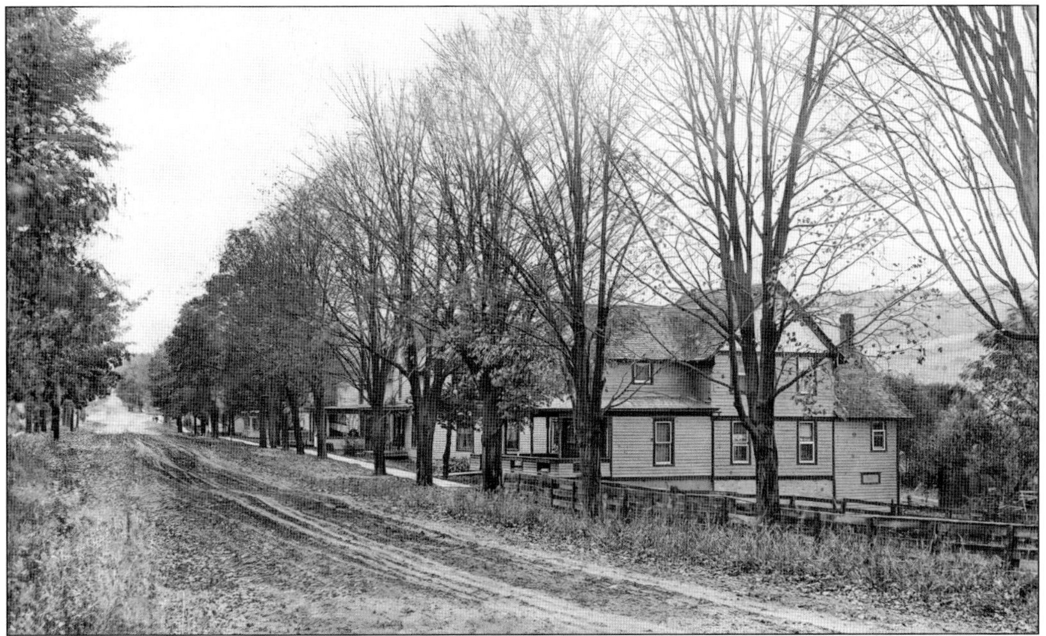

Taken close to Kellogg Road looking south, this picture shows a tree-lined Main Street in Springwater. Hitching posts can be seen between telephone poles, and ruts in the dirt road reveal the use of horse-drawn wagons and automobiles, evidence of the changing times in which old ways collided with modern advances made in the early 20th century.

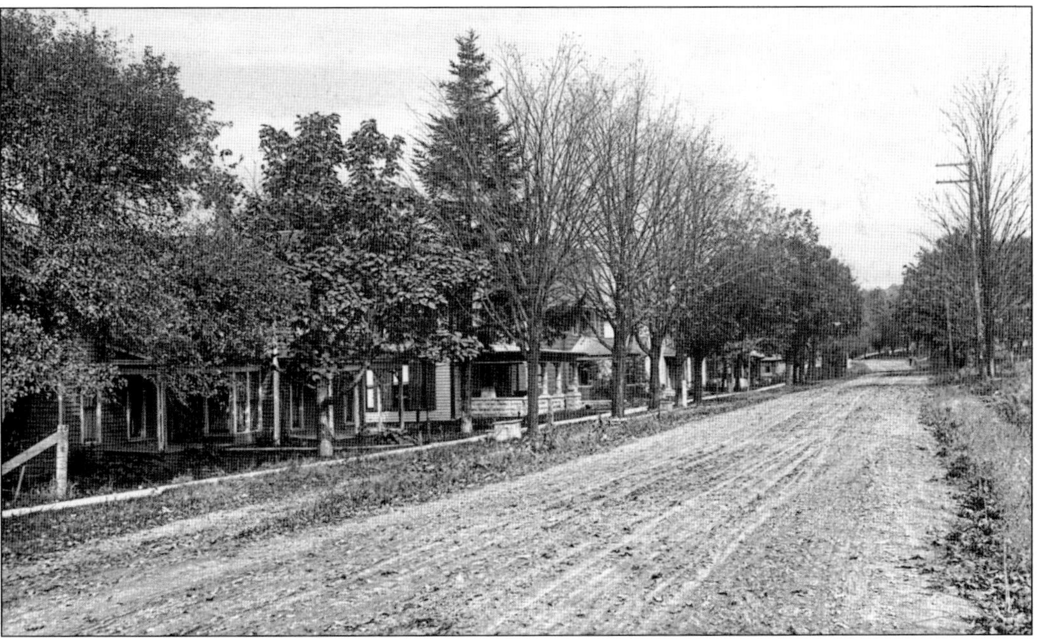

Looking north from the four corners on the west side of the road, this row of houses on Springwater's Main Street is just past where Allen and Whitlock's store and the Empire Hotel once stood. A 1902 Springwater map reveals that the Saltoc, Amos, Brown, Nixon, Grove, and Tucker families lived in these houses at that time. The homes are still standing. The second home from the left now has an enclosed porch, but the stone base and pillars are still visible.

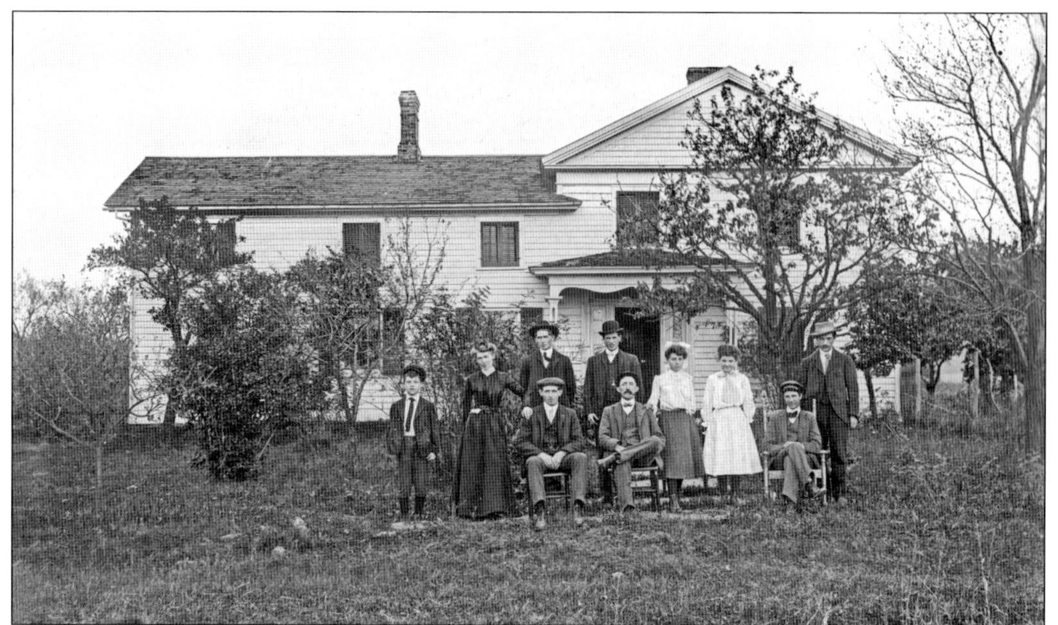

Melvin Ford and his family pose outside their house in Springwater in September 1904. From left to right are (seated) Floyd Ingraham, Melvin Ford, and Arthur Ford; (standing) an unidentified boy, Carrie Ford, Otto Ingraham, Leon Ford, Gertrude Ford, Veda McClellan, and Wells Ford. Melvin Ford was the brother of Floyd Ingraham's mother, Nettie.

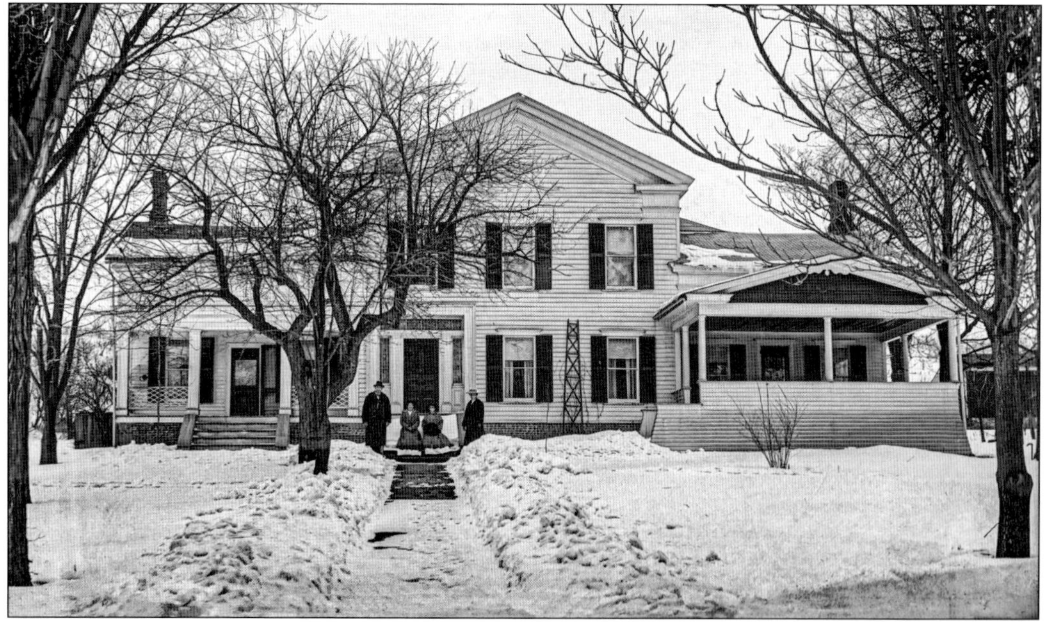

This home, built by the late 1800s, is listed as a boardinghouse in early documents. The Densmore family owned it by 1902. Located between the Methodist church and the Densmore Building on the east side of Springwater's Main Street, the home remains standing today. The family out front may be Horace H. and Emma Densmore with two of their nieces. The Densmores adopted their niece Lena Dubois of Omaha, Nebraska, after her parents died when she was six years old. In the 1930s, it was operated by Ethel Perry as the Eagle Hotel.

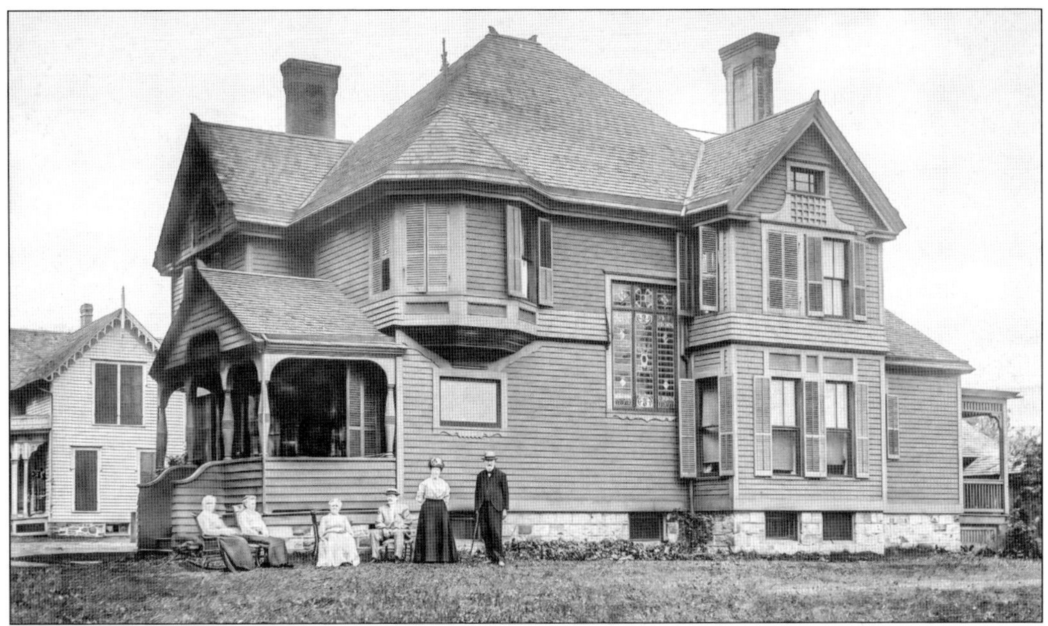

This beautiful home, built by Henry K. Cooper, was on Main Street in Springwater near where the town hall is now. H.K. Cooper was a civil engineer. When the Rochester and Corning Branch of the Erie Railroad was built, he supervised its surveying and construction. He also served as a department chief in the quartermaster general's office in Washington, DC, during the Civil War. His home in Springwater was built in the late 1800s and burned sometime in the mid-1900s. The people pictured here are unidentified.

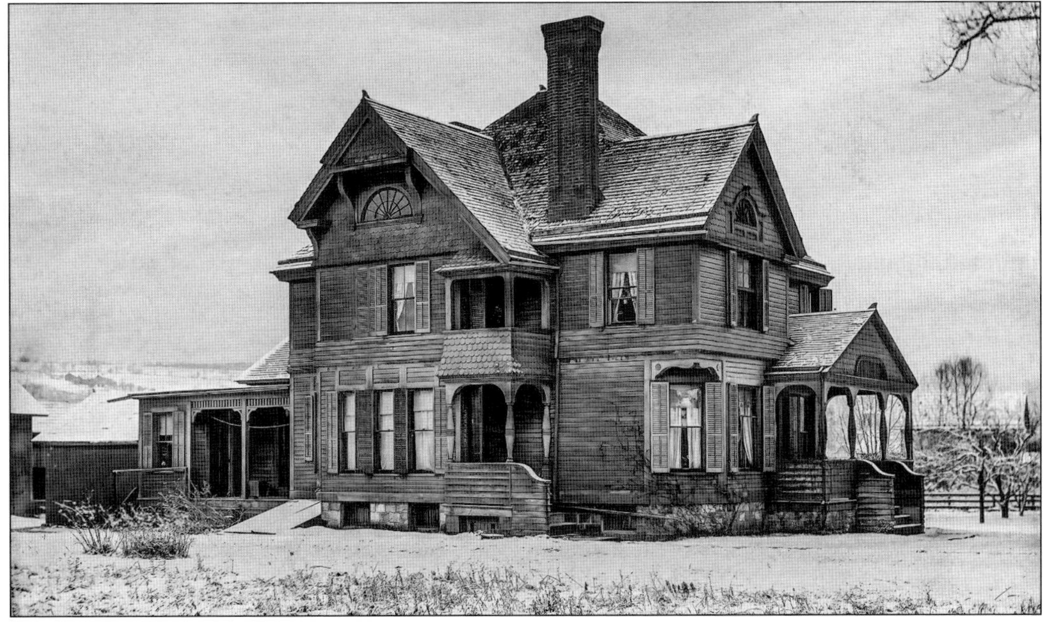

This is another view of the house on Main Street that was home to the Henry K. Cooper family. Born in 1830, Cooper was married first to Mary J. Putnam. Following Putnam's death in 1870, he married Mattie Snyder, daughter of Alonzo Snyder. Cooper's only child, Elizabeth, died in 1896. Cooper died in 1916 and is buried in Mount Vernon Evergreen Cemetery.

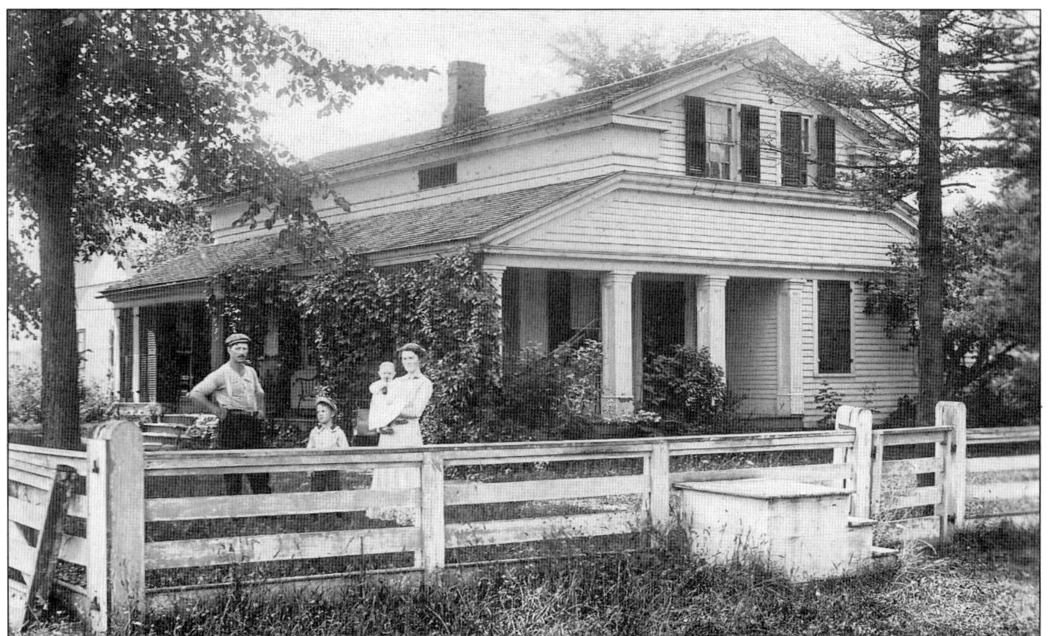

This home was built by Joseph Kellogg of Springwater in the mid-1800s. Nathan A. Kellogg, Joseph's son, later owned the property, which was known as the Kellogg homestead. Sometime after 1907, A. Barton Hyde moved here. He is pictured here with his wife, Lizzy, and their sons Glenn and Ellis outside the home around 1918. The home still stands on Kellogg Road. (Courtesy of Joyce O'Neil and Rick Osiecki.)

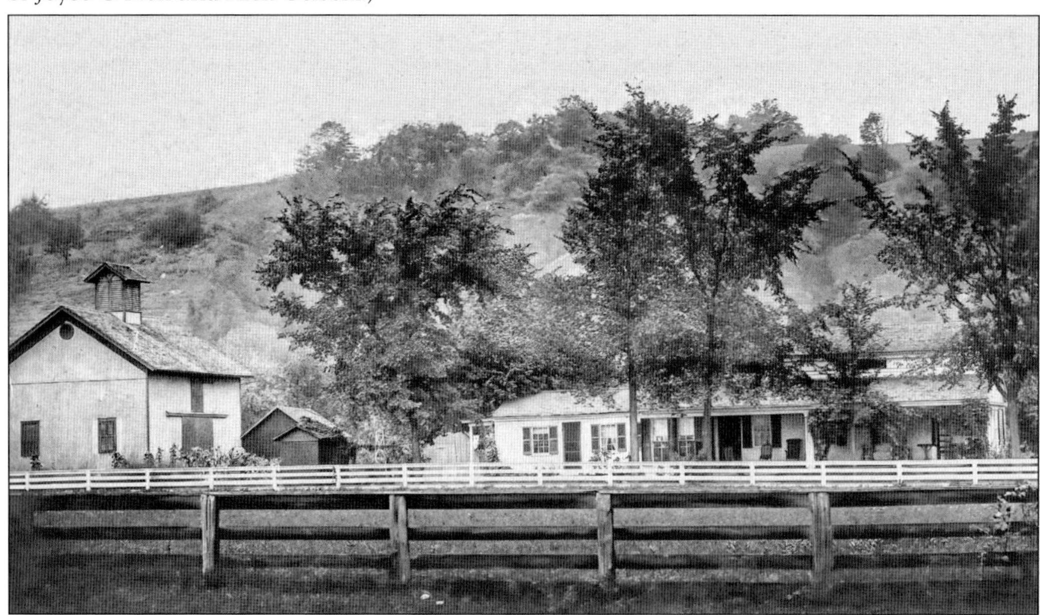

Pictured here is the Kellogg home on Kellogg Road with its large, beautiful porch and a barn at left. West Hill rises behind the home, and although it cannot be seen here, Kellogg Road turns left just after the house to follow the hill up to Mount Vernon Evergreen Cemetery. At least two generations of the Kellogg family lived in the home as well as the Barton Hyde and Charles Hanson families of Springwater. (Courtesy of Springwater–Webster Crossing Historical Society.)

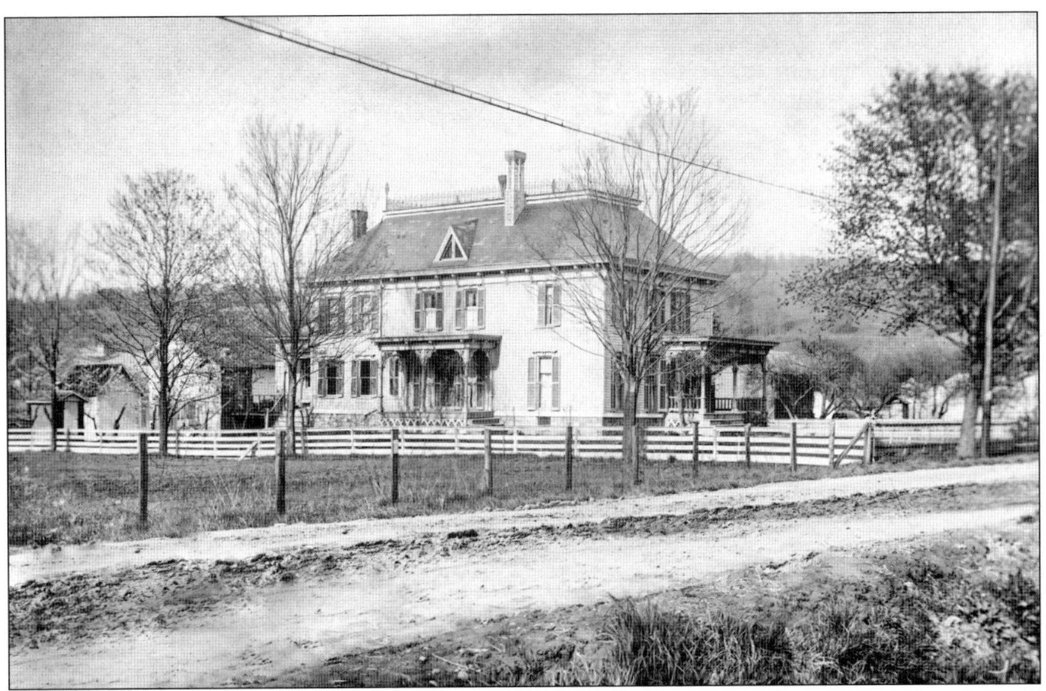

Built around 1900, this home on Mill Street in Springwater remains standing. Euretta (Sunderland) and Winfield Scott Earnest married and built the house on her family's farmland. It stayed in the Earnest family until 1932, when it was purchased by Cecil and Jane Saunders Miller. Ron Mastin is the current owner.

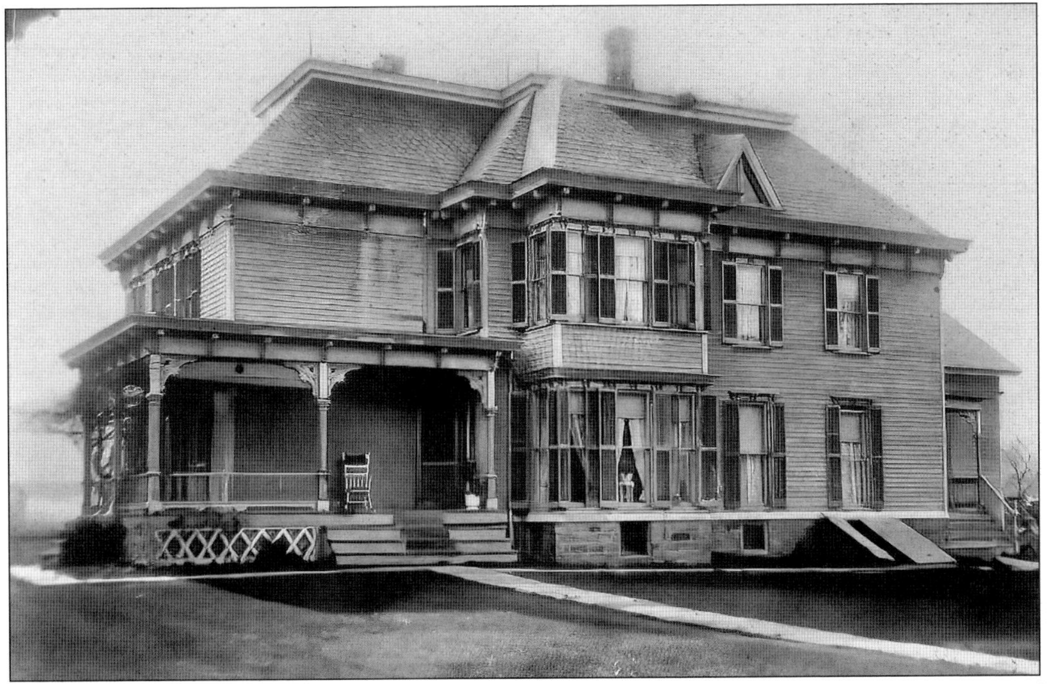

Here is another view of the Earnest/Miller home on Mill Street in Springwater. (Courtesy of Springwater–Webster Crossing Historical Society.)

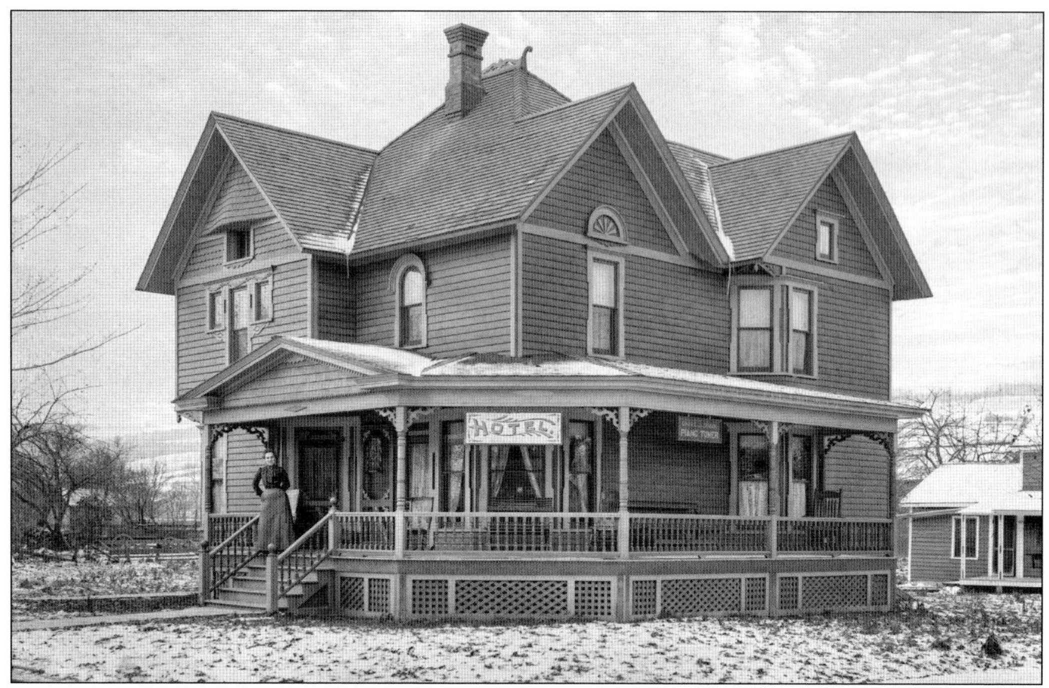

This house still stands on the corner of School and Mill Streets in Springwater. It was a hotel and home of Dana Jackman in 1891. Advertisements for his services list Jackman as a piano tuner, repairer, and regulator. The house became the Robinson home by 1902. This is one of Floyd Ingraham's earlier photographs.

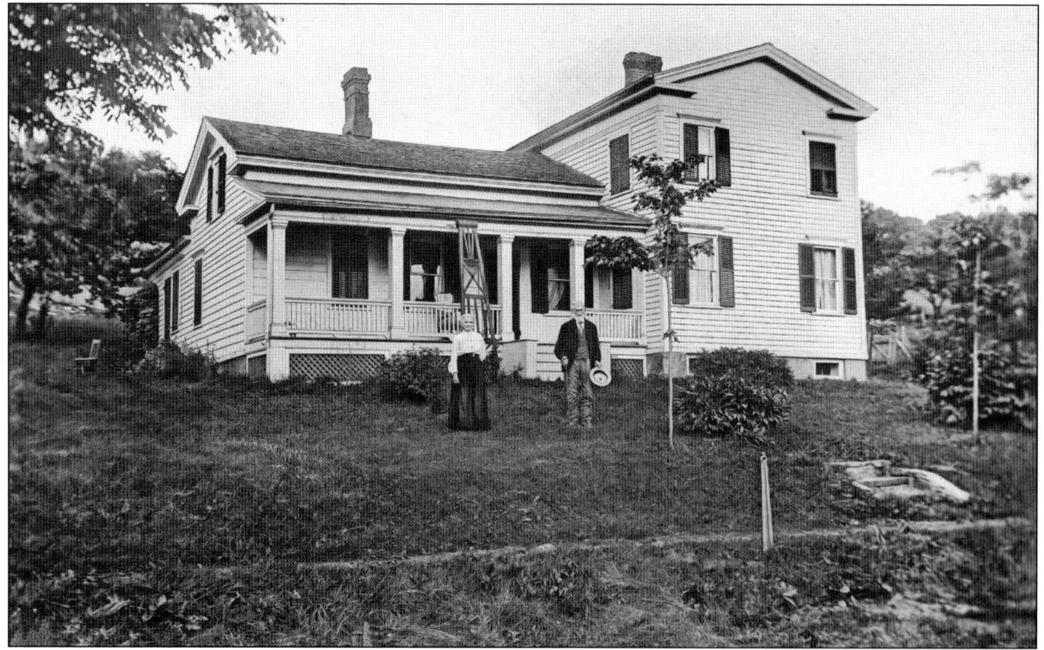

This home still stands on North Main Street in Springwater. It was the home of Ed and Phedora Sharp Holmes by 1930. The Holmeses came to Springwater from Conesus. Their son Francis "Bill" Holmes married Grace Fisher; they were the parents of Joyce O'Neil, a contributor to this book.

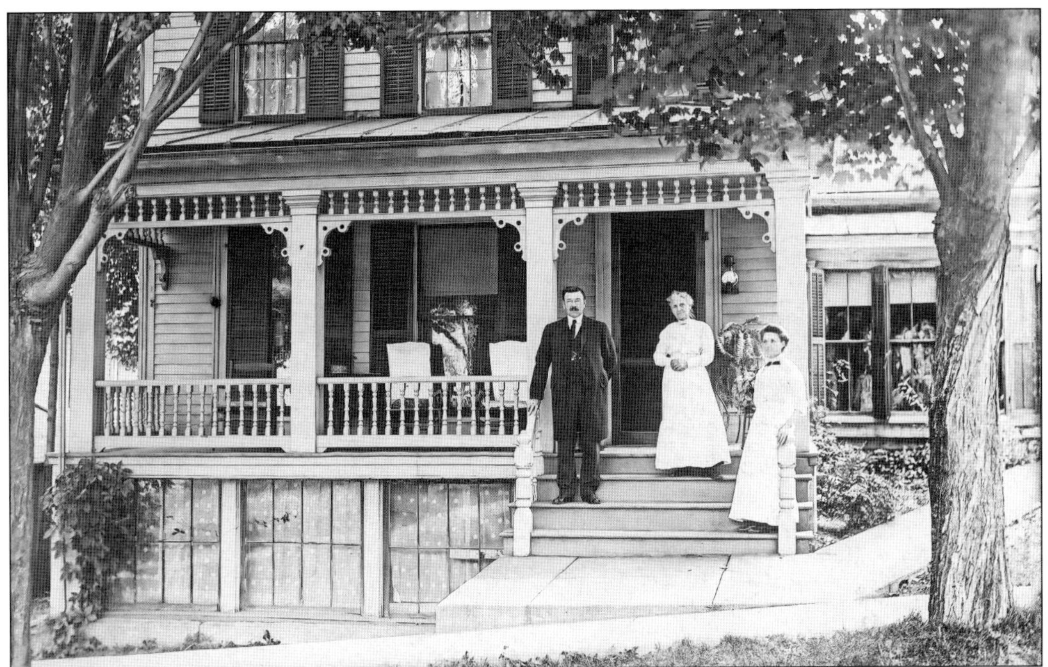

This house stands behind the Densmore building on East Avenue in Springwater. A doctor's home and office for many years, the man on the left may be one of the many physicians who served Springwater during Floyd Ingraham's lifetime. One was Dr. Albert Baker, who served the community for decades until his death in 1918 from pneumonia contracted during the flu epidemic.

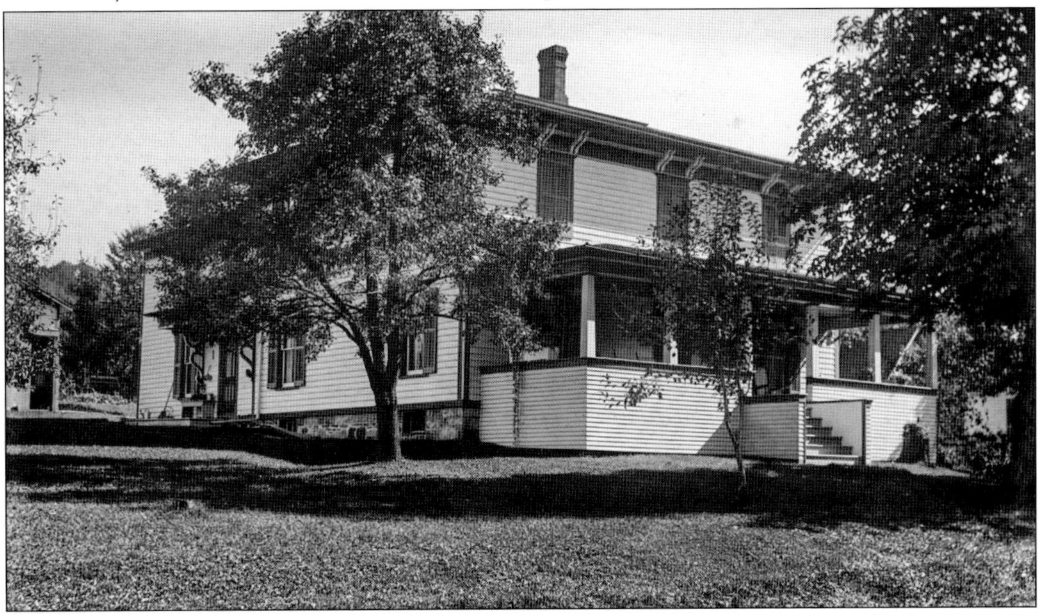

Erwin Erastus Wemett lived in this house on Main Street in Springwater in the early 1900s. He was the son of Erastus and Elizabeth Wemett. Born in 1875 in Springwater, he resided there most of his life. He married Laura Elmina Partridge in 1897, and they had three children, E. Harrison, E. Elizabeth, and George Erwin. Erwin operated an automobile dealership and was a real estate agent. He died in 1952 in Wayland. The Wemett house still stands on Main Street.

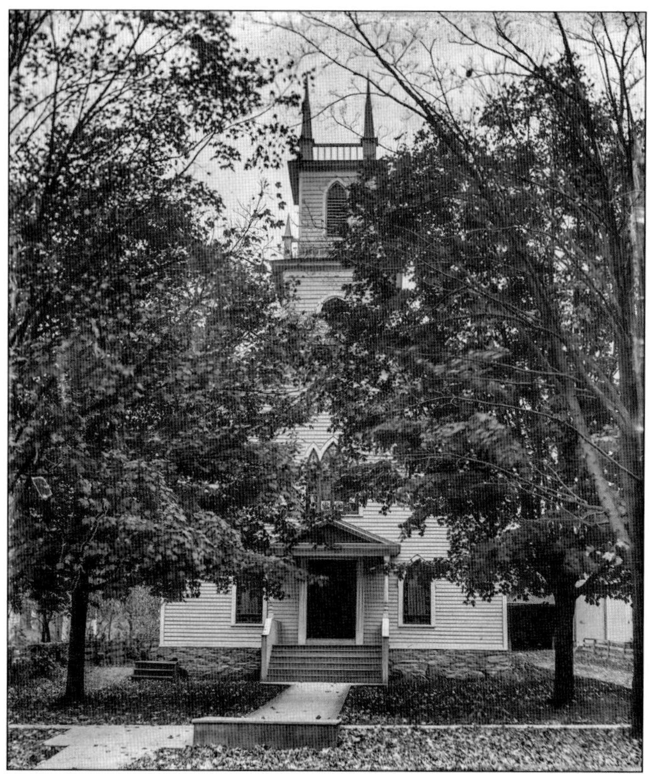

Ground was broken for the Springwater Methodist Episcopal church in 1833. It was dedicated in April 1834 and was the first church in Springwater. Now a United Methodist church, it still holds regular services and remains active in the community. Anna (Cork) Ingraham, wife of photographer Floyd Ingraham, was a member of this church until her death in 1981.

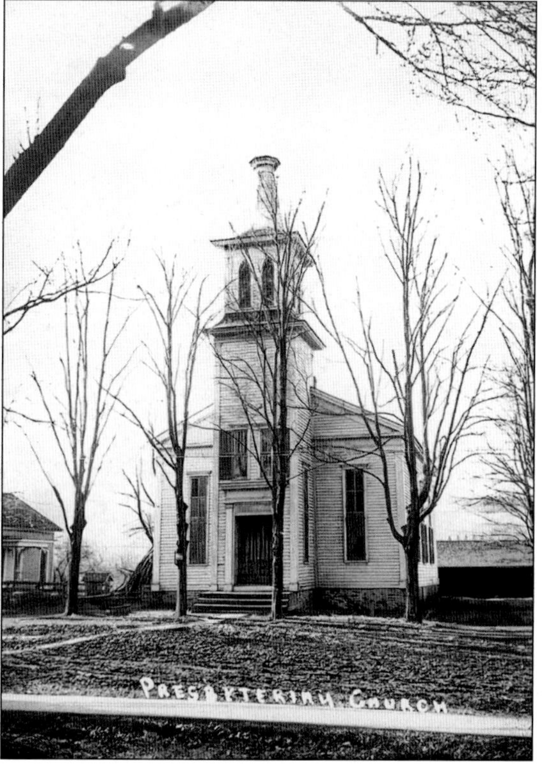

The Presbyterian church of Springwater was organized first as a Congregationalist church on February 10, 1821. In 1827, it came under the care of the Presbytery of Ontario County. Located on Main Street, it had a parsonage. This church no longer exists.

Floyd Ingraham attended the Advent church on Mill Street in Springwater. He did the wallpapering inside, seen here. The building remains, though the steeple is gone and it is no longer used as a church. The building has been used as a business location in the past. (Courtesy of Springwater–Webster Crossing Historical Society.)

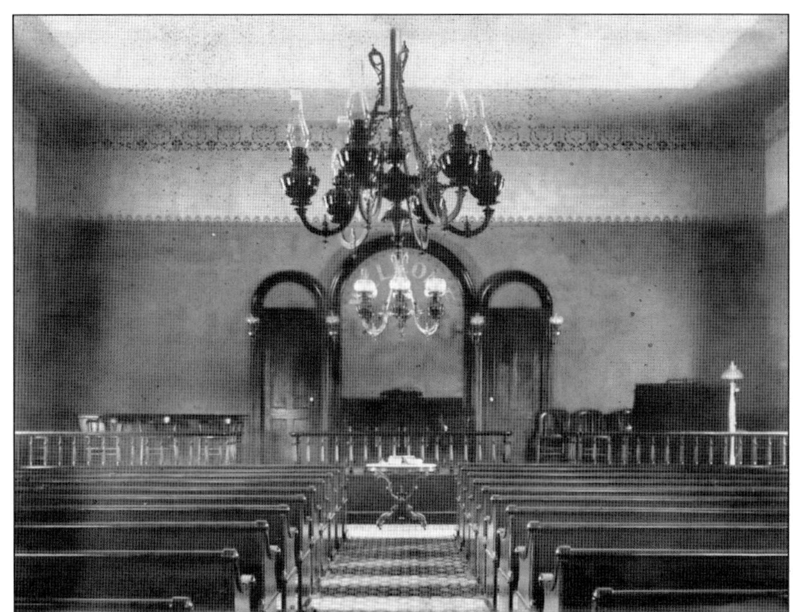

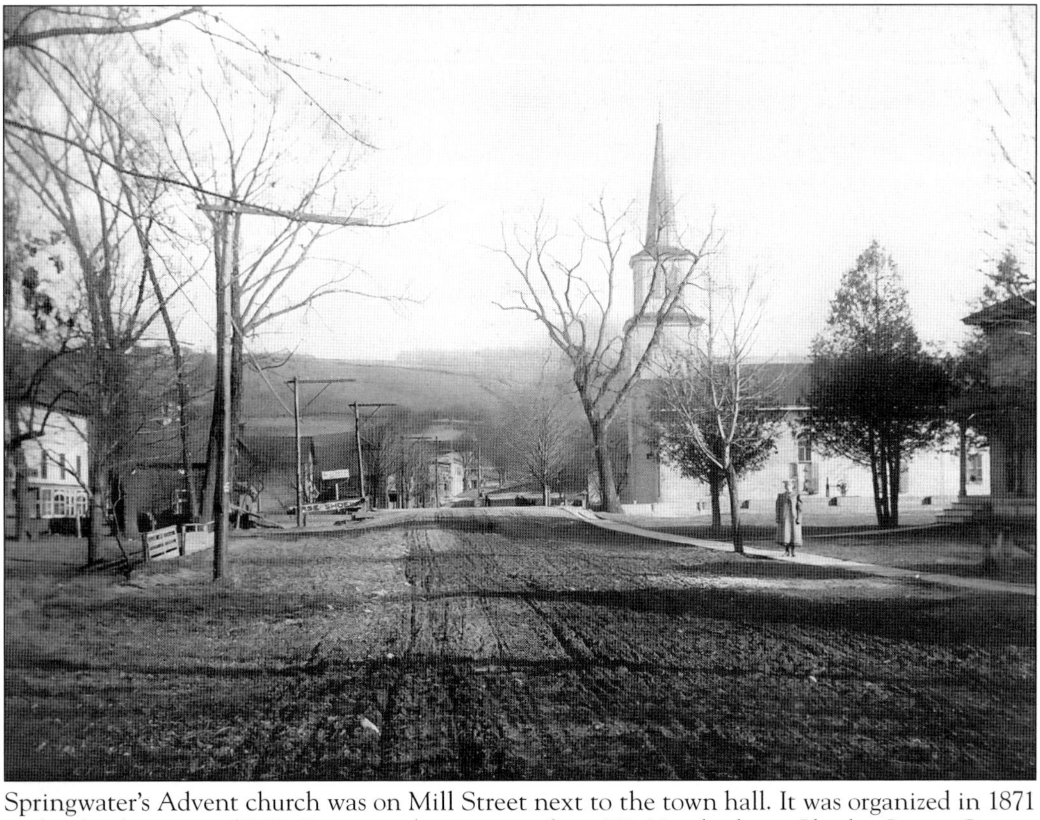

Springwater's Advent church was on Mill Street next to the town hall. It was organized in 1871 under the direction of D.H. Grover with assistance from J.D. Hendershott, Charles Green, George Davis, and Orson Walbridge. The congregation was active in Springwater, holding regular services and hosting church picnics and community events. Floyd Ingraham was raised in this church and attended until his death in 1920. (Courtesy of Joyce O'Neil and Rick Osiecki.)

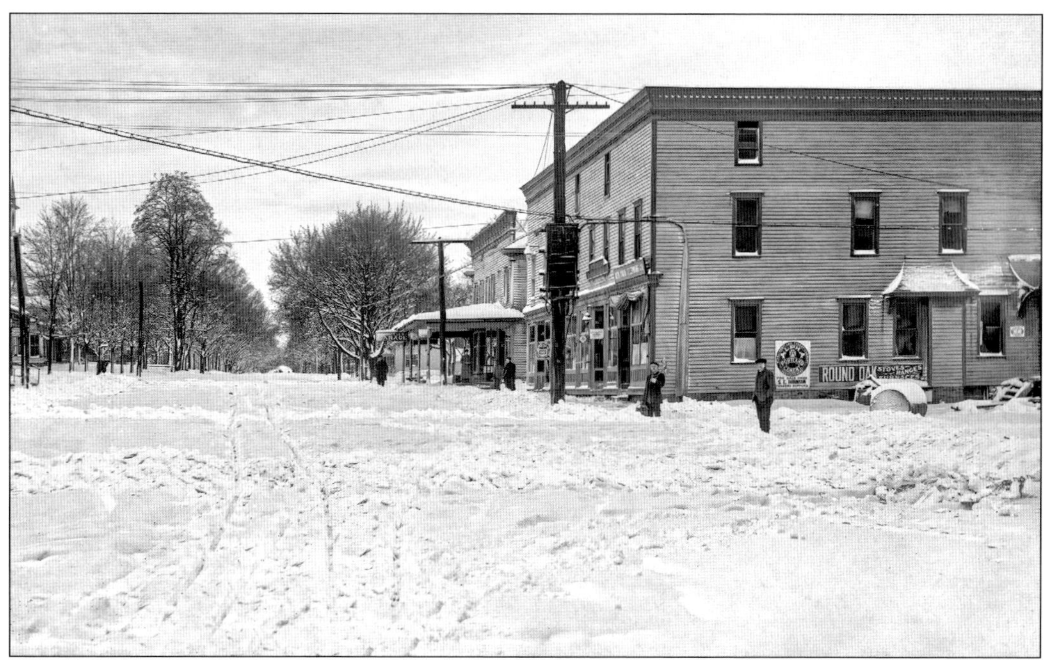

This view of the intersection of Main and Mill Streets in Springwater in winter shows the Marvin Building on the corner, home to many businesses and organizations including the IOOF. Floyd Ingraham and his son Kenneth were members.

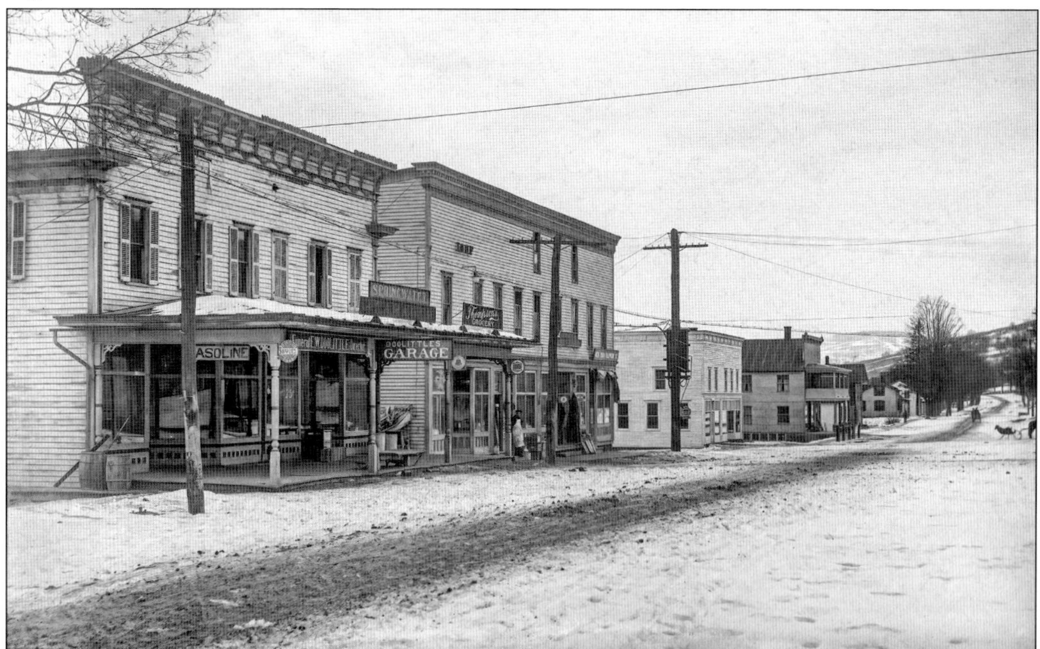

Looking northwest on Main Street in Springwater, these buildings at the intersection of Mill and Main Streets were home to some of Springwater's many businesses. The Laumbahr Building held a gas station and Doolittle's garage and funeral business. The Marvin Building just north of it held Thompson's Grocery, the telephone company, and the IOOF hall. Both buildings are now gone, and a gazebo has taken their place.

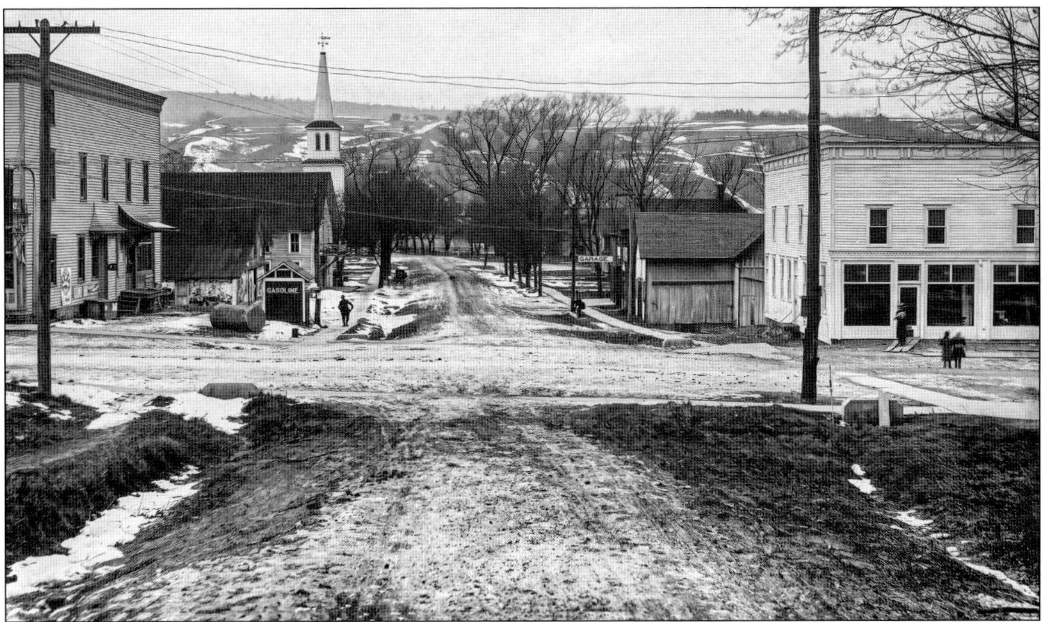

This picture of the four corners was taken from East Avenue looking toward Mill Street in Springwater. At the intersection on the left is the Marvin Building. On the right is the building that replaced Allen and Whitlock's store after it burned in 1909. At different times it was a grocery store, barbershop, antique shop, and the post office. The steeple of the Advent church can be seen just after the opera house, which became town hall. Across the street from it is Higgin's Garage.

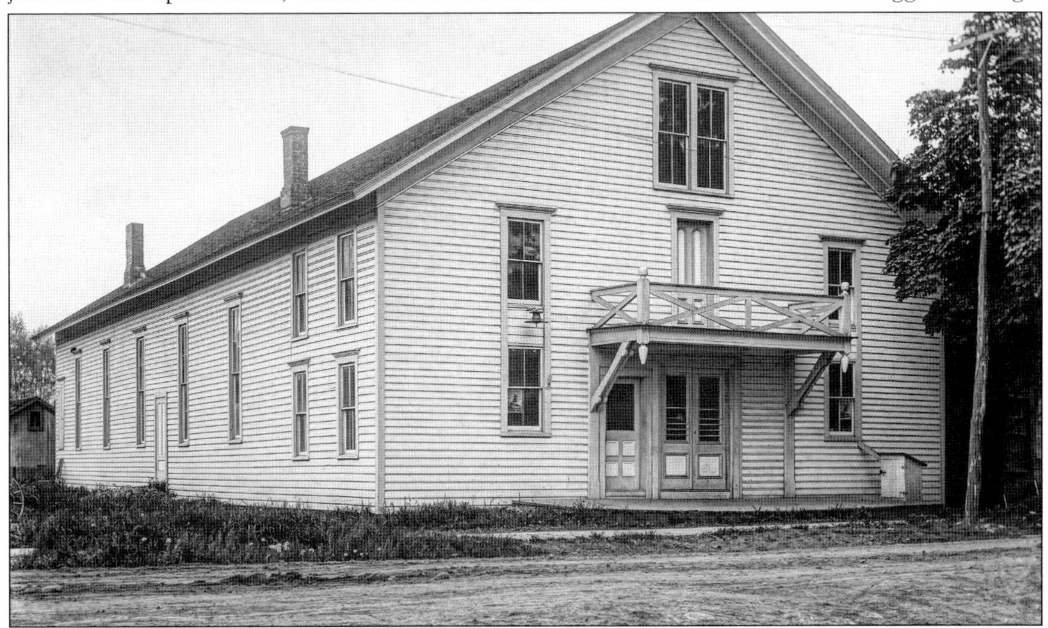

Springwater's town hall on Mill Street was built in 1885 and used as a roller-skating rink with a stage where musicians played for the skaters. In 1911, it was purchased by Springwater as a township and community building. The town hall became the location for voting, meetings, legal proceedings, school commencements, basketball games, conventions, dances, and flower shows. In the 1920s, silent motion pictures were shown here. The town hall was torn down in 2020.

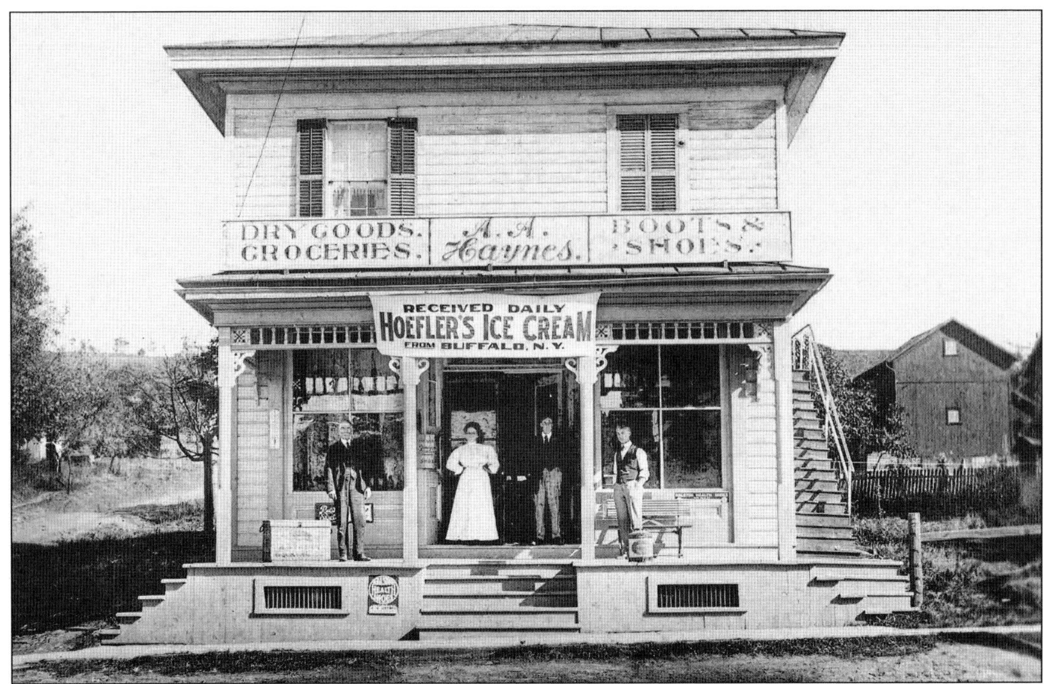

The A.A. Haynes store first opened on Main Street in the Laumbahr Building around 1897 when Aubrey A. Haynes arrived in Springwater from North Cohocton. The business later moved across the street to the location seen here. Haynes had a collection of mounted birds and animals in his barbershop. He operated first as a general store and then represented the chain of Red and White grocery stores. Haynes died in 1936. (Courtesy of Jane Schryver.)

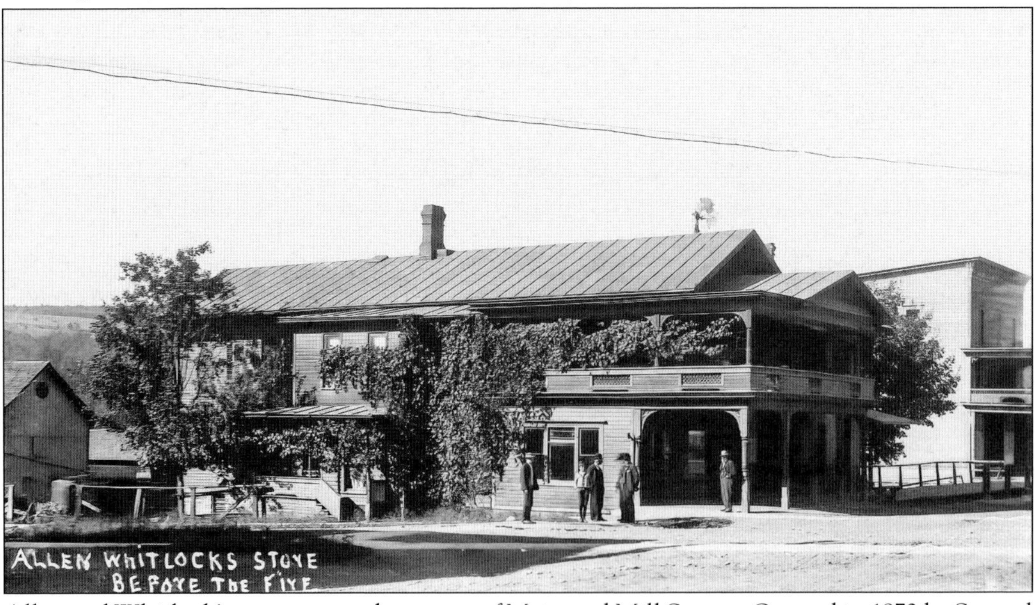

Allen and Whitlock's store was on the corner of Main and Mill Streets. Opened in 1873 by Samuel Whitlock and his brother in law H.E. Allen, the store sold everything from hardware to grocery items to clothing. The people standing outside are unidentified. Taken in 1909, this photograph also shows the Empire Hotel at right. (Courtesy of Joyce O'Neil and Rick Osiecki.)

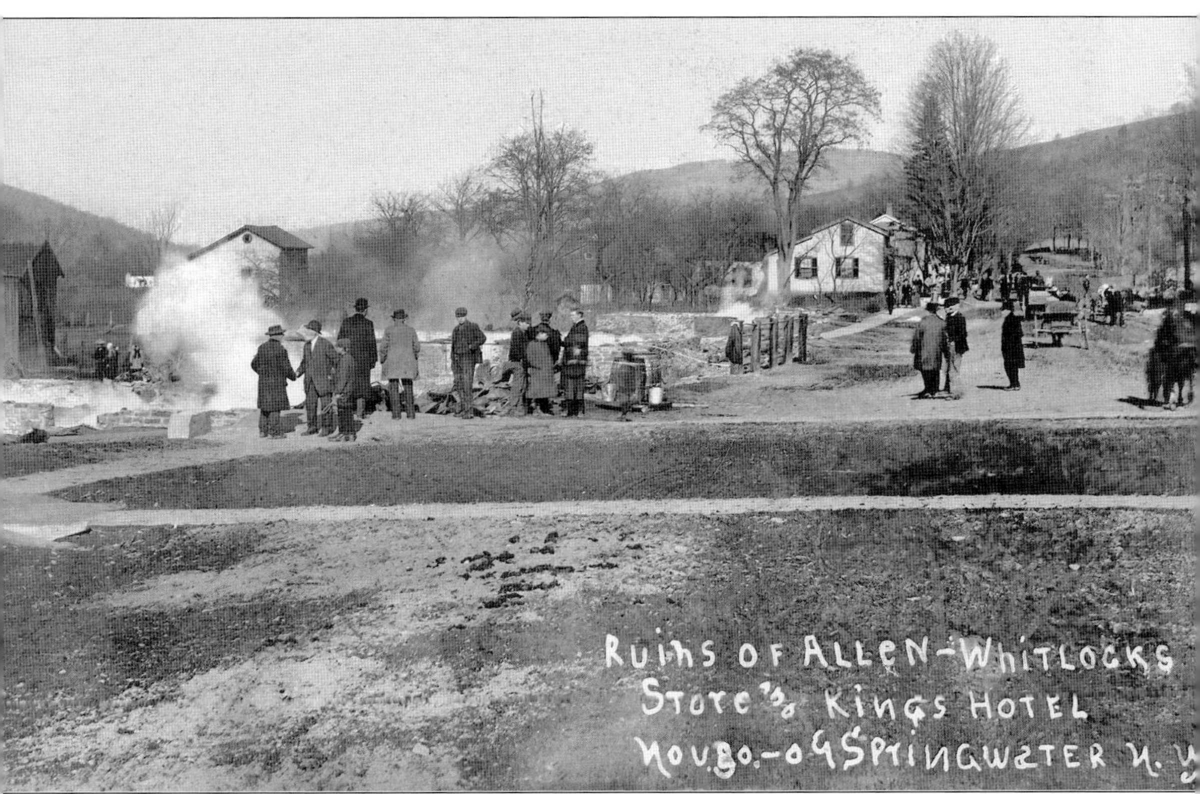

During the evening of November 30, 1909, fire consumed Allen and Whitlock's store, the Empire Hotel, the Robinson brothers' lumber sheds and yards, and Macabbee Hall on Main Street in Springwater. Samuel Whitlock was walking through his store with a lantern when Christmas decorations caught fire. Whitlock escaped through a cellar. His wife and Loretta (Whitlock) Allen, who lived above the store, jumped from windows and were caught by the crowd below. Springwater had no fire department at the time, so neighbors formed a bucket brigade and tried to save what they could. The massive fire scorched and blew out the windows of the Densmore Building across the street. In April 1912, Springwater residents organized a fire company to replace the bucket brigade system. H.H. Densmore installed a water system that same year to provide indoor plumbing and simultaneously bolstered the new fire company's effectiveness. The Springwater Volunteer Fire Company used water from the Densmore water system (later sold to the township) to save homes and lives. The Springwater Fire Company was incorporated in 1947. Today, Springwater's Station 54 serves over 2,400 residents of the township. (Courtesy of Douglas Morgan.)

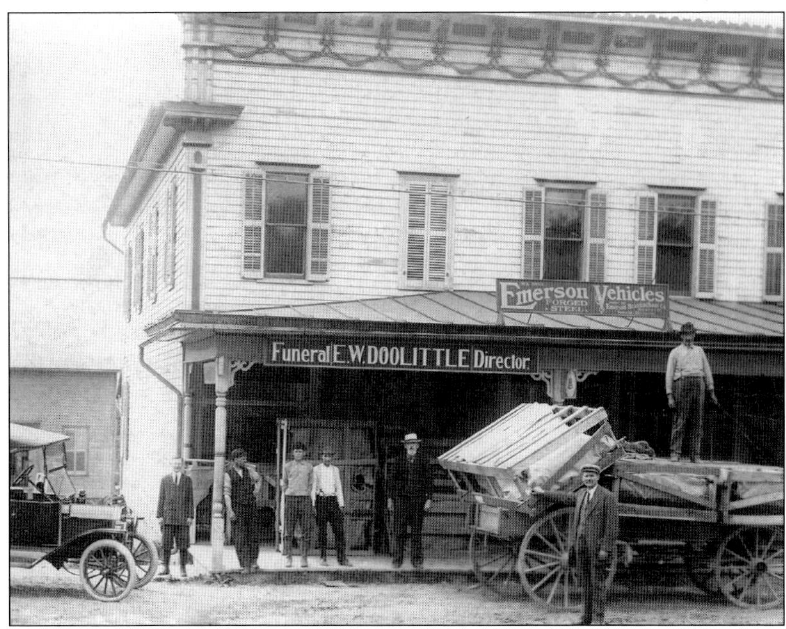

Edwin W. Doolittle operated his business out of the Laumbahr Building on Main Street. He and his wife, Emma, moved from Canadice to Springwater, where they opened an auto parts business and garage. Doolittle was also a funeral director and did repair work and odd jobs in the community. (Courtesy of Joyce O'Neil and Rick Osiecki.)

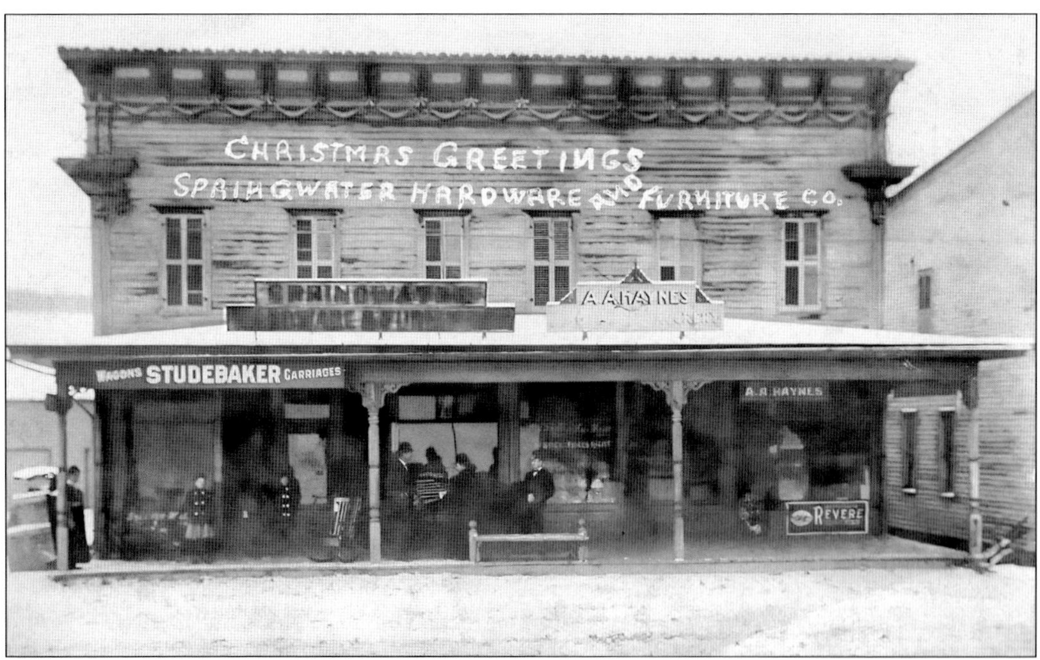

The Springwater Hardware and Furniture store was next to the A.A. Haynes store's first location in the Laumbahr Building on Main Street. The building no longer exists. Floyd Ingraham took photographs of many businesses and printed them as postcards. This one was a Christmas greeting card for customers in the early 1900s. (Courtesy of Joyce O'Neil and Rick Osiecki.)

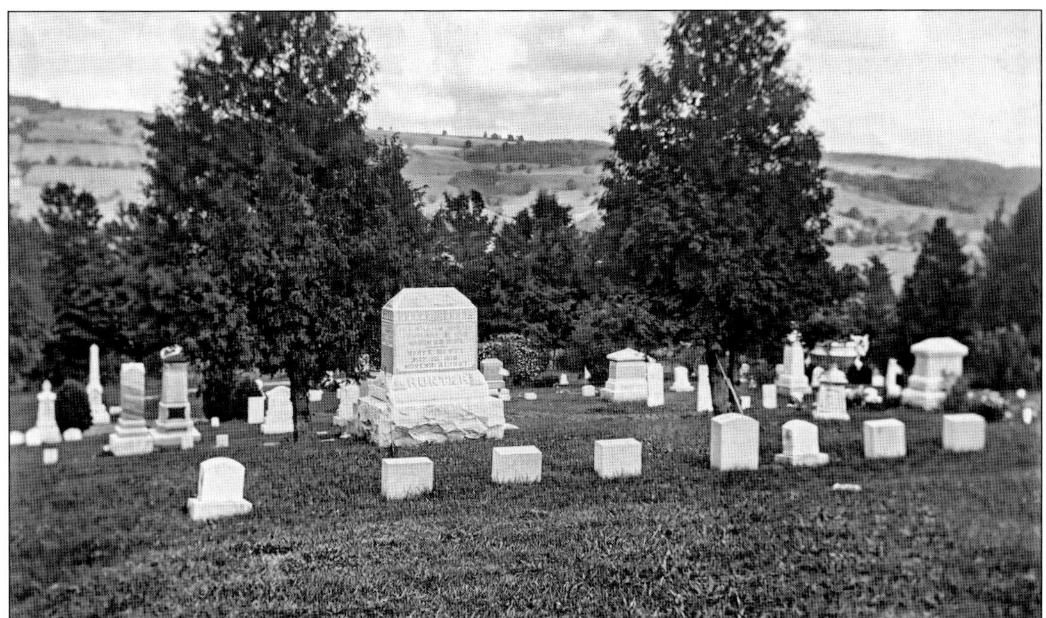

Mount Vernon Evergreen Cemetery is on Kellogg Road in Springwater. The earliest grave is that of Jane F. Stickney, who was born in 1790 and died on January 24, 1819. Floyd Ingraham photographed this cemetery often, one of eight in the township. His father, brother, nephew, son, and daughter-in-law are all buried here. Ingraham himself is also interred here near a path by a row of tall evergreen trees.

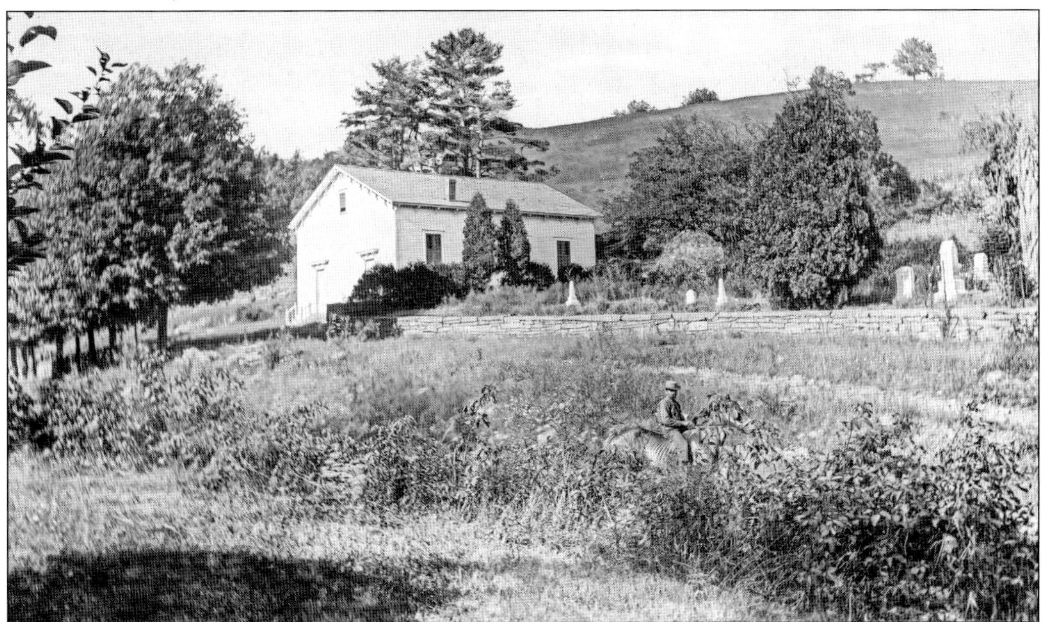

The Old South Church and cemetery on New York State Route 63 in Sparta, New York, was formed in 1808. It was the first church in Sparta and among the oldest in western New York. The church was used as the Sparta School and is still standing, though now privately owned. This view from the field behind the church shows the cemetery that contains the graves of early pioneers and Revolutionary War soldiers.

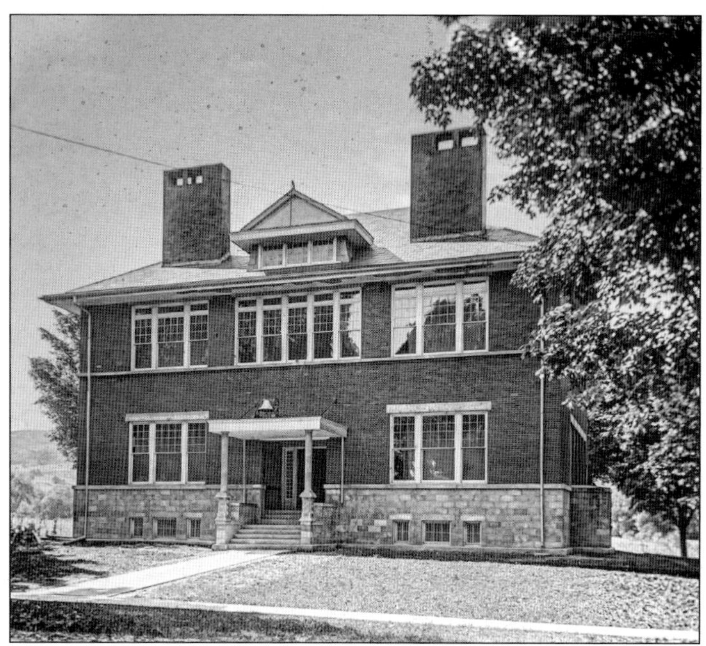

School No. 2 was formed in the mid-1800s on Main Street in Springwater. In 1874, a new building was erected on School Street. The two-story wooden building was used until this brick structure was constructed in 1912. Floyd Ingraham was one of the men who built the Springwater Union School, most likely using his masonry skills to construct its foundation. It became the school that Ingraham's son Kenneth attended and graduated from. The building is now the home of the American Legion Post 905.

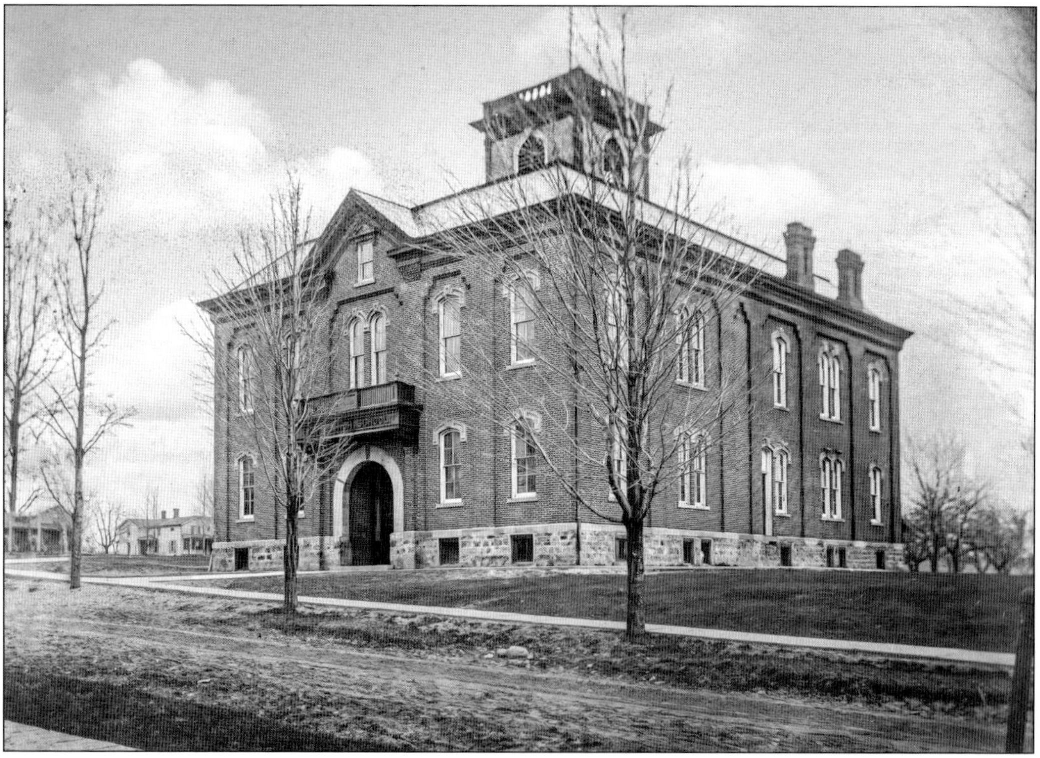

Livonia High School opened its doors in January 1876. First called the Livonia Union School, it graduated its first class of two students in 1882. In 1893, the building was expanded, and the bell tower changed to what is seen here. A third floor was added later. Students were charged for their education, and room and board if needed. In 1928, the district constructed a new school, and the building seen here was used as a gymnasium and auditorium space.

Canisteo Academy was at the corner of Greenwood and Academy Streets in Canisteo, New York. Formed in the late 1860s by Rev. Lewis Laine, who felt there was a need for higher education, the original brick building opened in September 1871. This picture was taken before 1914, since the grade school that would be constructed next to it that year is missing. A new school was erected on the Canisteo Academy site in 1935, and the original building was demolished in 1937. (Courtesy of Ron and Sharon Ingraham.)

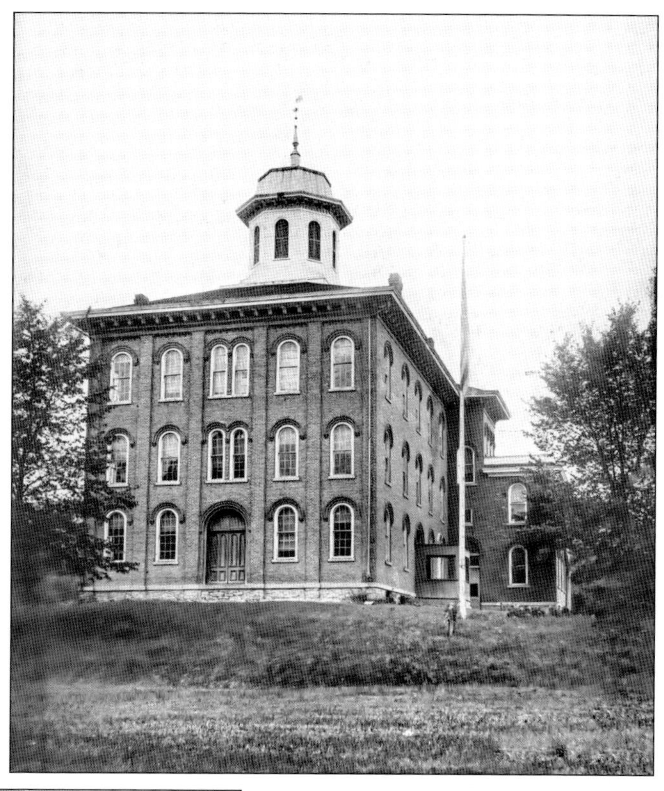

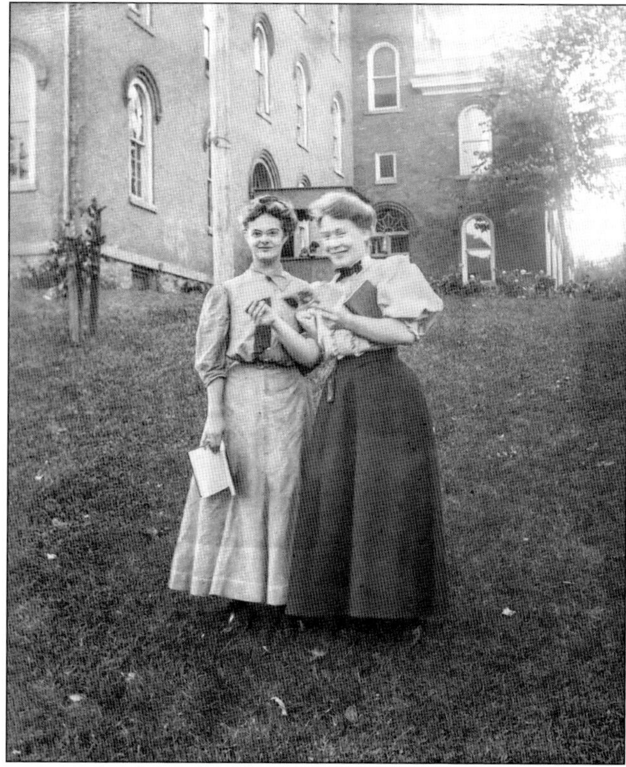

Elizabeth "Bess" Smail (right) of Springwater and an unidentified classmate stand outside of Canisteo Academy. This academy, like others in the region, provided higher education. Graduates could receive a teaching certificate.

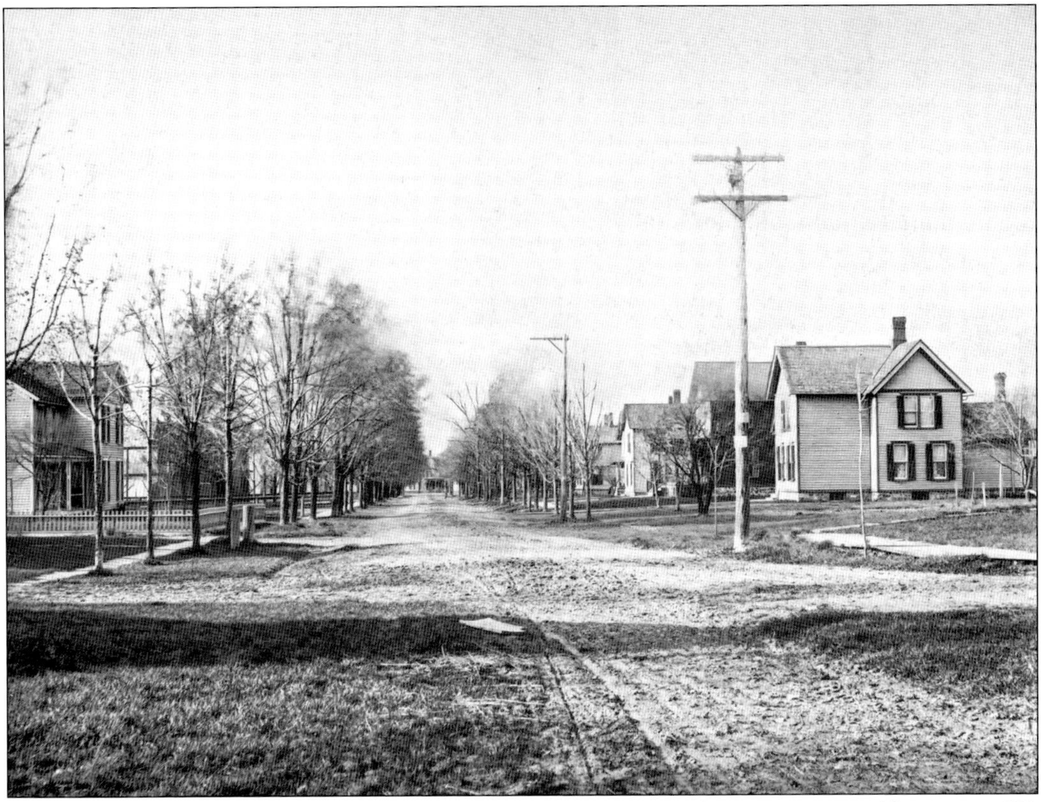

School Street in Springwater is parallel to Main Street. The road was constructed between 1872 and 1874. At the end of School Street is Mill Street. The Ernest home on Mill Street can be seen in the distance here. Halfway down School Street, on the left, the Springwater Union School would be built in 1912. It is now the American Legion building.

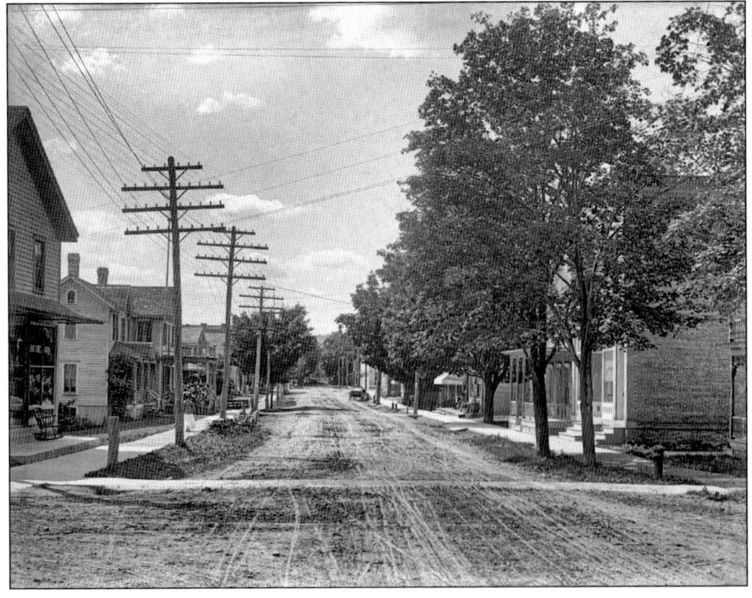

Springwater had electricity by 1900 and telephone lines installed in 1902. This view of Main Street shows utility poles carrying telephone and electrical lines to homes and businesses. Storms toppled lines in several newsworthy weather events, but they were soon up and running again, connecting Springwater to the outside world by phone and offering the modern-day convenience of electricity.

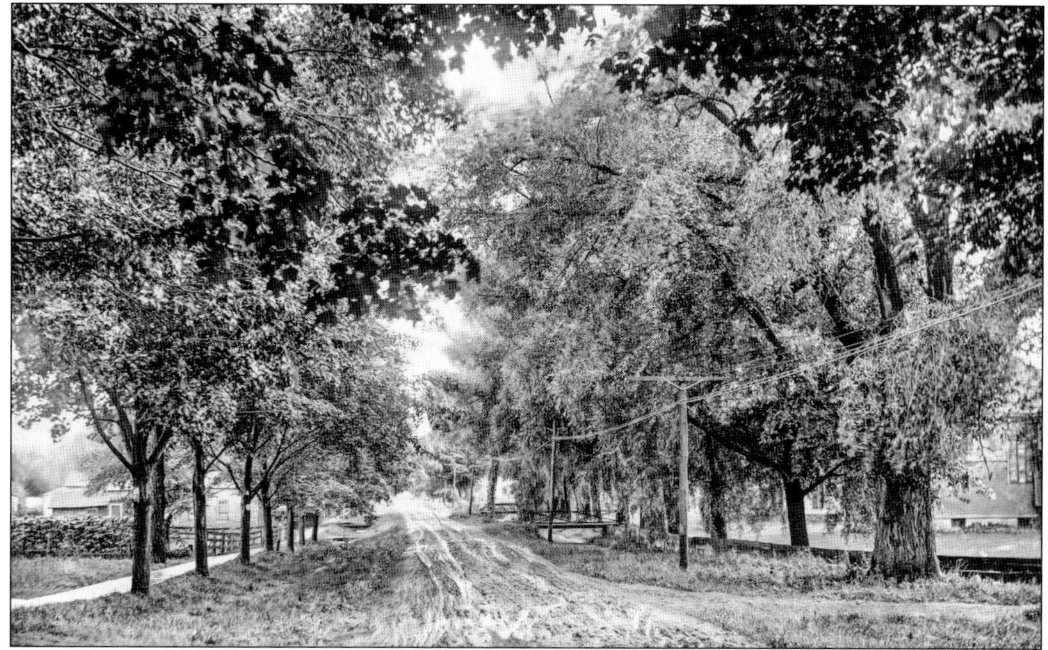

This view of tree-lined Main Street is looking south toward the intersection of what today is Depot Road. On the right, just behind the trees, is the Henry K. Cooper home that is shown on page 35. The small bridges on the side of the road allowed access to the road and unimpeded flow of one of Springwater's many streams.

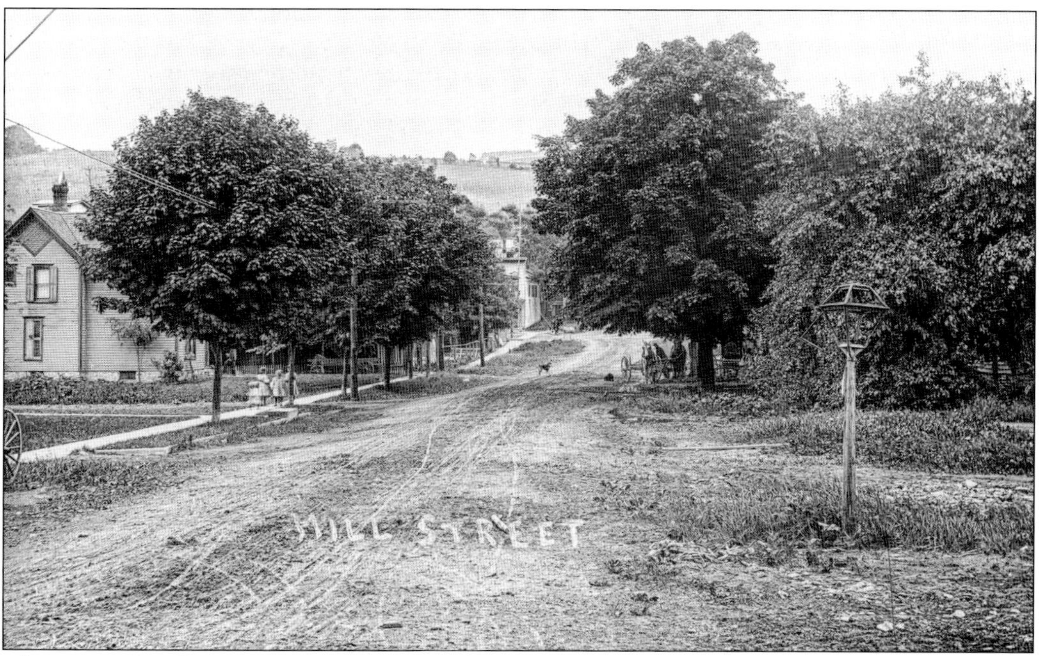

This view of Mill Street in Springwater looking toward Main Street is an excellent example of a village street scene in early-20th-century Finger Lakes communities. Girls stand on a sidewalk at left, a streetlamp can be seen at right, and men around a horse-drawn carriage wait beneath trees near where a horseshoe business was located, as a dog meanders across the street.

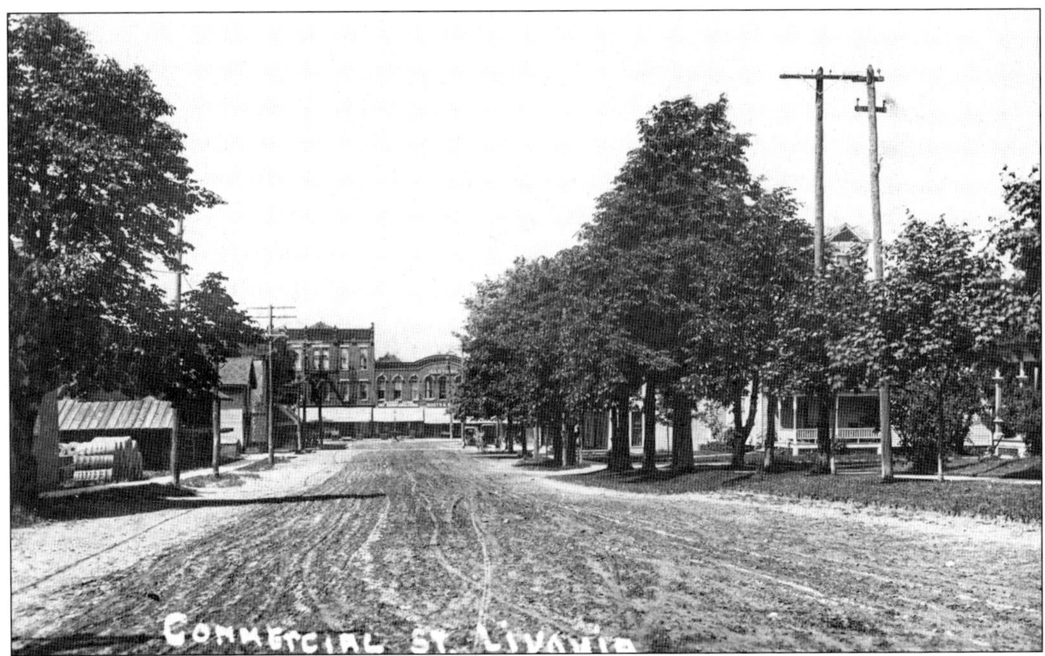

This view of Commercial Street in Livonia is looking toward Main Street. The Trescott Building, constructed in 1879, is at the end of the street. Trescott Hall hosted lecturers, comedy acts, and musical entertainment in its third-floor auditorium. Many businesses operated in the building. On March 12, 1930, a fire started in B.C. Black's store and quickly spread. Attempts to sound a siren failed, and by the time word spread, it was too late to save the Trescott Building. The fire, the worst since 1878 when buildings on the same site burned, consumed much of Livonia's business section on the north end of Main Street. Livonia rallied and rebuilt. Today, other businesses occupy the location where the Trescott once stood.

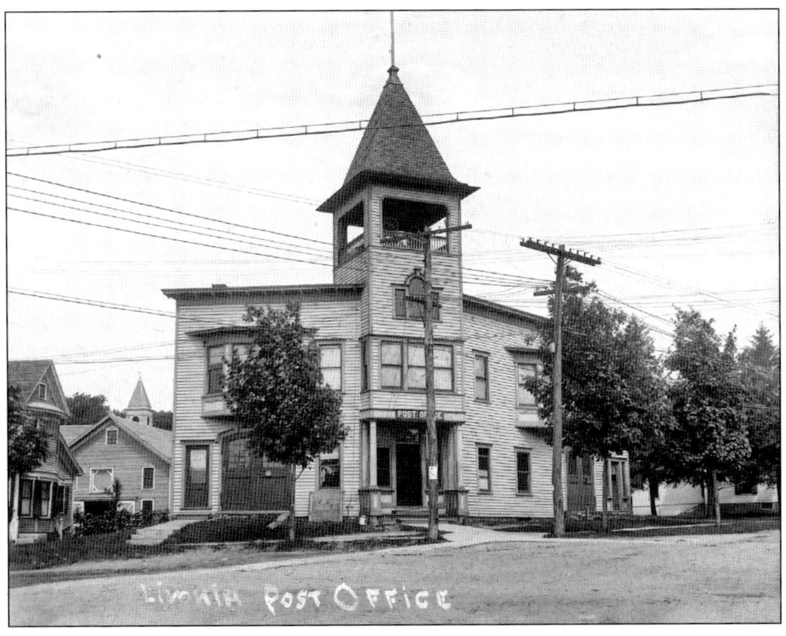

Livonia was formed from Pittstown on February 12, 1808. It lies near the north ends of Conesus and Hemlock Lakes. The name is derived from a Russian province and was proposed by Col. George Smith. The first settler in the town was Solomon Woodruff, who arrived in 1789 and built a log cabin. The post office first opened on April 9, 1811.

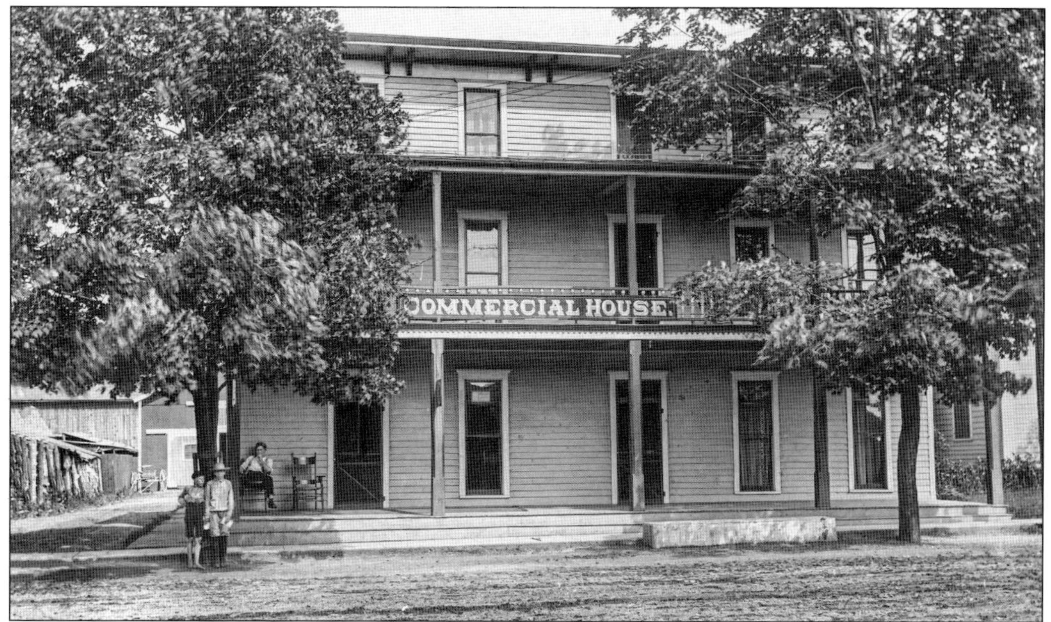

The Commercial House in Livonia was built in 1860 by Zebulon Woodruff as a home. It later became an inn called the Church House. During Prohibition, the inn's bar served ice cream. Now called the Livonia Inn, the building remains with its original hand-dug basement, cistern, and livery stable. It still welcomes guests, operating now as a restaurant and lounge. This c. 1907 photograph shows the famed Commercial House porch where many speeches were given.

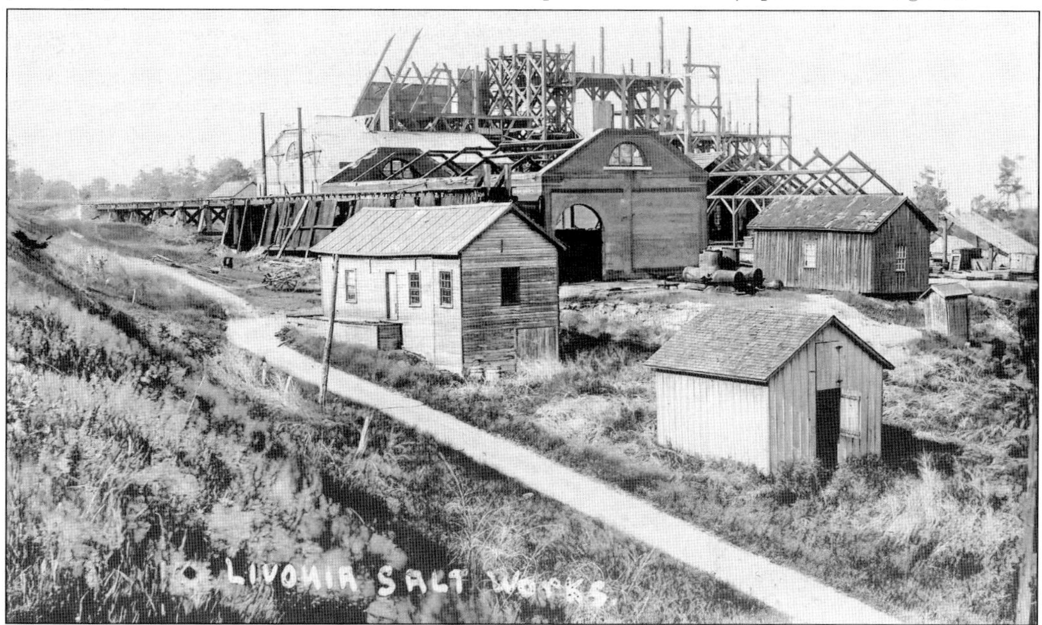

A salt well was put in north of Livonia by M.L. Townsend in the late 1800s. There, a solid bed of salt was discovered, the thickest in western New York. Townsend bought and leased hundreds of acres one mile south of Livonia and built a salt mine, completed in 1892. The mine was later sold to the Retsof Salt Company, which became the International Salt Company. Livingston County has produced more salt than any other county in New York. (Courtesy of Ron and Sharon Ingraham.)

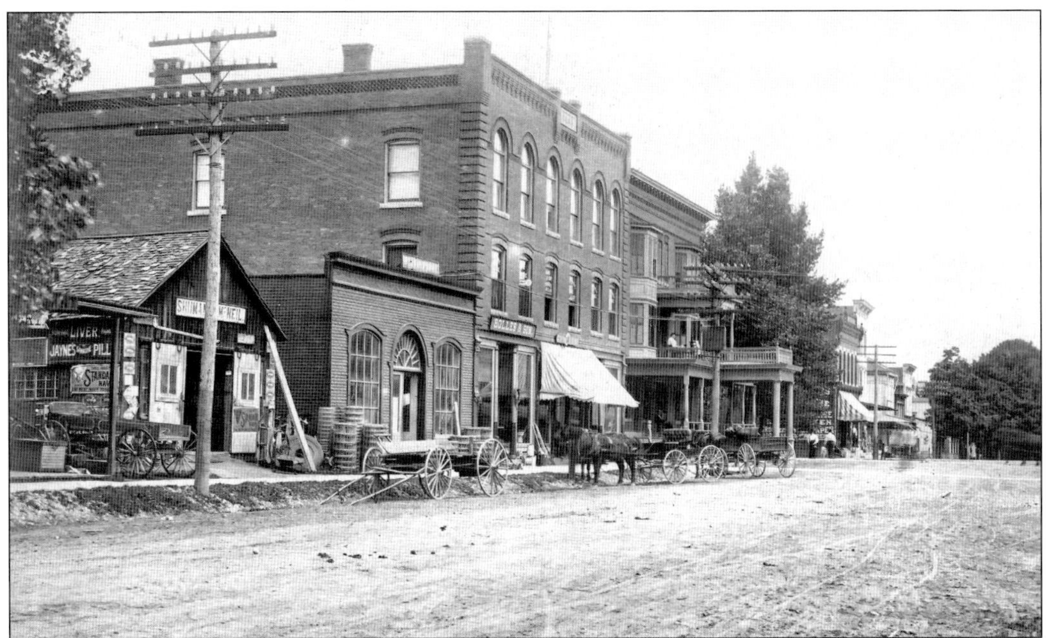

The G.R. Grandby Building was constructed in 1896. It held Bolles & Son Hardware on the first floor, and the telephone company on the second floor. Located on Main Street in Naples, New York, it is still standing, although the annex seen at left is gone. The annex has a sign above it advertising Wiard Plows. John C. Bolles took over the store for his father. He ran and organized the Naples Fair, built a movie theater, and owned a Ford dealership on Main Street. He served as the town supervisor and was elected Ontario County sheriff. (Courtesy of Ron and Sharon Ingraham.)

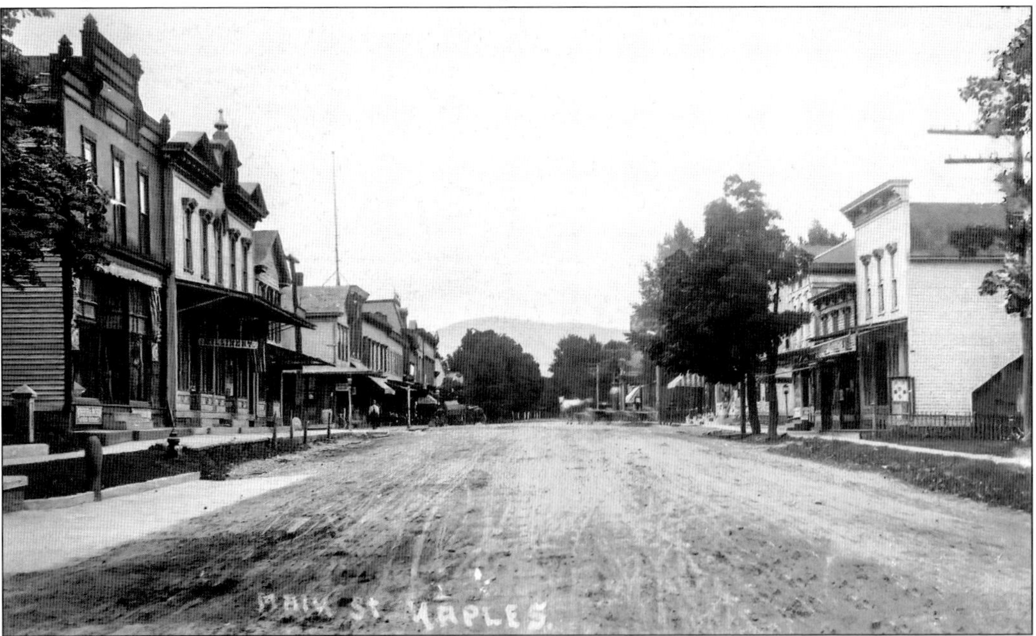

Naples was founded in 1798. It was first called Watkinstown, then Middletown, and was named Naples in 1808. The town became known for its vineyards and wineries. It has beautiful views of Naples Valley and Canandaigua Lake from its hills. This view of Main Street faces south around 1910.

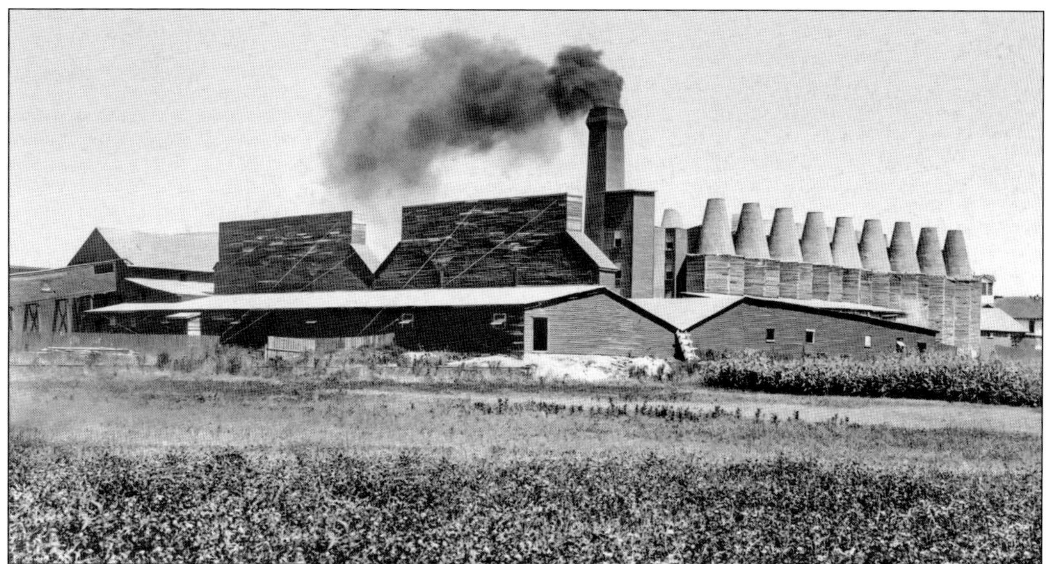

The Wayland Cement Works was built in 1892 after Thomas Millen and sons discovered marl deposits. In its first decade, the factory provided many jobs, and Wayland's population doubled. The cement works, with its large conical kilns, operated until 1907. In 1914, the Wayne Power Company used the building to house generators that supplied surrounding communities with electricity. The building was razed in 1941. (Courtesy of Ron and Sharon Ingraham.)

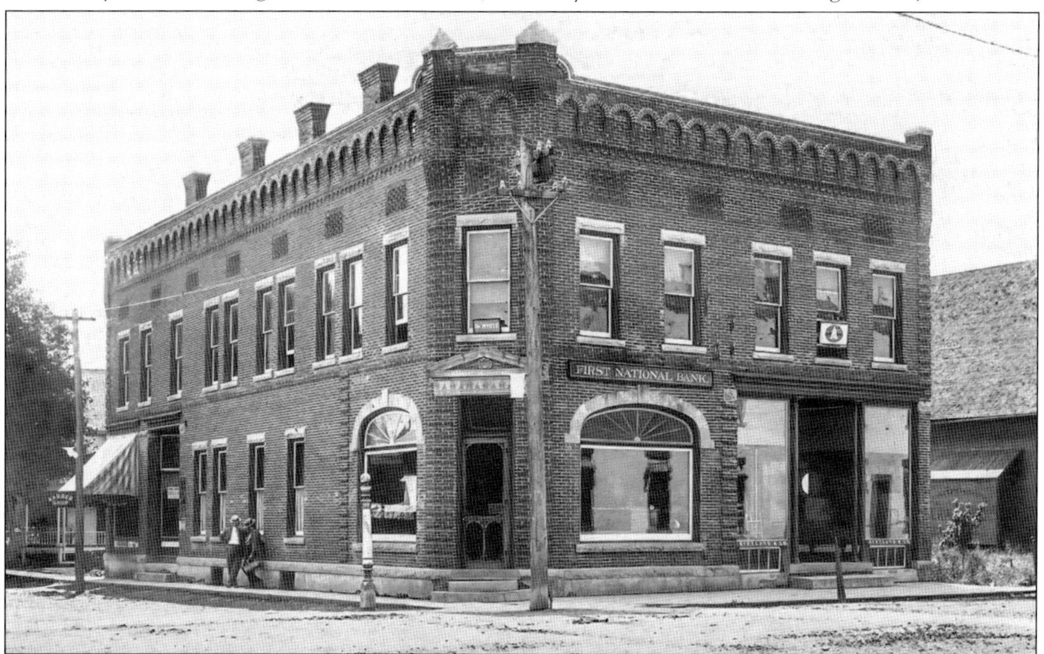

The First National Bank of Wayland was built in 1899. On the corner of West Naples and Main Streets, the bank was one of Wayland's prominent brick buildings. Brick was used in the early 20th century after several fires devastated Wayland's businesses. As a mint, the bank printed $713,340 worth of national currency here until 1935. Brown-back notes from the bank are quite valuable today. The building seen here was demolished in 1967. (Courtesy of Springwater–Webster Crossing Historical Society.)

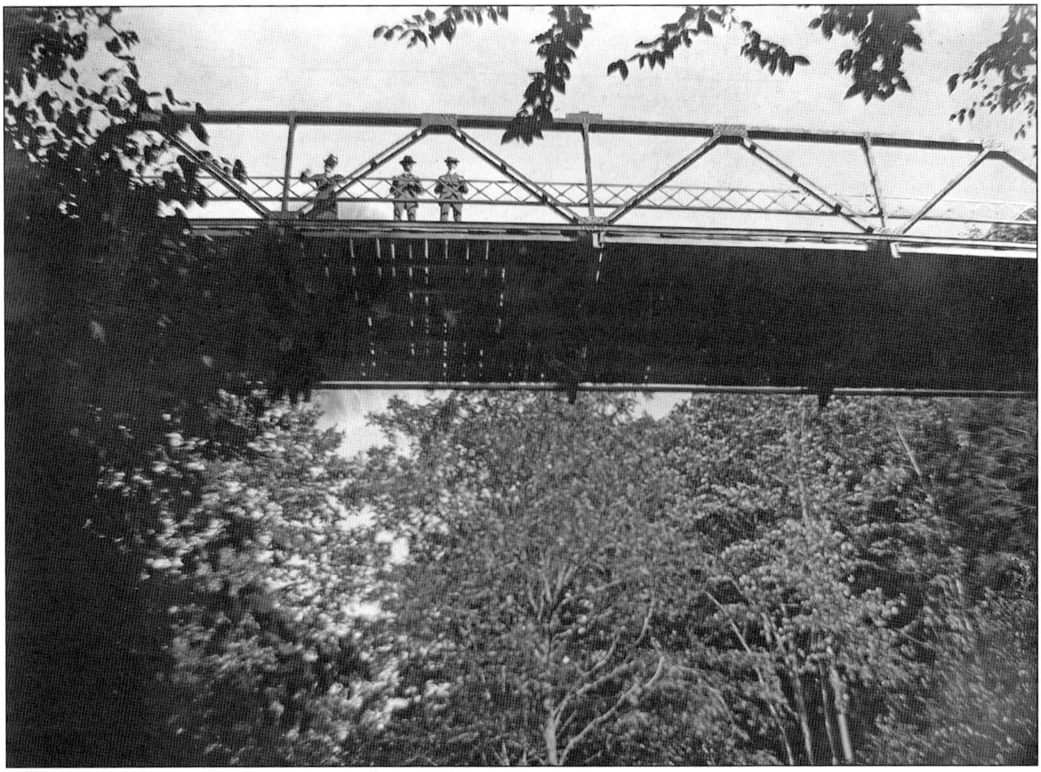

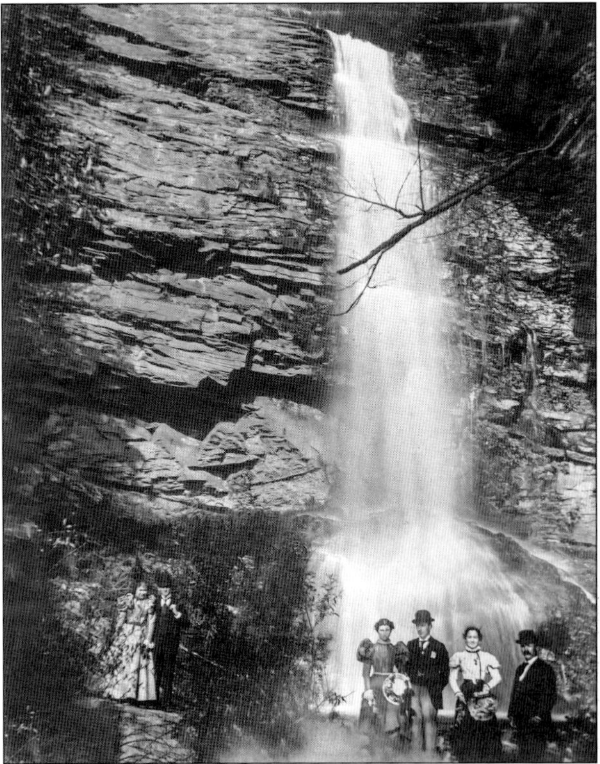

In 1840, Gordon Thayer and Orson Walbridge built the first covered bridge across Reynold's Gull. A second wooden bridge was built to replace the first in 1873. It collapsed and fell into the bottom of the gull, and a steel bridge, pictured here, was constructed. It was built in 1902 by the United Construction Company and stood until 1952.

This waterfall in Reynolds Gull is one of many tributaries that flow from the Hemlock Lake watershed. New York has over 2,000 waterfalls, many of which are in the Finger Lakes region. One local resident said she had counted 90 streams in Springwater. Many Finger Lakes communities have waterfalls, streams, rivers, and lakes in abundance, making this region one of the most beautiful places to hike and explore in the northeastern United States.

This tunnel is a mystery, as it has not been identified. Many similar tunnels exist in and around Springwater. Tunnels were built with sandstone or limestone in the late 1800s and early 1900s to carry roads or streams. Tunnels like this freed up tributaries to travel on to their destinations while providing sound support for passing trains above.

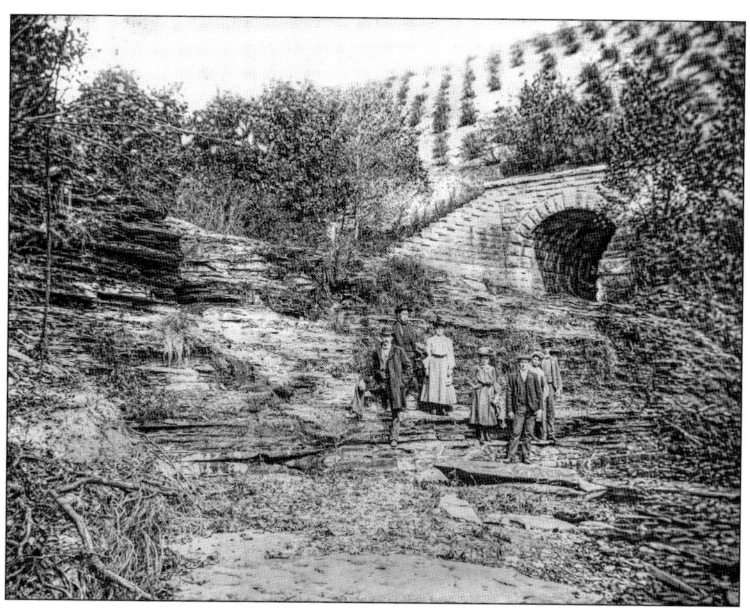

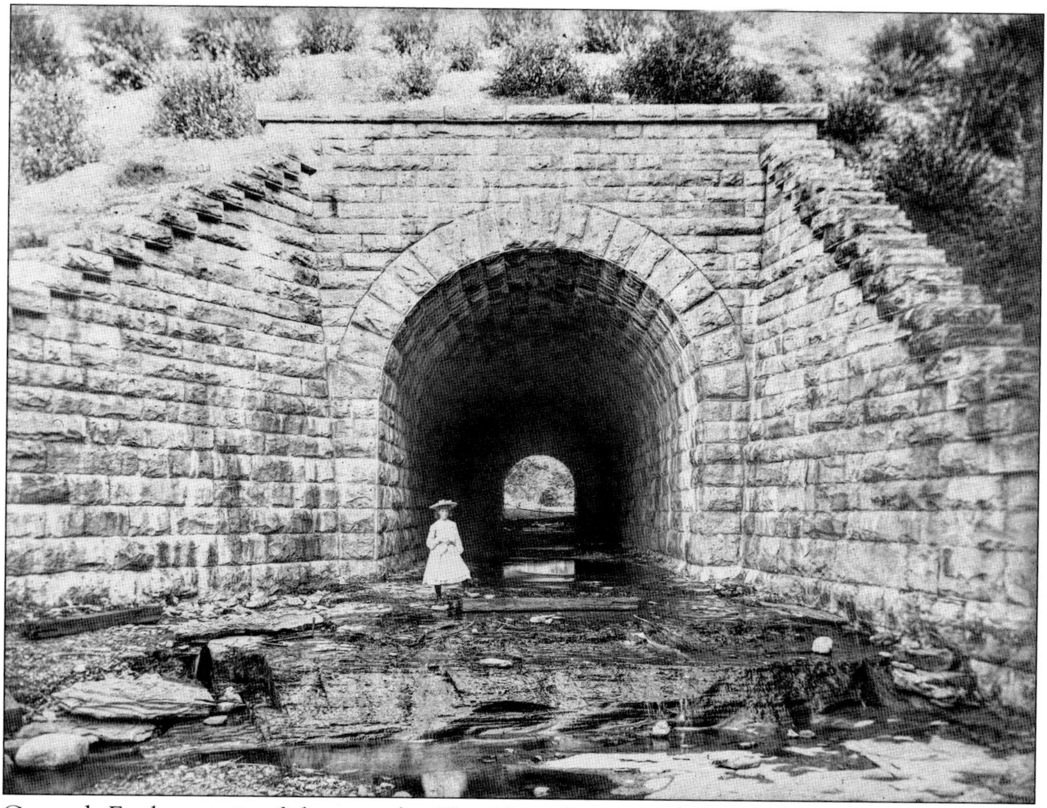

Gertrude Ford, a cousin of photographer Floyd Ingraham, stands outside of a tunnel in the Finger Lakes region. Ingraham took several photographs of this tunnel, some with his friends and family in the pictures. A similar tunnel can be seen at Corbett's Glenn, New York.

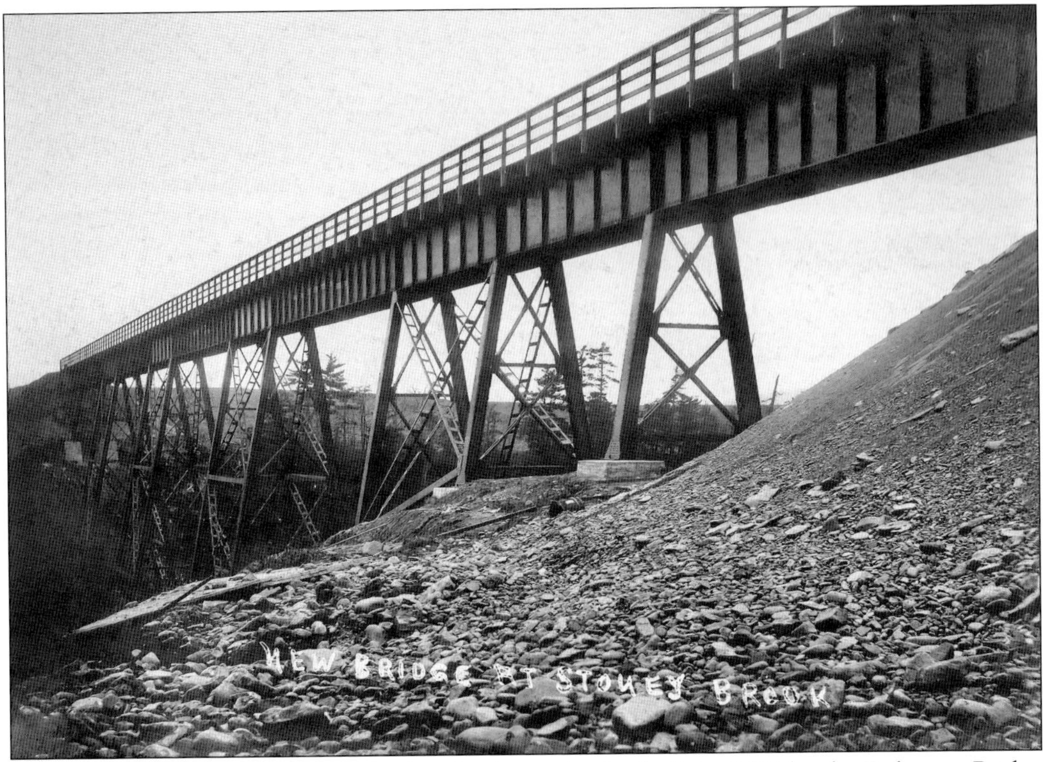

This bridge at Stony Brook Glen replaced a former bridge built in 1883 by the Delaware Bridge Company. Called the Pittsburgh, Shawmut & Northern Railroad Bridge when it was completed in 1907, this deck plate girder bridge rose 245 feet above the gorge. The deck plate description refers to structural steel plates that form I-beams that crisscross to form girders (or trusses) that hold up the structure. In the 1940s, this was the second-highest railroad bridge in the United States. It was 640 feet long and contained 1.3 million pounds of steel. It was abandoned in 1947 and eventually demolished. (Courtesy of Springwater–Webster Crossing Historical Society.)

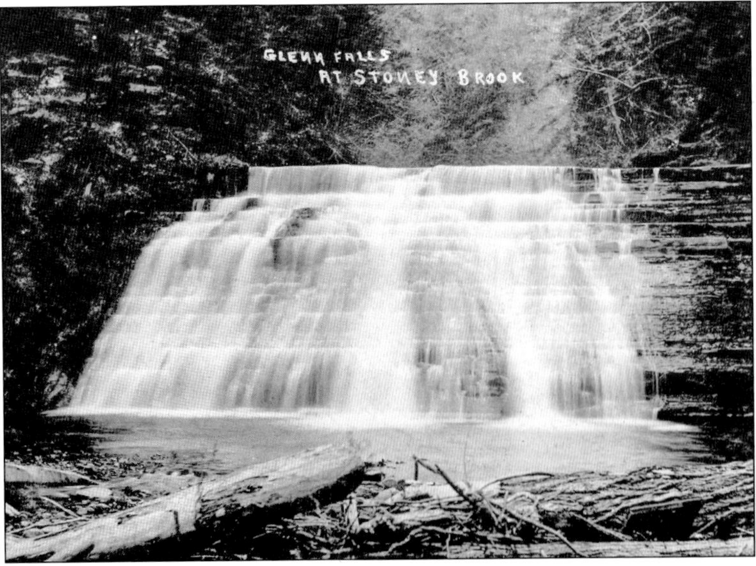

Stony Brook State Park is in Steuben County, south of Dansville. Frequented as a tourist spot in the late 1800s, it initially had 250 acres that included a gorge, waterfalls, picnic areas, and nature trails. Stony Brook Glen was where Mary Jemison and the Seneca tribe hid during General Sullivan's raid in 1779. (Courtesy of Ron and Sharon Ingraham.)

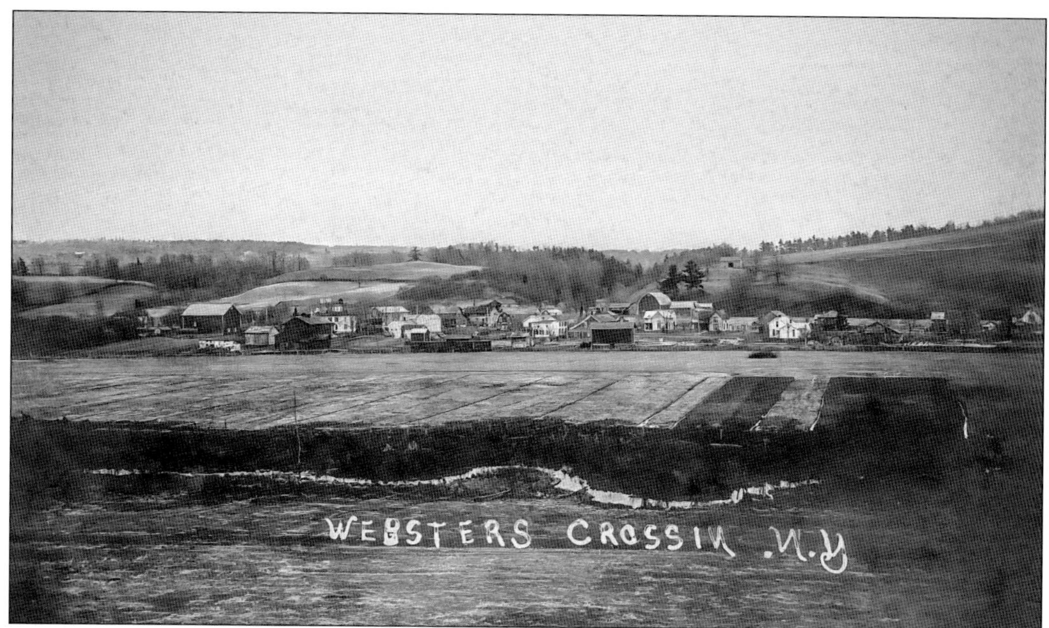

Webster Crossing, New York, was founded by Elisha Webster, who came there in 1845. Originally known as Webster's Crossing, local residents say the name of the hamlet today depends which way one drives into it. One sign has the possessive spelling, Webster's Crossing, and the other reads Webster Crossing. It is in Springwater Township on New York State Route 15. Webster Crossing was a small community in the early 1900s, with churches, schools, mills, shops, a blacksmith shop, and a New York & Erie Railroad depot. By the mid-1900s, it was also home to a large dairy operation. (Courtesy of Springwater–Webster Crossing Historical Society.)

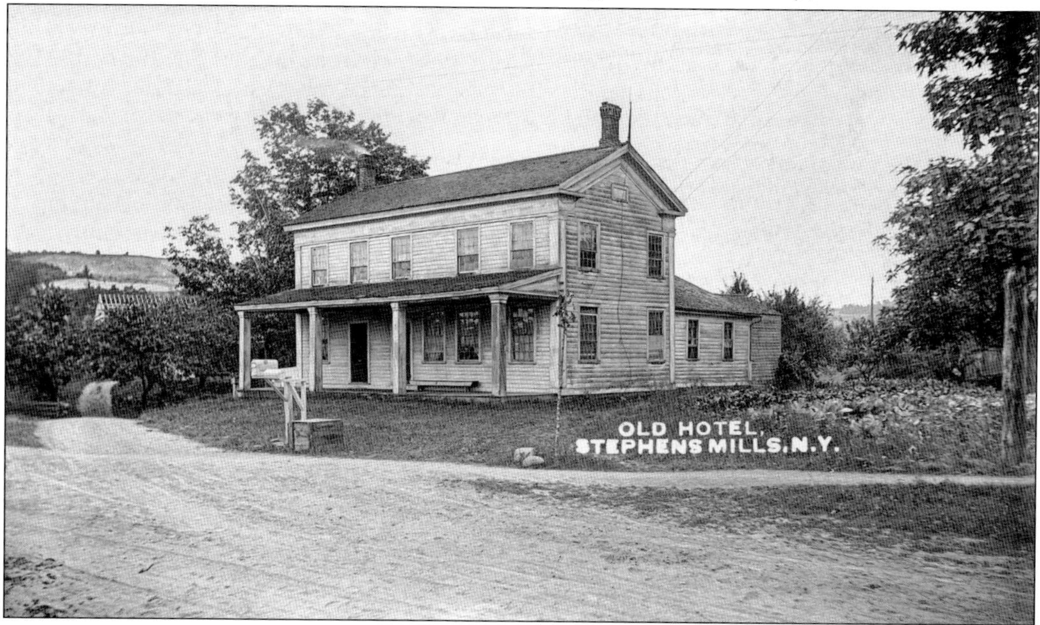

This building still stands in the small community of Stephen's Mills. Located on New York State Route 21 between Loon Lake and North Hornell, New York, it was a place to rest for travelers. Stephen's Mills is now part of the township of Fremont in Steuben County.

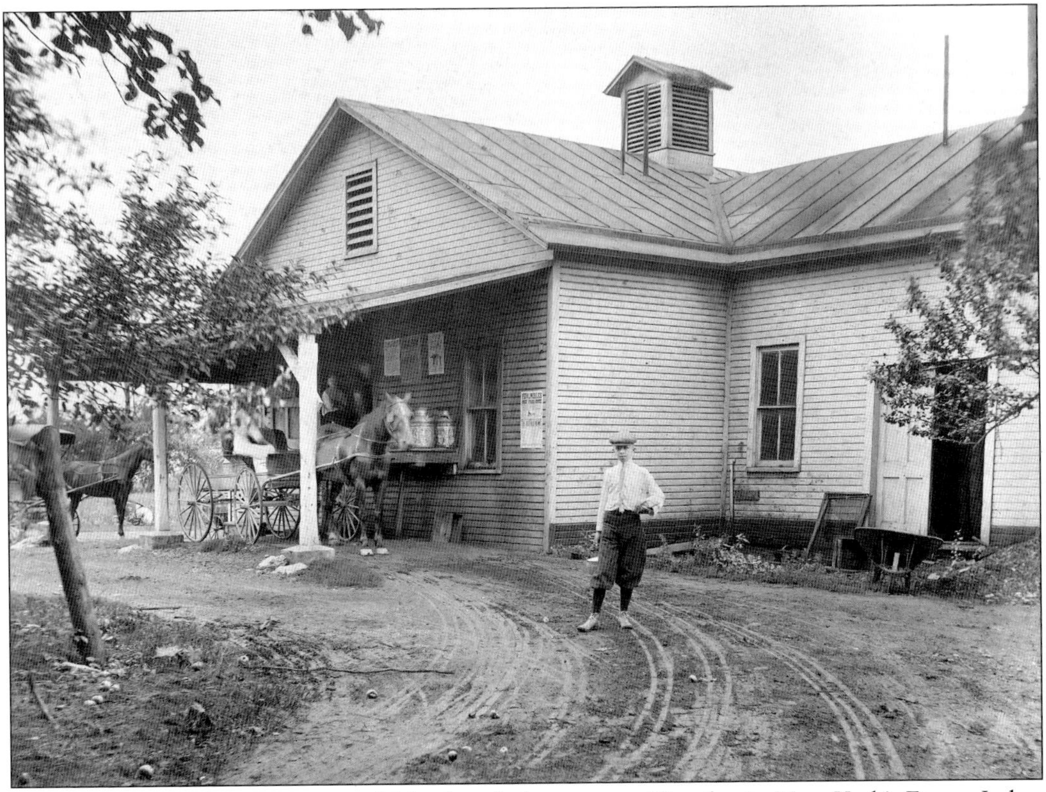

Cheese plants and creameries could be found about every 10 miles in New York's Finger Lakes region during the early 20th century. Dairy farms were abundant throughout the state. From around 1895 until 1910, a small creamery on the Earnest/Miller farm made butter and cheese from the milk of the local farmers' herds. Milk was delivered daily from the farm to the creamery by horse and buggy in 10-gallon cans.

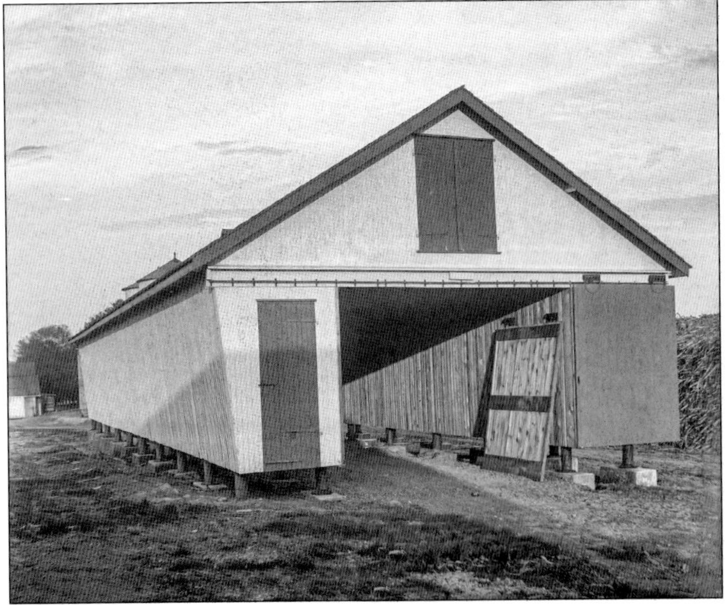

The pictures on this page are unidentified but are examples of scenes that were common in the Finger Lakes region in the early 20th century. Pole barns were easier and cheaper to construct because they used fewer materials and allowed for recycling materials, such as utility poles. This type of barn was larger and longer and could accommodate large machinery. Pole barns were not without problems, as the poles were often compromised and susceptible to rot.

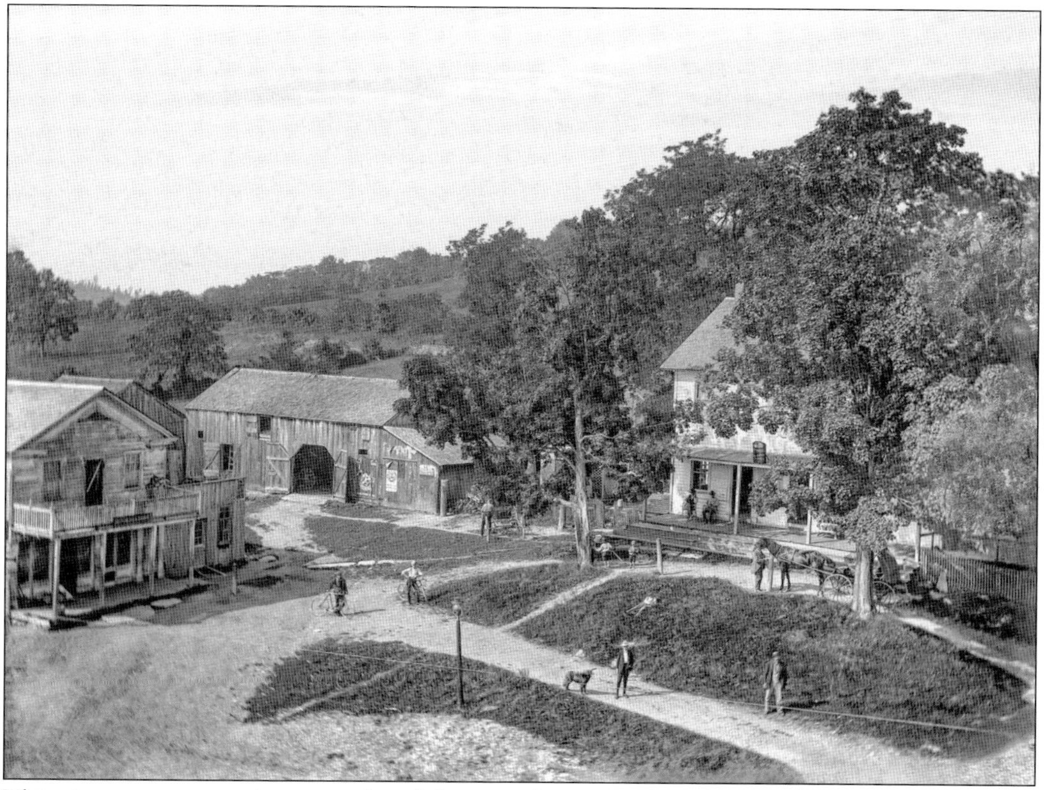

This picturesque scene has more detail than can be seen at first glance. The house has a sign on its porch roof that indicates it is an inn of some kind. The barn and carriage house has a buggy just inside its doors. And a balcony-clad building may have been used as a mercantile or dining establishment that welcomed traveling guests in need of a meal or dry goods. Although its location is still not identified, it is very much in keeping with Floyd Ingraham's style of photography and the Finger Lakes region he loved to photograph.

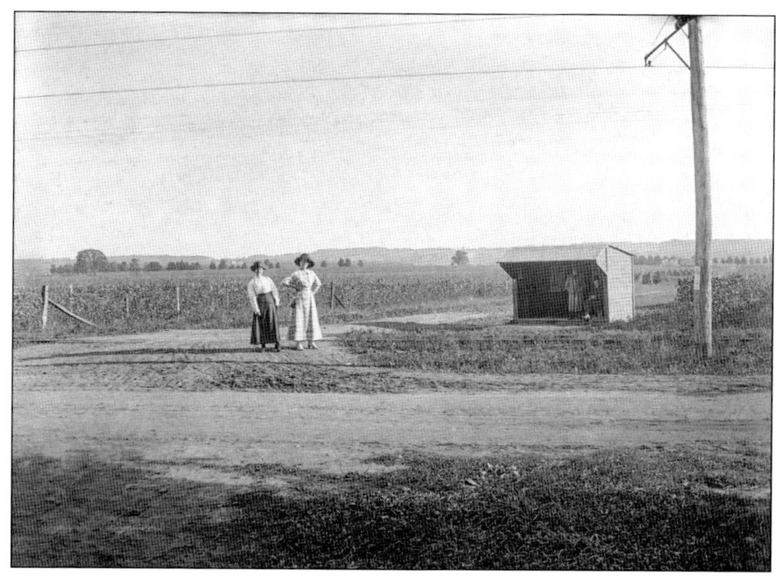

Two women wait for a trolley. Their traveling companions sit in the trolley shelter. On the wall inside are poster advertisements for street cars or trolleys. These shelters were installed in the Southern Tier region in the late 19th and early 20th centuries, allowing for transportation from Finger Lakes villages to larger train stations or nearby towns.

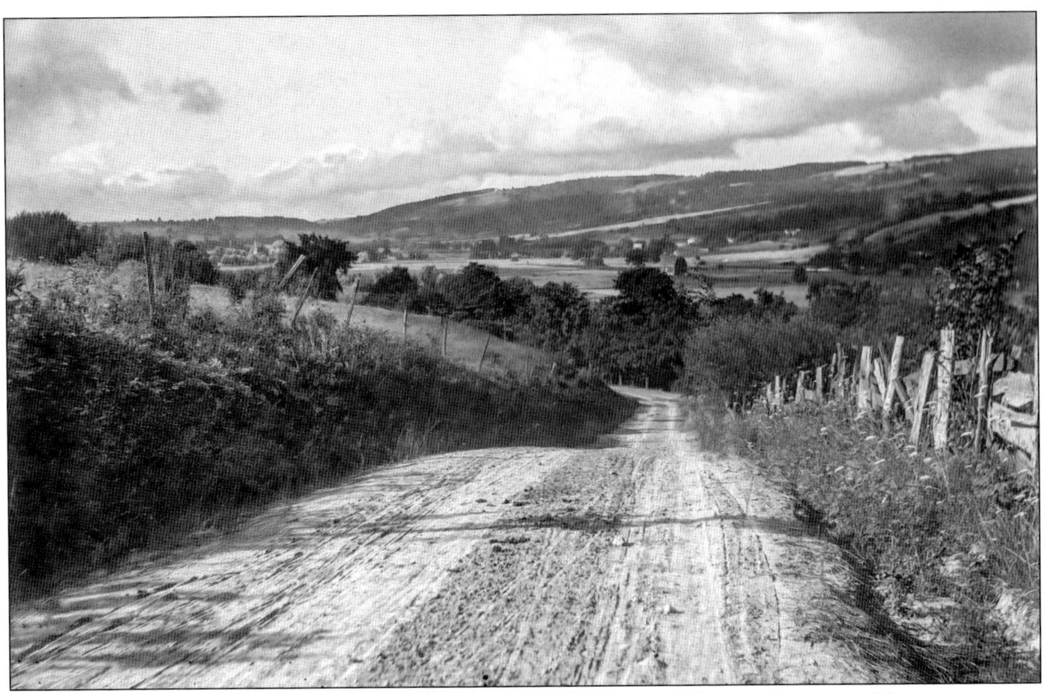

Many roads in the Finger Lakes region have beautiful views. The road pictured here was most likely Wheaton Hill Road in Springwater. The view is looking west. When followed down to the bottom, this road connects with Springwater's Main Street, now New York State Route 15A.

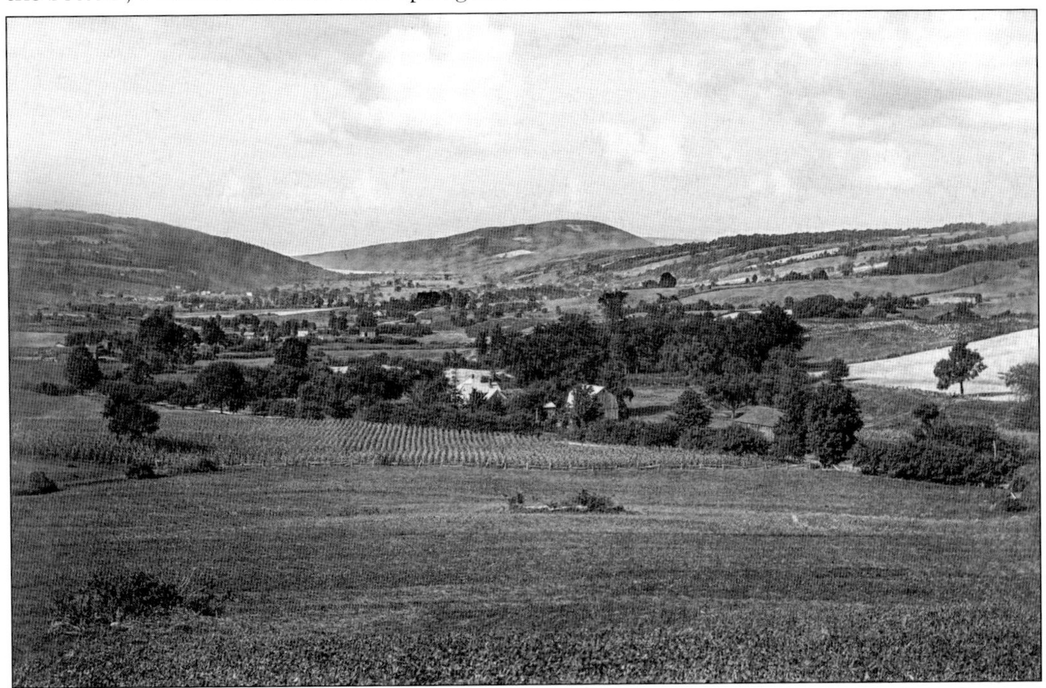

Bald Hill is seen here flanked by Hemlock and Canadice Lakes. This view was most likely obtained from Limekiln or Marvin Hill Roads, whose elevations would have given Ingraham a beautiful distant view of Bald Hill to the north.

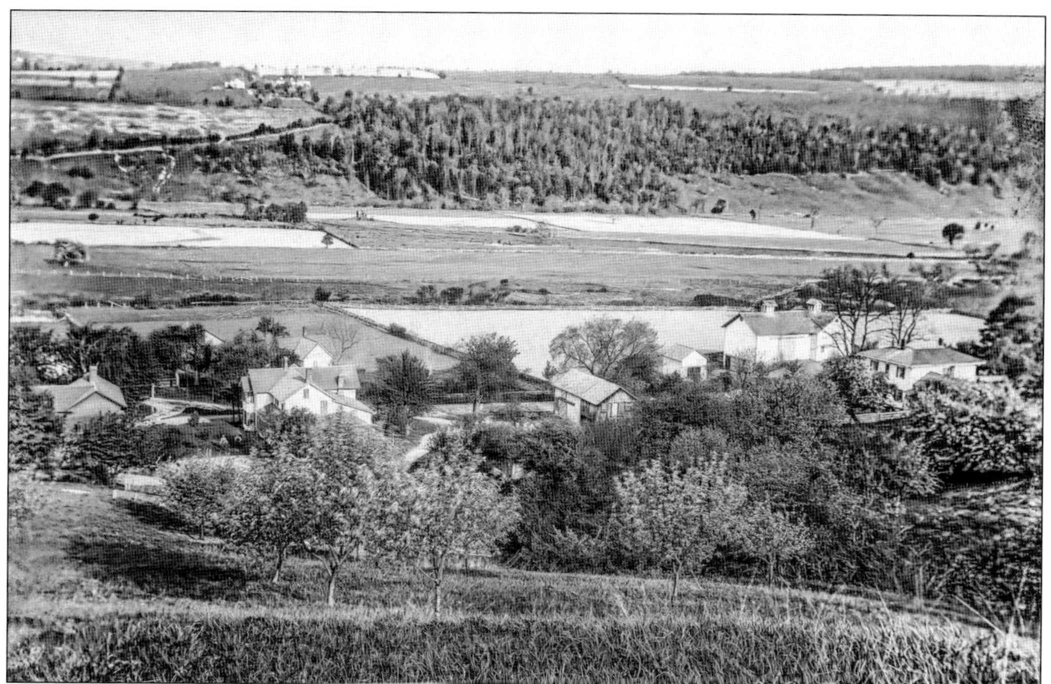

Kellogg Road is seen in this view looking west toward Marrowback Road, which rises in the distance. Houses, barns, and fields lie nestled in the valley. Floyd Ingraham took this picture from the hill behind his home, offering himself an elevated view of his early-20th-century agricultural community.

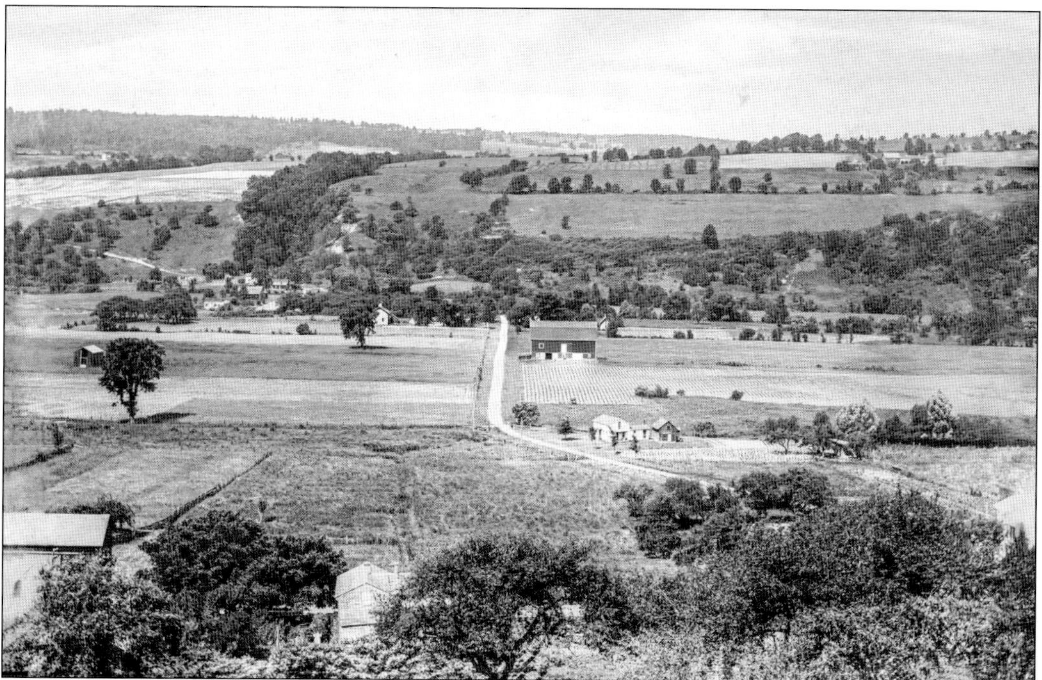

This view of Kellogg Road is looking east toward Main Street. It would have been taken on or around Marrowback Road. The Ingraham farm is at the end of the road and on the hill.

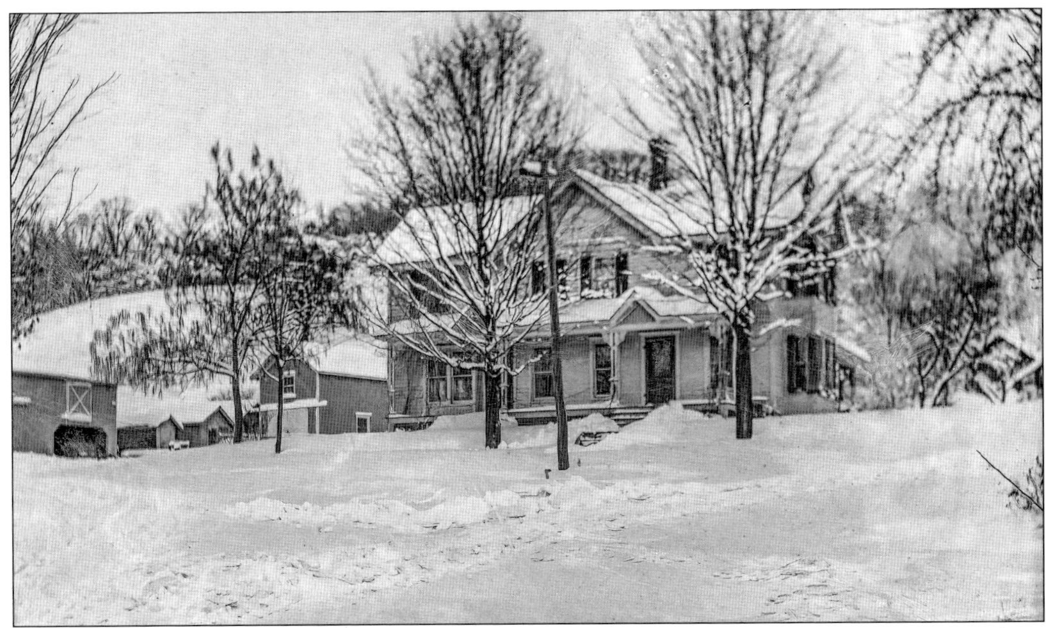

The Ingraham home on Main Street in Springwater is seen here blanketed in snow. Ingraham took pictures in all seasons, and his portrayal of Springwater in winter reveals the natural beauty of the place he loved. It is also a sobering reminder of the last horse-drawn sleigh ride that Ingraham would take from this same house on a winter night as his family and neighbors rallied to bring him to the hospital in Dansville, where he later died.

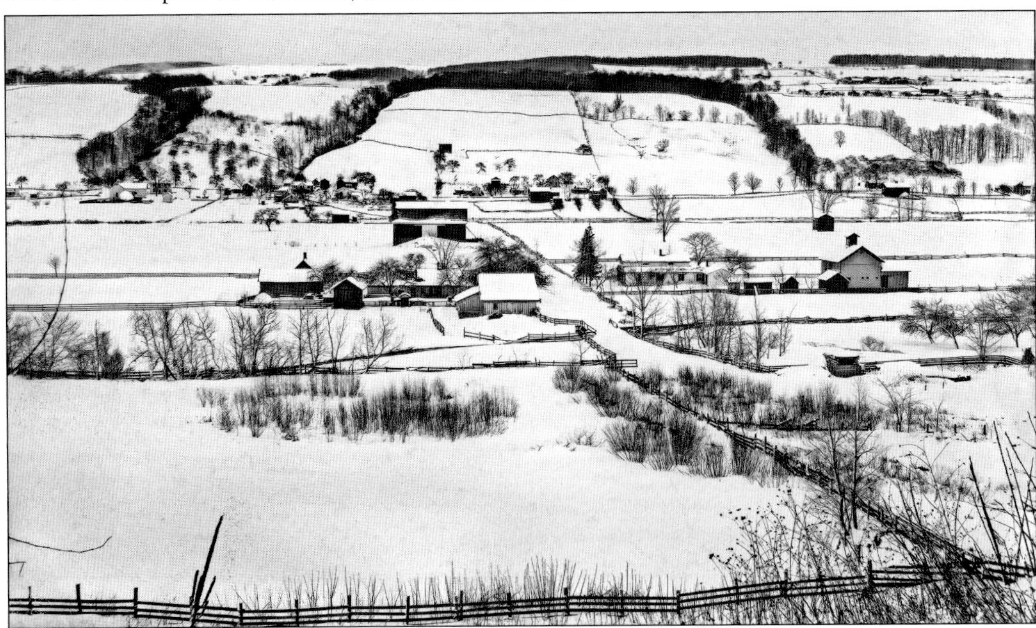

Taken from Marrowback Road, this view faces east on Kellogg Road as it leads to Main Street. It has been said that those who live surrounded by beauty often take it for granted. One has only to look at Floyd Ingraham's pictures to see that was not true of him. Ingraham's photography of the community and landscape of his birth captures not only a time and place, but also his deep personal feelings of love and respect for where he lived.

Three

Finger Lakes Families

During the first two decades of the 20th century, Floyd Ingraham photographed hundreds of individuals and families in his community. The following pages contain a small sampling of his portraits. Ingraham's photographs are an early-1900s snapshot of the people of the Finger Lakes region. They offer not just a pictorial record of individuals, but also a historical record of cultural significance.

Springwater had a population of over 2,000 at the turn of the century. The town experienced some of the effects of the 1918 flu epidemic and the migration of people to larger towns to find work.

Springwater had many industrious young people and close-knit families. Law and public opinion supported the patriarchal family at the end of the 19th century. Men were the leaders in local government, law, business, and family structure. Women married in their 20s, many times to older men. Women were expected to help on the farm, work in the home, cook, clean, and bear and raise children.

Before the rise of the women's right's movement, Springwater was already seeing a movement of its own. Local women rose to lead community organizations and societies, own businesses, run church charities, and express their unique voice in journalism and politics.

Children were expected to help the family. They worked alongside their parents in the garden and on the farm. Students walked to schoolhouses, and school schedules were set around farming needs, often closing for weeks during harvest.

The population in Springwater and the surrounding area included mostly citizens of European descent. Most families were farmers. With the coming of the railroad, the value of farms rose and they expanded as they were able to distribute their crops easily to towns and cities. As a result, across the United States the number of farms tripled from the late 1800s to the early 1900s. The first decade of the 20th century was a prosperous time for farmers in the Finger Lakes.

The elderly often lived with their children and still operated as heads of the house. Adults did not retire, they simply worked until they could not work anymore.

Hardworking and industrious, the families of the Finger Lakes region lived relatively simple lives compared to today. Floyd Ingraham's portrait photography reveals the spirit of a tenacious generation seen in the lines on their faces, the determination in their gaze, and the fierce bonds that held them to the land and each other.

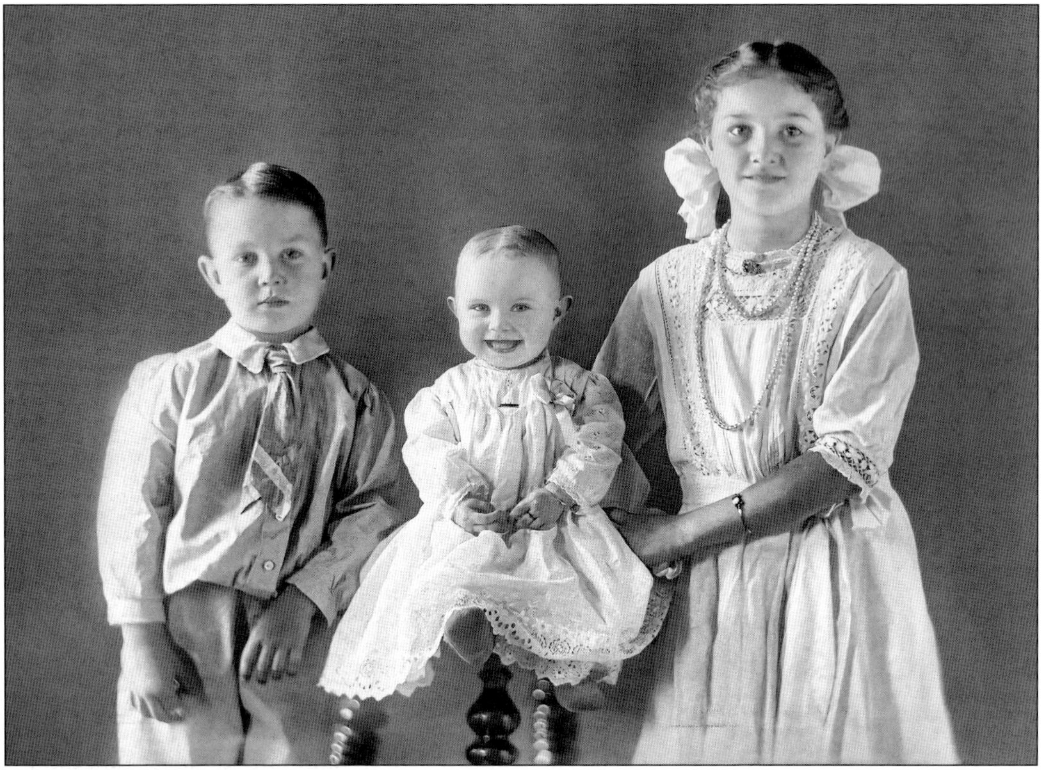

Pictured here from left to right are Glenn and Martha Hyde, the children of Barton and Lizzie Hyde, with Ethel Hyde, daughter of Lewis and Libbie Hyde. Ethel lived with her parents in a house on Main Street in Springwater, just down the road from the Ingraham residence. Her brother Barton and his wife and children lived on Kellogg Road.

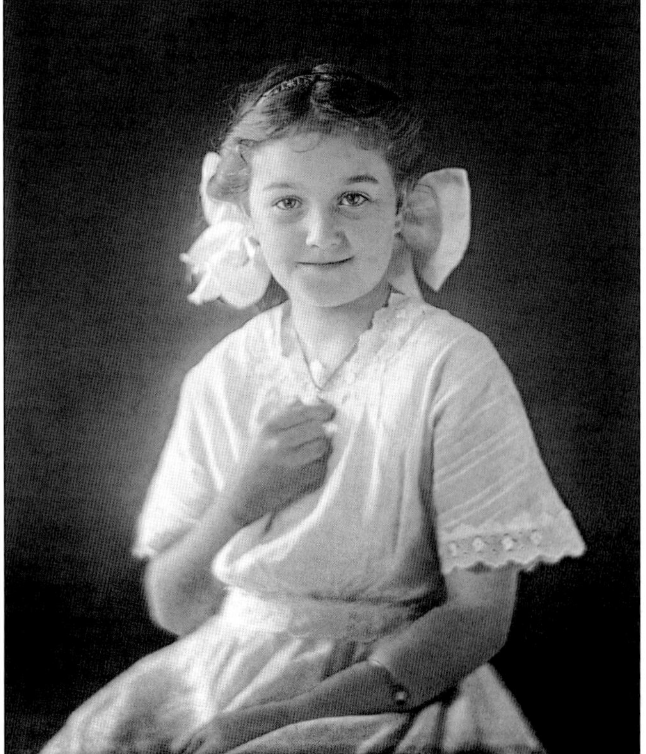

Ethel Hyde was born on June 23, 1903, in Canadice, the second child of Lewis and Libbie (Pursell) Hyde. She married Kenneth Beers, her childhood sweetheart. They attended the Springwater Union School and Rochester Institute of Business together. Kenneth and Ethel Beers settled in Rochester and had three sons.

A. Barton Hyde was born on June 4, 1887, the son of Lewis and Libbie (Pursell) Hyde. He married Elizabeth "Lizzie" May in 1907. He was a farmer and rural mail carrier. The couple had three children: Glenn, Martha, and Ellis. One year after Floyd Ingraham's death from appendicitis, Hyde had a similar surgery at the same hospital and survived. He was also a witness at the wedding of Floyd Ingraham's widow, Anna (Cork) Ingraham, to Floyd Caskey. Hyde died on May 10, 1941, and is buried in Mount Vernon Evergreen Cemetery. (Courtesy of Springwater–Webster Crossing Historical Society.)

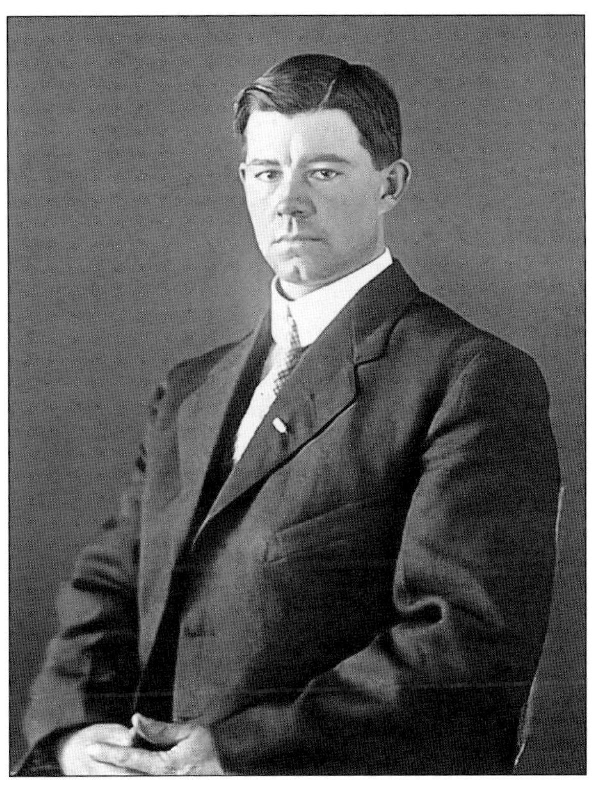

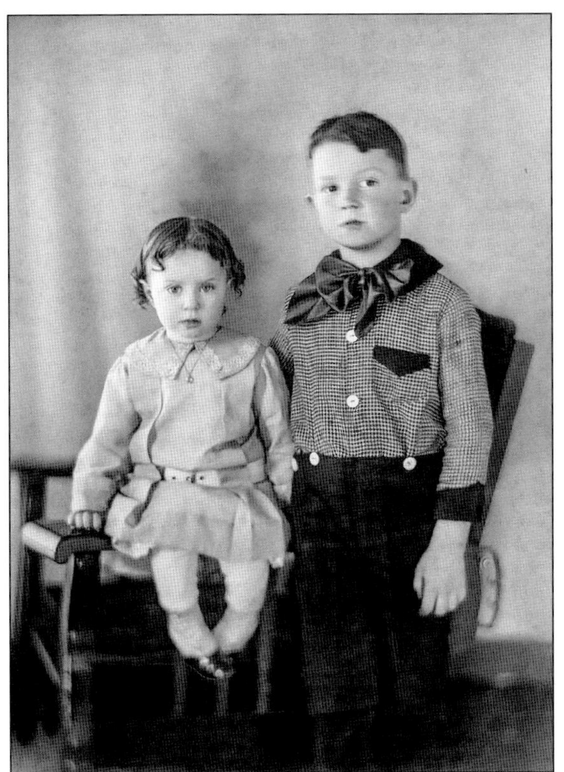

Two of Barton and Lizzie Hyde's three children, Glenn and Martha, are pictured here. Glenn F. Hyde, born in 1909, was a schoolteacher and later a bookkeeper for the creamery in Webster Crossing. He also became justice of the peace in Springwater. He died at age 33 when he was crushed beneath a truck in an accident on Loon Lake Road. Glenn was married to Melva Perkins and left behind a baby daughter. His sister Martha was born in 1914. She married William Luther, and they had four daughters. Martha died in 1989 in Hemlock, New York.

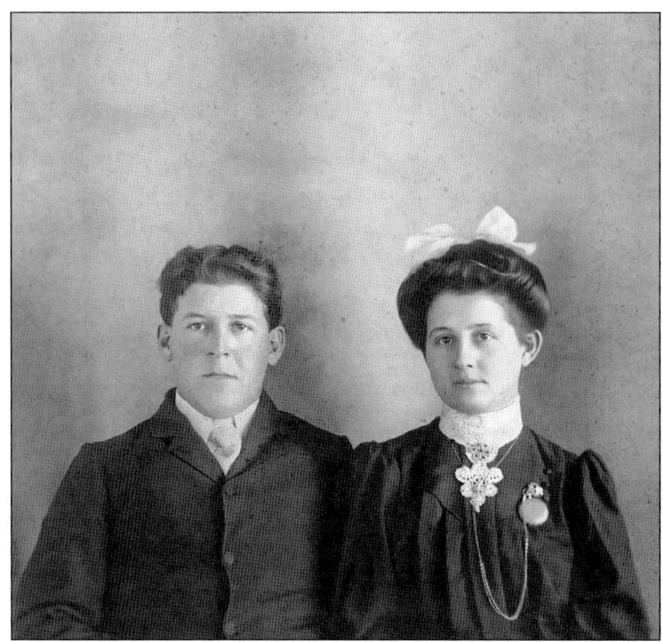

Roy Swan and Destie Glover were married on January 22, 1905, in Springwater. Roy Garfield Swan was born in 1881 to Cyrus and Mariette (Cornell) Swan. Destie Glover, daughter of Edgar and Maria Glover, was born in 1883. Swan was employed by the City of Rochester as gatekeeper at Canadice Lake for 40 years. He served as supervisor and assessor for the town of Canadice and was a school trustee. He died in 1962. Destie (Glover) Swan died in 1958. Roy and Destie had two daughters, Lunette and Geraldine. (Courtesy of Springwater–Webster Crossing Historical Society.)

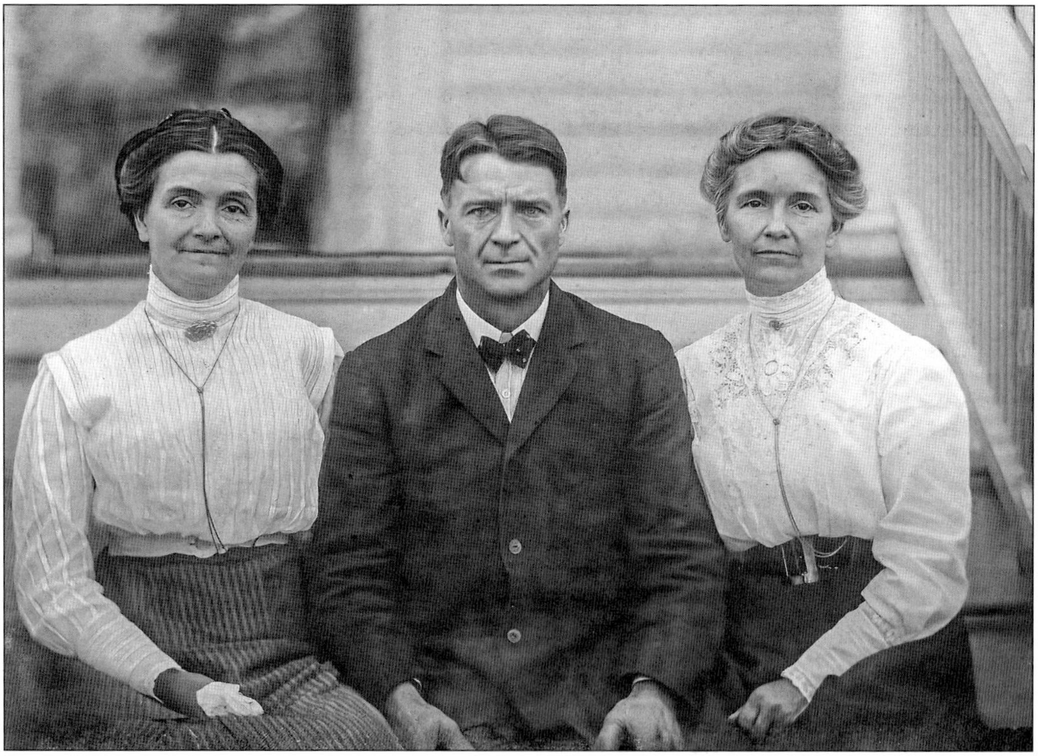

Ruth, Stuart, and Phebe Bush were the children of Scott and Anna (Henry) Bush of Canadice. Ruth (left), born in 1893, married Peter Ray Barnard in 1921. He died five years later, leaving her with a young daughter, Jane. Stuart, born in 1890, married Alma Wheaton in 1912, and they had one son, Winfield. Phebe (right), born in 1888, married Thomas Huxley Gibbs in 1912, and the couple had one daughter, Lois.

Oscar Benedict (1886–1950) married Maude Henry, daughter of Clark and Eliza Wright of Canadice. Benedict worked locally for Allen and Whitlock's store and H.H. Densmore in Springwater. He later became a prominent businessman and worked at companies in New Haven, Connecticut, and Rochester, New York. Oscar and Maude had two children. Maude died suddenly in 1922. Oscar relocated to Buffalo and married Elizabeth Reidel. He died in 1950.

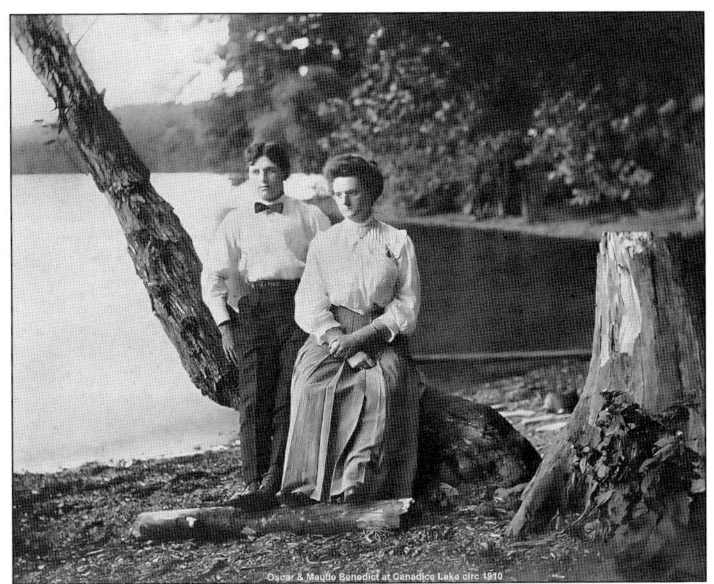

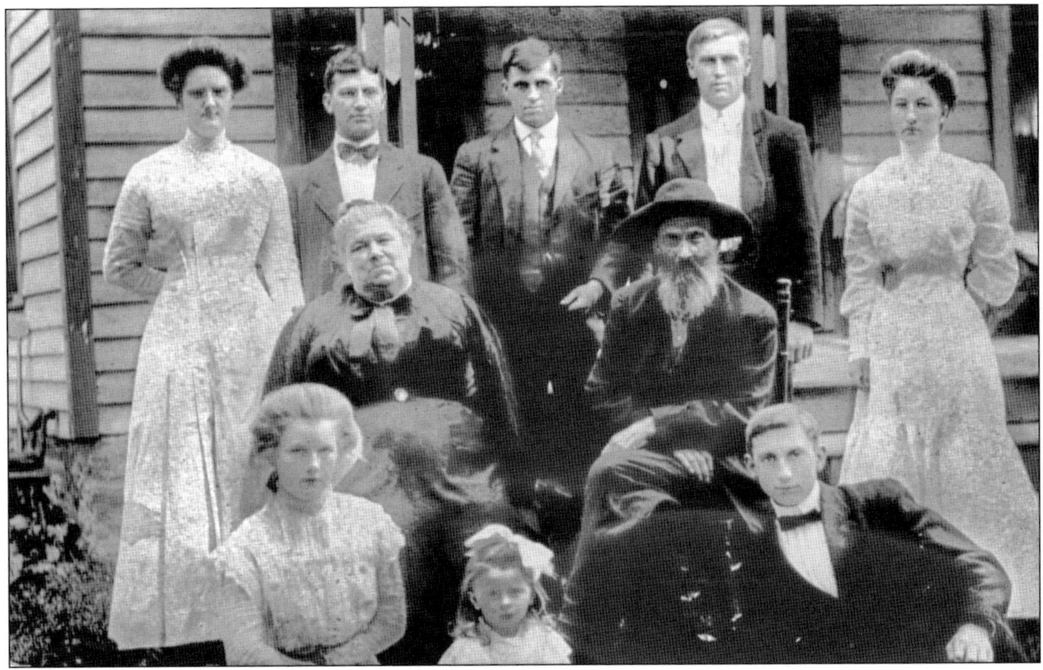

Abijah Dewitt Benedict was born in Otsego, New York, and served in New York's 10th Cavalry Regiment during the Civil War. He married Sarah Mallery in 1870, and they settled in Springwater by 1880. They had five children: George, Oscar, Clinton, Edward, and Harriet. Pictured are, from left to right, (first row) Hattie, Ethel (George and Nellie's daughter), and Edward; (second row) Sarah and Abijah Benedict; (third row) Maude (Oscar's wife), Oscar, Clinton, George, and Nellie (George's wife). Some of Edward Benedict's letters home to his family during World War I were printed in the *Cohocton Daily Times*. He died at age 33 of tuberculosis as a result of being gassed in Germany. (Courtesy of Ron and Sharon Ingraham.)

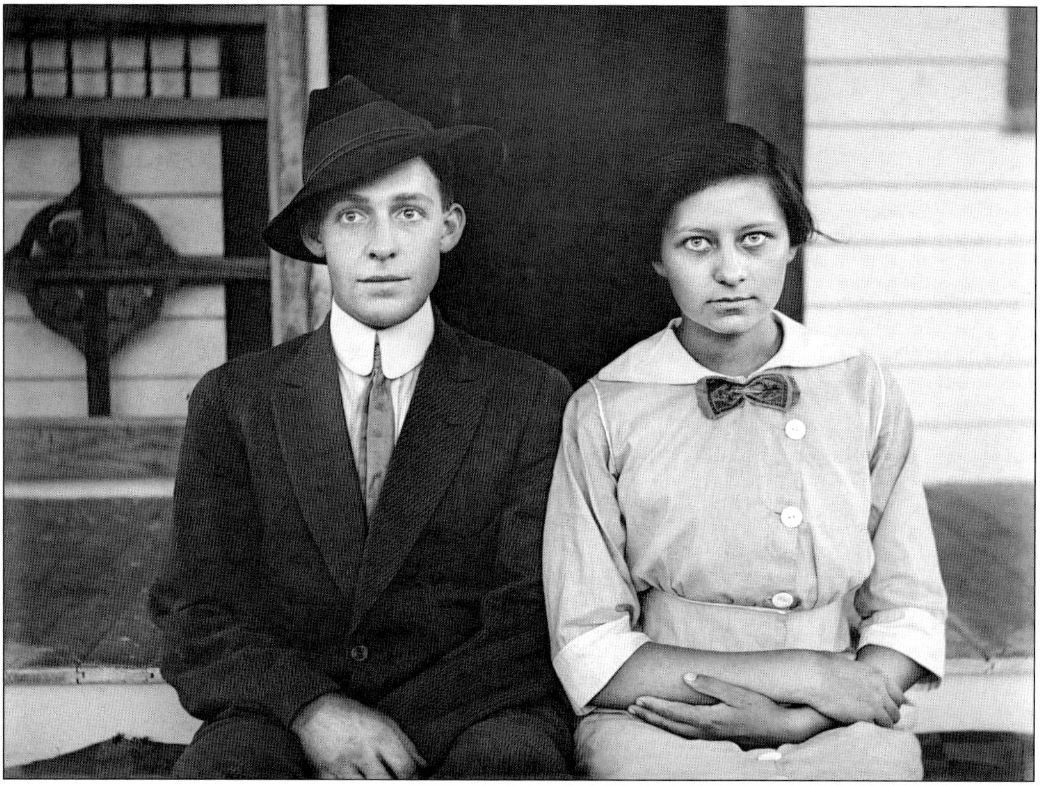

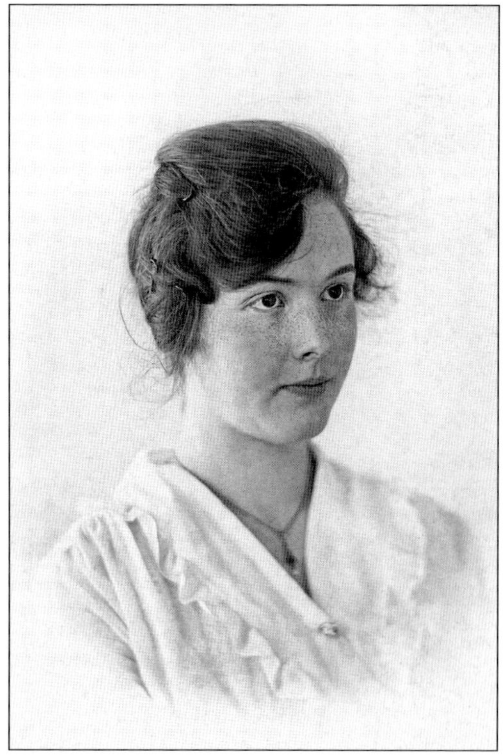

It is unknown when or how Eleanor Graves came to be with the Ford family. Shown here with Leon Ford, Eleanor Graves was named as an adopted daughter of Leon's parents, Melvin and Carrie Ford. She was born in 1890 and worked as a camera maker for Kodak in Rochester. She married Robert Andrews in 1936. She died in 1972. Leon Louis Ford, the son of Melvin and Carrie (Miller) Ford, was born on October 15, 1889. He first married Elizabeth Hulbert of Hornell. Following their divorce, he married Mary Helen Tobin. They had a son William, and Leon was a stepfather to Mary's two daughters. Leon Ford died in 1970.

Gertrude Ford was the daughter of Melvin and Carrie Ford. Born in 1892, Gertrude Ford was a cousin of Floyd Ingraham. Although the Ford family moved away, they frequently returned to Springwater. An automobile accident in 1956 left Gertrude with serious injuries. Her brother Arthur was driving the car, and another woman involved was killed. Gertrude married Fred Stoik; they had no children. She worked as a saleswoman for a bakery and died in 1993. (Courtesy of Ron and Sharon Ingraham.)

Arthur Ford was born in 1885 to Melvin and Carrie Ford. In 1911, he married Celia Jackman of Wayland, the daughter of Bernard and Mary Jackman. Arthur and Celia had one son, Leon, and settled in Rochester. Arthur worked as a teamster and a chauffeur, and did maintenance for the railroad. He died in 1971.

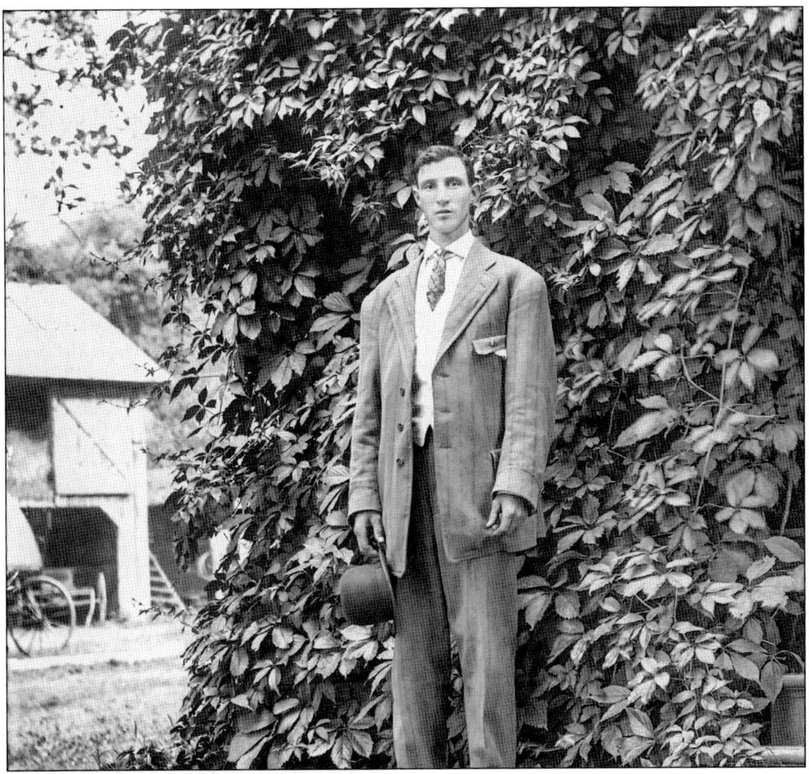

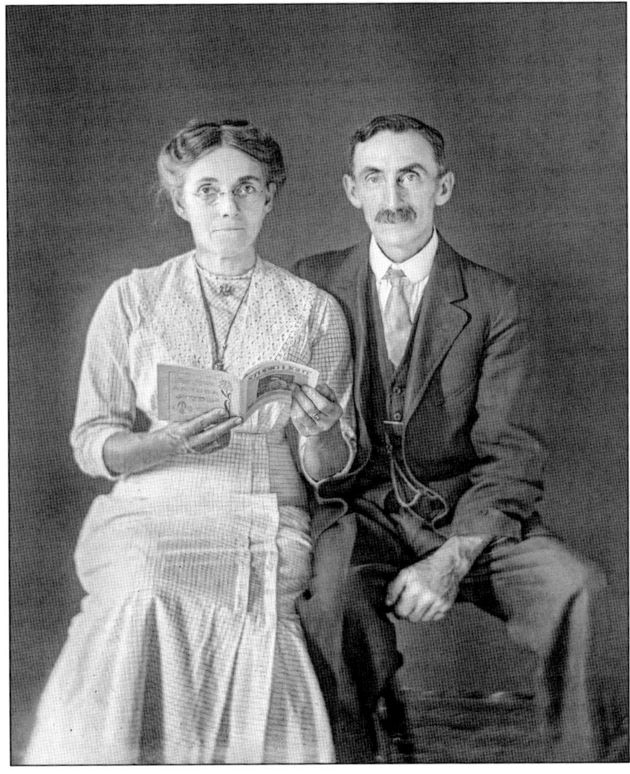

Melvin Christopher Ford and Carrie Miller were married in 1859. Melvin Ford was born in 1859 to John Ford and Louisa Charlotte Lyon. Carrie (Miller) Ford was born in 1862 to Ward and Elizabeth (Smith) Miller. Melvin and Carrie Ford had four children. Although they lived in the Dansville and Greater Rochester area, they visited friends and family in Springwater often. They eventually moved to Wayland. Melvin died in 1944, and Carrie died in 1947.

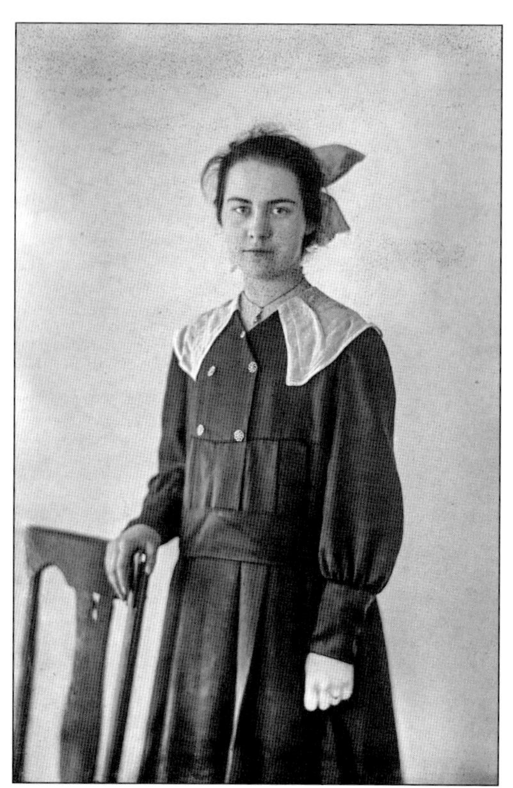

Melva Seward was the daughter of Frederick Dirgen Seward and Minnie Belle Caskey. Born on November 6, 1903, in Springwater, she grew up on the family's farm on Mill Street with sisters Clara and Lucille and brothers Horace, Arthur, and Harold. She married Arthur William Snyder on August 28, 1928, and the couple moved to Rochester. They had two sons, Norman and Gary. Melva and Arthur Snyder relocated to St. Louis, Missouri, and then Dallas, Texas. Melva died on August 9, 1992.

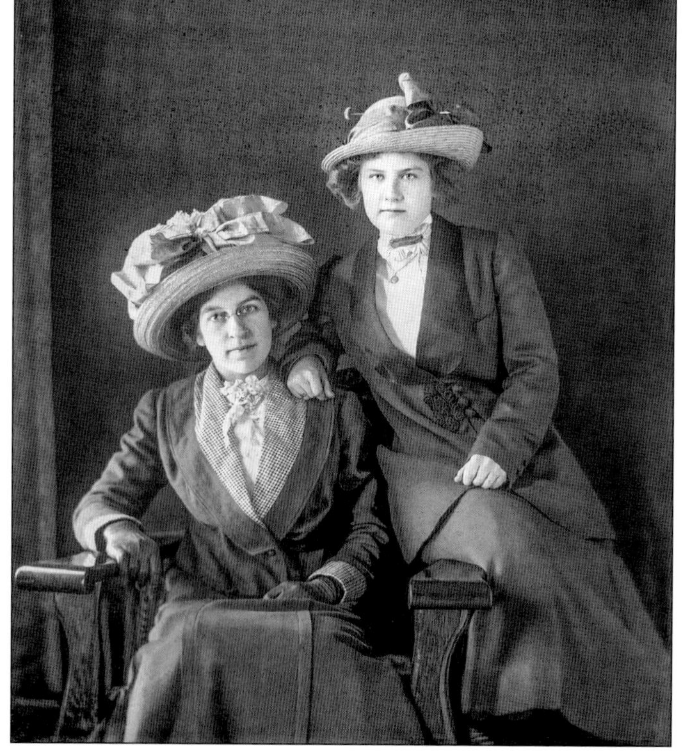

Harriet "Hattie" Benedict was born in 1896 to Abidja and Sarah (Mallory) Benedict. She worked for a time as a telephone operator in Atlanta, New York. She married and later relocated to Ohio. Pictured here with Hattie (right) is Clara (Seward) Mack. Mack was the daughter of Fred and Minnie (Caskey) Benedict and became a respected writer and journalist.

Clara Seward was born on September 9, 1898, in Canadice to Frederick and Minnie (Caskey) Seward. She married Charles Hubert Mack in 1918, and the couple resided in Springwater. Hubert Mack died in 1949, after one day of illness, at the age of 55. Clara then married Guy Bennett in 1951, and the couple made their home in Wayland, New York. Clara (Seward Mack) Bennett had no children.

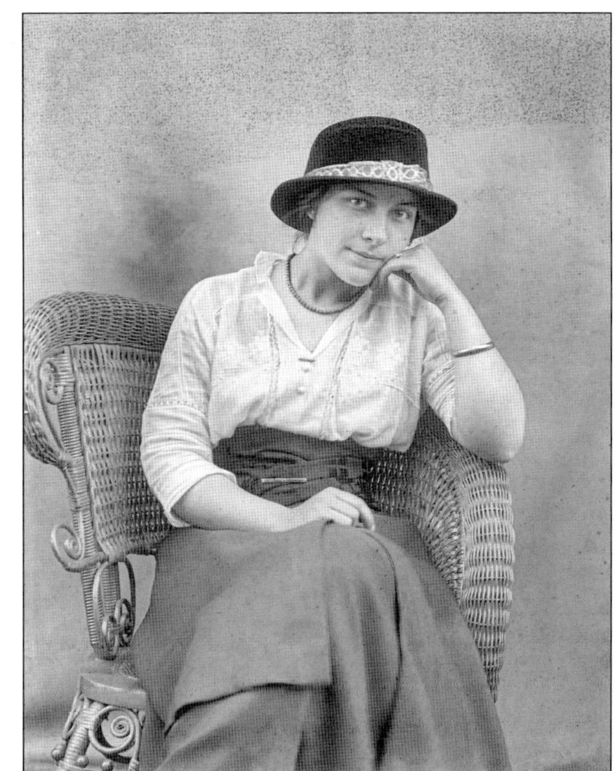

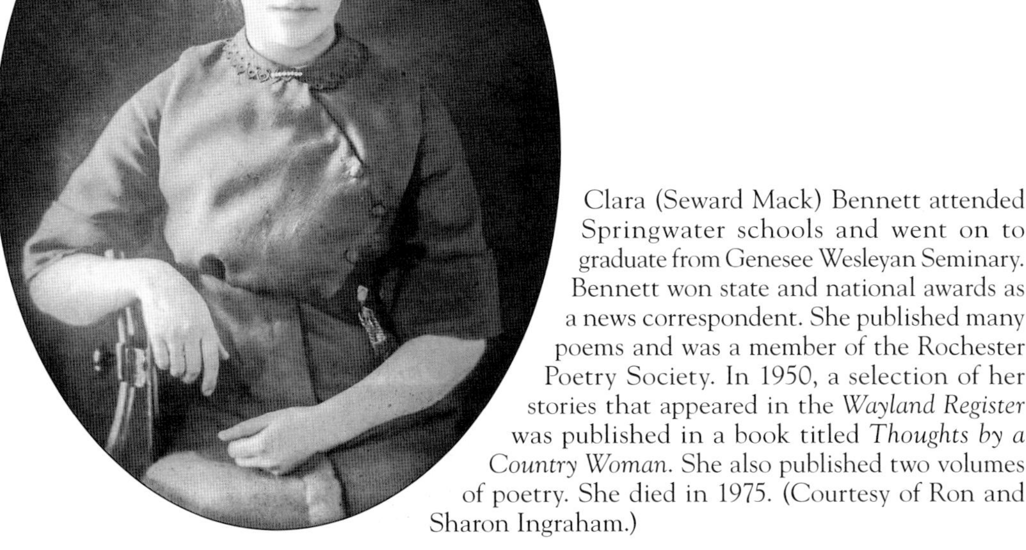

Clara (Seward Mack) Bennett attended Springwater schools and went on to graduate from Genesee Wesleyan Seminary. Bennett won state and national awards as a news correspondent. She published many poems and was a member of the Rochester Poetry Society. In 1950, a selection of her stories that appeared in the *Wayland Register* was published in a book titled *Thoughts by a Country Woman*. She also published two volumes of poetry. She died in 1975. (Courtesy of Ron and Sharon Ingraham.)

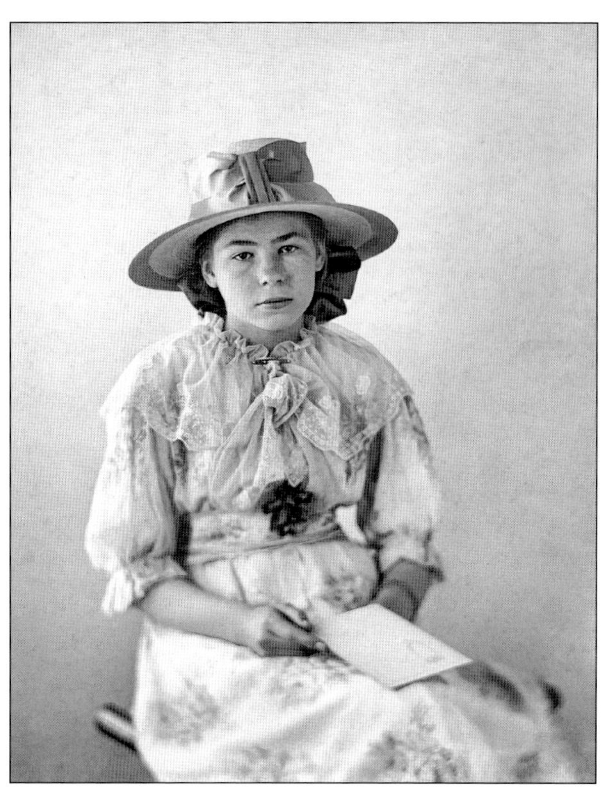

Alma Allene Buckner was born in 1894 to James and Minnie (Beers) Buckner and raised in Springwater. Allene married Edward Patrick Finn in May 1921 and moved to Dansville, where she worked as a linotype operator for the F.A. Owens Publishing Company and the Genesee Country Express. Allene (Buckner) Finn died on August 27, 1982, and is buried in Dansville.

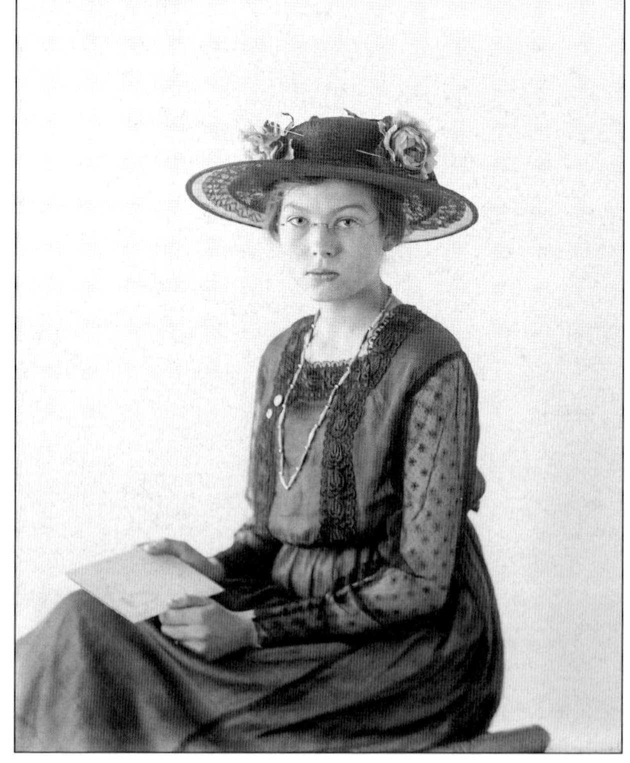

The daughter of James Buckner and Minnie Beers, Marion Buckner was born in September 1899. Marion was a Bell Telephone operator in Springwater. She later relocated to Rochester. She married Walter Webber in 1922. He died a year later. She married Walter McTurk of Pittsburgh, Pennsylvania, in 1926. The couple had one son, Ralph, and lived in Rochester. Marion (Buckner) McTurk died on April 30, 1982.

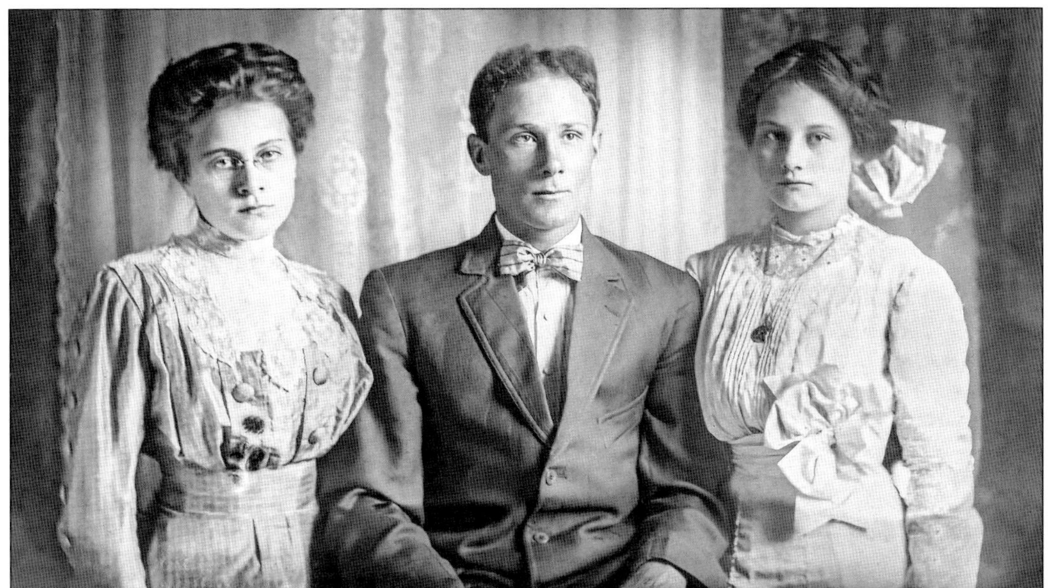

The children of Charles and Anna Snyder, Alma "Allie" and Elizabeth "Lizzie," are pictured here on the left and right, respectively, of John Nicholas Wolfanger, their stepbrother; he was called Nicholas. He was the son of Anna from her first marriage to Nicholas Wolfanger Jr., who died of diphtheria 17 days after his son was born. Nicholas grew up in Springwater and was a farmer. He married Carrie Lawrence and had two daughters. He lived for a time in East Aurora but returned to Springwater after his wife's death.

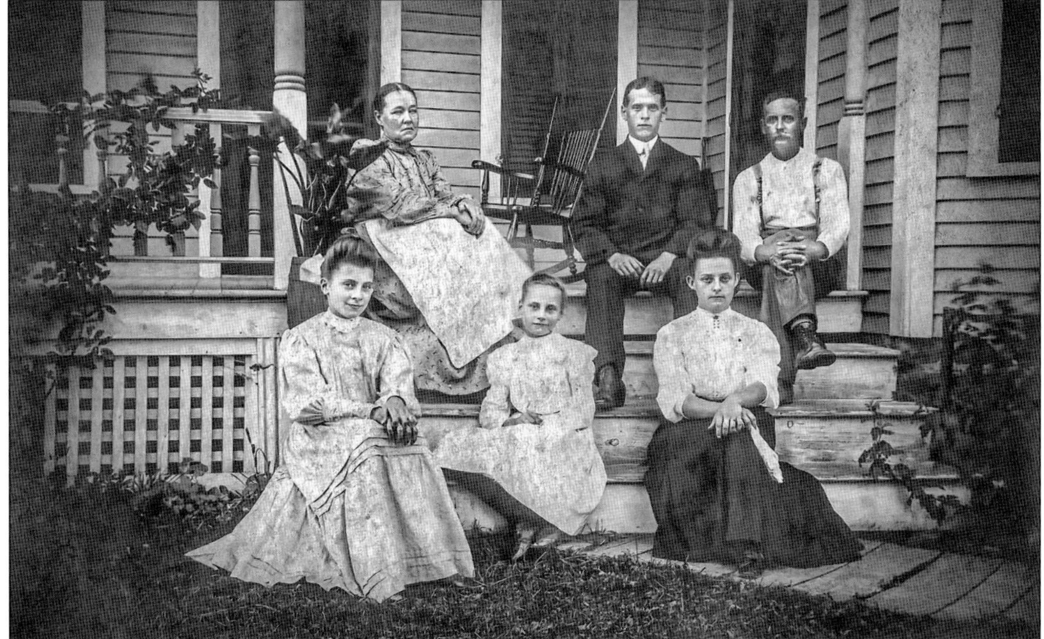

Charles H. Snyder married Anna Smith Wolfanger, a German immigrant who was widowed with a son, John Nicholas Wolfanger. The Snyders had two daughters together, Alma and Elizabeth. Anna (Smith Wolfanger) Snyder died in 1923, and Charles Snyder died in 1924. Their children settled in Springwater. (Courtesy of Ron and Sharon Ingraham.)

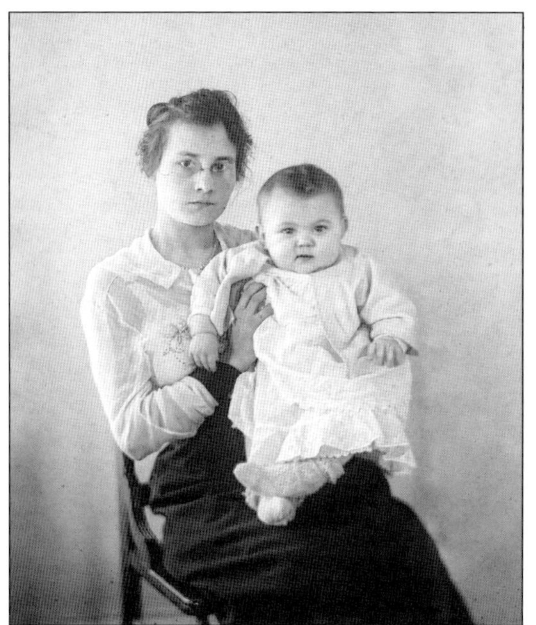

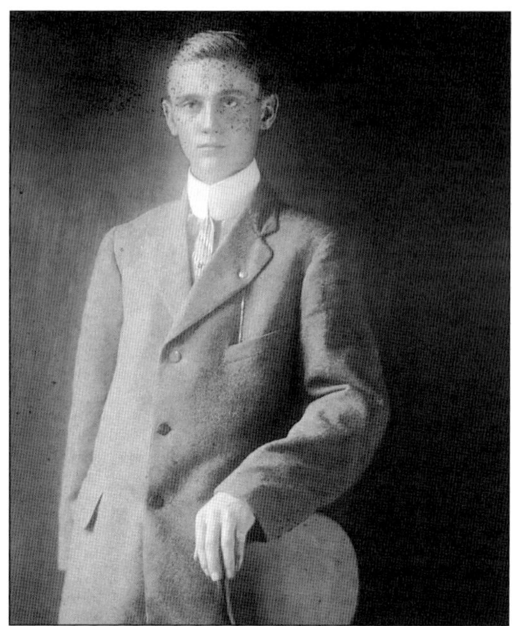

In 1916, Elizabeth "Lizzie" Snyder, seen holding an infant at left, married Pearl Robinson, right, the son of Sheldon and Anna (Bailey) Robinson. Pearl died from injuries suffered in an auto accident in September 1917. Lizzie gave birth to their daughter, whom she named Pearl, in May 1918. Lizzie married Walter Fairbrother in 1925, and had a second daughter, Lorraine Fairbrother. Elizabeth (Snyder) Fairbrother died in 1976. (Both, courtesy of Ron and Sharon Ingraham.)

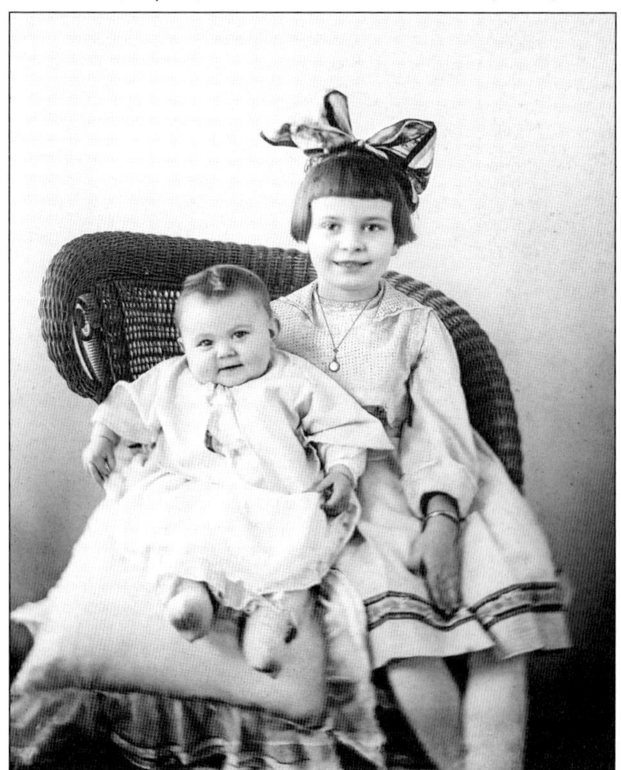

The Robinson brothers married the Snyder sisters of Springwater. Their children, cousins Evelyn (right) and Pearl Robinson, are in this portrait. Pearl was the daughter of Pearl and Elizabeth Robinson. Pearl's father passed away seven months before her birth. Evelyn was the daughter of George and Alma Robinson.

George Robinson married Alma "Allie" Snyder in 1910. Robinson was born in 1890 to Sheldon and Anna (Bailey) Robinson. They operated a hardware business for 40 years in Springwater. Alma Snyder was born in 1891 to Charles and Anna (Smith) Snyder of Springwater. George and Alma had one daughter, Evelyn, pictured here in 1912. George ran an insulation company in Morris, New York, for many years before his death in 1964. Allie died two years later in 1966.

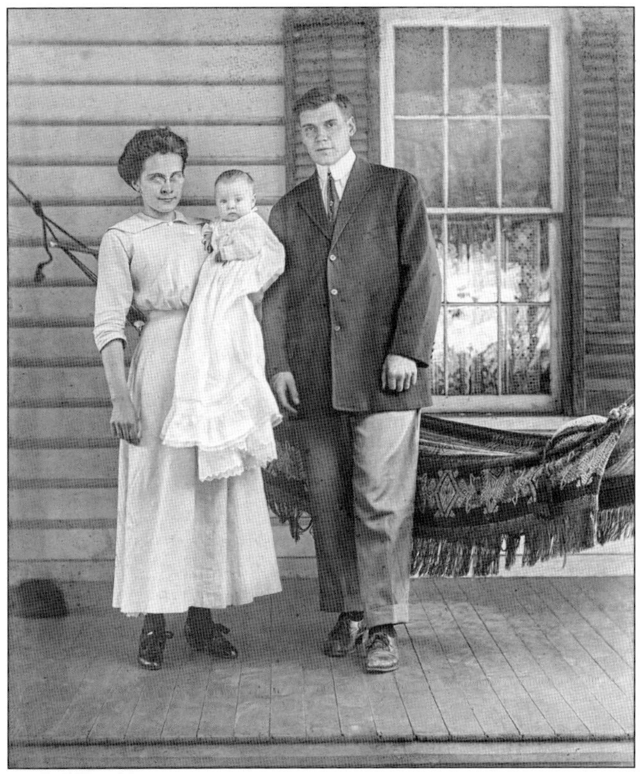

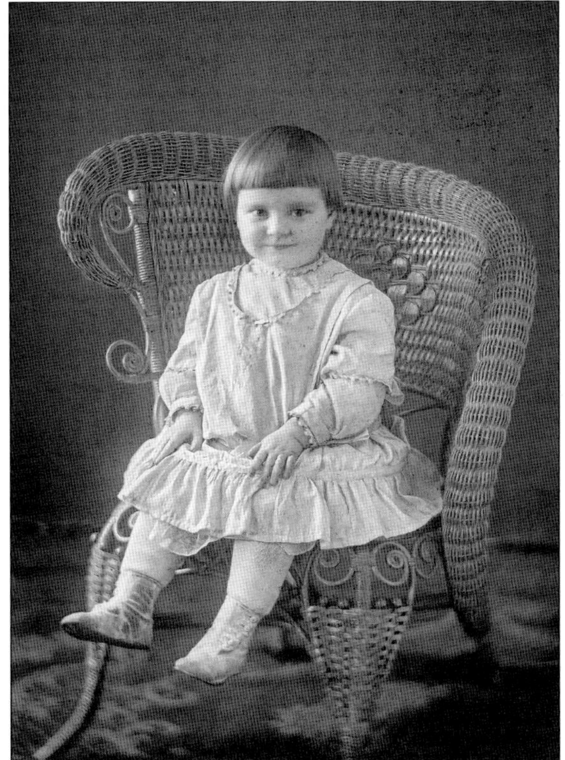

Evelyn Robinson was born to George and Alma (Snyder) Robinson on June 7, 1912. She married William Gilbert of Livonia in 1937. They lived on School Street in Springwater and had no children. Evelyn (Robinson) Gilbert served for a time as receiver for the Springwater Water Company and was a teacher for many years at the Springwater Union School. She died in 1988.

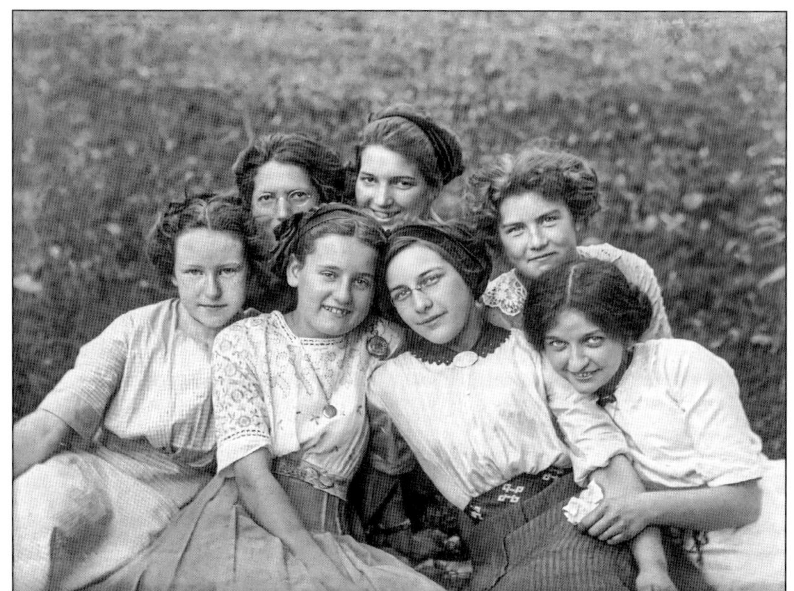

Friends in this portrait are, from left to right, (first row) Mildred Marvin, Ellen Doolittle, Clara Seward, and Agatha Schlenker; (second row) Maude and Myra Doge and Hattie Benedict.

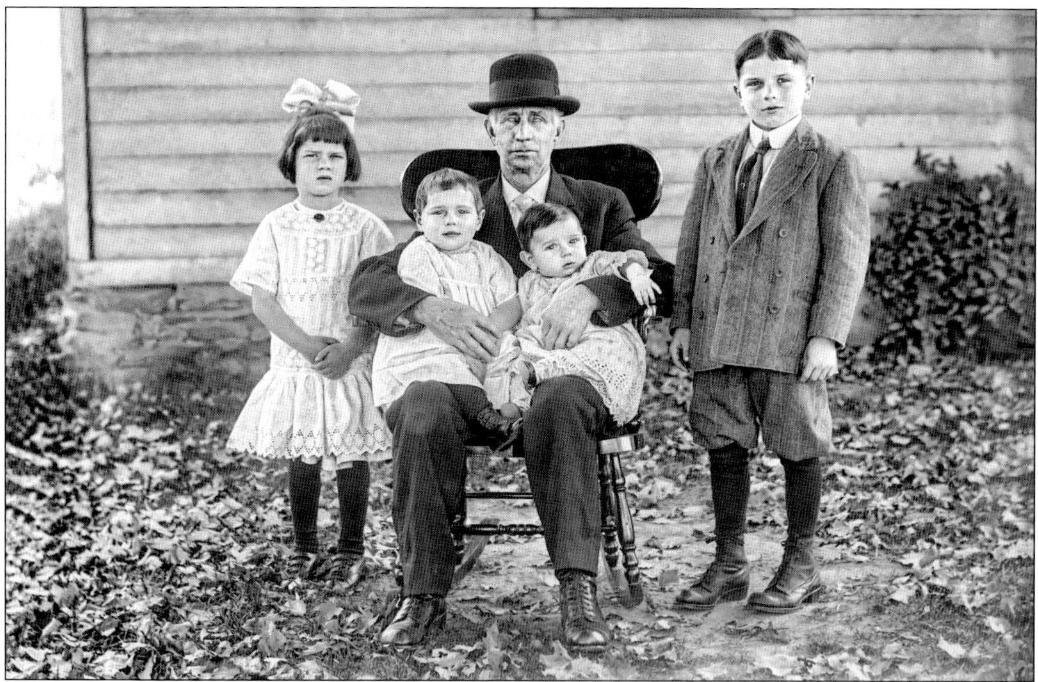

William Magee posed for this portrait with his nephew George Richardson's children in 1914. George and Ethel (Mastin) Richardson had six children, five living to adulthood. They are, from left to right, Dorothy, Beatrice, Alonzo, and Claude Richardson. Dorothy was born in 1909 and married Harvey Hillman. Bernice was born in 1911 and married Peter Hoffman. Alonzo was born in 1913 and married Dorothy Mae Perkins. Claude was born in 1906 and married Evelyn Jacot. Another sister, Beulah Mae, was born after this picture was taken. William Magee, seated at center, was married to Polly Richardson. He was one of the neighbors who came to the aid of Floyd Ingraham in January 1920. Magee's team pulled the sleigh carrying Ingraham to the hospital in the snow.

Elizabeth Mary "Libbie" Ingraham (1883–1965) was the only daughter of Lester and Francis Ingraham. She was a cousin of Floyd Ingraham, and this picture was taken by him in 1901. Libbie was raised in Springwater and married Daniel Thrasher in 1903. They settled in New Jersey, where she had two children, Mildred Isabelle and Carlton. Her husband died in 1923 when Libbie was 40. She never remarried, and died in 1965.

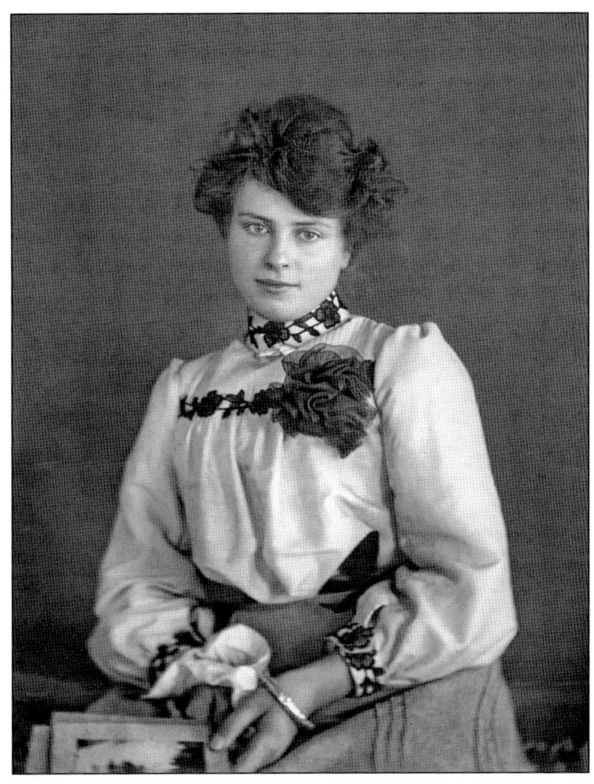

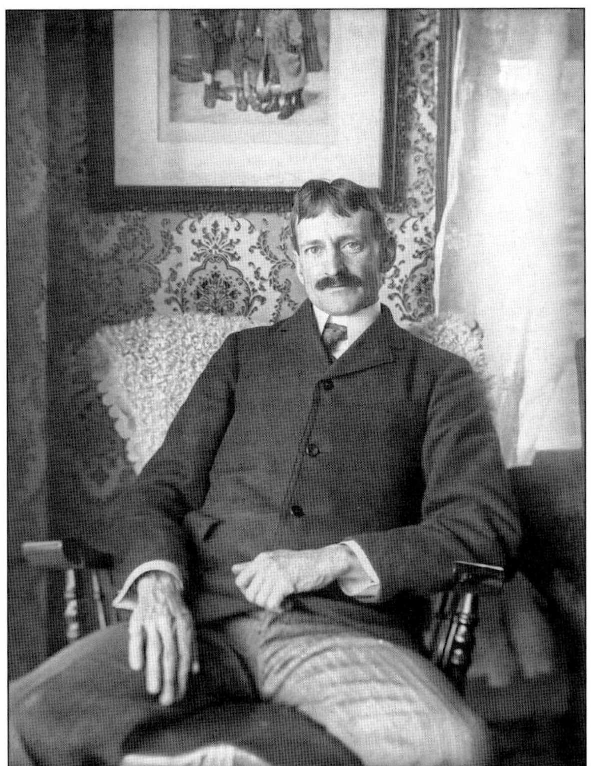

Dr. Herburt DeLancey Knickerbocker was born on November 2, 1867, in Watertown, New York. He was a member of the Farrington Medical Clinic in Watertown by the age of 20. He also served in the Spanish-American War and was a homeopathic doctor in Springwater. Later, he moved to St. Albans, Vermont. It was there he met and married Nellie J. Tinker. Dr. Knickerbocker relocated to Springwater in 1899. There he had a large medical practice and was a health officer, manager of the Bell Telephone office, and a member of the board of education. Through his influence, the Springwater Union school was established. After returning to Watertown in 1909 due to failing health, he died on November 8, 1910.

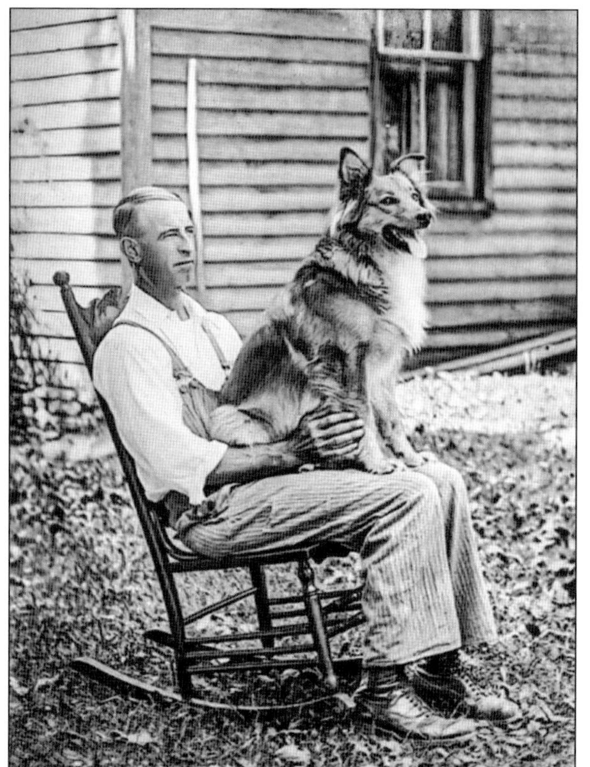

William H. Wilcox was born on December 22, 1869, to Eber and Marilla (Robinson) Wilcox. He was a descendant of Stephen and Phebe Robinson. Wilcox married Minnie Salter in 1895. They had one son, Glen Allerton Wilcox, born in 1897. The couple divorced in 1904. Wilcox then married Minnie Elizabeth Wiley in 1909. They were the parents of Helen Wilcox, born in 1917. (Courtesy of Ron and Sharon Ingraham.)

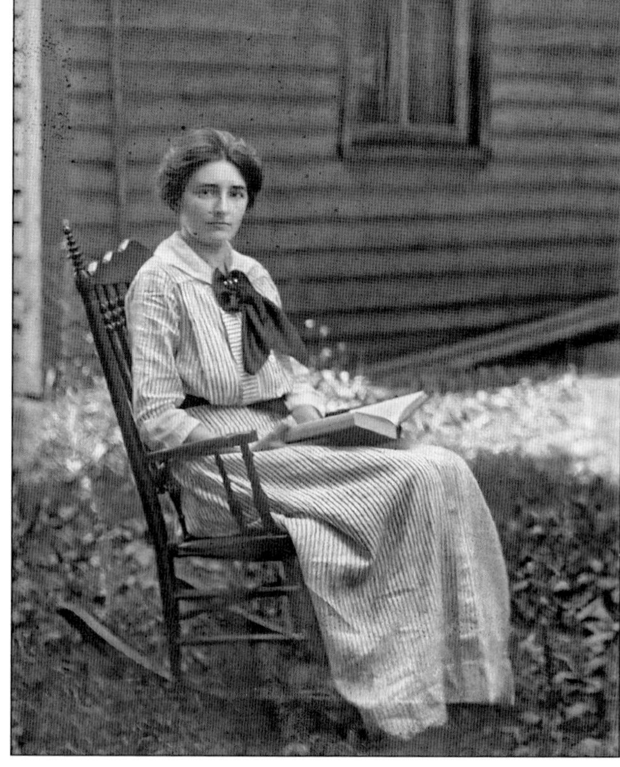

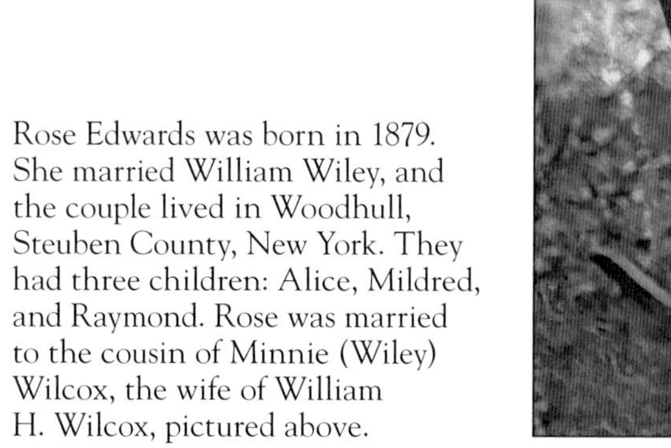

Rose Edwards was born in 1879. She married William Wiley, and the couple lived in Woodhull, Steuben County, New York. They had three children: Alice, Mildred, and Raymond. Rose was married to the cousin of Minnie (Wiley) Wilcox, the wife of William H. Wilcox, pictured above.

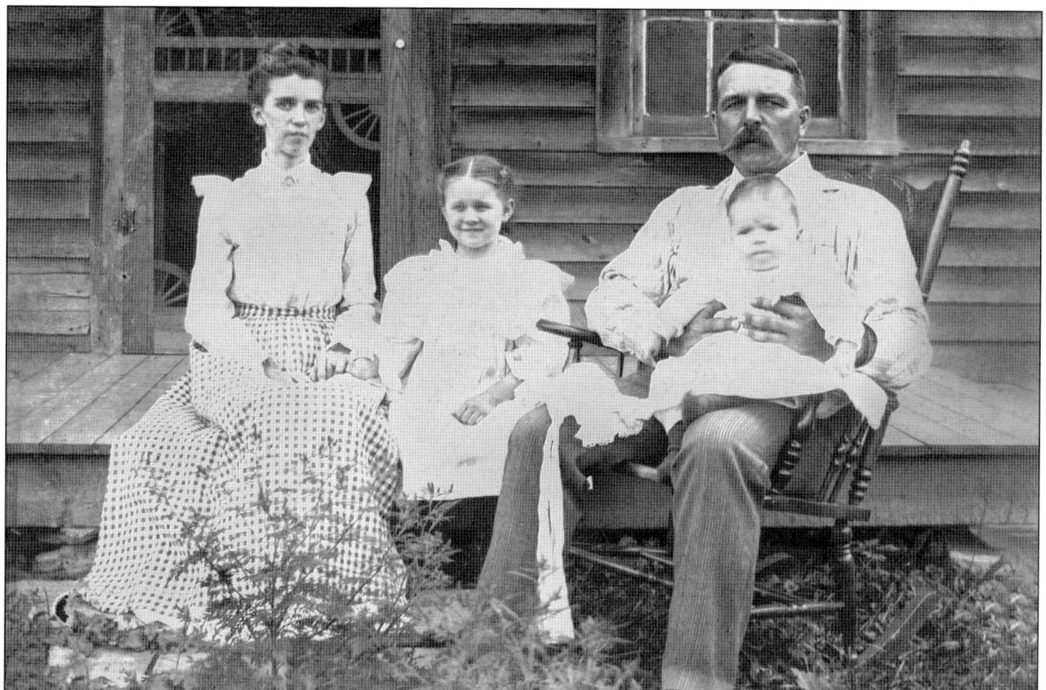

Franklin Hiram Ingraham, son of Hiram and Mary Ingraham, was born in 1859. He married Emiline McNair, who died in 1890. He then married Emiline's sister Carrie, who died in 1895 from complications in childbirth. Ingraham named his daughter Carrie after her. Ingraham was married a third time to Mary Bessie Hayward in 1897. They are pictured here with Carrie and the couple's infant daughter, Lura Pauline (called Pauline). Ingraham was a prominent resident of Canadice, and he served on the town board, was a justice of the peace, and held the office of superintendent of highways. He died in 1939. (Courtesy of Ron and Sharon Ingraham.)

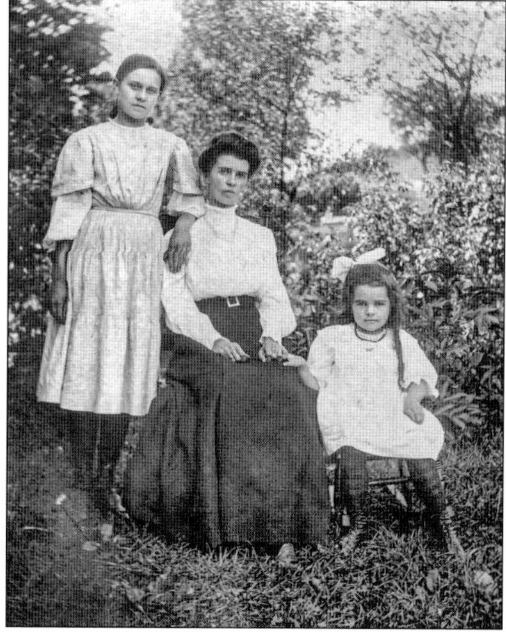

Bessie (Hayward) Ingraham is pictured here with Carrie (standing) and Pauline Ingraham. Bessie was born Mary Bessie Hayward in Canadice. She was the daughter of Frank and Stella (Hawks) Hayward. In 1897, she married Franklin Ingraham, a widower with a young daughter, Carrie. The couple settled in Canadice. Bessie Ingraham died in 1962. (Courtesy of Ron and Sharon Ingraham.)

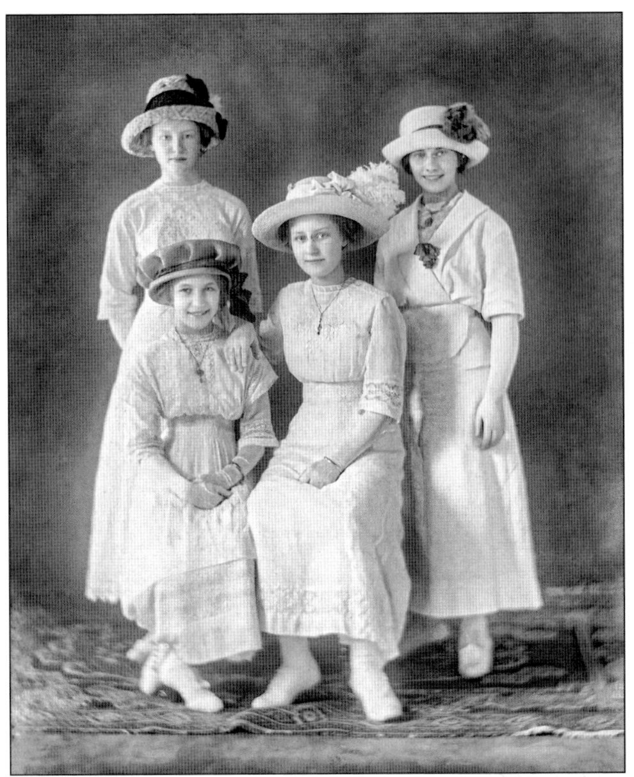

The Marvin sisters are seen here with Irene Haynes (seated, far left) and Clara Seward (standing, far right). Mildred Marvin (standing, far left) was born in 1899 to Frank and Cora Marvin. She married Harold Seward, brother of Clara. They had two sons, Gary and Norman. Ruth Marvin, sister of Mildred, is seated at right. Irene Haynes was born in 1899, the daughter of Aubrey A. and Rose (Capron) Haynes. A.A. Haynes owned a store on Main Street in Springwater. Irene Haynes married William Schofield and moved to Brooklyn, New York.

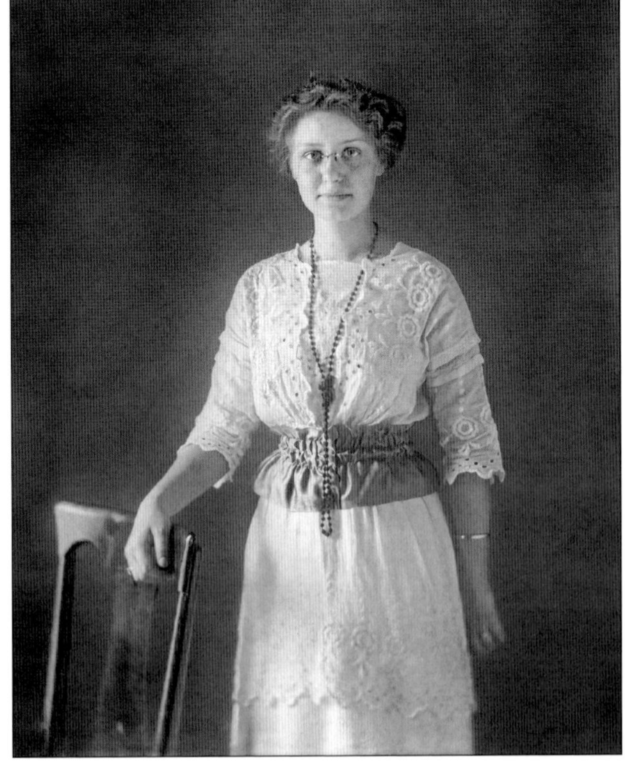

Ruth Marvin was born in 1897. She attended school in Springwater and teacher training school in Atlanta, New York. She was one of two students in her class of 10 to receive her teaching certificate and was a teacher at Wright's School in Springwater. She later continued her education at Genesseo Normal School. She married Robert Downing in 1926. The couple lived in Avon, New York, and had two daughters, Virginia and Betty. Ruth (Marvin) Downing died in 1987.

Gladys Walker and her twin siblings Alexander and Ward are seen here. They were three of nine children born to Erwin and Maude (Smart) Walker. Gladys was married for only one week to Harley Loveland when she died at age 24 on August 17, 1924. The newspaper reported that her death was due to acute indigestion. Alexander and Ward were born in 1902. Alexander married Leola Hoffman; he died in 1965. Ward married Helen Kurtz; he died in 1964. (Courtesy of Donna Walker.)

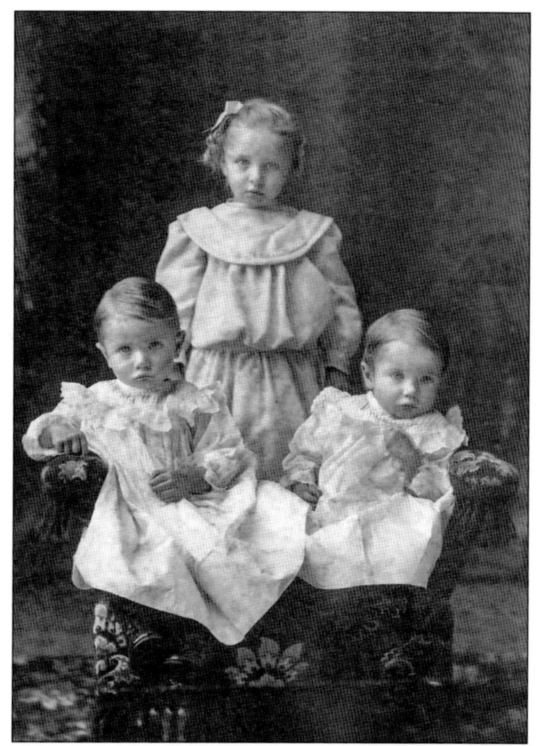

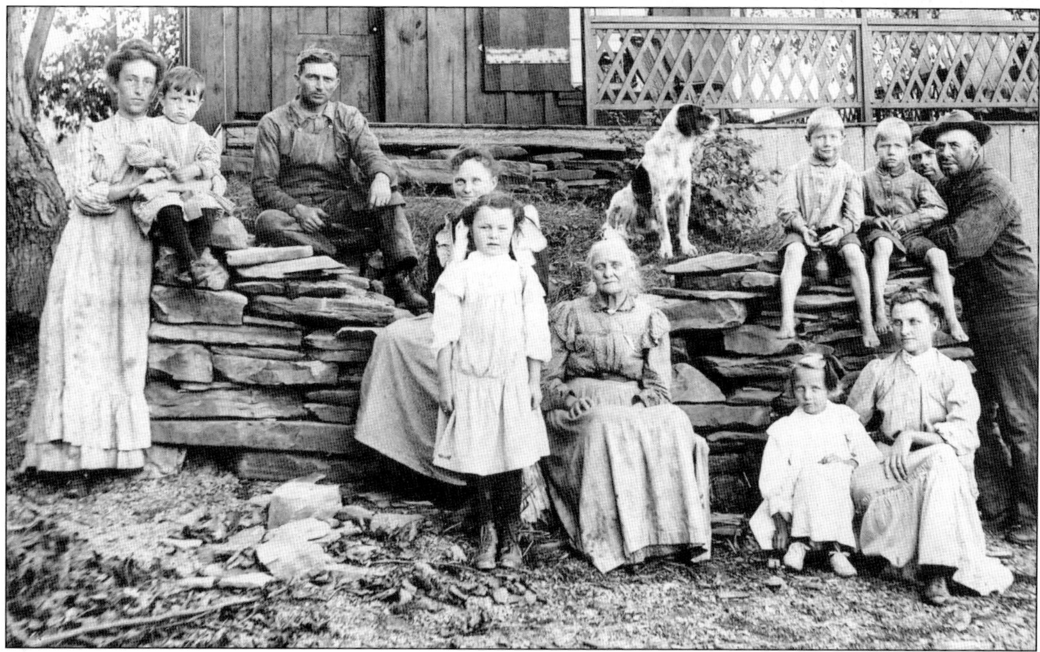

Four generations pose here outside a house on Canadice Lake. From left to right are Myrtie (Walker) Fuller, J. Kirk Fuller, Bert Fuller, Julia (Bill) Walker, Hazel Walker, Alvira Celestia (Clark) Whitman, Gladys Walker, Maude (Smart) Walker, Alex and Ward Walker, Erwin Walker, and Judson Walker. The Walker family of Springwater are descended from Ezra and Harriet (Stewart) Walker, who came to Springwater in 1820. (Courtesy of Donna Walker.)

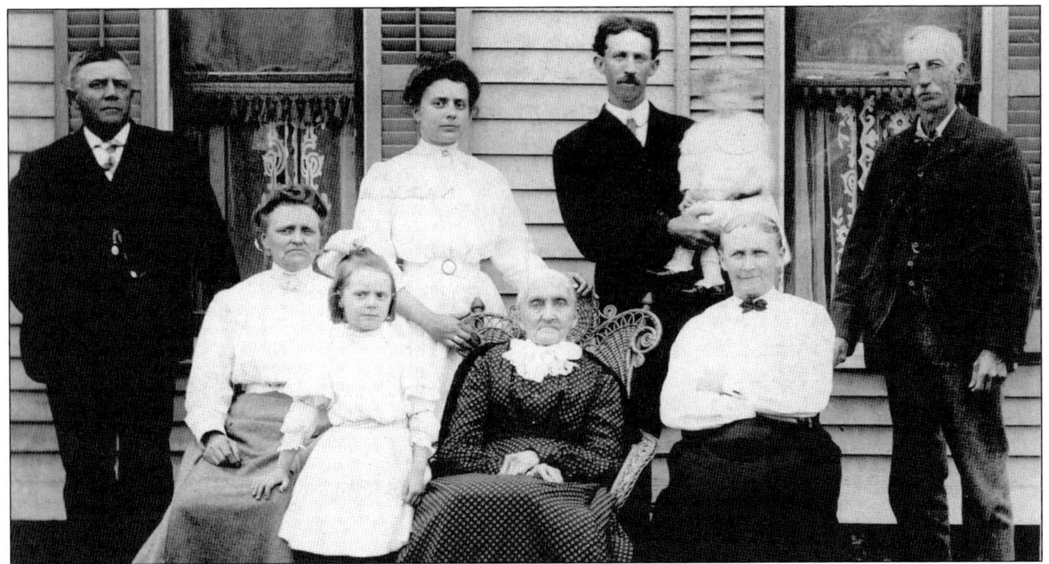

The Van Riper and Higgins families are pictured here. From left to right are (seated) Jane Eliza (Lewis) Van Riper, Louita Higgins, Phylinda (Thatcher) Lewis, and Mary (Purcell) Higgins; (standing) Edgar Van Riper, Ida May Higgins, George Higgins Jr. holding Kenneth Higgins, and George Higgins Sr. George Higgins Jr. married Ida May (called May) in 1901. He owned and ran Higgins' Garage in Springwater and also served as Springwater town clerk and justice of the peace before being elected town supervisor. (Courtesy of Ron and Sharon Ingraham.)

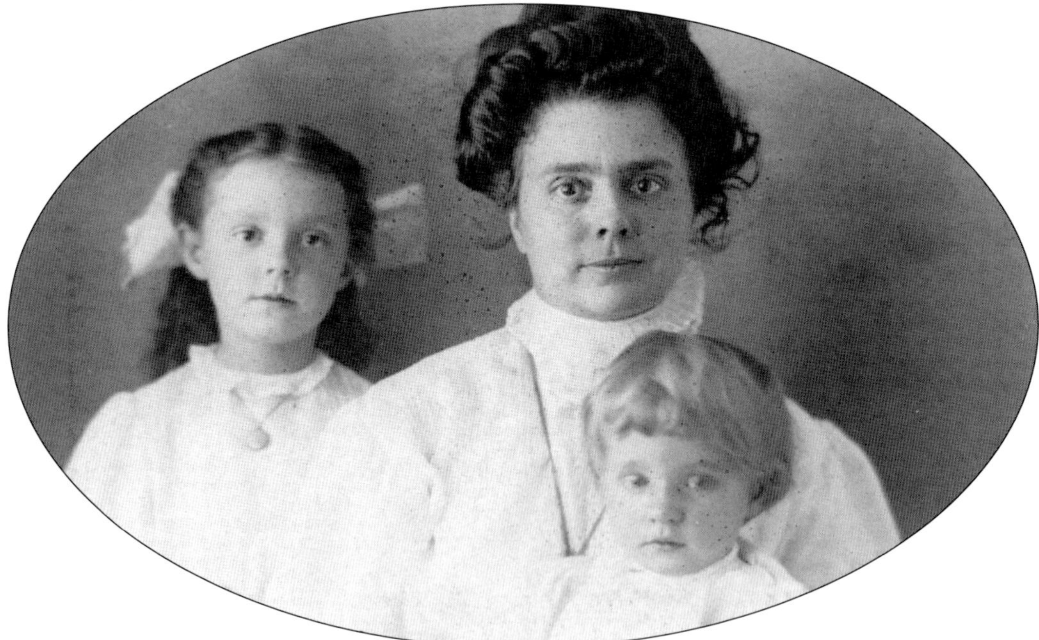

Ida May Van Riper was the daughter of Edgar and Jane (Lewis) Van Riper. She was born on May 1, 1882, in Yates, New York. Her father sold flower seeds and bulbs and was well known throughout the state for his flowers. Her mother, Jane, was an award-winning florist, and her displays were featured at fairs and flower shows. May is seen here with her two children, Louita and Kenneth Higgins. (Courtesy of Ron and Sharon Ingraham.)

Louita May Higgins, born in 1902, was the only daughter of George and May (Van Riper) Higgins. The Higgins family lived on the corner of Main Street and Kellogg Road in Springwater, just across from their friend Floyd Ingraham. The Higginses' first house burned in 1911, and they rebuilt in the same location later that year. The house is still standing. Louita became a schoolteacher and returned often to Springwater. She had no children. She died in 1989 and is buried near her parents in Mount Vernon Evergreen Cemetery.

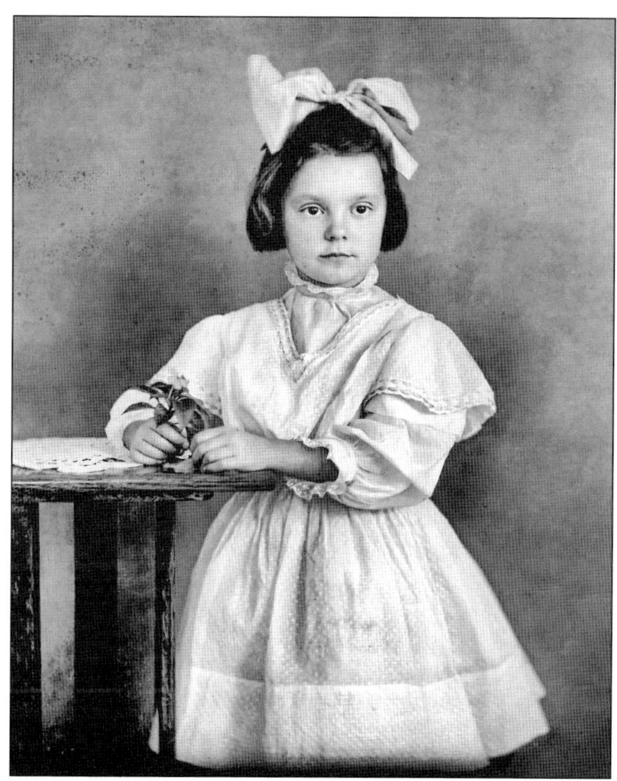

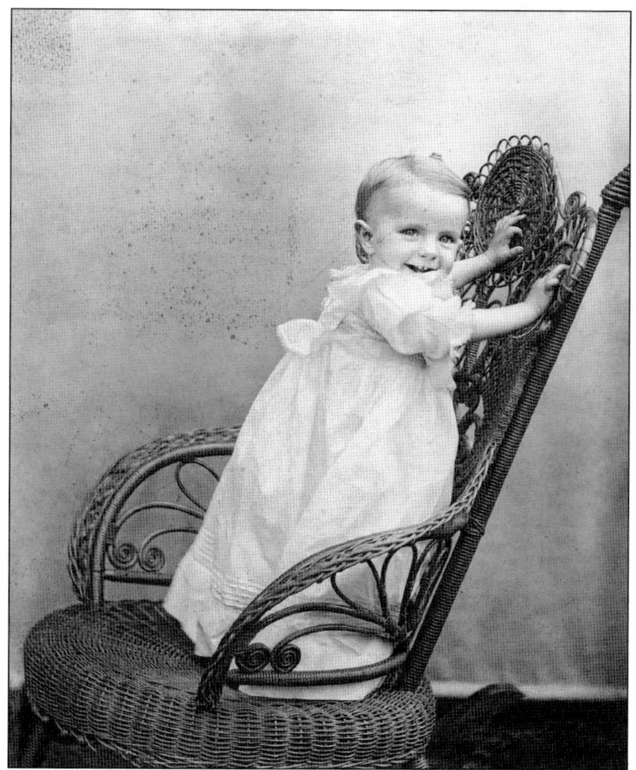

Born on July 19, 1906, Kenneth Higgins was the youngest child of George and May (Van Riper) Higgins of Springwater. He attended high school in Lima, New York, and after college became a teacher. He married Ruth (Bowne) Morgan and the couple had one son, Gary. Kenneth Higgins served in World War II. He was a member of the board of education in Middletown, New York, and the director of Camp Wilderness in Springwater. He was a representative for the New York State Boards Association and a volunteer for his local fire department. He died in 1991 and is buried in Mount Vernon Evergreen Cemetery.

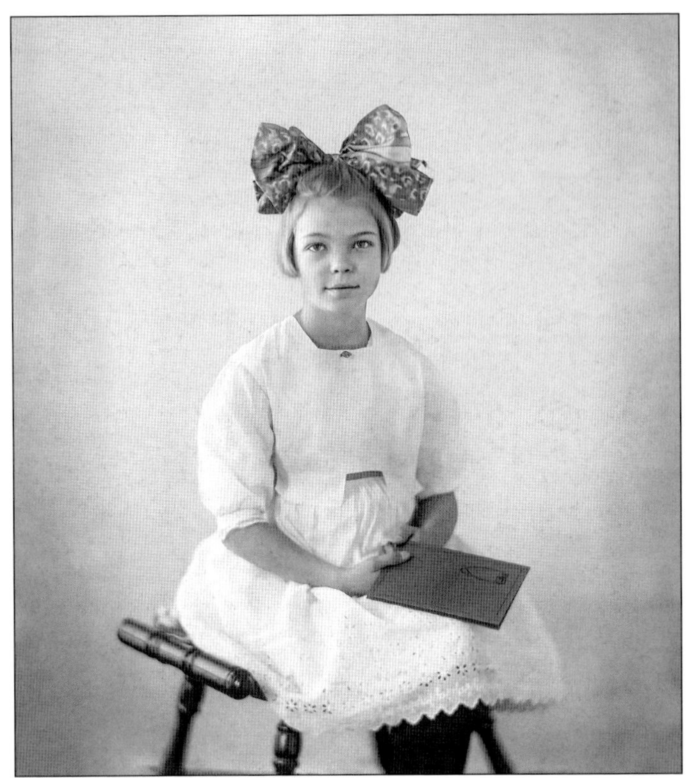

Madge Hansen was born on July 14, 1910, in Springwater. The only child of Charles and Amanda Conrad Hansen, Madge grew up in Springwater on Bell School Road. She married Lee McIntyre on July 2, 1938. They lived on Kellogg Road in Springwater and had no children. Madge worked for the post office and became postmaster of Springwater. She died in 1999 and is buried in Mount Vernon Evergreen Cemetery.

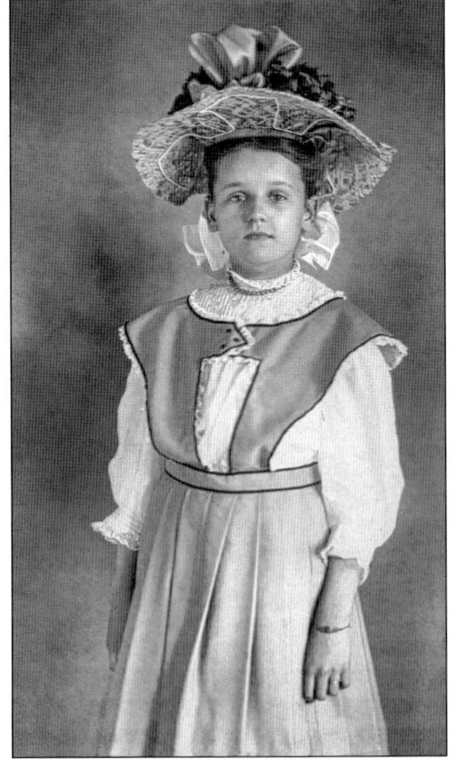

Ellen Flossie Doolittle was born on August 16, 1896, to Edwin and Emma Eldridge Doolittle. Born and raised in Springwater, she married Harold S. White on July 4, 1920. The couple lived in Conesus and had two children, Maxine and Warren. Ellen was a schoolteacher for many years and also worked at the Cannon Miller Radio Factory in Springwater. (Courtesy of Ron and Sharon Ingraham.)

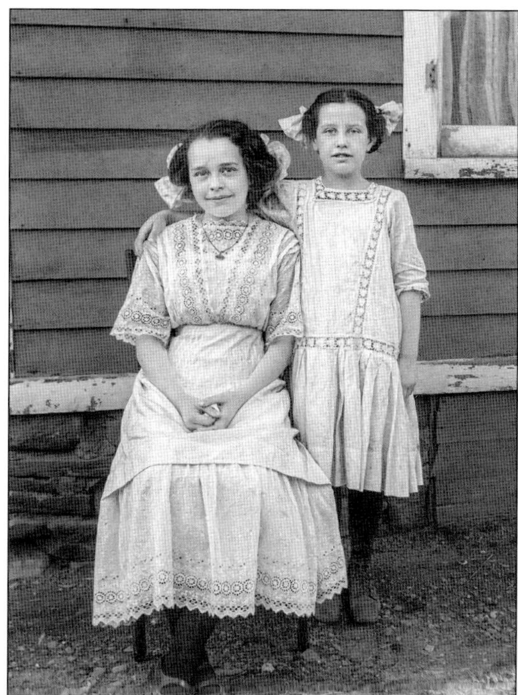

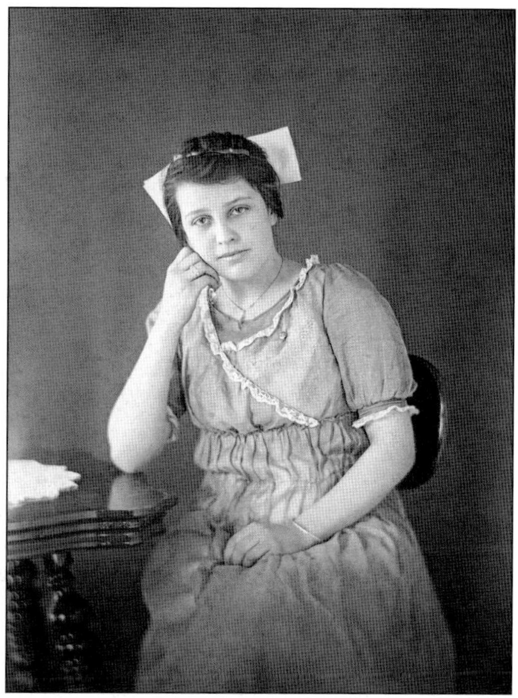

At left, Myrtle (left) and Hazel Perkins were two of nine children born to Allen and Ella Perkins of Springwater. Hazel Ella Perkins (at right) was born on May 2, 1901. She married Thomas Gordon Leeson in 1918 in a small ceremony in the Methodist church parsonage on Main Street in Springwater. The couple lived in Conesus and Springwater. They had eight children, two of whom died in infancy. Hazel (Perkins) Leeson died in 1947.

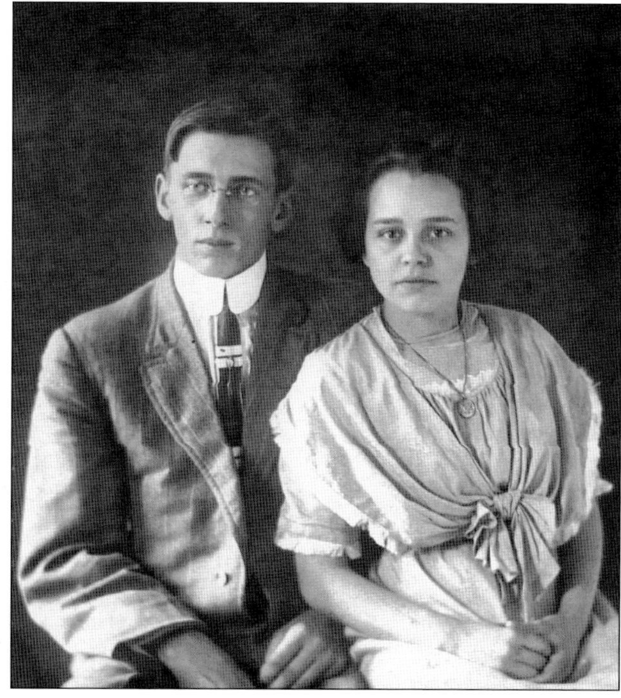

Myrtle Emile Perkins was born in 1894 in Springwater. She was a schoolteacher and a member of the Springwater Grange. She married Reginald Armstrong of Hornell, seen here. He died at age 30 in 1924. She then married Ray Thomas of East Bloomfield, New York. Myrtle (Perkins) Thomas died in 1994. (Courtesy of Ron and Sharon Ingraham.)

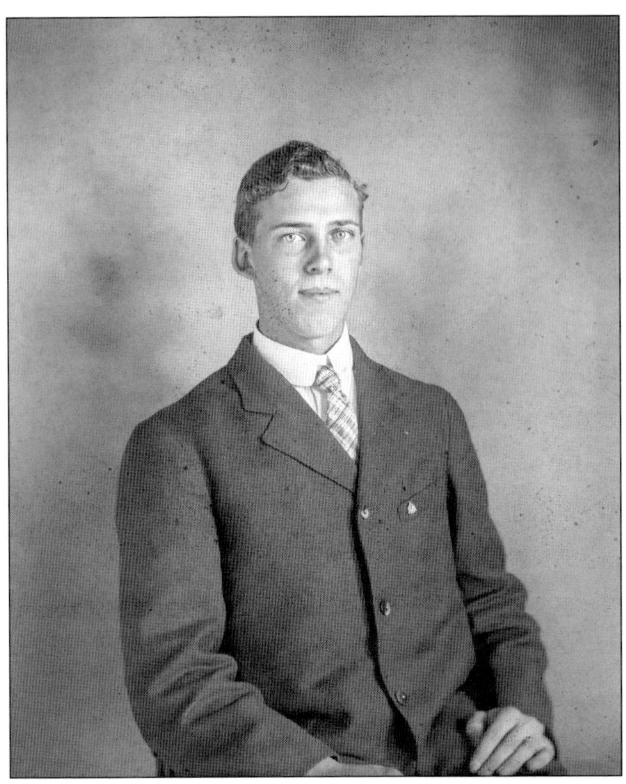

George Johnson was born on March 25, 1889, in Canadice, New York, to Alfred and Ella (Smith) Johnson. George married Leata Rutherford in 1925, and they had no children. George worked as an engineer at Gunlocke Chair Factory and died in 1943.

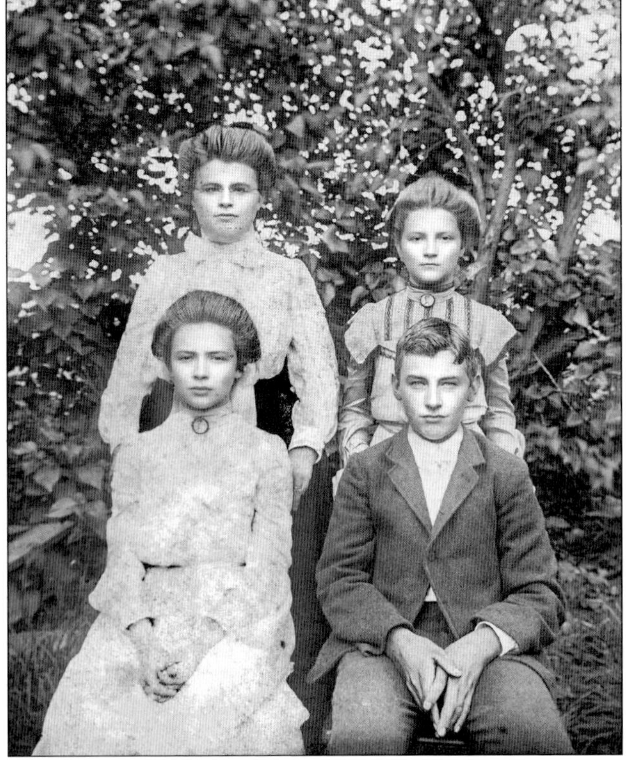

Pearl (standing, left) and George Johnson (seated, right) were the children of Alfred and Ella (Smith) Johnson. Pearl was born in Canadice on March 6, 1888. The Johnson family moved to Springwater by 1900. Pearl married Albert I. Sparks in 1912. They had no children. Pearl worked as a nurse in Elmira, New York. She died in 1934. Pictured with the Johnson siblings are Iona and Ethel Kruse, daughters of Charles and Clara (Smith) Kruse. Iona (standing, right) was born in 1889. She worked as a teacher before marrying Joseph A. Henderson. They settled in Ossining, New York, and had eight children. Iona died in 1976. Ethel (seated, left) was born in 1891. Never married, she worked as a bank clerk and a stenographer. She died in 1952. (Courtesy of Springwater–Webster Crossing Historical Society.)

Grace E. Johnson of Springwater was born on July 3, 1885, to Eugene and Blanche Johnson. Grace was honored as a 50-year member of the Springwater Grange and a member of the Daughters of Rebekah. She worked for more than 25 years as a telephone operator in Springwater beginning in 1911, nine years after Springwater had telephone lines put in. She became chief operator, working in the office in the Marvin Building on Main Street. Grace never married. She died on January 3, 1969, at the age of 83. (Courtesy of Ron and Sharon Ingraham.)

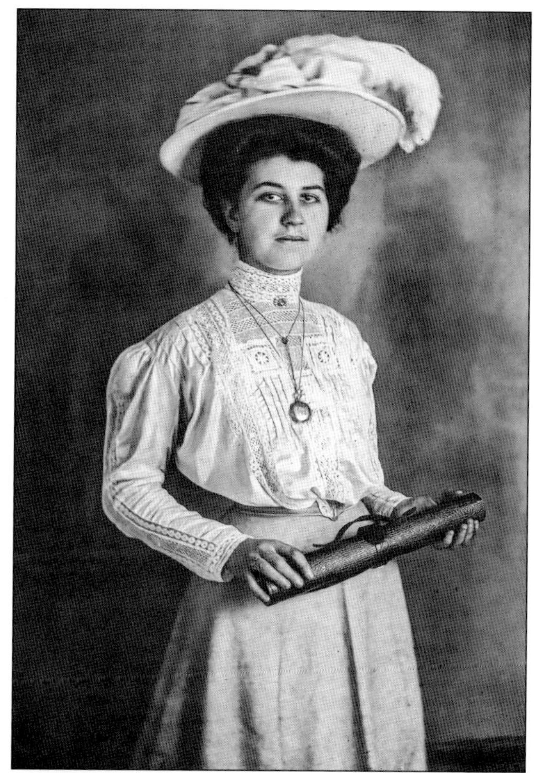

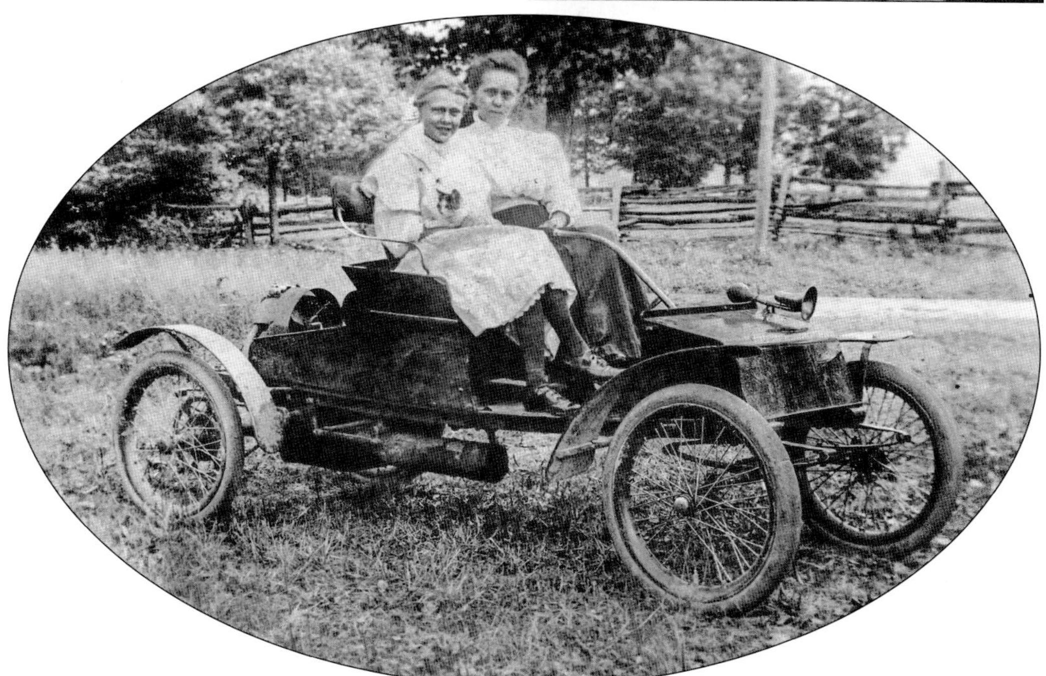

Blanche H. Johnson, the wife of Eugene Johnson, and her daughter Grace sit in Bert Johnson's automobile. Bert Johnson was one of the first in the area to purchase an automobile. The model seen here is believed to be a Waltham Orient Buckboard. (Courtesy of Ron and Sharon Ingraham.)

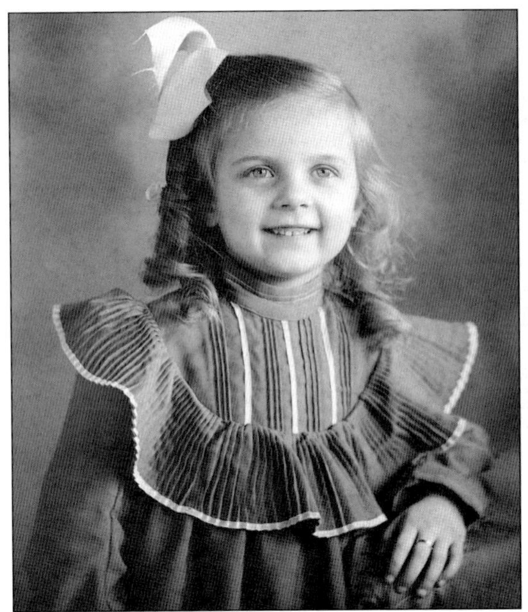

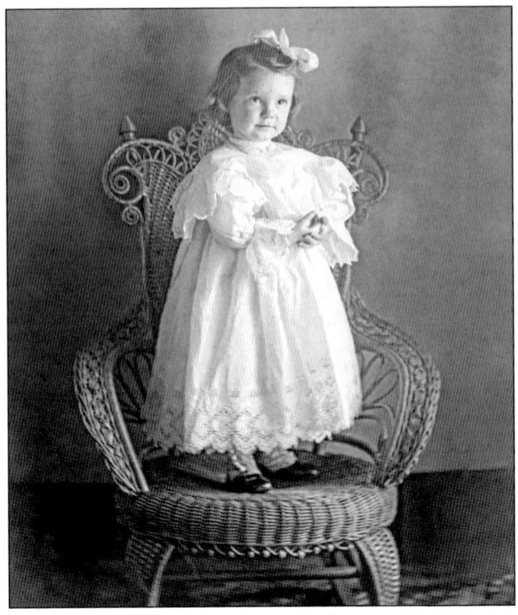

Gladys Fidelia Jackman (left) was born on April 18, 1901, and Farolin Irene Jackman (right) was born on May 12, 1904, in Springwater to William and Irene (Andrews) Jackman. Gladys and Farolin's great-grandfather Ira Jackman came to nearby Canadice on an ox sled with his family and all their belongings. The Jackmans later moved to Newport, Rhode Island. Gladys married Charles Donovan in 1922. She had one son, Charles. Gladys died in 1988. Farolin married Robert J. Kyle and had five children. Farolin died in 1992.

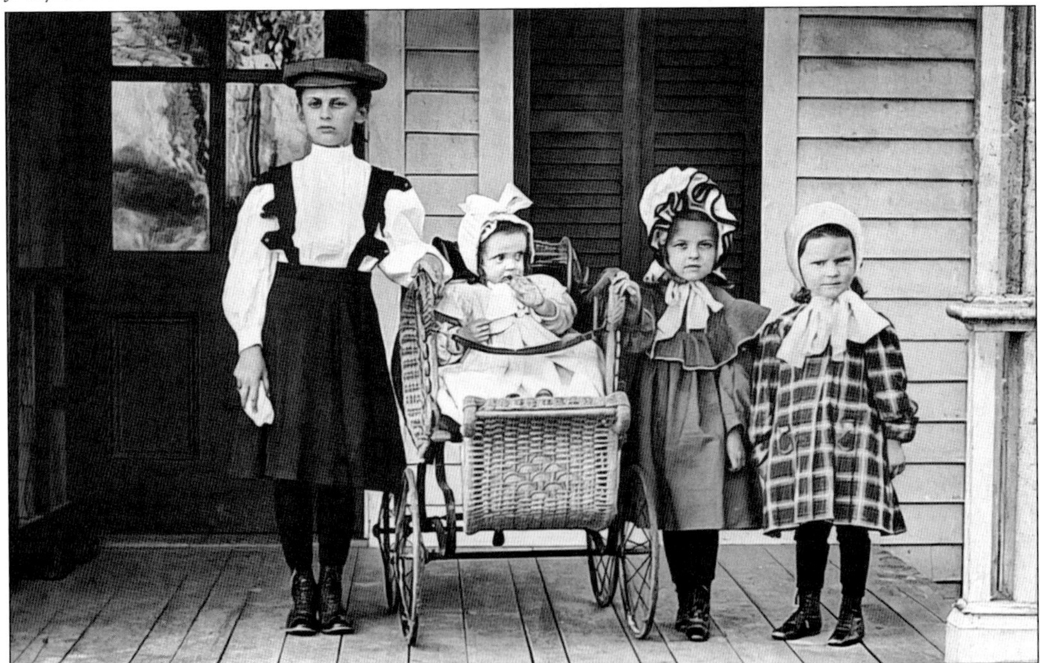

From left to right, Florence, Farolin, and Gladys Jackman and friend Louita Higgins pose on a porch. The wicker baby carriage was typical of the period. Fancy bonnets, wide collars, bows, and button boots were in fashion for young girls at the time.

Fanny Delphine Bielby was born in 1862 to Thomas and Catherine Downing. Catherine died when Fanny was an infant, and Fanny was raised by her grandparents. She married Alfred Gardner in 1982 in Fairport, New York. They had a son, Forrest Alfred, and a daughter, Mildred. Alfred died in 1908. Fanny married to Chester B. Jackman in 1910, and the couple resided in Springwater for 15 years before moving to East Avon, New York. Fanny died in 1936, ten months after her husband.

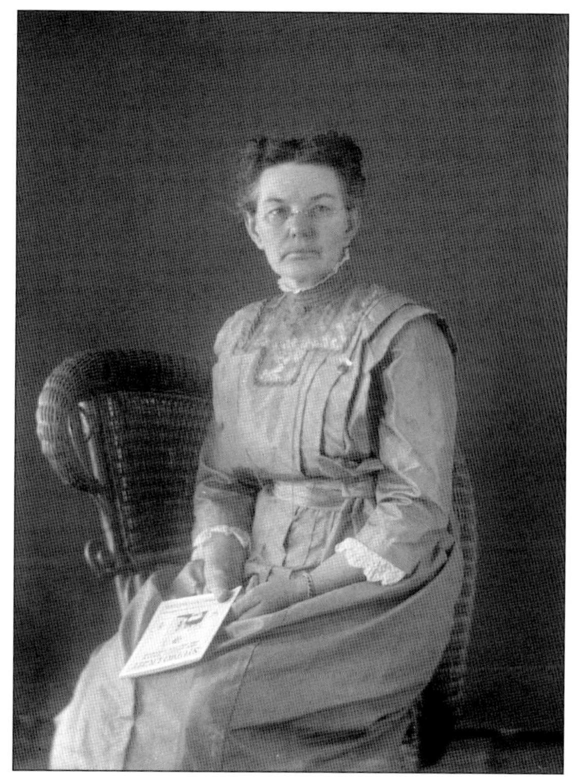

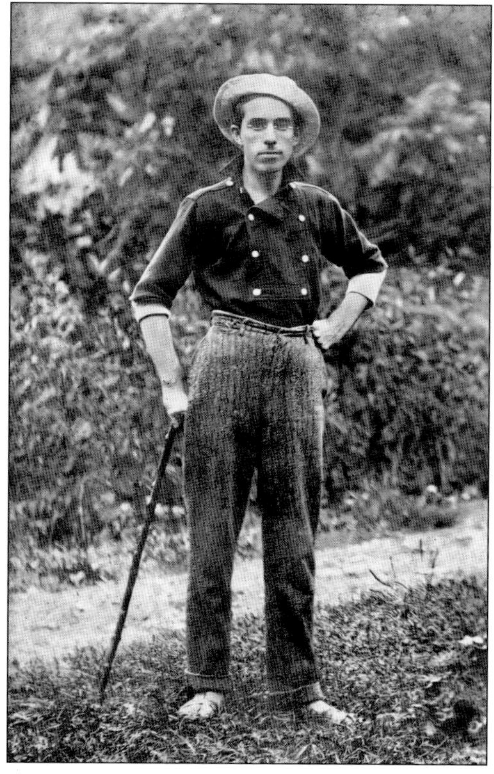

Albert Duane Jackman was born on April 18, 1882, to Albert and Annie May (Sherman) Jackman in Canadice. This picture was taken in 1906. Duane attended the North Cohocton Atlanta High School and the seminary at Lima. He taught school in Springwater. He was educated abroad and traveled extensively. He worked in New York City and Miles City, Montana, before moving to Forest Lake, Illinois, where he was a city clerk. He married Grace Taylor and had two daughters. A. Duane Jackman died at the age of 56 on February 11, 1939, in Illinois. (Courtesy of Ron and Sharon Ingraham.)

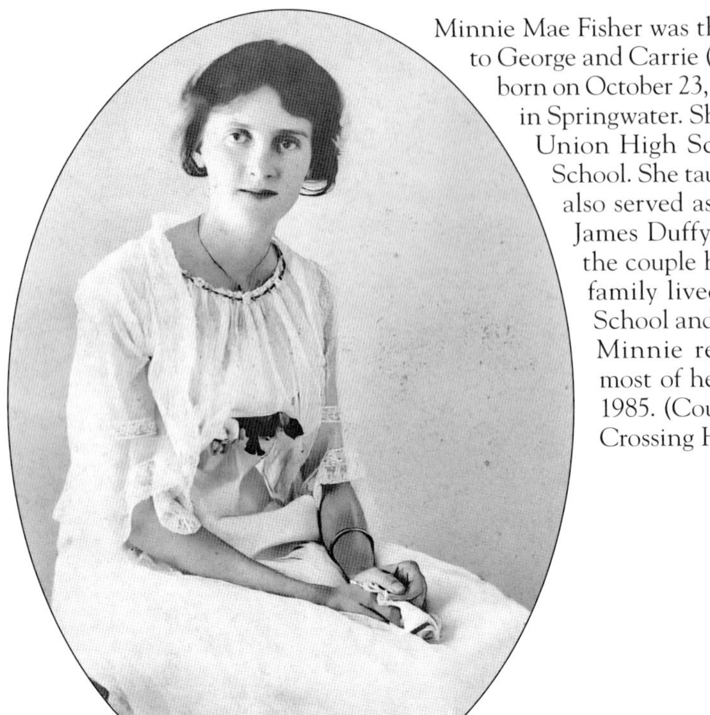

Minnie Mae Fisher was the oldest of five children born to George and Carrie (Wheaton) Fisher. Minnie was born on October 23, 1899, on the Fisher family farm in Springwater. She graduated from Springwater Union High School and Genesseo Normal School. She taught school in Springwater and also served as the town clerk. She married James Duffy in 1919 in Springwater, and the couple had three children. The Duffy family lived in a home at the corner of School and Howe Streets in Springwater. Minnie remained in Springwater for most of her life. She died on January 4, 1985. (Courtesy of Springwater–Webster Crossing Historical Society.)

Marguerite Wheaton, daughter of John and Sarah (House) Wheaton of Springwater, was born on July 13, 1897. Marguerite was the aunt of Minnie Mae Fisher. After Marguerite's graduation from the Geneseo Normal School, she taught at Dansville High School. She was also an accomplished musician. She married Carl Gross of Naples, New York, in 1923. The couple settled in Naples and had one daughter, Shirley. Marguerite (Wheaton) Gross died on August 3, 1983, in Naples.

Eva Cora Fisher was one of eight children born to Purley and Eva Fisher, on November 7, 1898, in Springwater. Eva attended Springwater schools and graduated from Genesseo Normal School, receiving a teaching certificate. She married Henry Benson of Buffalo. The Bensons made Buffalo their home and had one son, Richard. Eva (Fisher) Benson died on January 22, 1993. (Courtesy of Ron and Sharon Ingraham.)

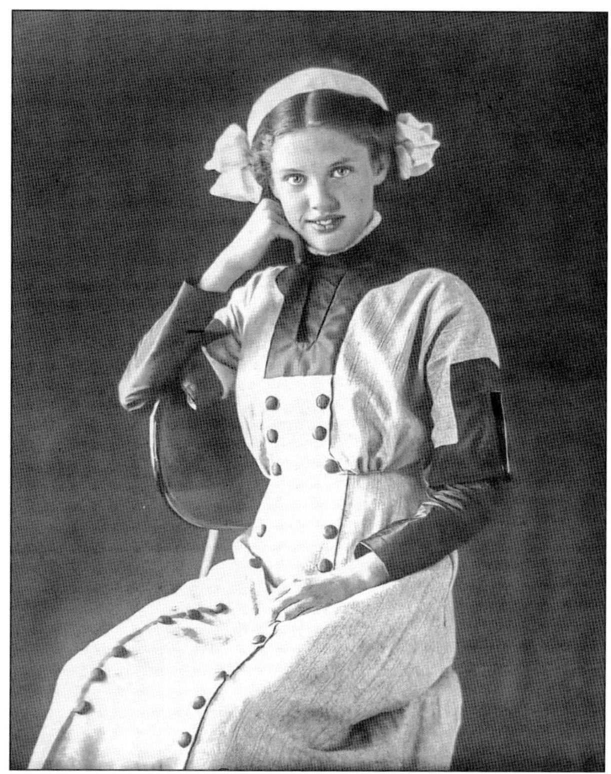

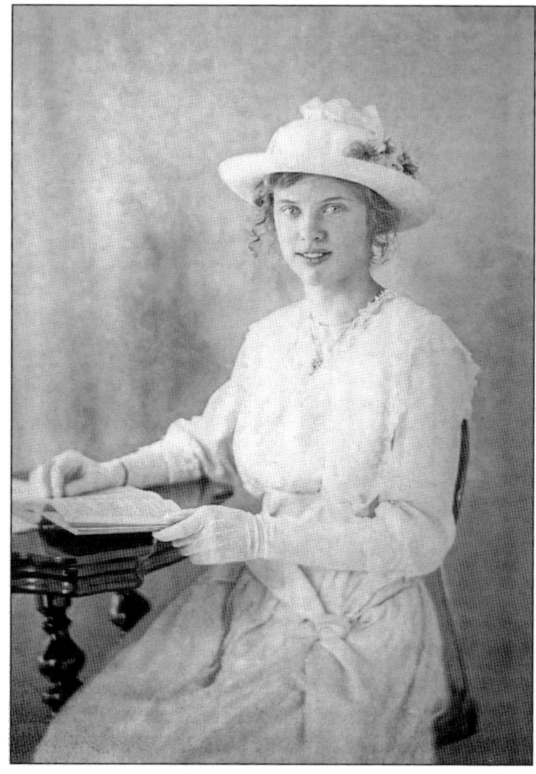

Eva (Fisher) Benson, seen here, was five years old in December 1903 when her family had a devastating house fire. The Fisher family had started a fire in the kitchen stove to heat the house before going to bed. They were awakened by the kitchen roof falling in. Due to fierce winds, the fire quickly spread. They had recently had a telephone line installed and were able to call for help before evacuating. Neighbors came to their aid and were able to save a large horse barn, though it caught fire several times. The house and the family dog were lost. Neighbors took the family in, and the Fishers later rebuilt. (Courtesy of Ron and Sharon Ingraham.)

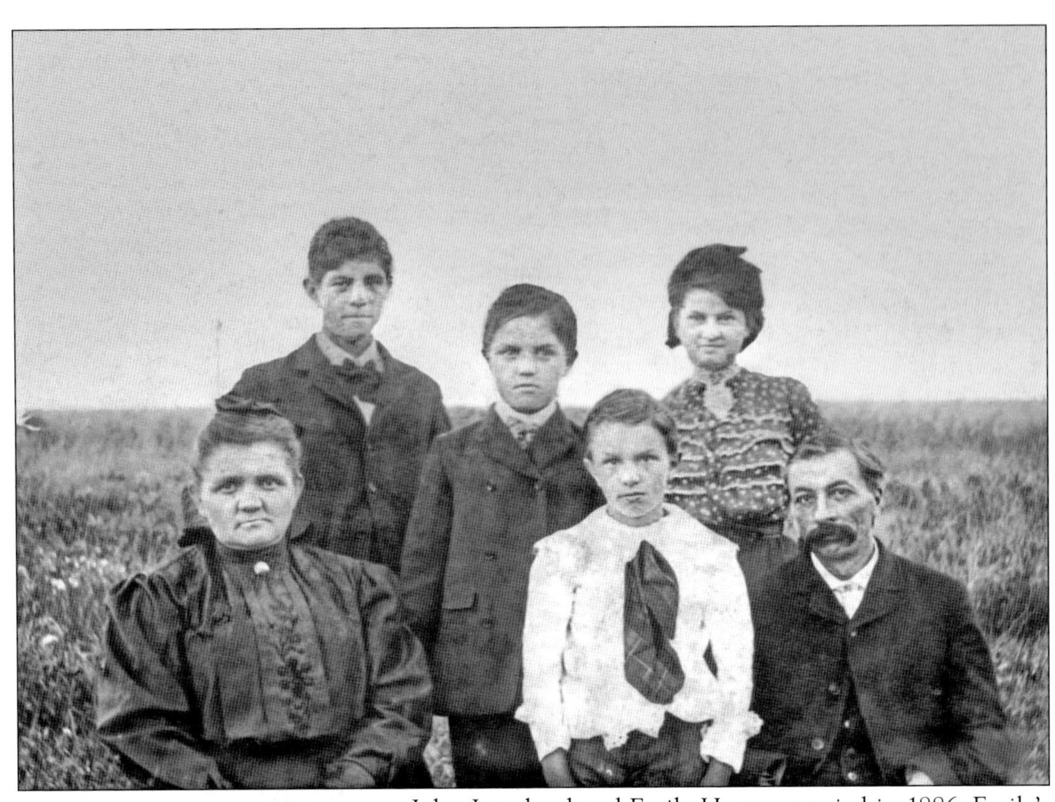

John Loveland and Emily Harter married in 1886. Emily's mother, Caroline Harter, died when she was two years of age, and she was adopted by the VanScooter family of Dansville. John Loveland was a carpenter and the son of William and Mary Louisa Loveland. Pictured here from left to right are Emily, William, Harry, Albert, Lottie, and John Loveland. The Lovelands lived in Wayland and Cohocton, New York. Emily died in 1931, and John in 1950. (Courtesy of Ron and Sharon Ingraham.)

Harry August Loveland was born on July 13, 1894, to John and Emily Loveland. He married Anna Alice Harrigan in 1931. They relocated to California in 1950. Harry Loveland died on March 1, 1968, in Los Angeles. (Courtesy of Ron and Sharon Ingraham.)

Bernice (left) and Alta Loveland were the daughters of Murray and Laura (Wagner) Loveland. Bernice was born on April 15, 1897, in Fremont, New York. She married Edwin Mehlenbacher in 1916. She had six sons and one daughter. She was active in the community and instrumental in raising war bonds during World War I. Bernice died on June 6, 1996. Her sister, Alta Irene Loveland, was born on December 7, 1907. Alta married Wallace Jackson, and the couple lived in Naples, New York. They had two children, Doris and Francis. Alta died on December 26, 1999.

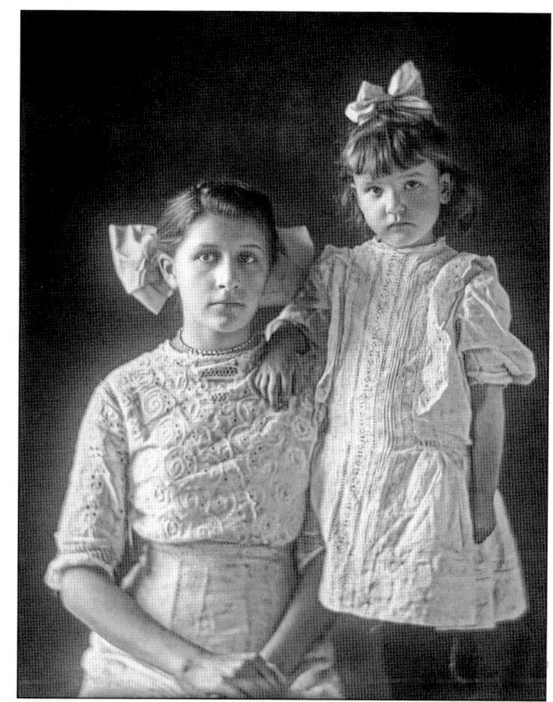

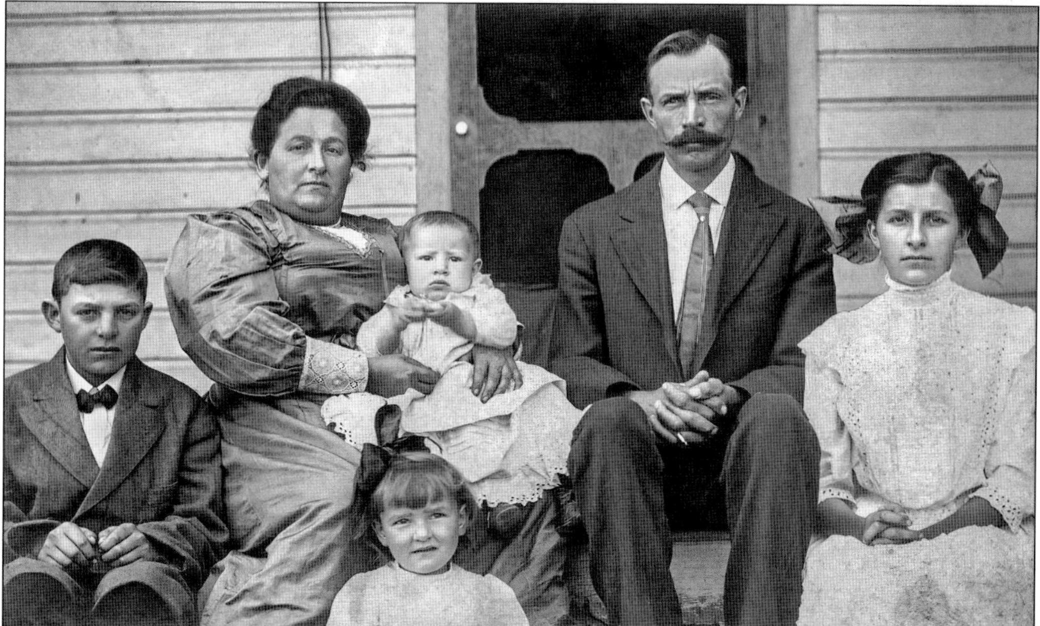

Murray and Laura (Wagner) Loveland are pictured here with their children. From left to right are (first row) Alta; (second row) Robert, Laura with Walter on her lap, Murray, and Bernice. The Lovelands had another son, Julian, sometime after this picture was taken. Murray and Laura married in 1935 in Stephens Mills, New York. Laura was the daughter of Wallace Wagner and Alma Hayward of Springwater. Murray was the son of William and Mary Louisa Loveland of Wayland. Laura died in 1933 and Murray in 1948. They are buried in Lakeside Cemetery in Wayland. (Courtesy of Ron and Sharon Ingraham.)

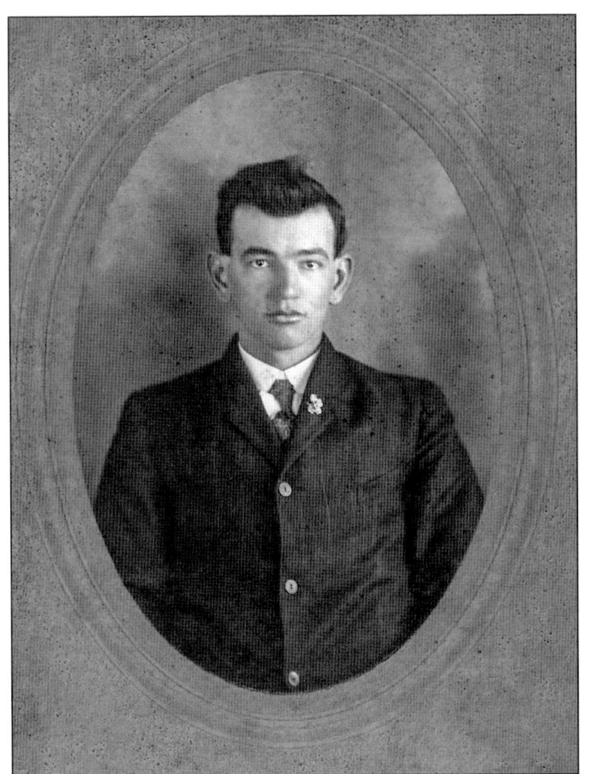

Herbert Everette Becker was one of 18 children born to John Franklin Becker and his second wife, Lucinda Jane Butler. He was born in Canadice on March 1, 1879. He was a farmer. Most of his large family farmed and were well known in the community. Herb married Anna Roberts of Sparta, New York, in 1911. They had no children. Herb Becker died on June 7, 1947, in Dansville. (Courtesy of Springwater–Webster Crossing Historical Society.)

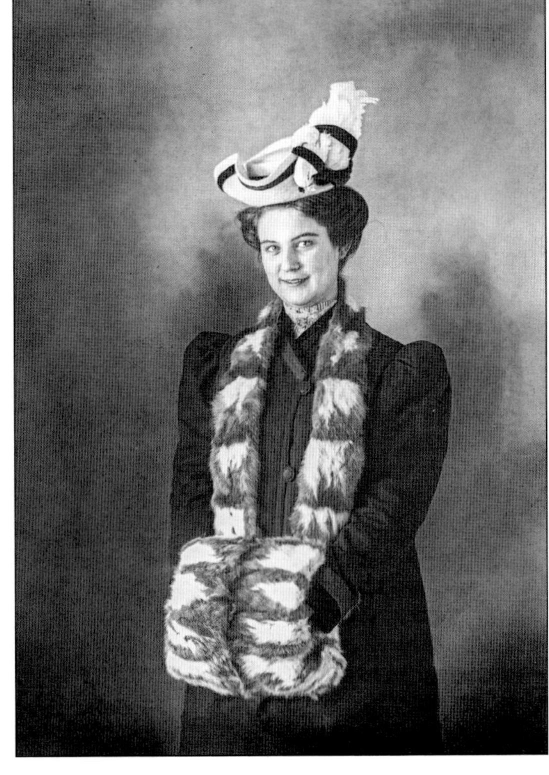

Harriet "Hattie" J. Crooks was born on August 20, 1889, in Canadice. The daughter of Richmond Crooks and Elizabeth Dalrymple, she was one of seven children. Hattie lost her mother when she was seven years old. She married Harrison Fremont Becker, and the couple had two children, Harland and Hazel. Hattie (Crooks) Becker died in 1944.

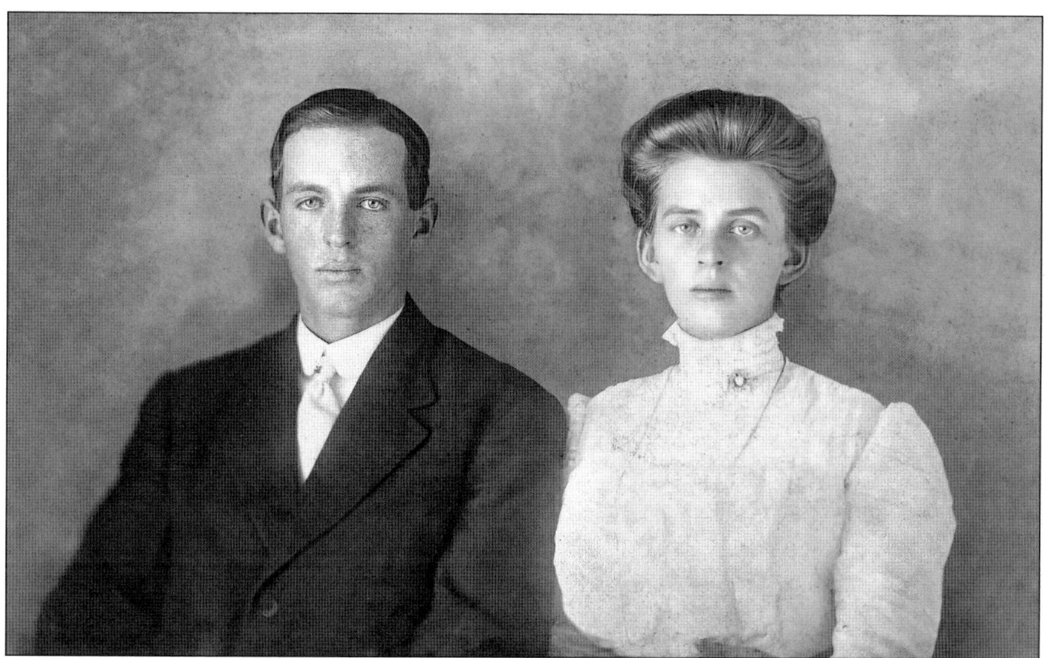

Spencer Dayton Becker (known as Dayton) and Esther Preston married in 1912. Dayton Becker was born on September 12, 1889, to Marion and Emma (Tague) Becker in Canadice. Esther, born in 1885, was the daughter of David and Maria (Kinne) Preston of Canadice. Dayton and Esther had three children: Fremont, Leah, and Clifford. Dayton Becker was a farmer and operated an insurance agency started by his father. He also was a teacher, town clerk for Canadice for almost 19 years, and served on several boards in the community. Dayton Becker died at age 63 on March 30, 1953. (Courtesy of Ron and Sharon Ingraham.)

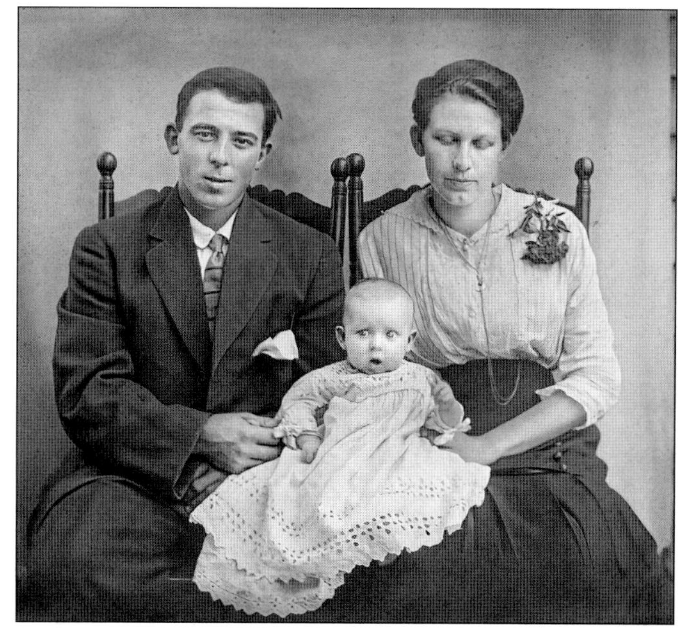

Robert C. Pragle and Iva Hattie Smith were married on May 24, 1913. Their daughter Leona Pauline Pragle, pictured here, was born on February 20, 1915. She was the first of the Pragles' 17 children, 13 of whom survived to adulthood. Iva took in children from New York City during the summer as part of the Fresh Air Fund organization. Iva died on May 3, 1939, three hours after falling ill at the age of 45. At the time, the Pragles of Wayland had the largest family in the area. Robert then married Florence Engle. He died on April 2, 1983, at the age of 92.

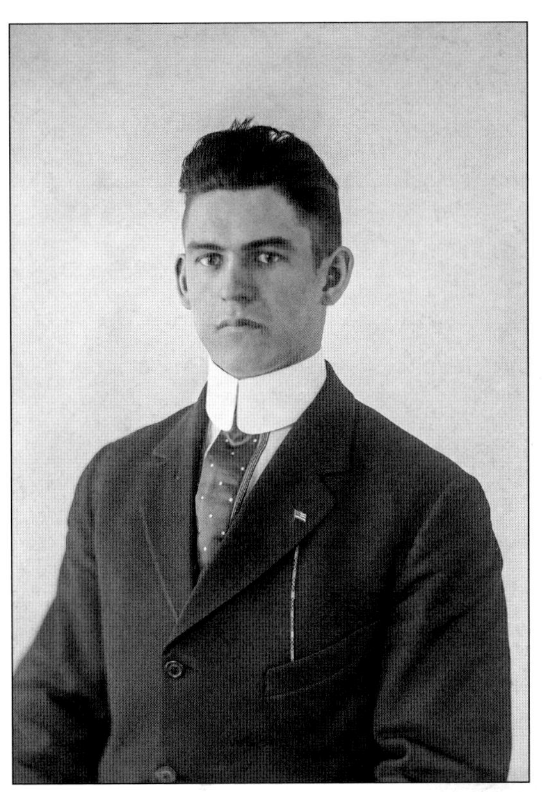

George W. Brokaw was born in Springwater on February 11, 1894, to Wilmer and Mary (Weed) Brokaw. When he died, he was the last living Springwater resident born in a log cabin. George joined the Army in 1918 and served as a machine gunner in World War I. He lived in Springwater for most of his life, marrying Catherine Steidle in 1919. They had two daughters. George ran a barbershop, sold poultry, was a mail carrier, and worked other odd jobs. He did not have electricity until 1934 and did not have a phone until 20 years later. He died in 1978.

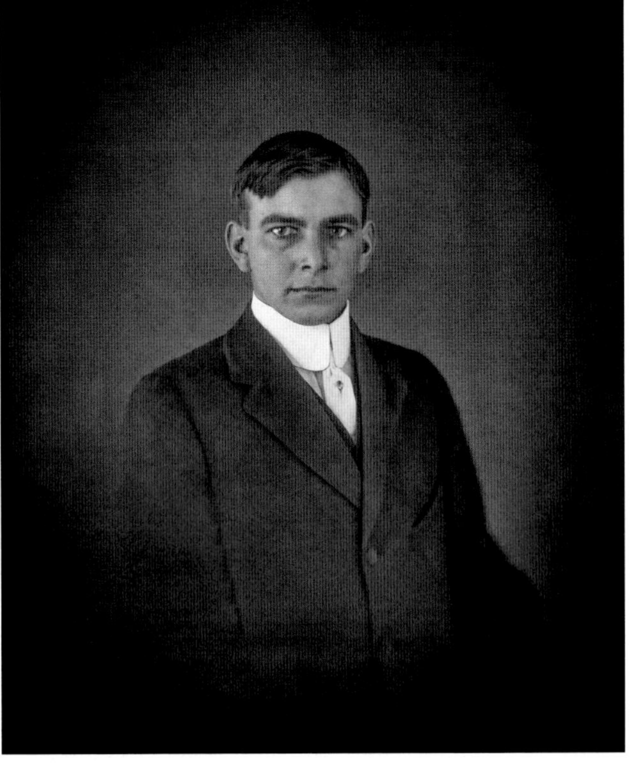

Fred S. Snyder was born on July 30, 1895, to Stanley and Dora Snyder in Springwater. He attended Geneseo Normal School, and after graduation taught at School No. 4 on Tabors Corners Road. Fred enlisted in the Navy in 1917 and trained in Norfolk, Virginia. He rose rapidly, earning the rank of ensign, while serving overseas during World War I. After returning home, he accepted a position in Washington, DC, with the Officer's Materials School. He married Ruth Goundry in 1918. On May 31, 1920, during a trip home from Norway with the Merchant Marine Service, he fell into the sea and drowned.

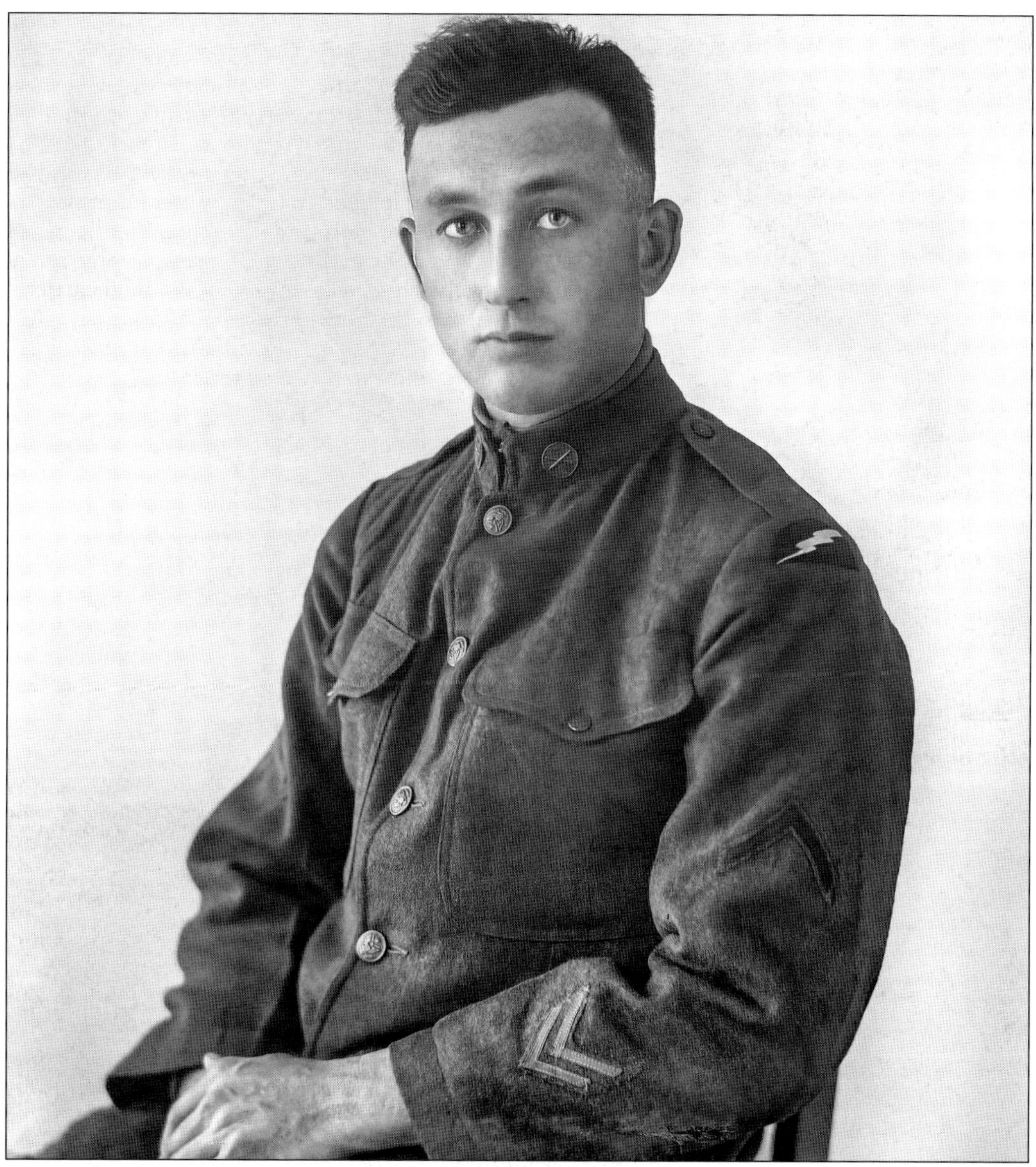

Renesselaer Grouse, son of Christian and Henrietta Grouse of Springwater, served in Battery E of the 307th Field Artillery Regiment—part of the 78th "Lightning" Division in World War I. Grouse rose to the rank of sergeant before being honorably discharged in 1919. During World War I, no state sacrificed more than New York. One of 10 soldiers who served in the American Expeditionary Forces in France were from New York. More than 250,000 military personnel from New York served at home or abroad. With more than 15,000 fallen soldiers, New York had the highest casualty count of any state and was one of three states that sent an entire National Guard division into battle, including half a division from western New York. Livingston County sent 1,700 men. Four brothers from the Tennent family of Caledonia, New York—Elbert, Donald, Walter, and David—enlisted, served overseas, and returned safely home. Of the three Kern brothers of Springwater—Jesse, Homer, and Clinton—only Homer returned. Livingston County welcomed soldiers back with open arms, parades, and honors. Dansville's Jackson Sanitorium was used as a hospital for soldiers. Hometowns and the Finger Lakes were havens of rest and healing.

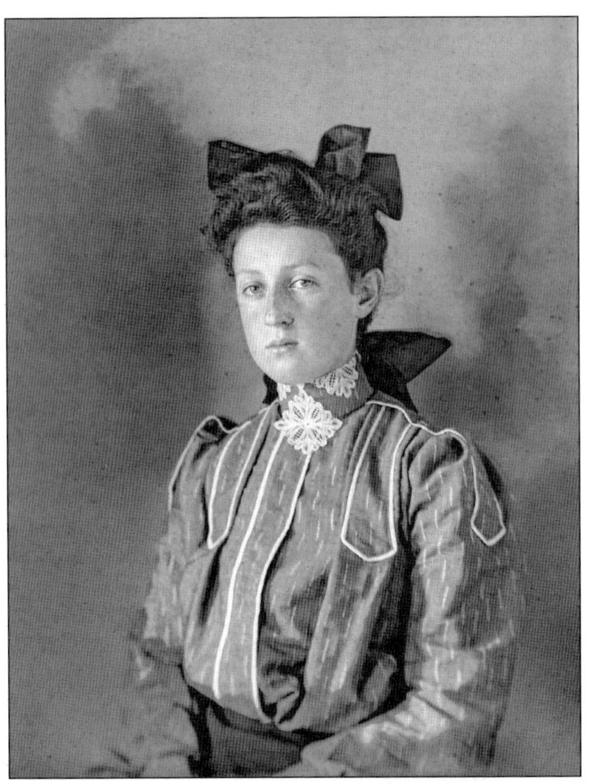

Ethel Baretta "E.B." Waite was born in December 1894 to Frank and Minnie (Sawdy) Waite of Springwater. Her father was in the construction industry. The family relocated to Rochester, and Waite eloped at age 15, lying about her age and marrying an older man. The marriage was annulled, and she went back home with her parents. Waite married Donald Cameron Doane at age 18, and they settled in the Rochester area. She had no children. Ethel (Waite) Doane died in 1970.

Frank Waite was born in 1861, the oldest of eight children born to Francis and Hannah (Brown) Waite of Springwater. Frank is seated at center in a striped tie with his parents on either side and surrounded by people who are assumed to be his siblings—Emma, Carrie, Lillian, Morris, twins Warner and Warren, and Edmund—along with their spouses and children. (Courtesy of Ron and Sharon Ingraham.)

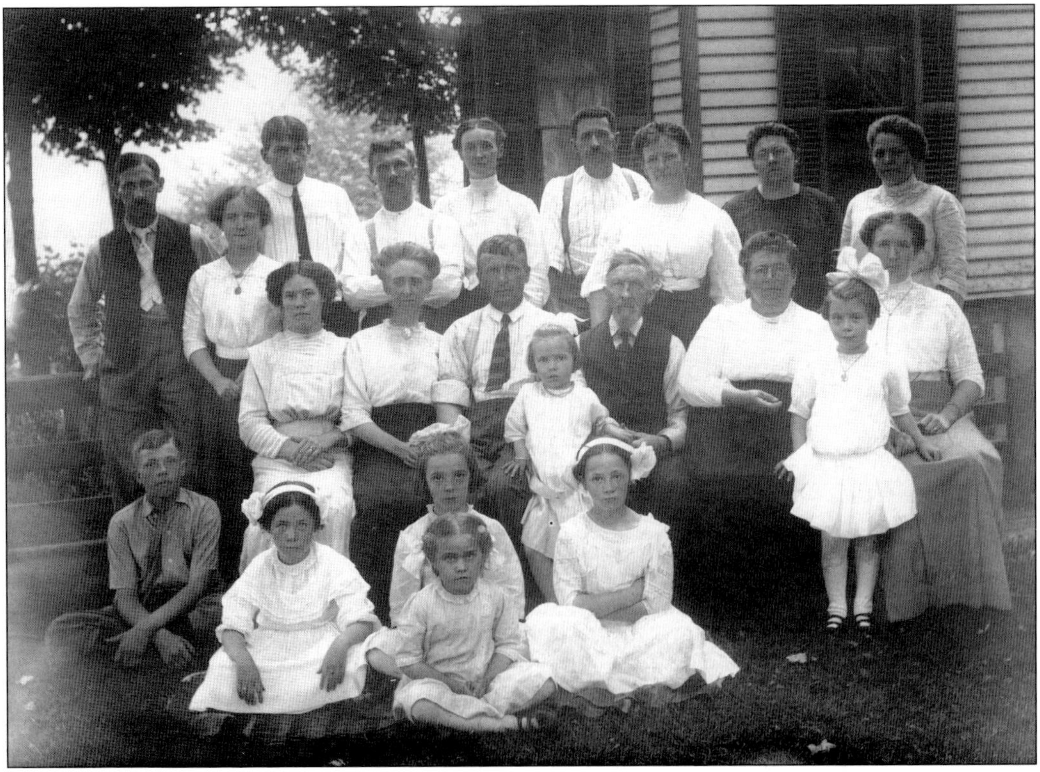

Born in 1895, Earl Armstrong lost his father, Henry Armstrong, at the age of three. His mother, Sarah (West) Armstrong, moved in with her family in Springwater for help with her three sons. Armstrong was boarding with families and working as a farm hand by age 14. He later worked as a silk weaver in Hornell. He married Laura Beebe, and they had one daughter, Phyllis. He and his brothers owned and operated Armstrong Brothers Inc. in Wayland, selling petroleum and oil-burning equipment for many years. Armstrong died in Rochester in 1993.

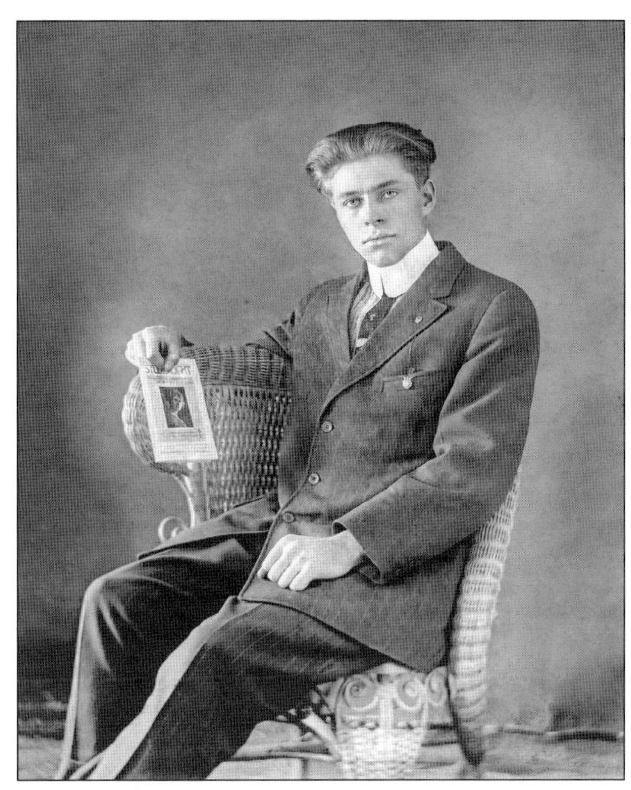

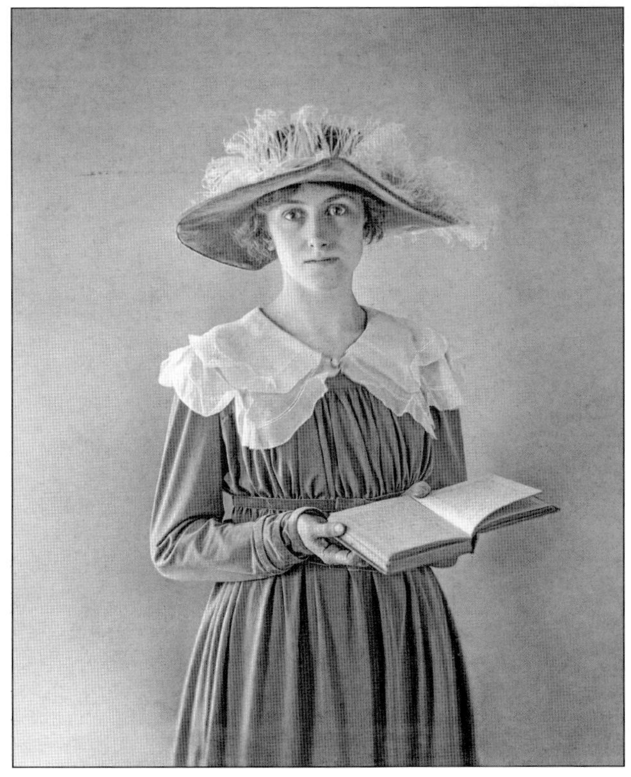

Laura Beebe was born in 1896. The daughter of Samuel and Minnie (Slaughter) Beebe of Oswego, New York, she married Earl C. Armstrong in 1915. The couple had one daughter, Phyllis Adele, who married Terrence Fox. Laura (Beebe) Armstrong died in 1986.

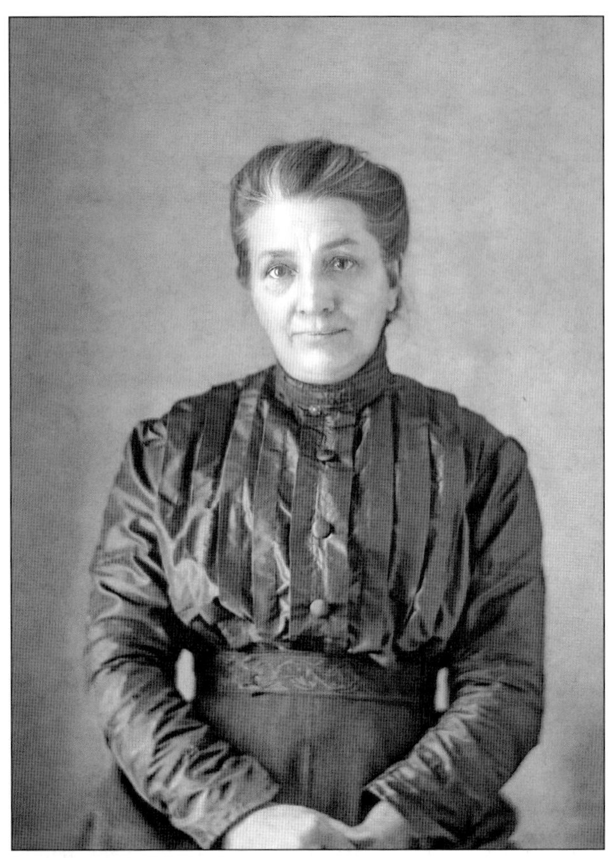

Born on August 26, 1854, in Wayland, Luthera E. Loveland was the daughter of William and Mary Louise (Warren) Loveland. She married Joseph Cork in 1873 and had six children, five of whom survived to adulthood. One of her daughters, Anna, married photographer Floyd Ingraham. Luthera (Loveland) Cork died on March 17, 1912, in Springwater.

The Cork family, pictured here, lived in Wayland and Cohocton, New York, before settling in Springwater by 1900. Joseph Cork, born in England, came to New York at the age of 11. He became a farm laborer in Geneseo and then Wayland. He married Luthera Loveland, and they had six children. A daughter, Clara, died at birth. Pictured here are, from left to right, (first row) Anna, Joseph, Luthera, and Louise Cork; (second row) Lester, Fred, and Charles Cork. Anna Cork was the wife of Floyd Ingraham. (Courtesy of Ron and Sharon Ingraham.)

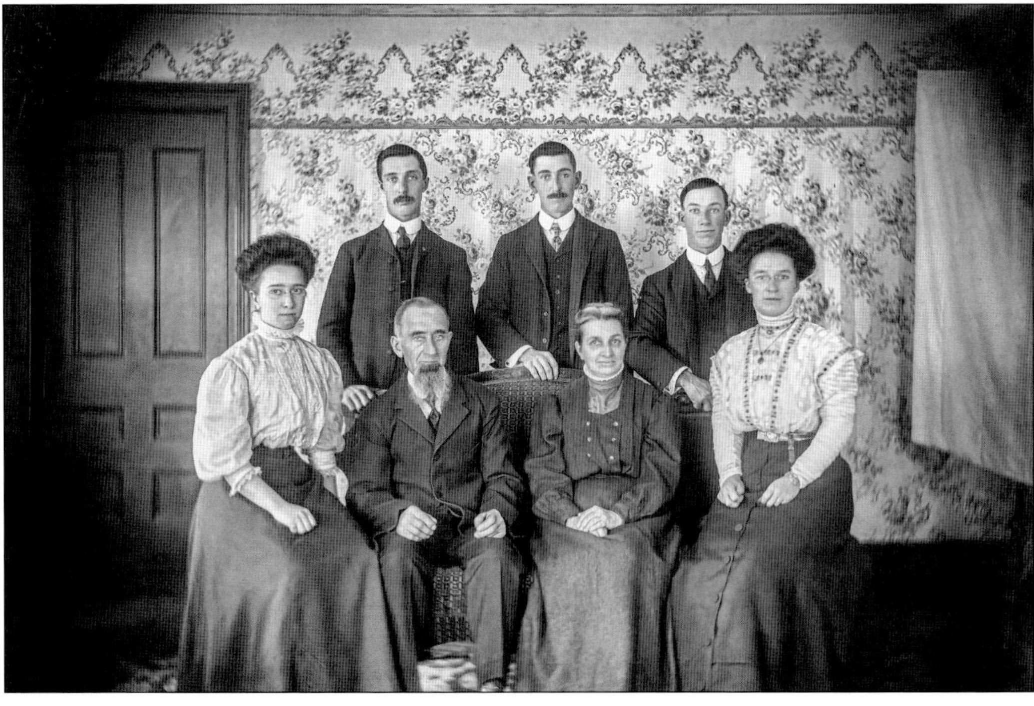

Four

Early-20th-Century Life

The residents of New York's Finger Lakes communities at the turn of the 20th century saw incredible changes and advancements in transportation, industry, and invention. They were ordinary people living simple lives in an extraordinary time. Within a few decades, they observed the expansion of the railroad, the introduction of electricity, running water in their homes, changes in manufacturing, and advancements in agriculture and transportation. The arrival of the automobile on their dirt roads that still were traveled on by horse-drawn carriages gave them unprecedented freedom to travel and explore communities that had been beyond easy reach.

The region saw growth and prosperity during this time as trains brought visitors from nearby cities like Rochester to enjoy the beautiful lakes. Boating and fishing were favorite pastimes, and families socialized in homes where they enjoyed games, music, skits, and dinner parties. Nearby Hemlock, Canadice, Honeoye, and Conesus Lakes were frequented by area residents and drew others from Rochester who arrived on the Rochester Main Line of the Erie Railroad.

Education made advancements as well. School, which was previously seen as an option, became a necessity. One-room schoolhouses were found in almost every community of the Finger Lakes region by 1900. Within the first two decades of the 20th century, schools were being consolidated and higher education became more common, giving students a variety of opportunities to make a living. Careers in agriculture were no longer seen as a foregone conclusion. More and more young people left the farm and rural communities to move into the city and work in other industries.

Hospitable and kind, residents of western Finger Lakes communities like Springwater opened their homes to visitors, hosted benefits and events for causes they valued, and did not hesitate to help when one of their neighbors was in need. The towns and villages that dotted the landscape of the Finger Lakes were tight-knit communities of people who depended on each other. In work and in play, they valued relationship. Rarely idle, they were hardworking, industrious, and loyal. Neighborliness and a strong sense of community characterized these hardworking 20th-century Americans who would birth what was later called "the greatest generation."

Floyd Ingraham's pictures preserved what life was like at the start of the 20th century and beautifully captured the spirit of the people of that time. The spirit of a generation who lived and thrived 100 years ago still lives in the people of the Finger Lakes region today.

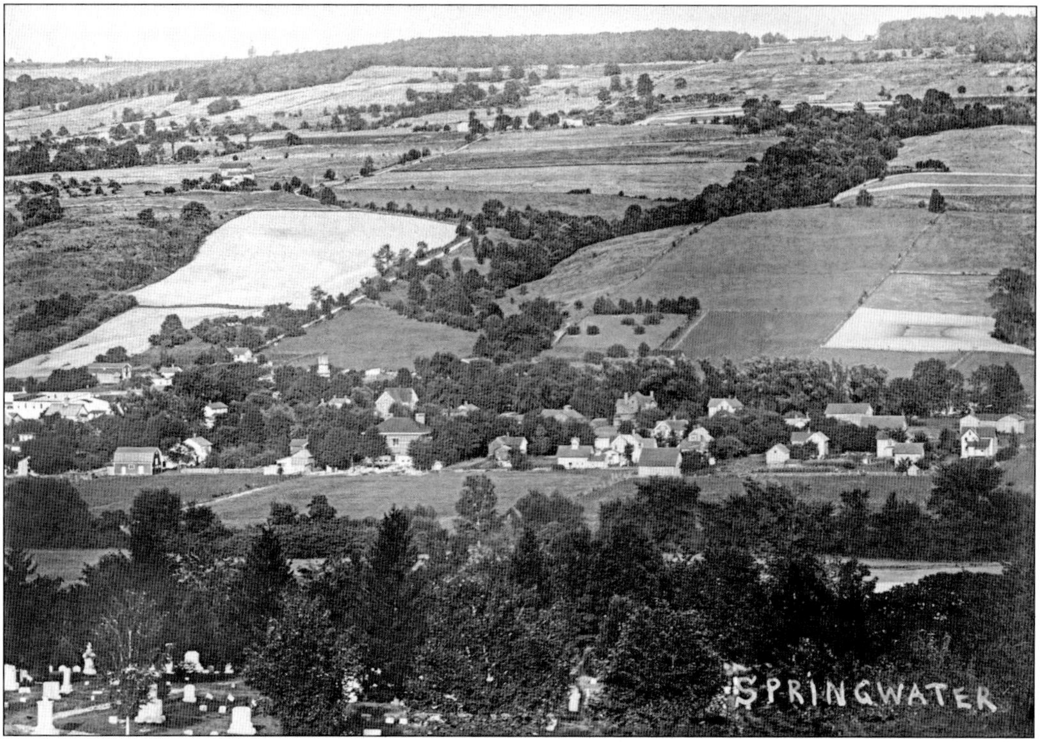

The Finger Lakes region of New York looks vastly different today than it did in Floyd Ingraham's lifetime. The village of Springwater is recognizable by the steeple of the Advent church, prominently placed on Mill Street, and by Mount Evergreen Cemetery, on a hill off Kellogg Road. Acres of farmland were a common sight in the 19th century. Loggers and early farmers stripped the hillsides of forest cover to market the valuable timber and to create open land for crops. Agriculture thrived for almost a century here, but by the mid-1900s, the condition of the land deteriorated due to erosion, topsoil loss, and farming practices that did not return nutrients to the soil. Farming declined, and landowners let much of the hills and valleys, especially land with steep slopes, return to forest. Today, approximately 70 percent of the Finger Lakes hillsides are forested compared to 20 percent in Ingraham's day. (Courtesy of Joyce O'Neil.)

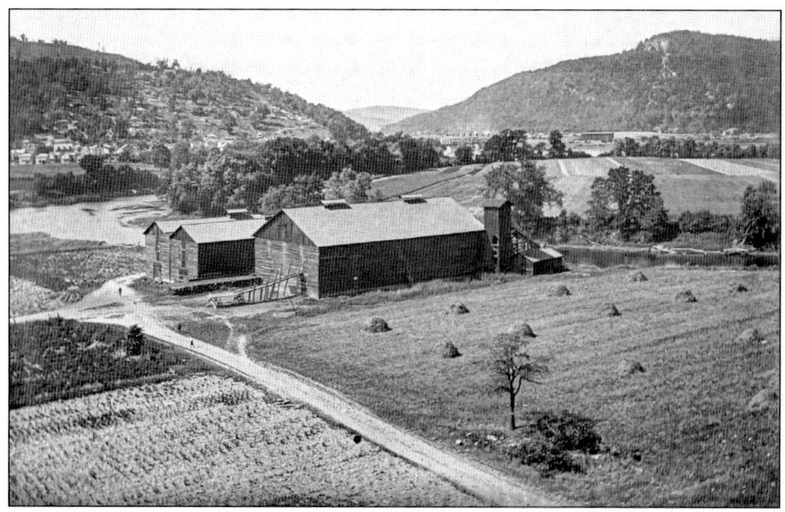

The location for this Floyd Ingraham photograph has yet to be identified, but the landscape is reminiscent of the Finger Lakes region. The building seen here may be a mill.

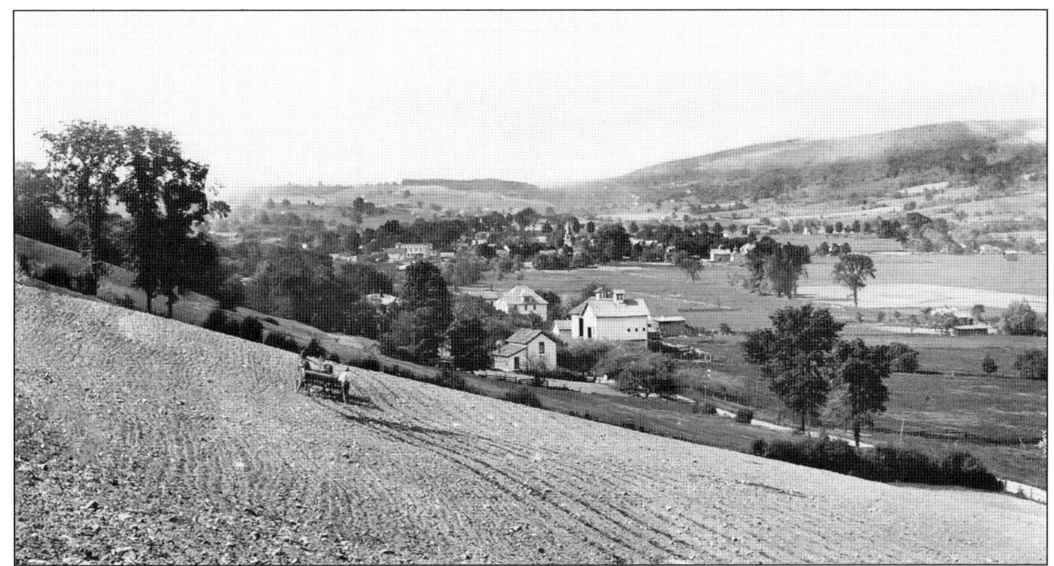

Horses provided the power that pulled heavy farm machinery, and were the primary mode of transportation for families through the turn of the 20th century. Here, a team of horses pulls a grain drill that would till the earth to prepare it for planting. Although tractors were in use in the United States by the end of the 1800s, less than 1,000 were being used in the first decade of the 20th century. This field was on Main Street, going north, just after the Ingraham home. The view is looking south over the valley and the town of Springwater. (Courtesy of Joyce O'Neil.)

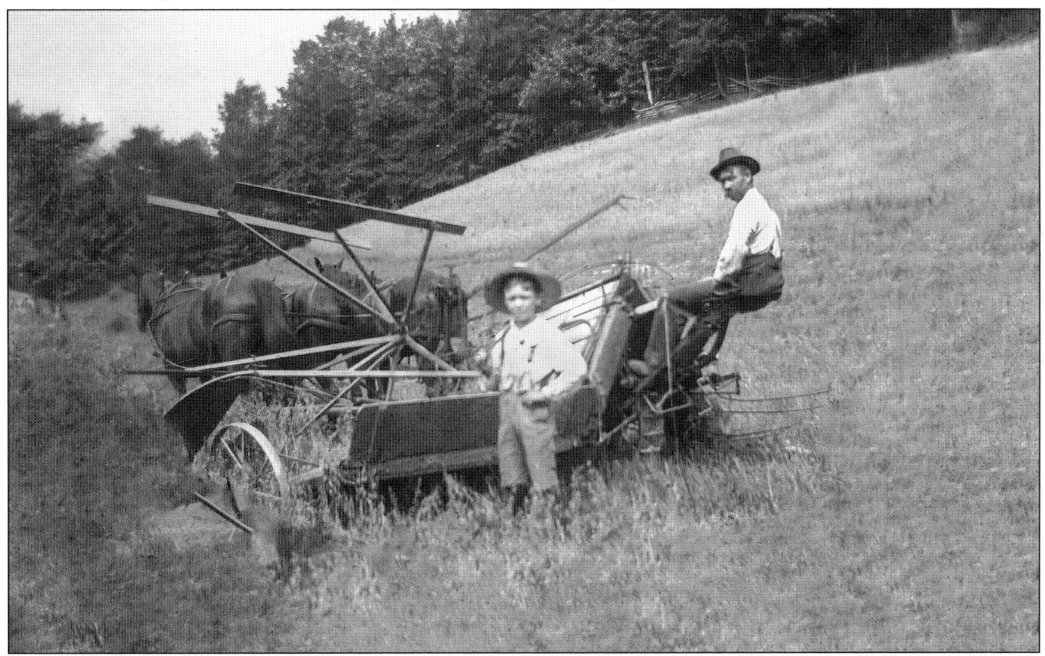

Using a grain binder, a man and boy work in a field near Springwater. A binder was used to cut small grains and bind the stalks into sheaves that were dried before threshing. Farming was a family affair. All hands were needed to get work done, and children began working alongside their parents from a young age. From the slope of the land in this image, this farm may have been just past the Ingrahams' home on Main Street.

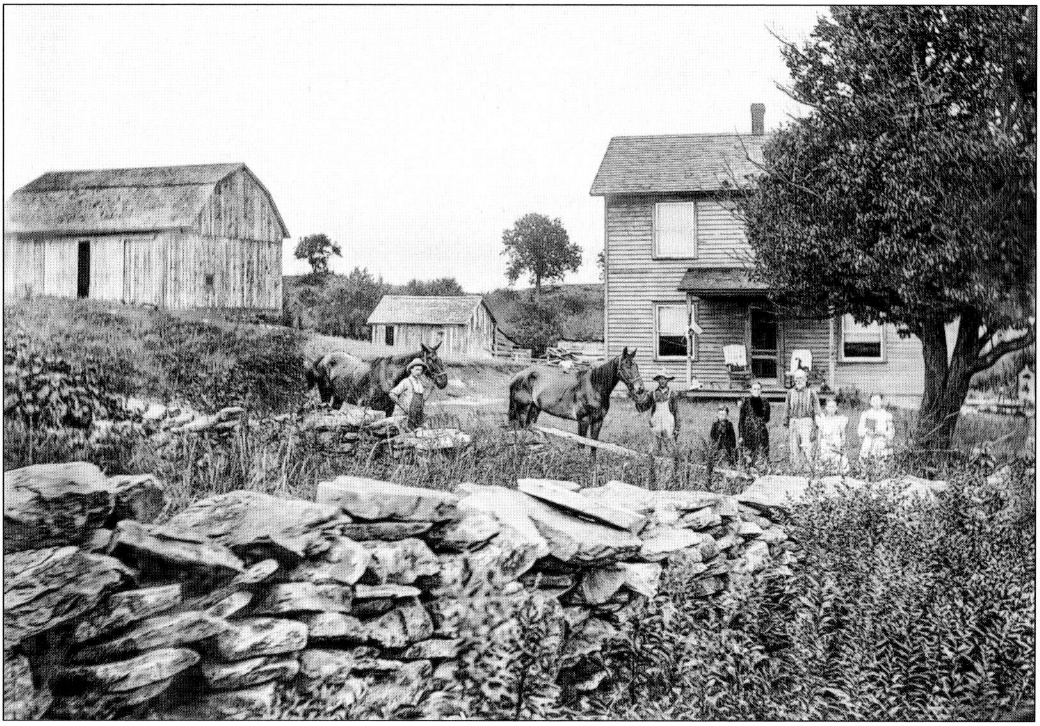

This unidentified family stands outside their home on a hillside farm. Farms of around 100 acres were common at this time. If a family could not afford to purchase their own land, they might farm rented land. Approximately one third of farms in Livingston County in the early 1900s were operated by tenant farmers. Single men were hired as farm laborers, and they often boarded with the family. Stone walls like the one seen here marked property lines and kept farm animals from straying.

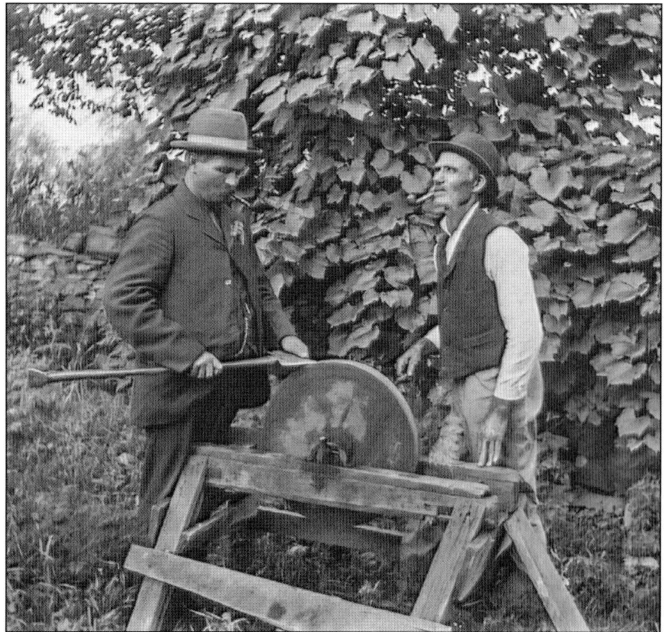

Grinding wheels like the one seen here were made from sandstone and were a necessity on the farm. Grindstones were used to sharpen knives, ax blades, scythes, and other farm tools. This one had a pedal or crank handle for speeding up or slowing the spin to control the sharpening process. The man on the right may be pumping the pedal for the man holding the ax on the left. Some grindstones were powered by a waterwheel. The user would lie on a plank above the stone, and the water of a stream or creek would turn it. This resulted in the phrase "nose to the grindstone."

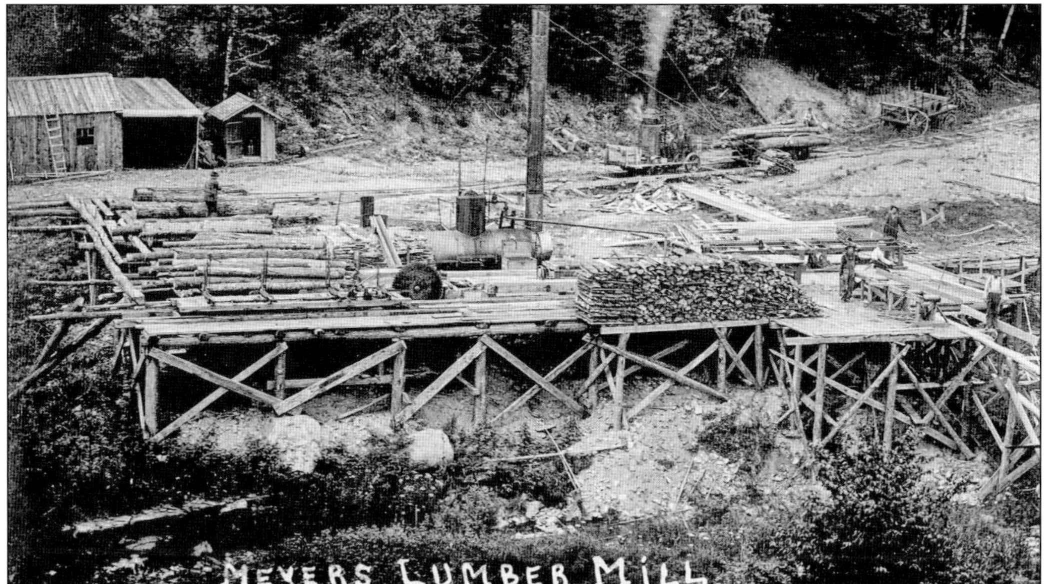

Meyers Lumber Mill was above Reynolds Gull in Springwater. There were many lumber mills in and around Springwater over the years, as lumber was plentiful. Reynolds Gull was home to several of them, including one owned in the 1800s by town historian Orson Walbridge. Around 1910, a man named Meyers came to Springwater and erected a sawmill just above Canadice Road at Reynolds Gull. To get the logs to the mill, he built a private railroad, visible in the background. Railcars were custom-made to haul lumber. Logs from below the mill were pulled up from the bottom of the gully. The sawed lumber could then be picked up by wagons or shipped by train anywhere. (Courtesy of Joyce O'Neil and Rick Osiecki.)

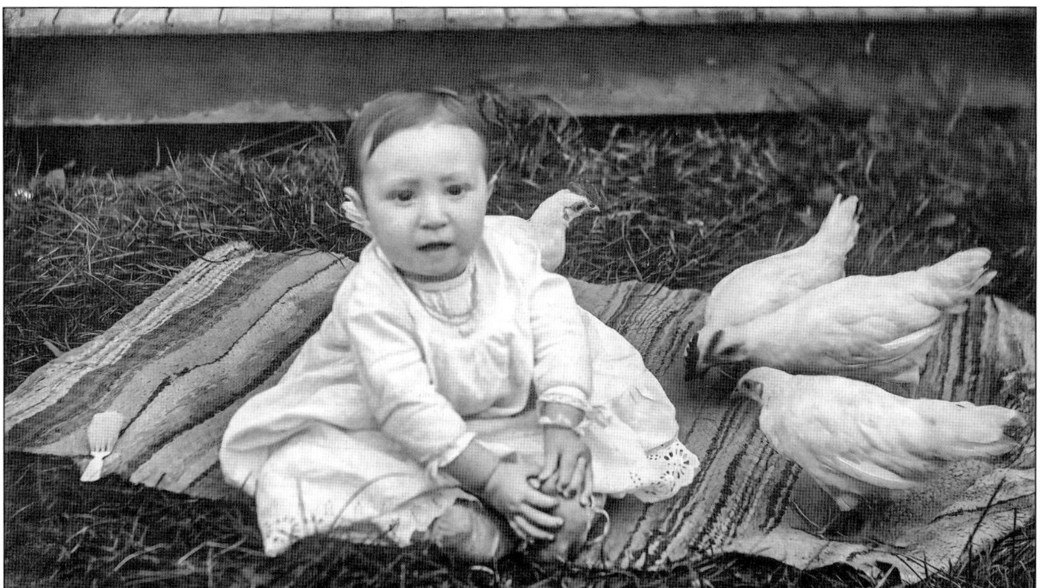

Kenneth Ingraham, son of photographer Floyd Ingraham, sits among the chickens. Children were engaged in all aspects of farm life and worked alongside their parents when they were old enough. Most families at the turn of the 20th century in rural communities had farm animals. Poultry was raised to provide meat and eggs for the family.

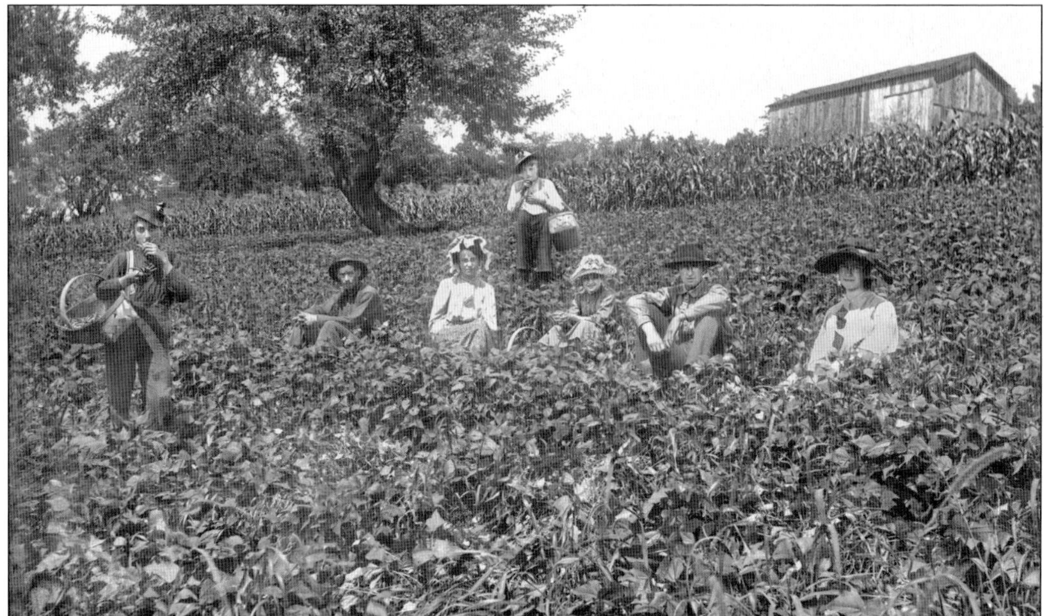

Harvesting beans at the Ingraham farm in Springwater are, from left to right, Burns Stephenson, Otto Ingraham, Blanche Ingraham, Ralph Miller (rear), Carrie Crooks, Floyd Ingraham, and Anna Cork. The Ingrahams had a large bean field, and many hands were needed to help pick them. A good bean crop could make a profit for farmers, but there were risks involved too. In 1904, an early frost and low overnight temperatures killed fields of beans. Many farmers with beans in the ground that September had all of their crops destroyed.

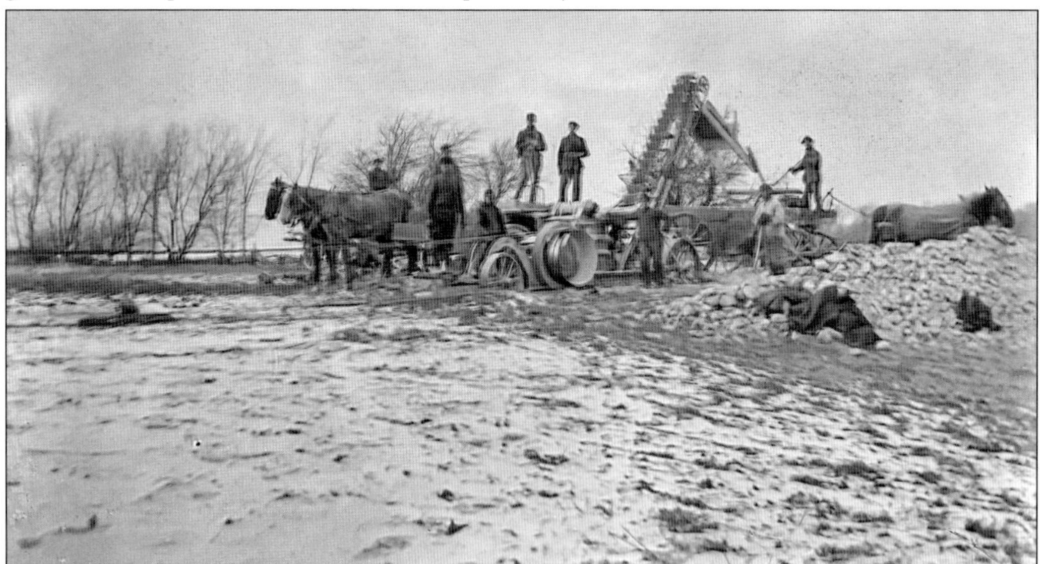

Threshing was done in late summer or autumn. The threshing machine separated the grain from the stalks and the hulks of the plant. It was a large and expensive machine. Often, several families would go in together to purchase a machine and help each other with the harvest. The threshing team would move from one farm to the next. It was hard and dirty work in the heat of late summer. While the men worked at threshing, women would prepare huge lunches to feed the crews. To "eat like a thresher" is a country term for someone who has a big appetite.

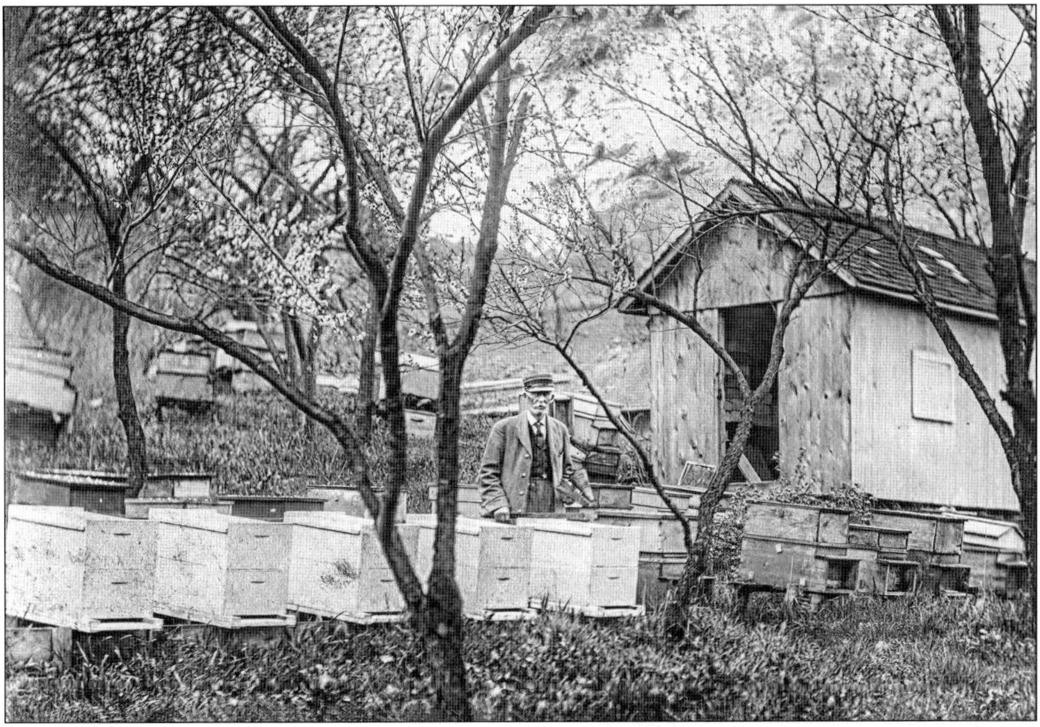

Beekeeping provided another harvest for farmers. Marchus Ingraham, Floyd Ingraham's father, kept 83 swarms of bees in Langstroth moveable frame hives. The simple box design allowed bees to move freely and make honey on screens that slide into the boxes on slats. Langstroth hives are still used by beekeepers today. In 1904, Ingraham yielded around 2,500 pounds of white honey for the season.

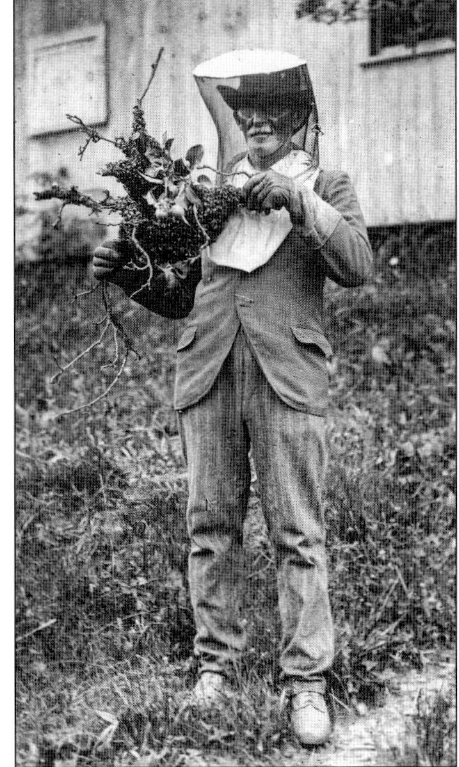

Marchus Ingraham is protected by his gloves and Alexander veil as he holds up bees swarming on a branch. He may be removing the swarm to add to his hives. Bees were kept to produce honey for the family's use, to be sold, and to aid in fertilization of fruit tree blossoms. It was a supportive crop for farmers. (Courtesy of Ron and Sharon Ingraham.)

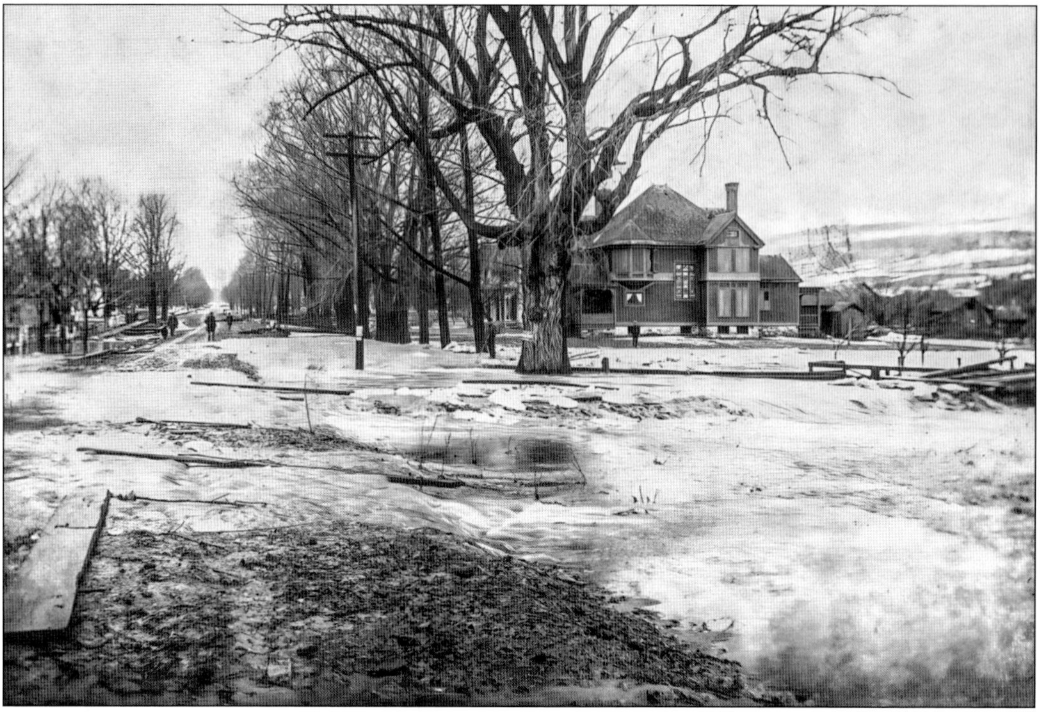

Floods were common in the region. In April 1904, a flood caused water to cover Main Street. It caused property damage and washed debris and topsoil down hillsides. In June 1916, a damaging flood destroyed property and took several lives, including that of Jennie (Haskins) Saxton of Hornell, New York, who was swept away with her family in an automobile that overturned in the water. Peter Head drowned when his house was washed away near Canisteo, and Levi Madison also drowned. The depth of the water registered at five feet near the Erie train depot, and 300 feet of train track was wiped out.

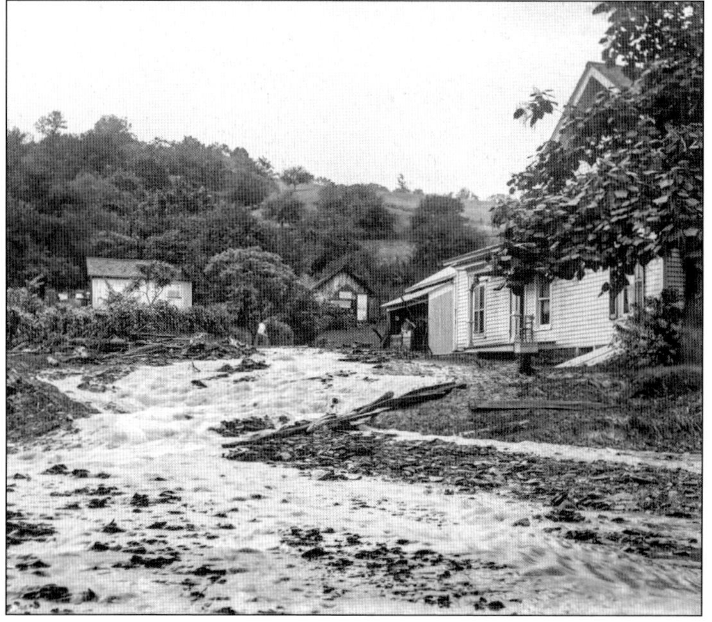

This view of the Ingraham home shows the runoff from a flood. Erosion and deterioration were a problem for hillside farming in the Finger Lakes. With trees and plant life cleared for farming, an intense rainfall would cause water to rush down unimpeded, bringing topsoil with it and causing property damage. Heavy spring rains brought floods almost every year to Springwater and surrounding communities.

B.F. Bailey's barn on Hemlock Lake Road in Canadice was destroyed by what the newspaper called a cyclone that came through the area in 1911. Trees were uprooted, and the storm also damaged other properties in the area, including a barn at the Cooper farm and two barns that housed threshing machines on A.W. Perkins's property.

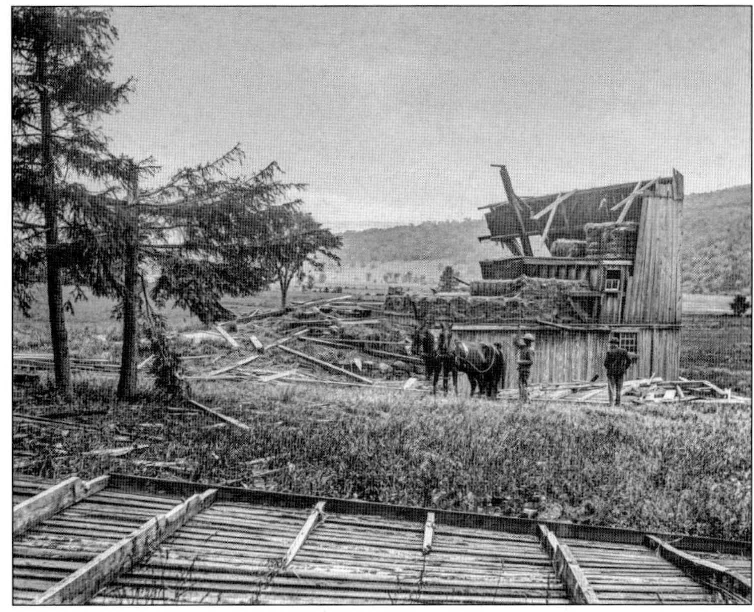

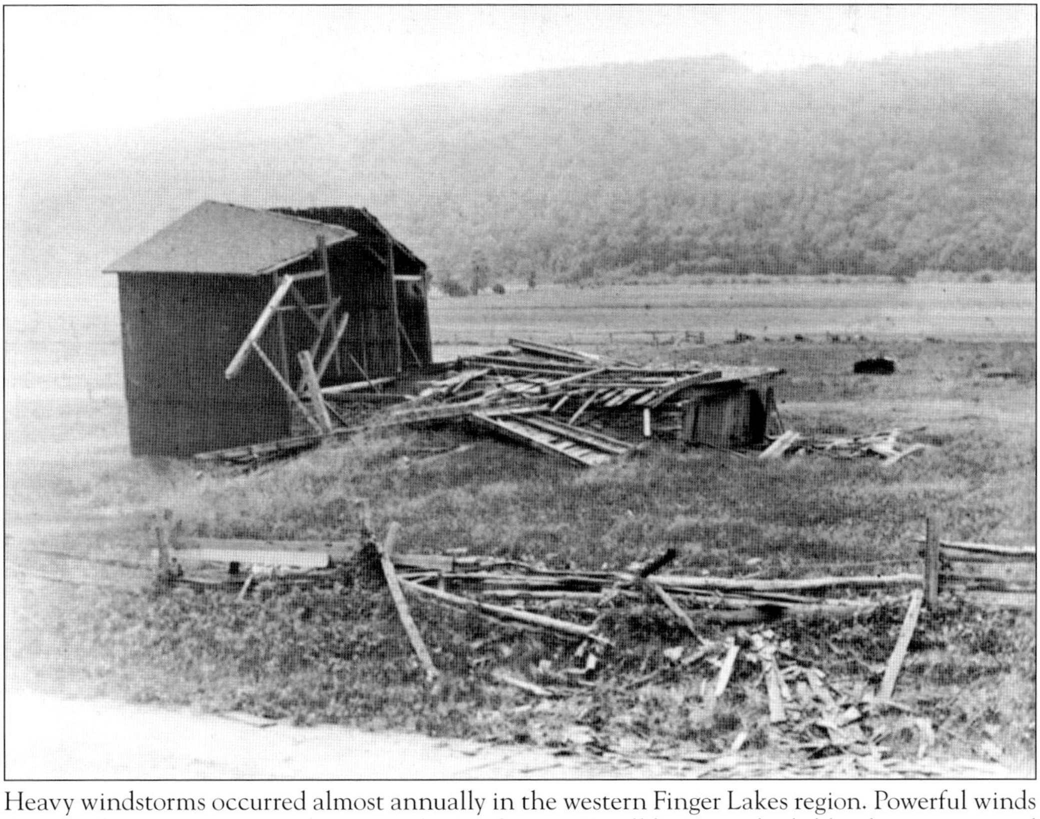

Heavy windstorms occurred almost annually in the western Finger Lakes region. Powerful winds destroyed property, uprooted trees, and ruined crops. Small barns or sheds like the one pictured here were no match for powerful tornado-like winds. Storms such as these caused much damage, as seen here from an early-20th-century tornado. Storms in Springwater in 1905, 1911, 1913, and 1918 caused significant damage in the area.

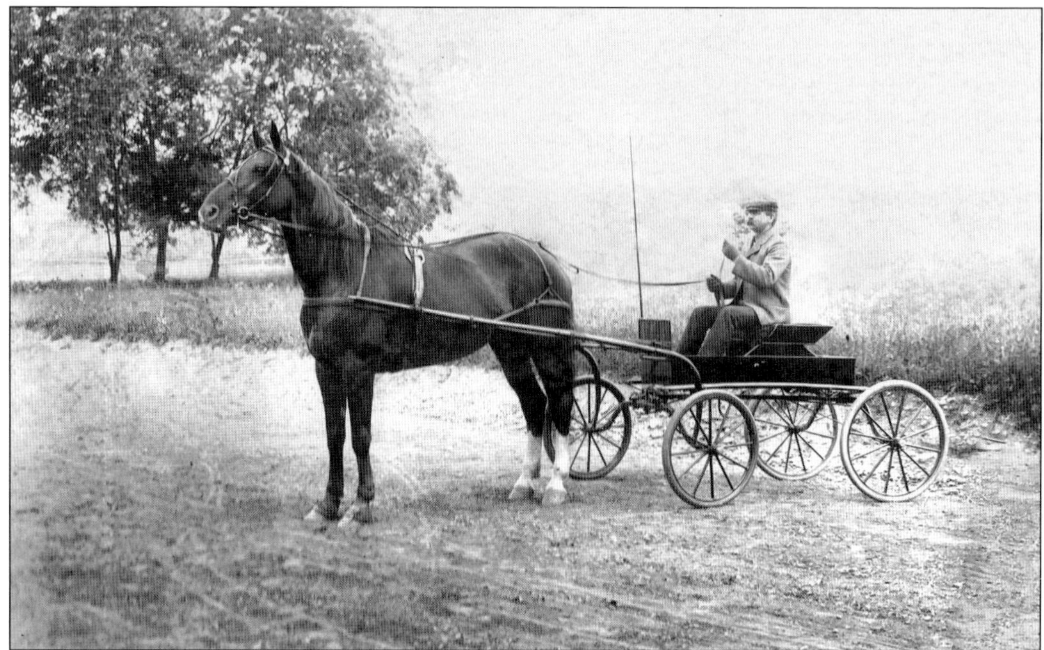

John Shetler was born in 1863. He is pictured here in his box buggy just a few years before he died in 1917 at the age of 53. Lightweight and faster than a wagon or carriage, it was perfect for a quick drive into town. Shetler was born in Pennsylvania and settled in Springwater and later Wayland. He married Clara Jackman, and the couple had nine children, including six sons and three daughters. (Courtesy of Ron and Sharon Ingraham.)

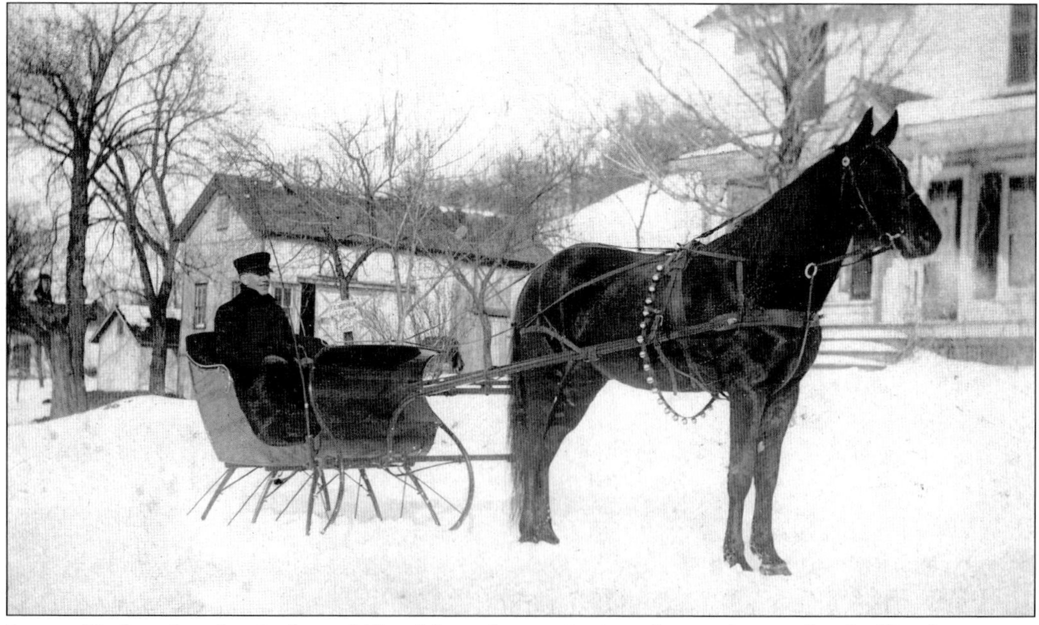

Lester Cork, a brother-in-law of Floyd Ingraham, sits in a horse-drawn sleigh. Sleighs were a necessity for winter travel. Floyd Ingraham was taken by sleigh to the hospital in Dansville, driven by another brother-in-law, Fred Cork, on January 21, 1920, the day before he died. (Courtesy of Ron and Sharon Ingraham.)

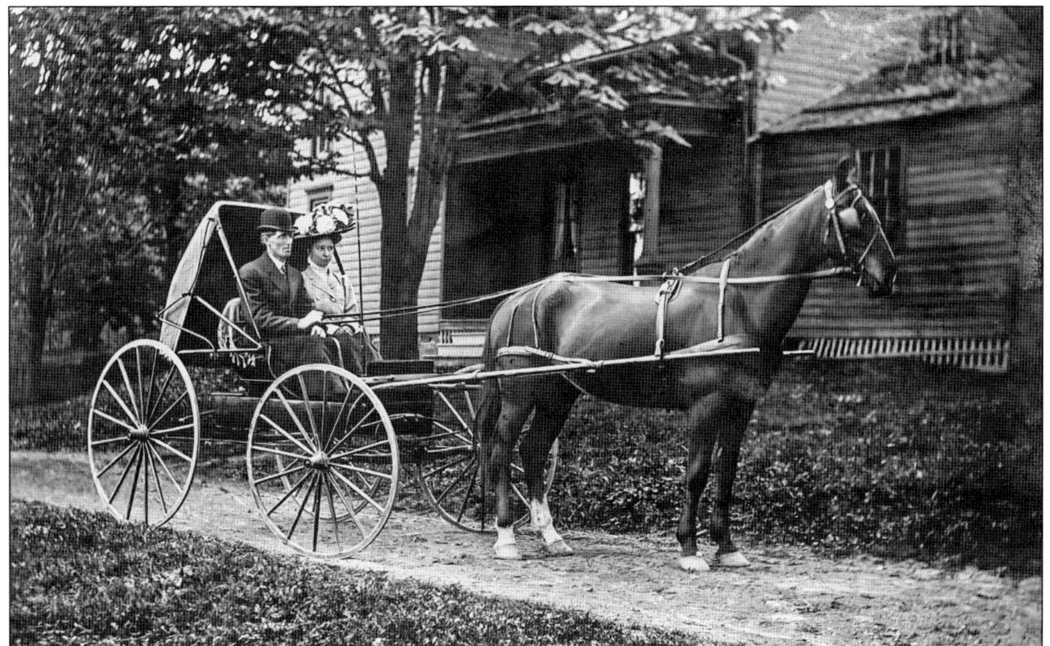

Floyd and Anna Ingraham traveled in a horse-drawn buggy to visit Anna's sister. The coal-box buggy was smaller and was mass produced in the United States by 1900, offering affordable and easy transportation for a few family members. (Courtesy of Ron and Sharon Ingraham.)

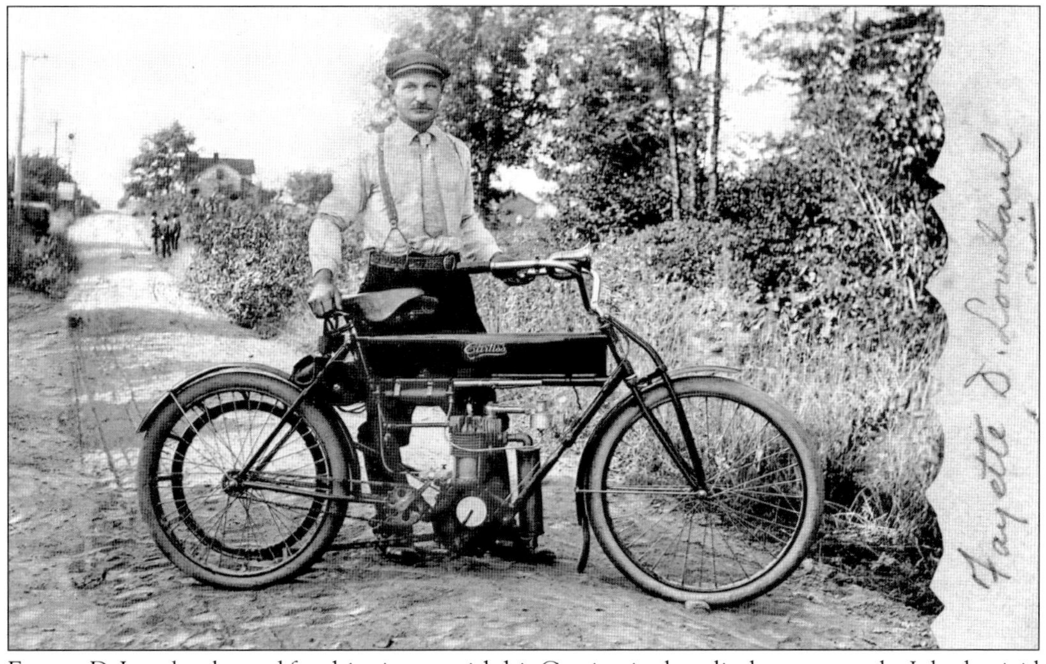

Fayette D. Loveland posed for this picture with his Curtiss single-cylinder motorcycle. It had a rigid rear frame, a simple can exhaust system, and a direct belt drive with no clutch. Floyd Ingraham took this picture and printed it as a picture postcard. He mailed it to Anna in September 1908. Fayette Loveland was Anna's uncle, the brother of Luthera Loveland. Fayette married Alta Kinner and lived in Wayland and later Hornell. (Courtesy of Ron and Sharon Ingraham.)

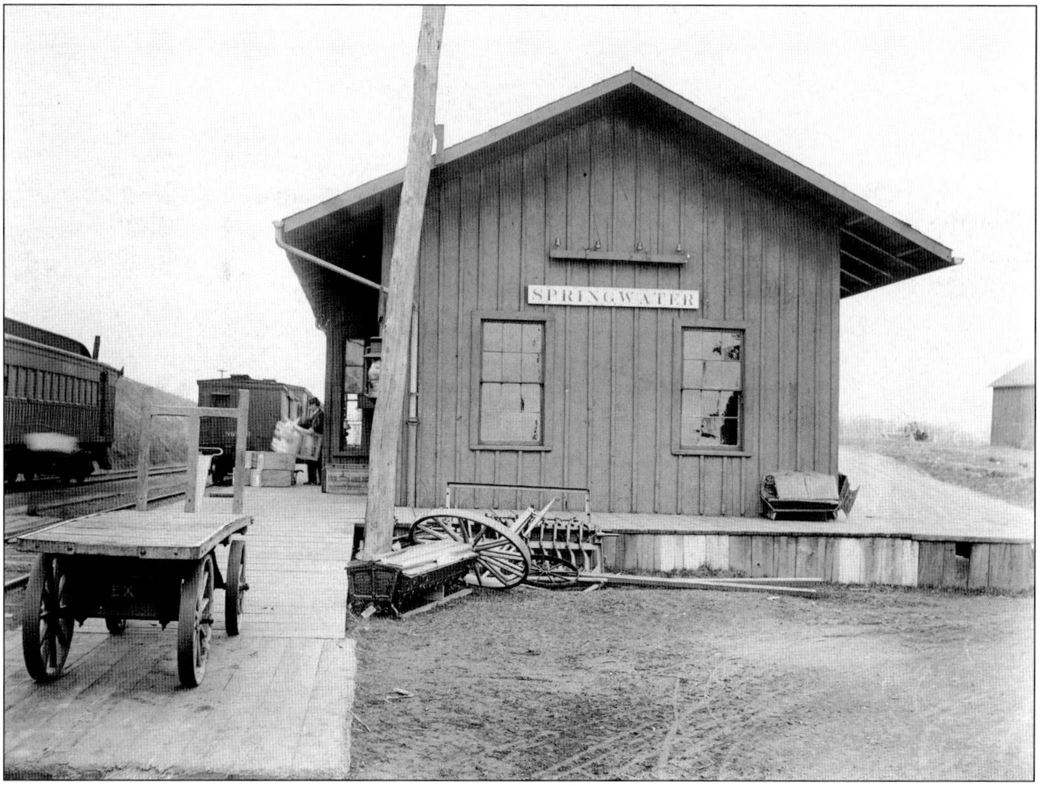

The Erie Railroad depot at Springwater was between Wayland and Conesus. It began operating in 1854. The 446 miles of track for the Erie Railroad was built as broad gauge, offering six feet between rails instead of the standard 4 feet, 8.5 inches. This enabled the railroad to carry larger items than others and gave the Erie an advantage over its competition. Erie Railroad's Rochester Branch ran from Corning to Rochester, Wayland, Springwater, Livonia, and Avon. In 1956, the Erie Railroad tracks were removed by the Interstate Commerce Commission to promote highway transportation. (Courtesy of Steamtown National Historic Site.)

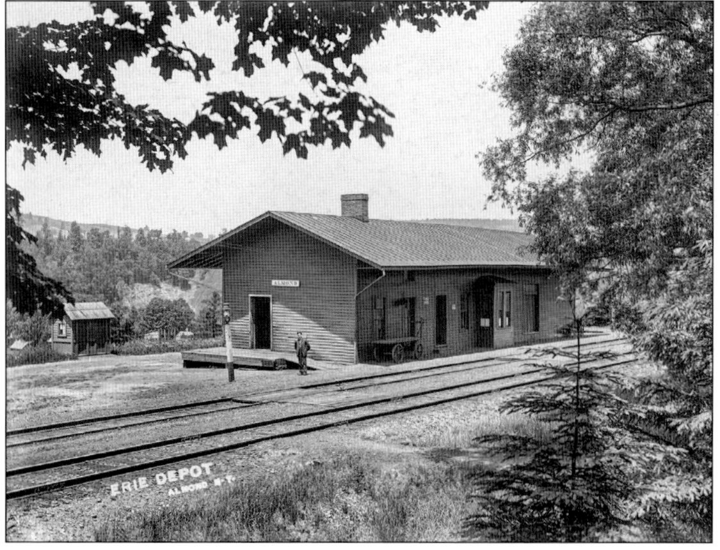

The Erie Railroad depot in Almond, New York, was halfway between Hornellsville and Alfred, New York. The Erie Railroad was influential in the development of New York's Southern Tier. It allowed for the shipment of goods and provided transportation for citizens. Chartered in 1832, it was finished in 1851. The New York & Erie Railroad was the second longest in the world when it opened in 1853.

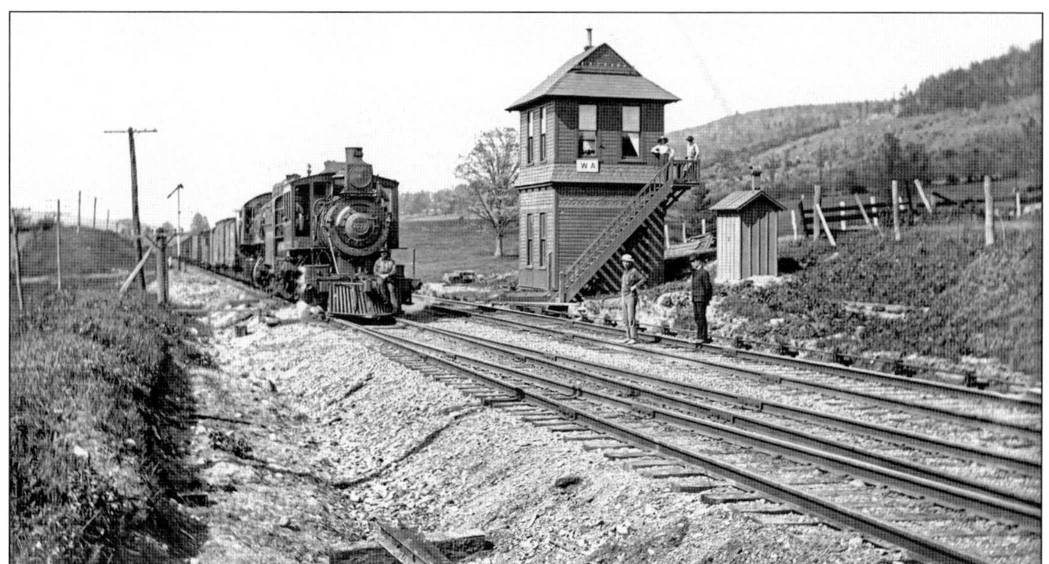

When the Southern Tier branch of the Erie Railroad was completed, a train traveled the entire route, stopping at each town. The railroad was met with fanfare and people who came to see it approach. Pres. Millard Fillmore and Daniel Webster spoke at many of the stops. In Binghamton, Webster said, "I can hardly say more than express the pleasure I have in seeing you and the western end of this great work of art. I have crossed the upper branches of the Delaware and the Susquehanna, and I know something of these rivers at their mouths: but never had I seen them as they issue from these lofty sublime and picturesque hills. It is a beautiful and a vigorous and a healthy country. May God bless you and enable you to enjoy all its blessings."

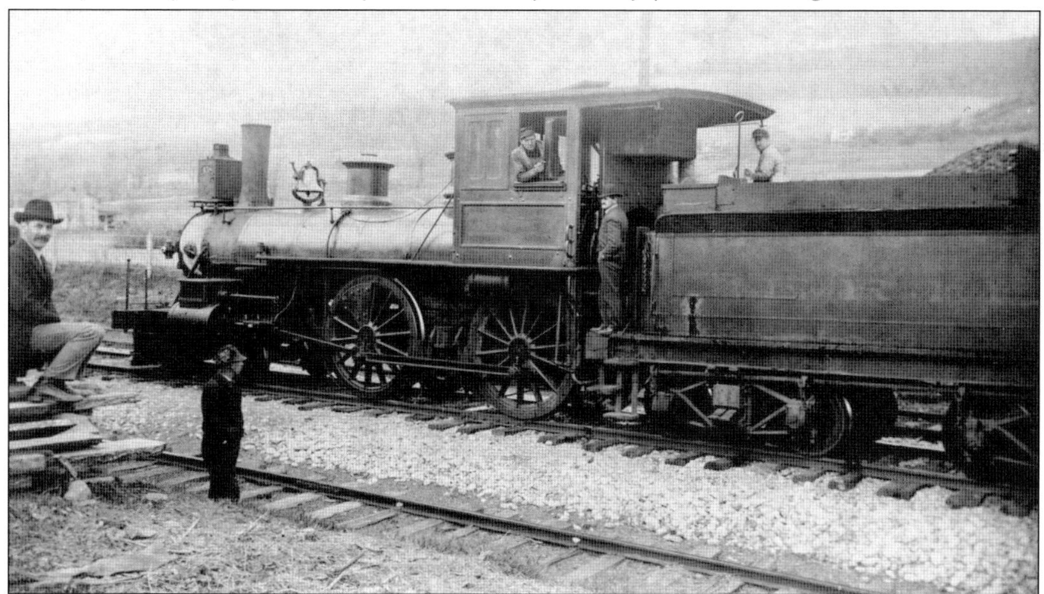

The train engine is seen here arriving in Springwater. Originally built by the Buffalo, New York & Erie Railroad, the tracks through Springwater were part of the Corning Branch. The high point of the Corning Branch was Springwater at 1,412 feet. This line connected Avon with Painted Post, New York, and went through Cohocton, Wayland, Springwater, Webster Crossing, and Conesus. The Corning Branch track was removed in 1956. (Courtesy of Ron and Sharon Ingraham.)

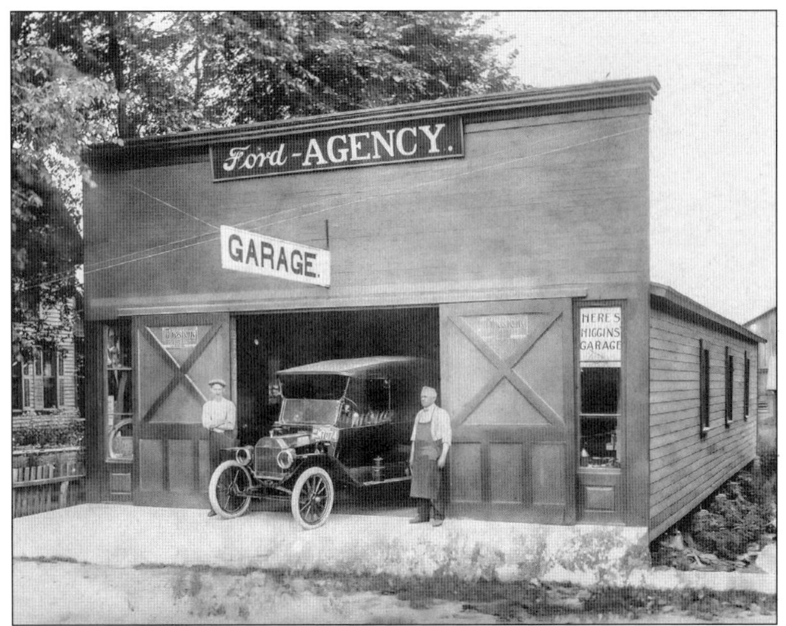

The Higgins Garage in Springwater was first on Mill Street, across from the town hall. Opened by George Higgins before 1915, it also served as the Ford dealership. The Ford touring car sold for $550 in 1913. Higgins's garage eventually moved into a white stucco building, which also operated as a gas station through the mid-1900s. (Courtesy of Joyce O'Neil and Rick Osiecki.)

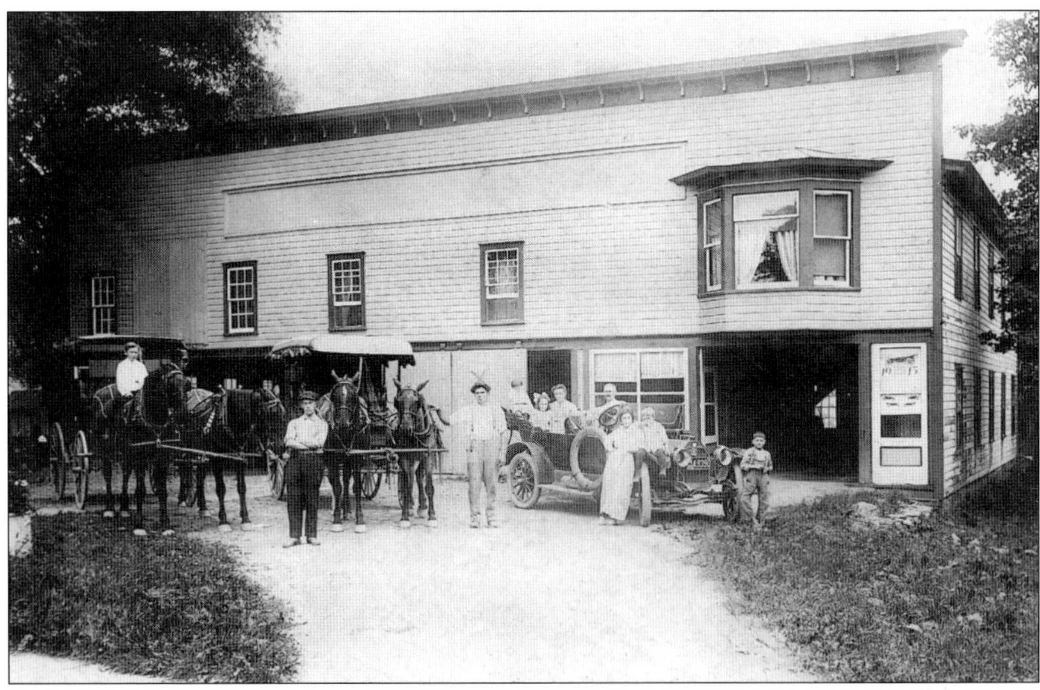

Taken in 1915 at a garage owned by Fred Seward on Mill Street in Springwater, this photograph shows the transition of transportation that took place in the early 20th century. George Richardson is standing by a horse with the Seward family in the car next to him. Richardson's son Claude is standing to the right of the car. Finger Lakes families traveled by horse, auto, and train to get where they wanted to go. This garage was owned by Merton Homes by 1920. It survived an automobile crashing into it and the overflow from a creek bed that ran under it. A large bee infestation in its walls prompted many unusual suggestions from area residents for how to get rid of them. The garage no longer exists. (Courtesy of Joyce O'Neil and Rick Osiecki.)

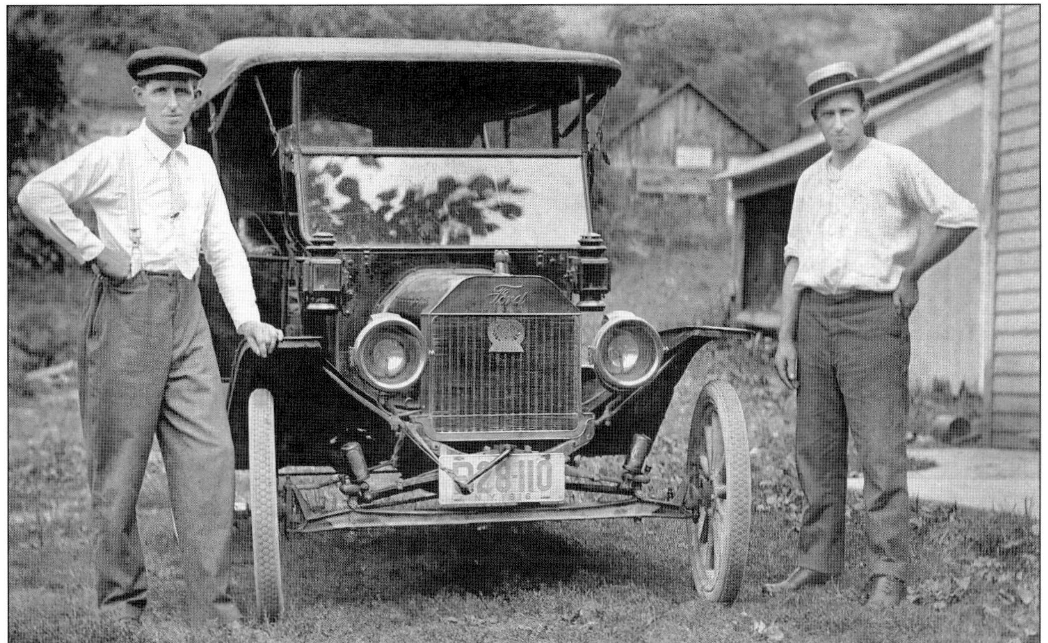

Photographer Floyd Ingraham, left, stands with his brother Otto Ingraham, right, near their Ford Model T touring car. Though the license plate reads 1916, this model is believed to be a 1914. Its square-shaped lights were standard in 1914 and became rounded in the 1915 and 1916 models. The car cost between $300 and $400 at the time. (Courtesy of Ron and Sharon Ingraham.)

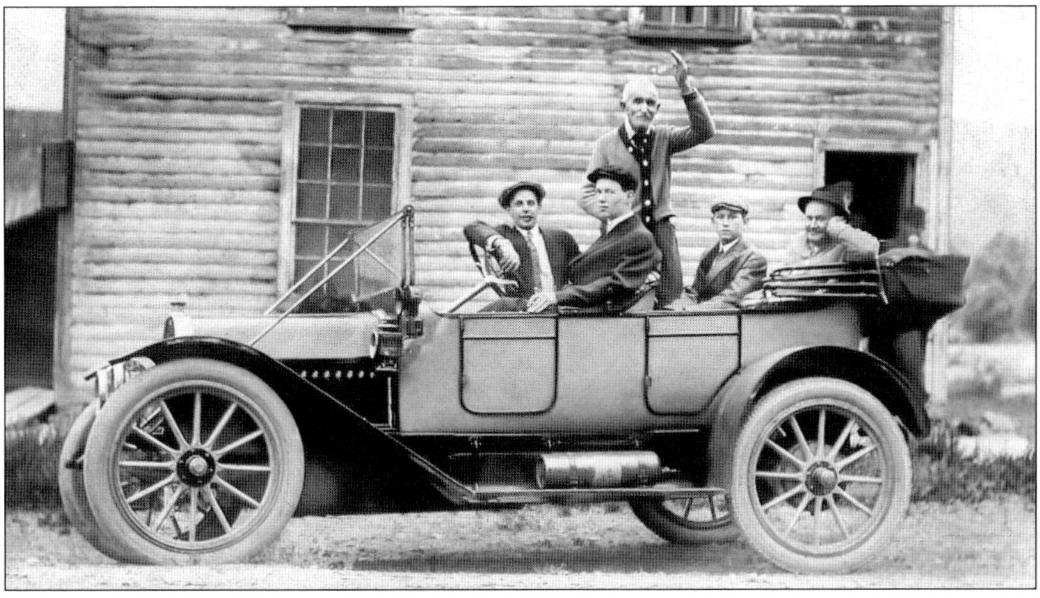

George Richardson leans on the steering wheel of this automobile in front of Merton Holmes's barn near Tabor's Corners in Springwater. Richardson was born on April 4, 1887, in Texarkana, Arkansas. As a young man, he made his way to Springwater and never left. He married Ethel Mastin in 1906, and they had six children. In the front seat next to George is Barton Hyde; the other men are unidentified. Richardson was deputy sheriff in Springwater. He died in 1977. (Courtesy of Joyce O'Neil and Rick Osiecki.)

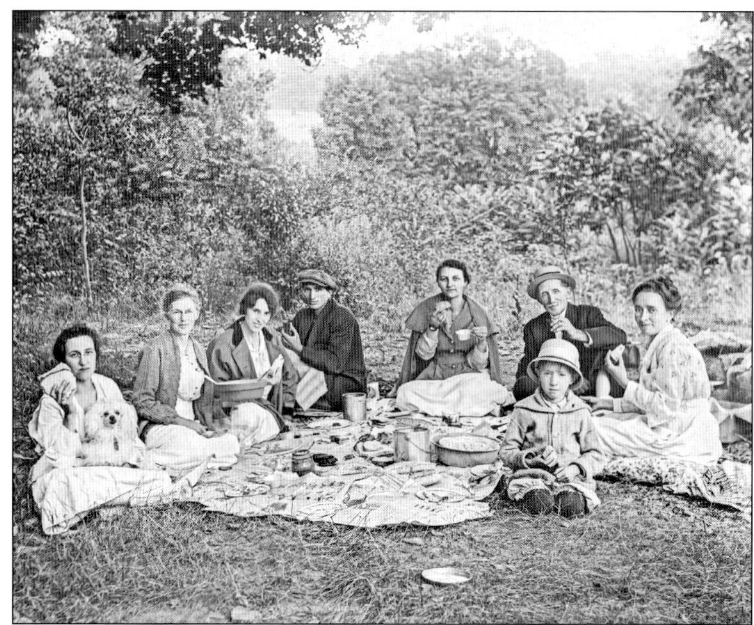

The Ford and Ingraham families are having a picnic at Barringer Point on Canadice Lake. Sitting on a quilt spread out on the grass, they enjoy fresh berries, cake, and sandwiches. From left to right are Louise Cork, Carrie Ford, Gertrude Ford, Leon Ford, Eleanor Graves, Melvin Ford, Anna Ingraham, and Floyd Ingraham's son Kenneth (front). Then, as today, food was very much a part of gatherings and events.

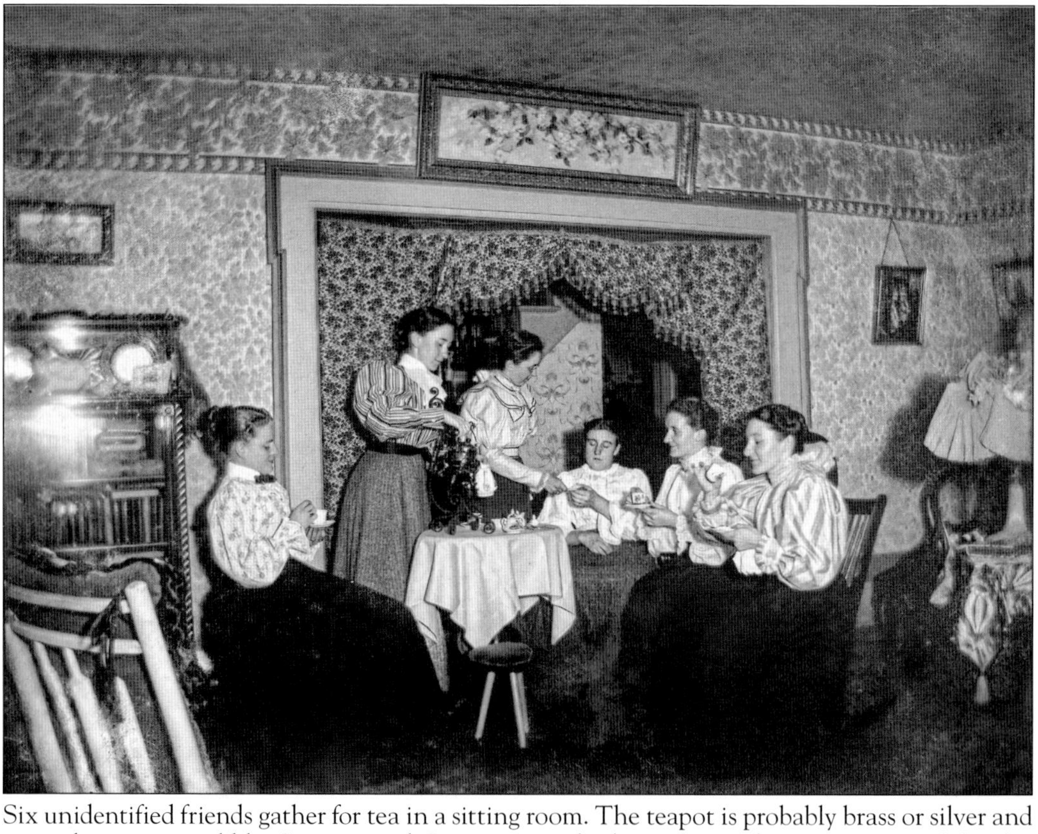

Six unidentified friends gather for tea in a sitting room. The teapot is probably brass or silver and is similar to ones sold by Sternau and Company in the late 1800s. The newspapers of the day were filled with listings of who called on whom. Several visits a week to friends and family were common in the time before cell phones and social media.

This view inside the Higgins home on Main Street reveals some unique features of an early-1900s home interior. Patterned wallpaper often covered not only walls but the ceiling too. Draped curtains adorn the entrance to an adjoining room, and pictures of Pres. Theodore Roosevelt and Vice Pres. Charles Fairbanks hang on the wall.

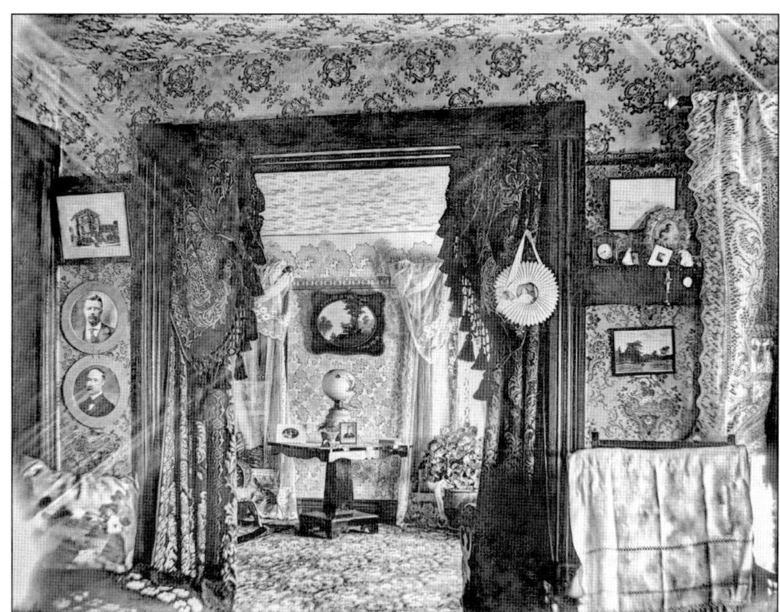

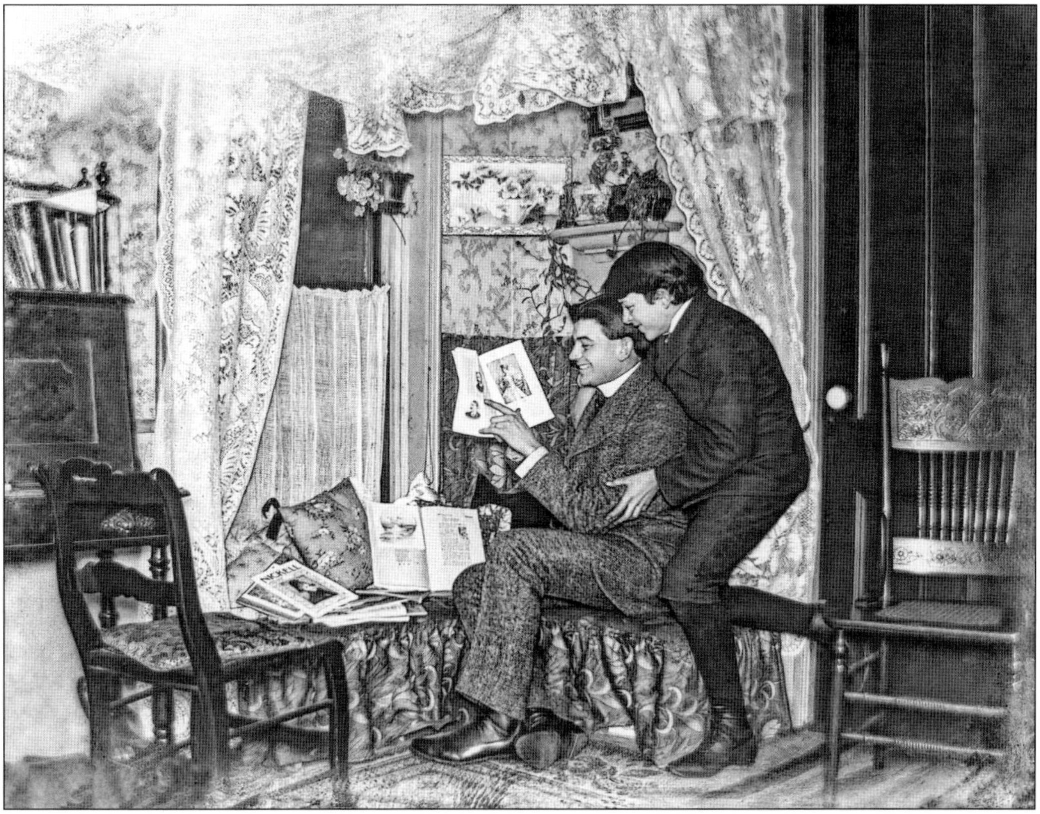

Homes were decorated lavishly with many patterns and fabrics. Here, a window seat that holds a corner bench serves as a reading nook. Unidentified boys find humor in a magazine, and a late-1800s copy of *Nickell* magazine lies nearby. Details around them reveal this is a loved spot by members of the household.

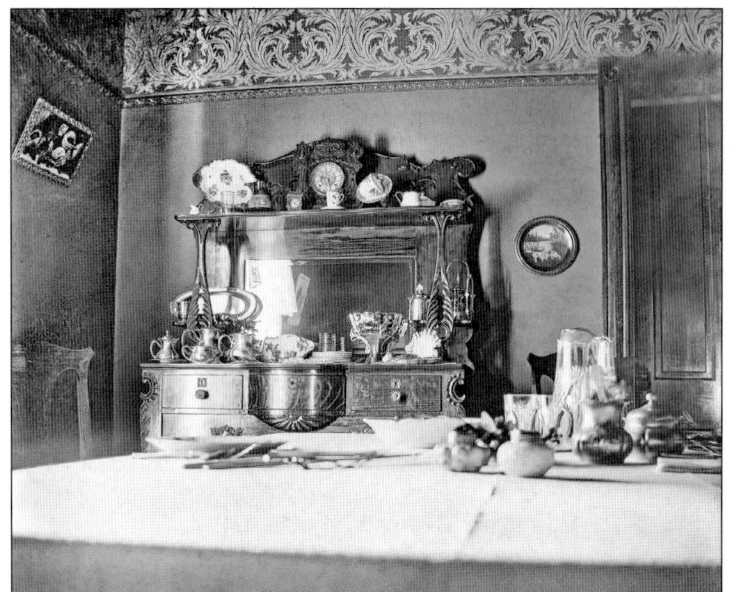

This beautiful sideboard reveals the ornate design of furniture that was common at the beginning of the 20th century. Scrolls, bevels, gilded handles, and locks all point to a late-19th-century piece. Taken from a unique view at the table, Floyd Ingraham may have rested his camera on the table itself to take the picture. Set for a meal, the lines of a pressed linen tablecloth can be seen, along with the china and crystal used by the family.

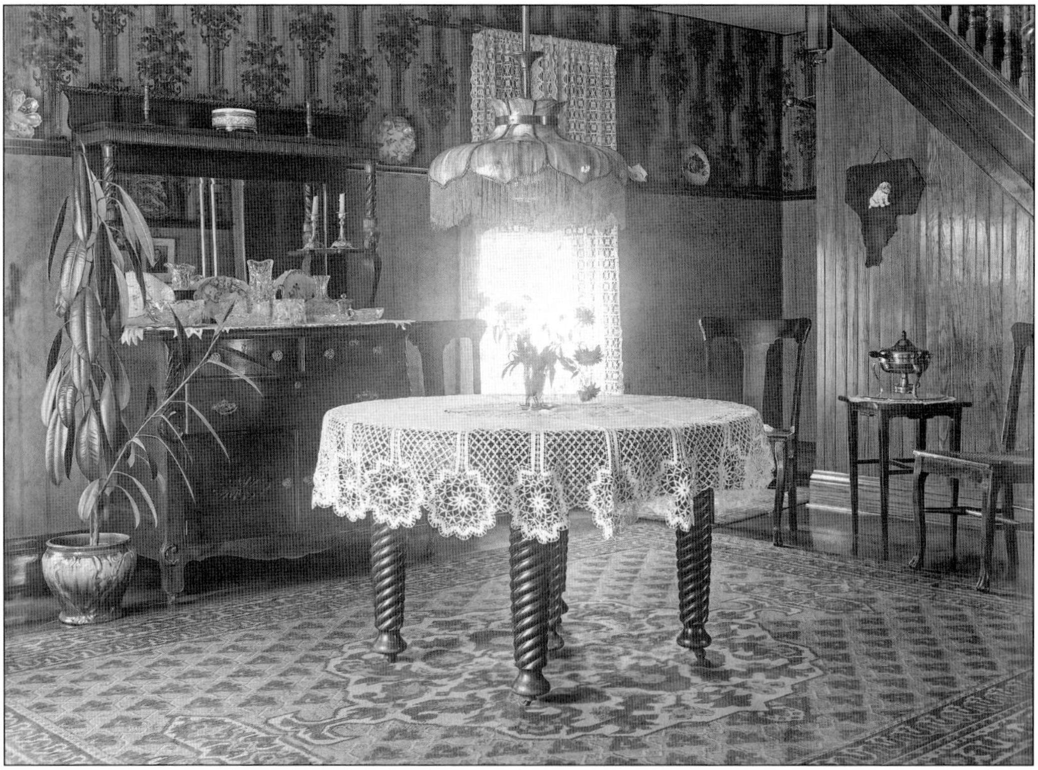

This dining room is from an unidentified home in the early 1900s. The sideboard is laden with crystal. A silver chafing dish rests on the table between two chairs waiting to serve up something warm. An art piece hanging on the wall features a puppy on a piece of rawhide. One of the most interesting pieces in the room is the Victorian period table with its five barley twist legs. When pulled apart, the table would expand so that leaves could be put in to provide additional seating, and the middle fifth leg offered stability.

Most homes had pianos. This one is at the Ingraham home, with the stool Floyd often used in his portraits recognizable at far left. The table that appears in several of his portraits is recognizable as well. The pictures on the bottom shelf of the table all face each other, and a woman who appears to be Floyd's grandmother Amanda (Jackman) Ingraham is in the picture facing out. She appears in a portrait on top of the piano as well.

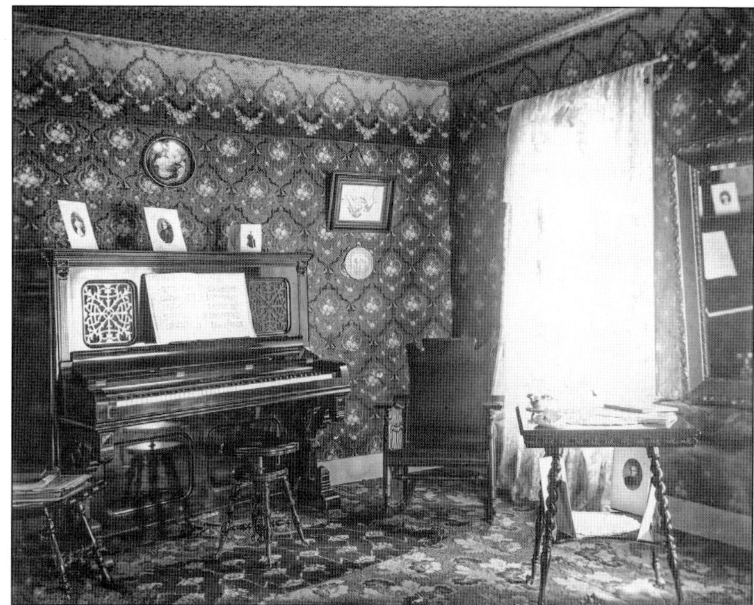

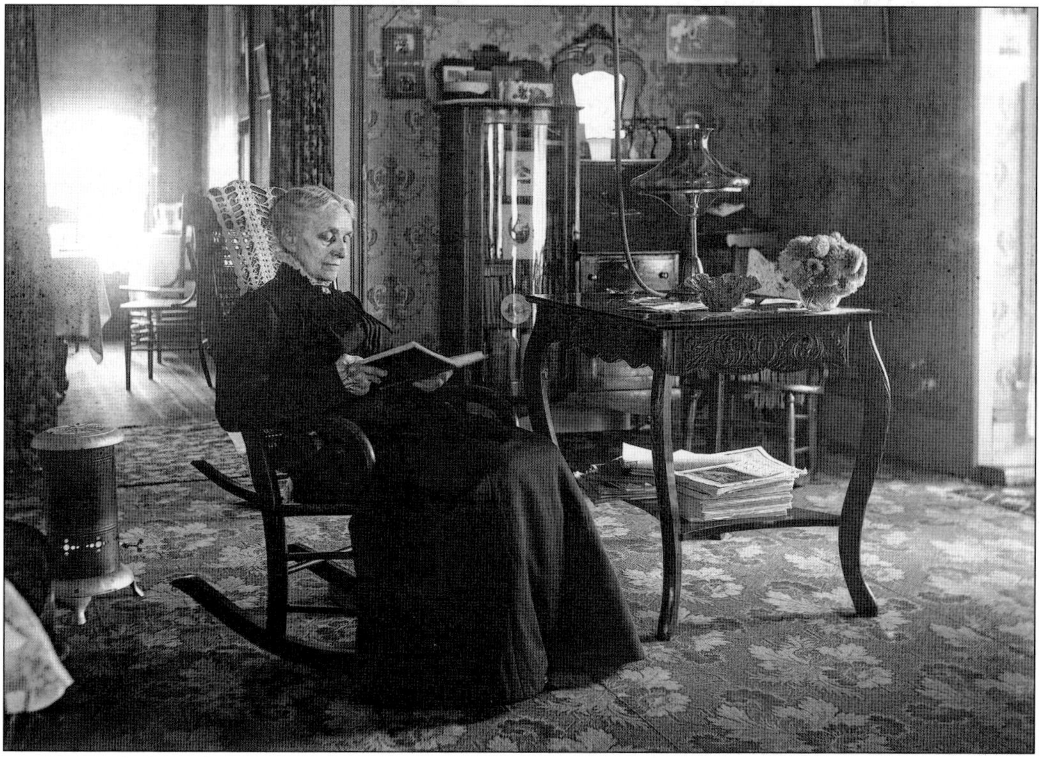

A woman believed to be Amanda (Jackman) Ingraham sits in the Ingraham parlor. Amanda Ingraham lived with Marchus and Nettie Ingraham for the last 16 years of her life. The magazine on the top of the stack beneath the table is *McClure Magazine*. A space heater is close by, offering added warmth as large farmhouses could be quite drafty. A gas lamp would have provided better lighting than candles once the natural light streaming through large windows faded. Amanda Ingraham died in 1907.

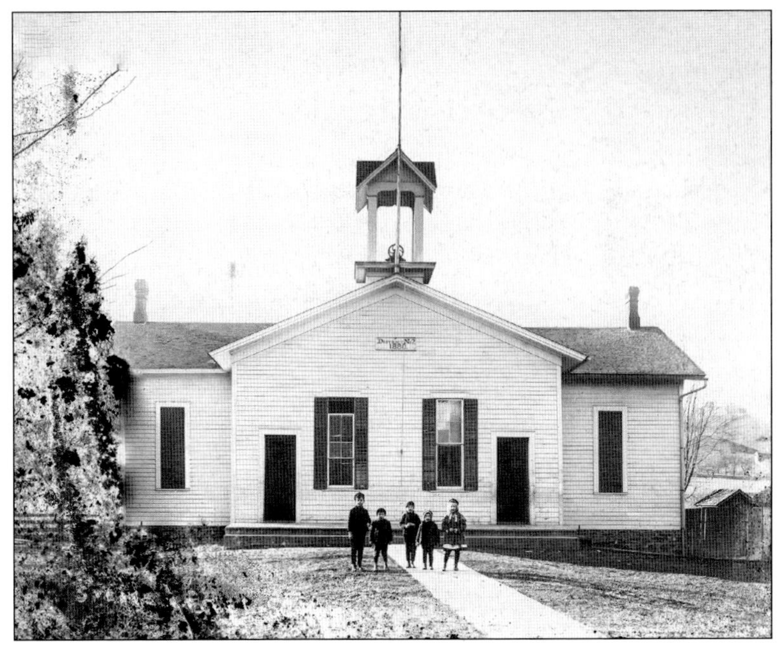

Springwater School No. 2 was established in 1880 on Main Street. It provided education for children until 1912, when a larger brick building was constructed. The building seen here is no longer in existence. The brick schoolhouse that replaced it, also called the Springwater Union School (page 48), was built on School Street.

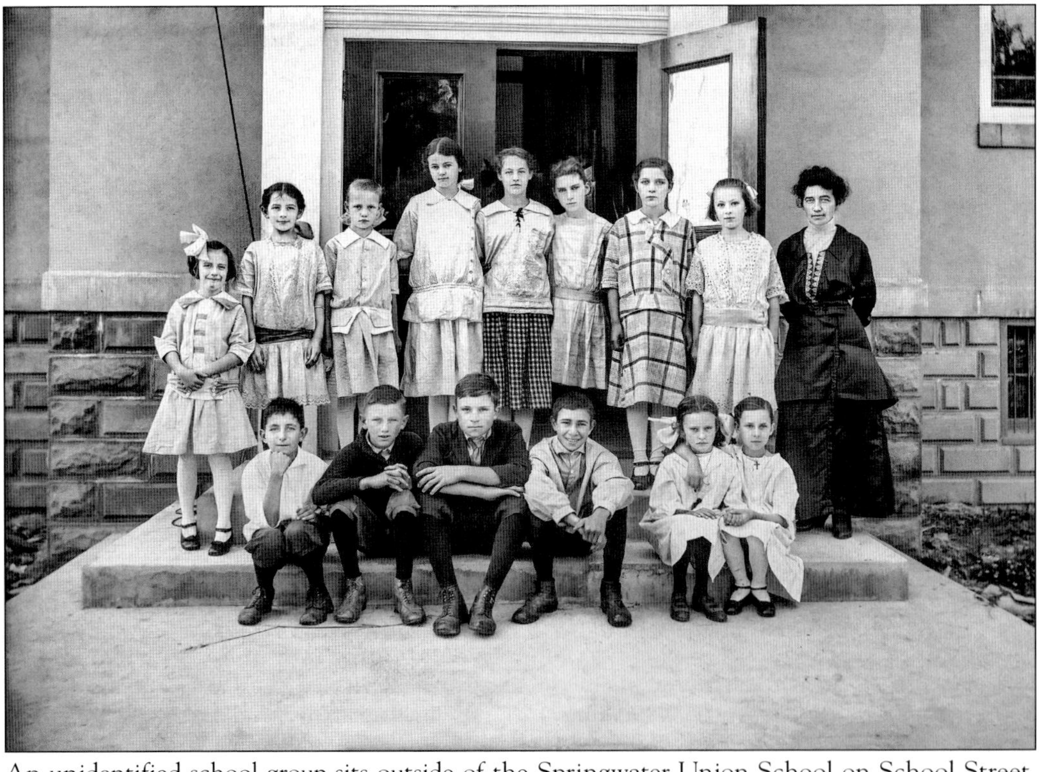

An unidentified school group sits outside of the Springwater Union School on School Street. This picture, taken sometime between 1912 and 1919, shows the front entrance to the building before skylights were put in on the sides. Students during this time would attend until grade eight. Some would go on to attend local high schools in Livonia, Cohocton, or Canisteo, New York.

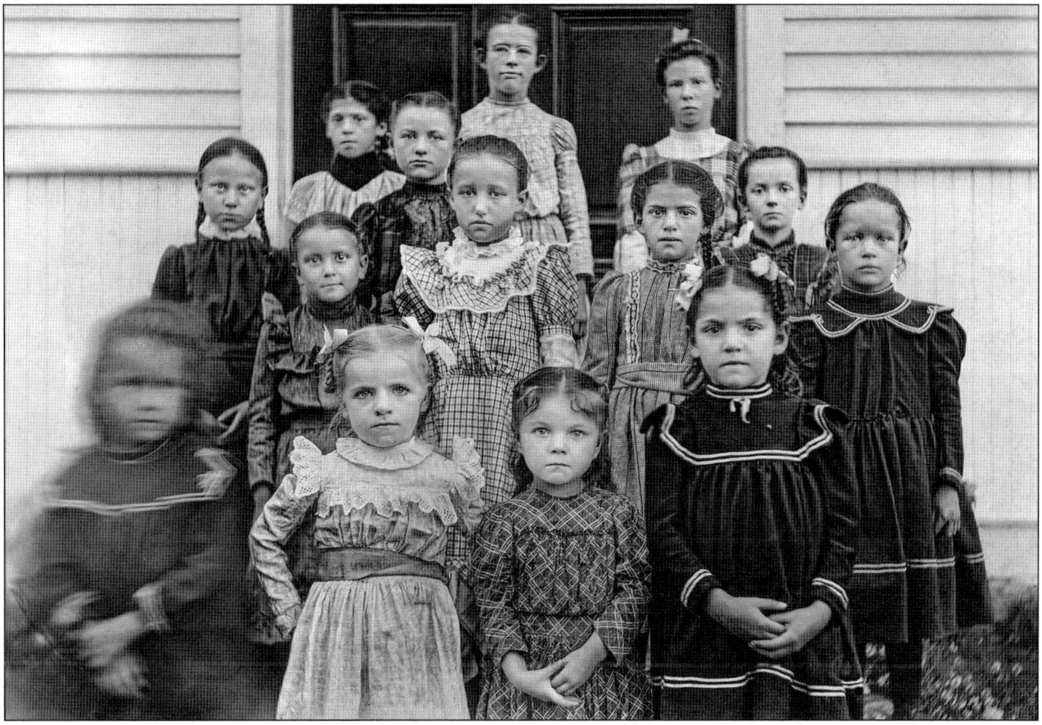

This group of students from the Finger Lakes area are unidentified and the schoolhouse is unknown. It is typical of small rural schoolhouses of the period, as it most likely had two rooms with all students for elementary grades in one area and all students for the upper grades in another.

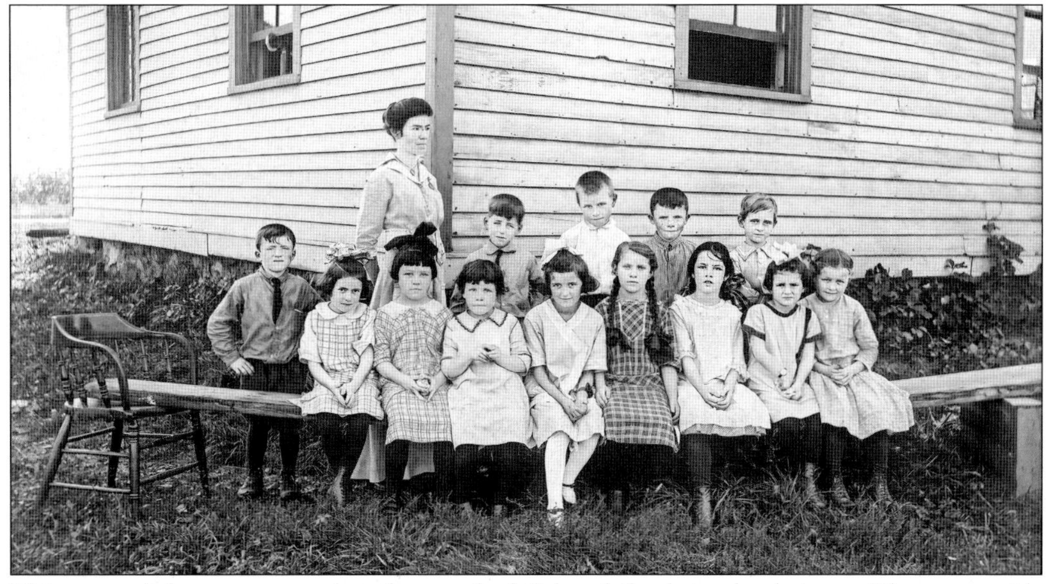

This group of classmates uses a board as a makeshift bench for their school picture. They are outside what appears to be a one-room schoolhouse. Though the location is unknown, many one-room schoolhouses dotted the Finger Lakes landscape, providing education in the basics of reading, writing, and arithmetic. In 1905, the school year averaged about 150 days. In rural communities, many weeks were given off since children were needed on the farm.

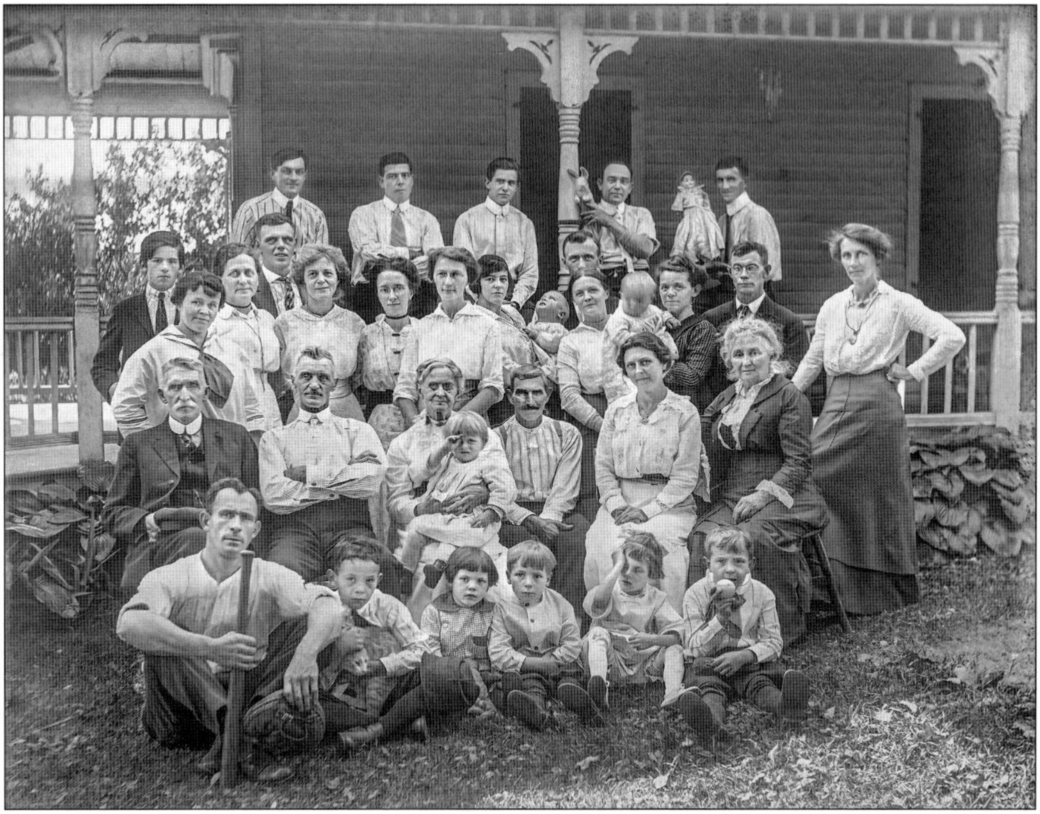

This photograph of an Ingraham family reunion may be the one held in July 1915 in Railroad Mills, a community that is a part of Pittsford, New York, near Rochester. Recognizable in this group is Marchus Ingraham (second row, far left) and Nettie Ingraham (second row, far right). Anna Ingraham, photographer Floyd Ingraham's wife, is in the center (third row, fourth from left). Family reunions were an annual occurrence, and large families would elect officers to coordinate the following year's events.

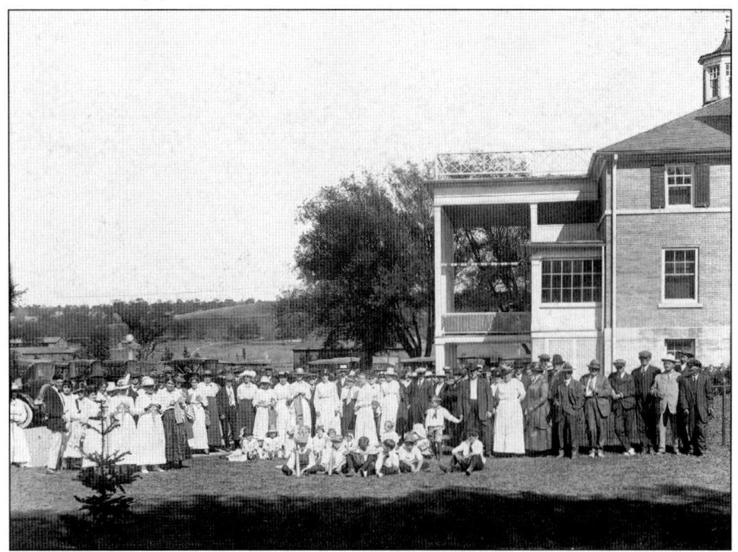

In the early 20th century, auto clubs began to spring up as a way for people to show off their automobiles and enjoy a social event. Often, money raised would go to a charity. Springwater's auto club held a winter ball and an annual summer picnic. This picture is of the Springwater auto club picnic at the foot of Hemlock Lake in 1917 or 1918. Roasted sausage links, wieners, corn, and baked goods were served up to hundreds of guests.

This ball game was played during the Wayland and Springwater Advent church Picnic at Jordon Ponds on Lawrence Gull Road in Springwater. The two churches got together many times for what was called a Union Picnic in the early 1900s.

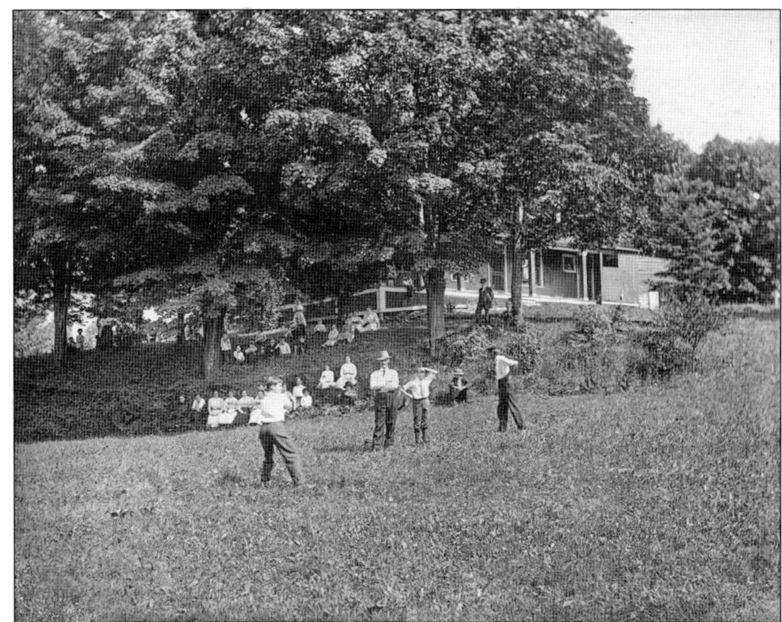

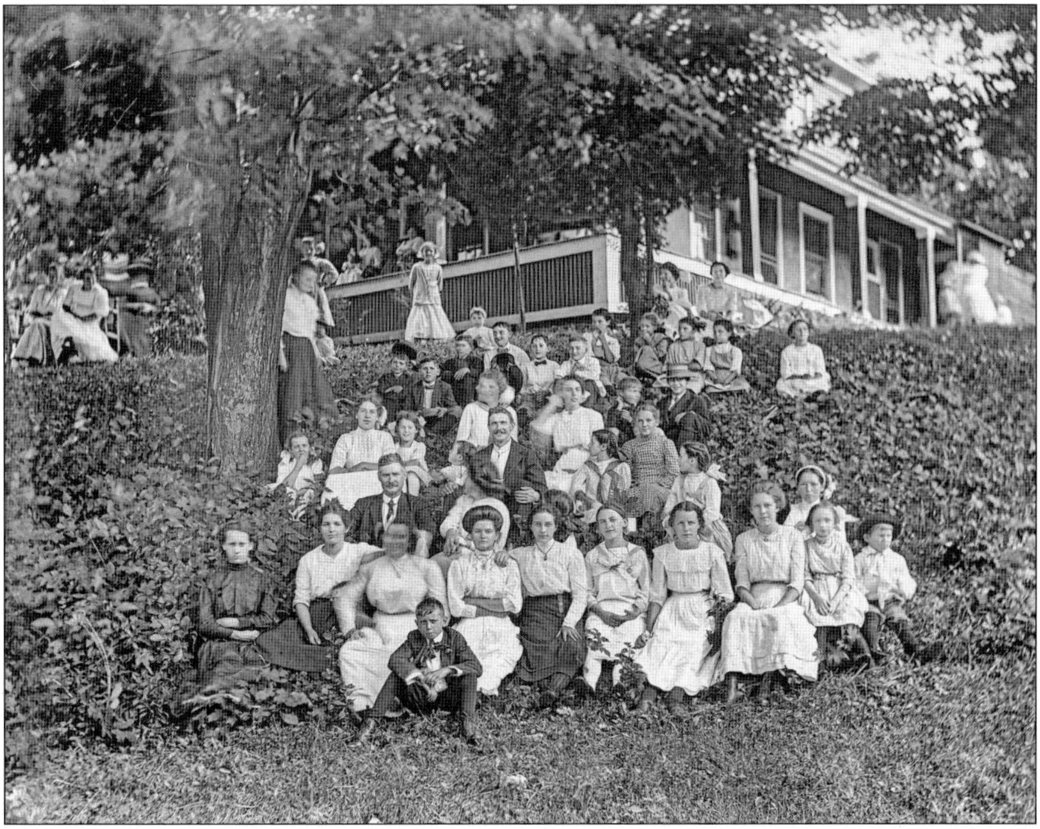

The occasion for this gathering at Jordon Ponds on Lawrence Gull Road was the Union Picnic of the Wayland and Springwater Advent churches. None of the people in the photograph have been identified except for Clara (Seward Mack) Bennett, who is seated in front, fifth from the left.

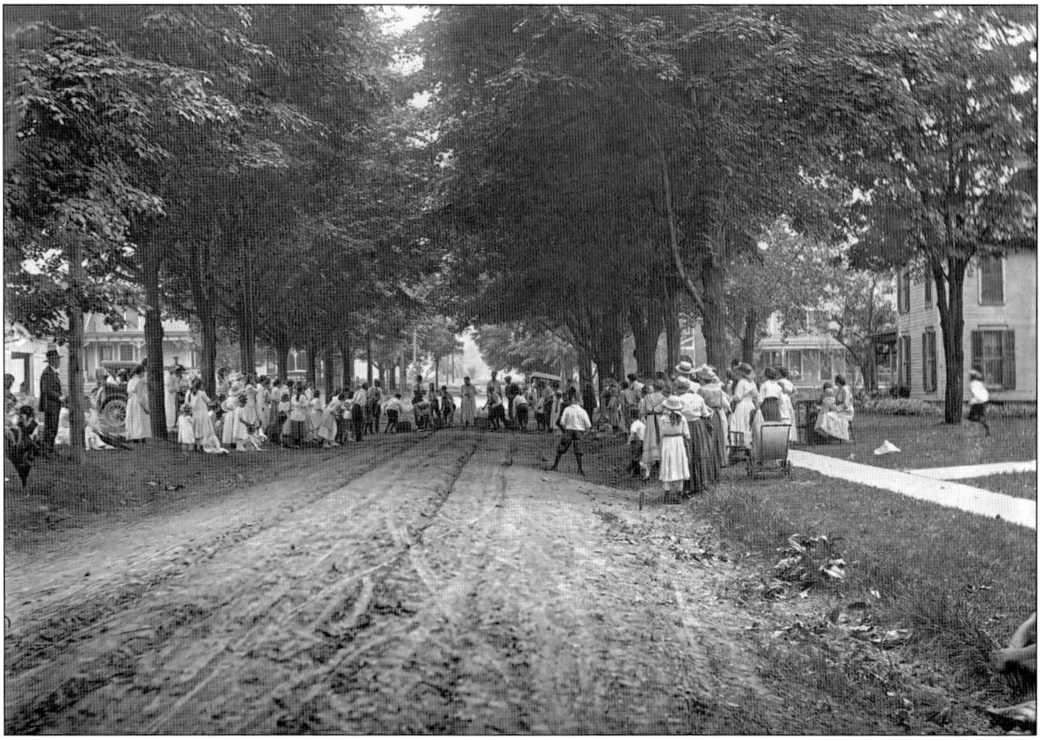

Street carnivals, festivals, and fairs were common in the warmer months. This image of a street carnival scene around 1910 in Springwater was taken just as a foot race was ready to begin on Main Street. In small rural towns like Springwater, work would stop for a moment, and everyone would come out to participate in community-wide events like this one. Springwater once again holds an annual community day as of the writing of this book. Floyd Ingraham's descendants help to plan it each year.

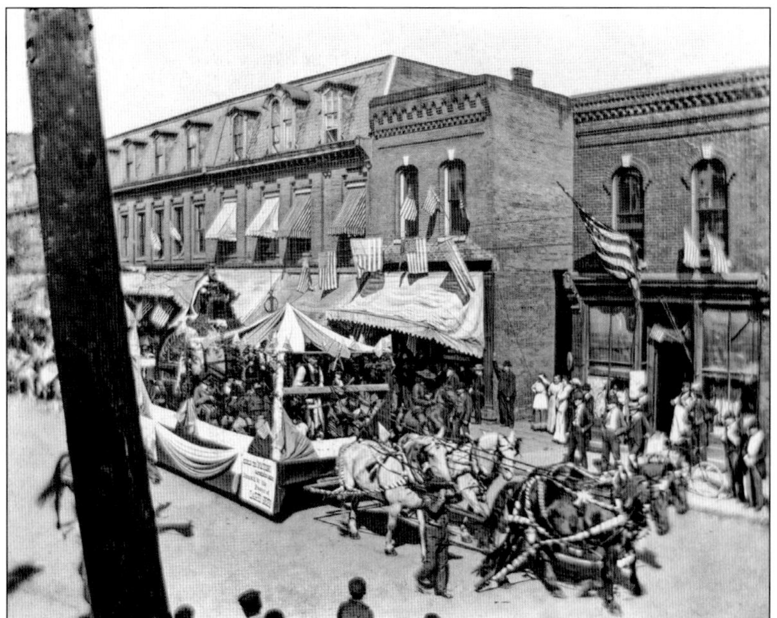

This parade in Hornell, New York, may have been for Memorial Day, or what was then called Decoration Day. The photograph was most likely taken on Canisteo Street. None of the buildings exist today. The float shown here is for the Schwarzenbach Brewery, which operated in Hornell from 1895 to 1920.

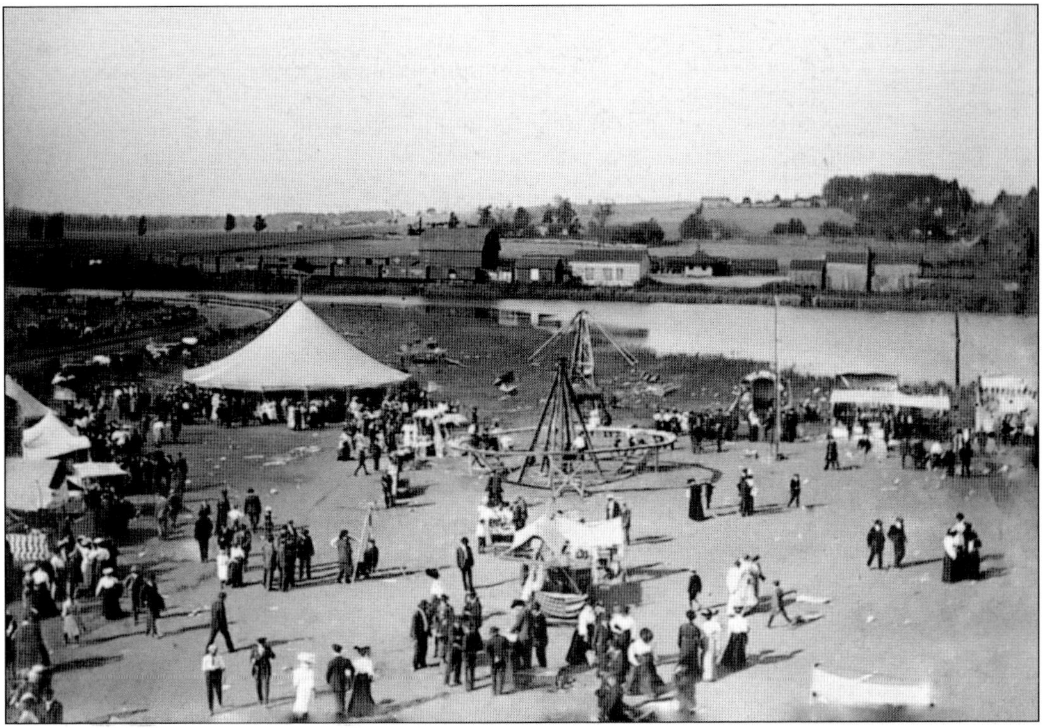

The Hemlock Fair began in 1866. It was also known as the Slab City Fair and the Little World's Fair. It grew to two days in 1877 and then became a five-day fair that is still held annually on dedicated fairgrounds in Hemlock, New York.

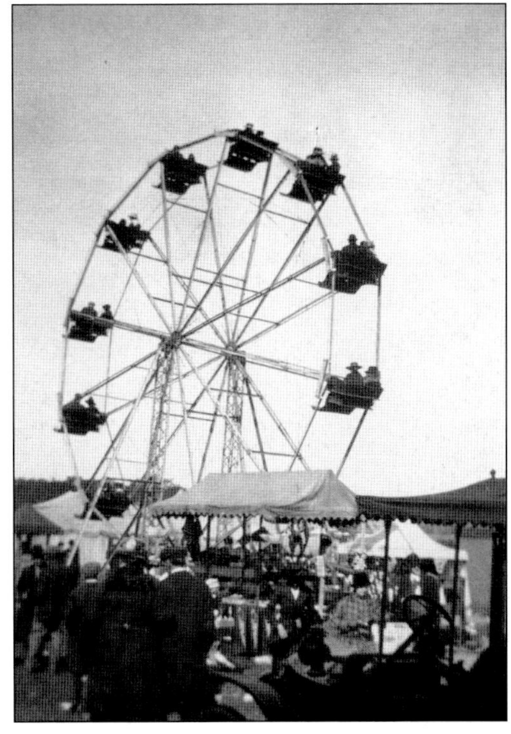

The Hemlock Fair not only featured amusements and food such as E.I. Adams's hot dogs and Kummi John's popcorn, turned by a small steam engine mounted on a wagon, it also had exhibits of livestock and poultry. In 1910, there were 444 classes and breeds of poultry shown at the Hemlock Fair. Another highlight of the Hemlock Fair was the horse races. In 1910, two horses named June and Lottie Hal were entered in the race. Lottie Hal came in first, and June came in second. However, June's owner contested and received first prize after it rained and Lottie Hal showed that her two white forelegs had been dyed to make her a solid brown color. This revealed that she was a horse that had been banned from running in the state of New York. (Courtesy of the Livingston County Historical Society.)

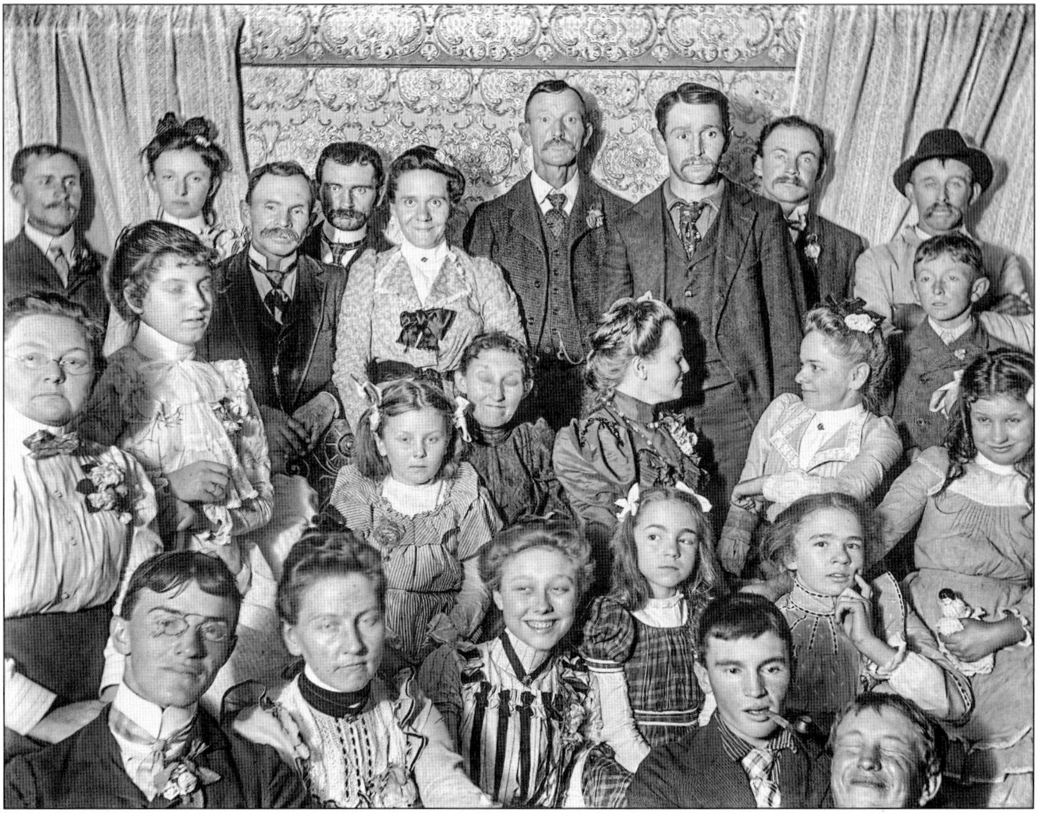

Floyd Ingraham's photograph of a Springwater house party offers a glimpse into everyday life in the early 1900s. Men, women, and children gathered in homes to share meals, stories, games, laughter, and music. People of all ages can be seen in this Norman Rockwell–esque photograph, a snapshot of Springwater's social scene at the start of the 20th century.

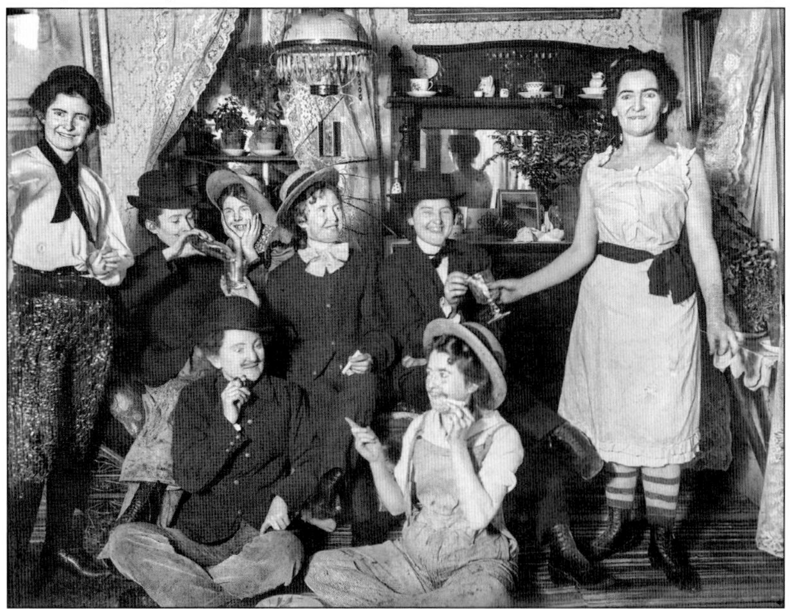

Skits were one of the ways young people would amuse themselves in Floyd Ingraham's day. Here, young women are dressed up for what appears to be a slapstick comedy routine.

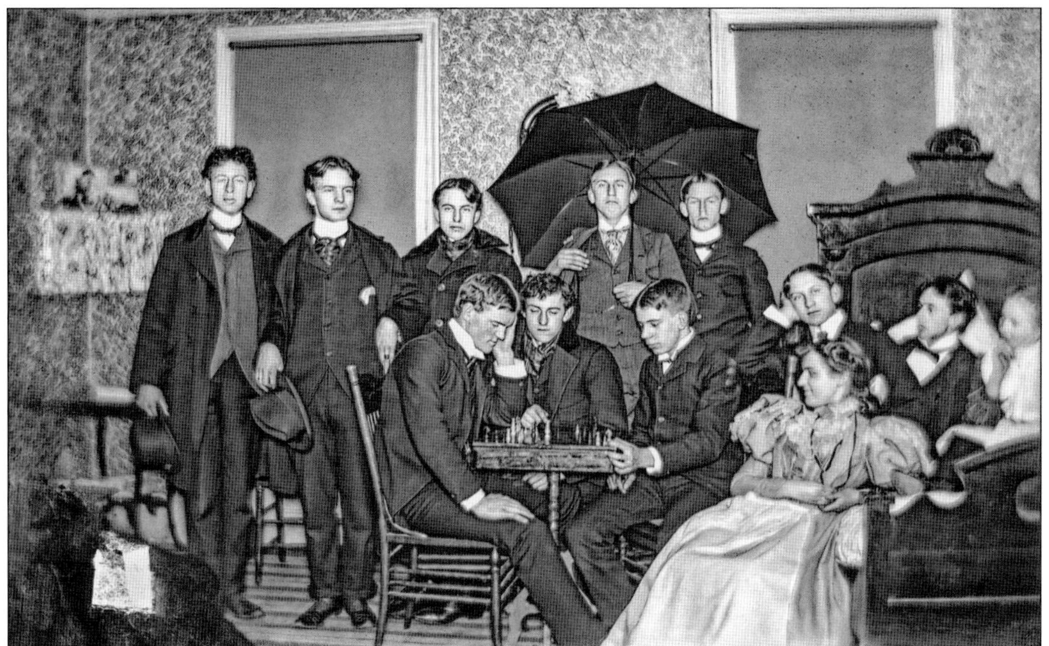

A group of young people gather in a bedroom to observe a chess match. Floyd Ingraham took several unique photographs of people in real-life situations. Although posed, his photographs of events and gatherings in his community are photojournalistic in nature. His images give a glimpse of how leisure time was spent. None of the people in this image have been identified.

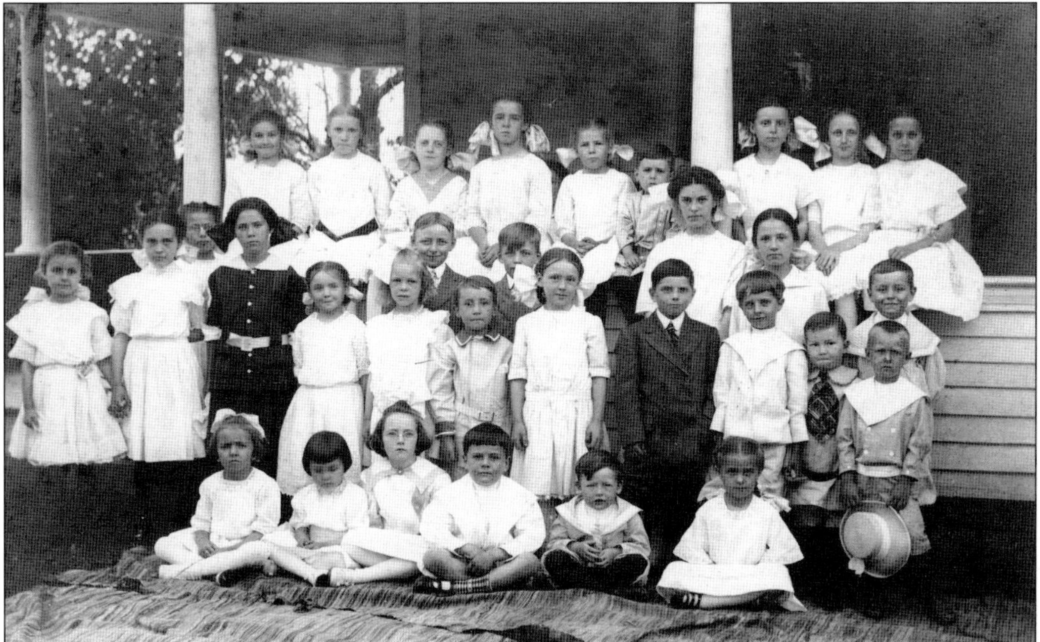

The occasion for this gathering was Louita Higgins's birthday party on August 20, 1913. Higgins was 11 at the time and living in Springwater at the corner of Main Street and Kellogg Road. Although many of the children seen here have not been identified, Ethel Hyde is in the back row at far left, and Louita Higgins is in the back row, third from right, near the pillar.

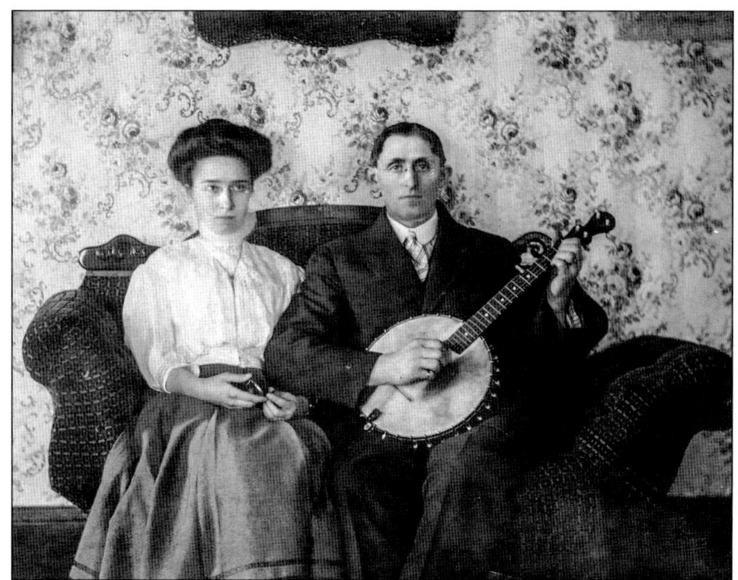

Anna and Floyd Ingraham loved music. Here, Floyd is pictured with his beloved banjo. Most certainly a favored possession, it appears to be a Buckbee five-string banjeaurine. J.H. Buckbee, who was called the "Henry Ford of Banjos," introduced the first mass-produced banjos in the United States. They were made from the early 1860s until the 1890s. Anna also loved music and kept lists of her favorite songs to play on her phonograph.

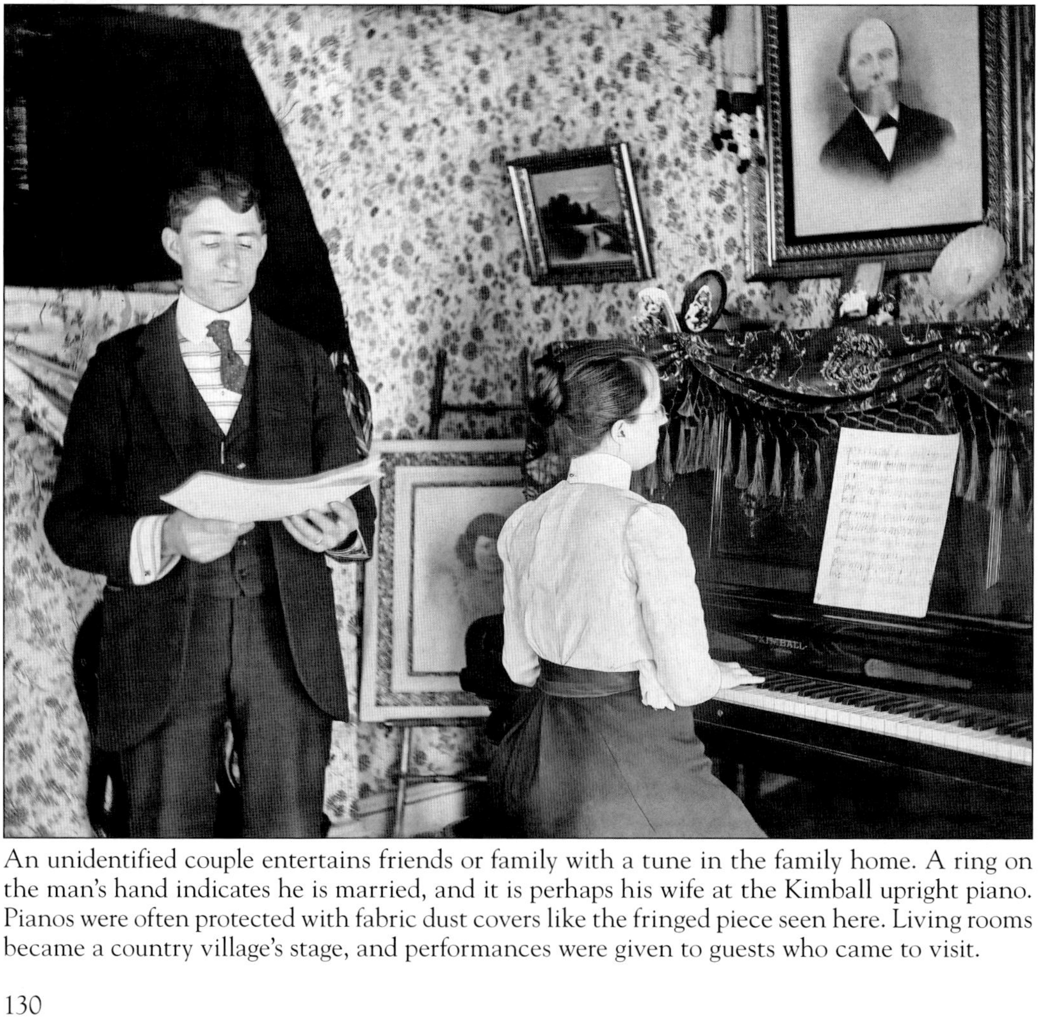

An unidentified couple entertains friends or family with a tune in the family home. A ring on the man's hand indicates he is married, and it is perhaps his wife at the Kimball upright piano. Pianos were often protected with fabric dust covers like the fringed piece seen here. Living rooms became a country village's stage, and performances were given to guests who came to visit.

Floyd Ingraham was photographed with the guitar, banjo, and fiddle in his pictures. It is clear he played several instruments and that music was very much a part of his life. Here, he plays the fiddle with his cousin Gertrude Ford, who is seen with the guitar. Ford would later become part of the Rochester Culture Club and entertain in her home.

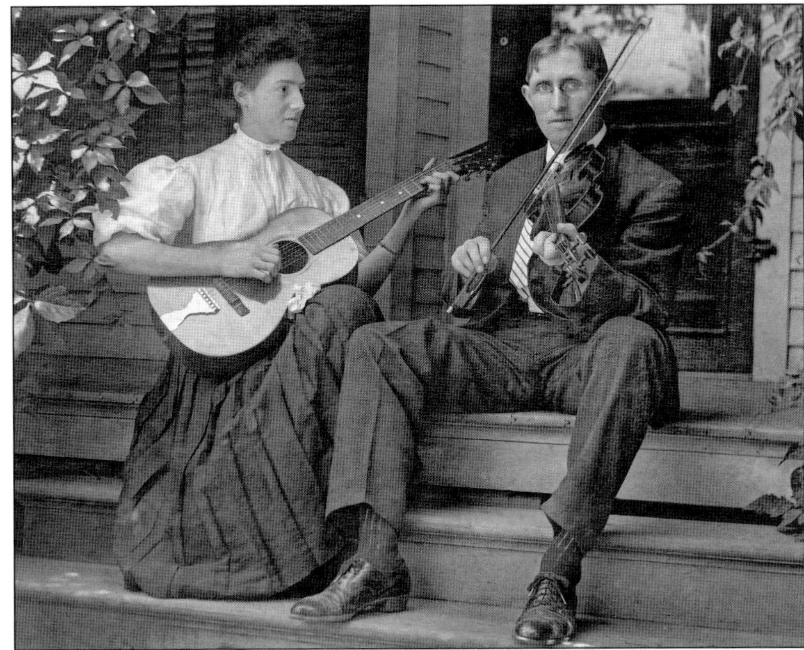

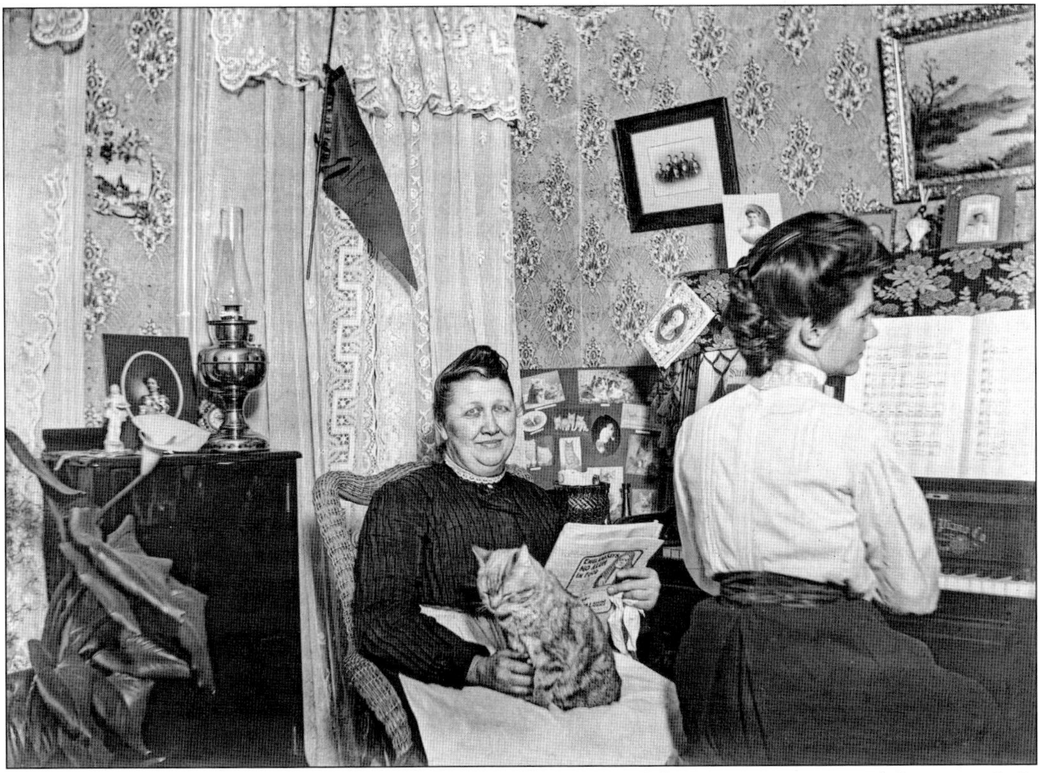

This unidentified early-20th-century woman enjoys time reading a newspaper with her cat while she listens to the young woman next to her play the piano. A collage behind her suggests a love of cats, and the many pictures displayed suggest a love for family. Many young women learned to play an instrument and entertained their family or played for community gatherings.

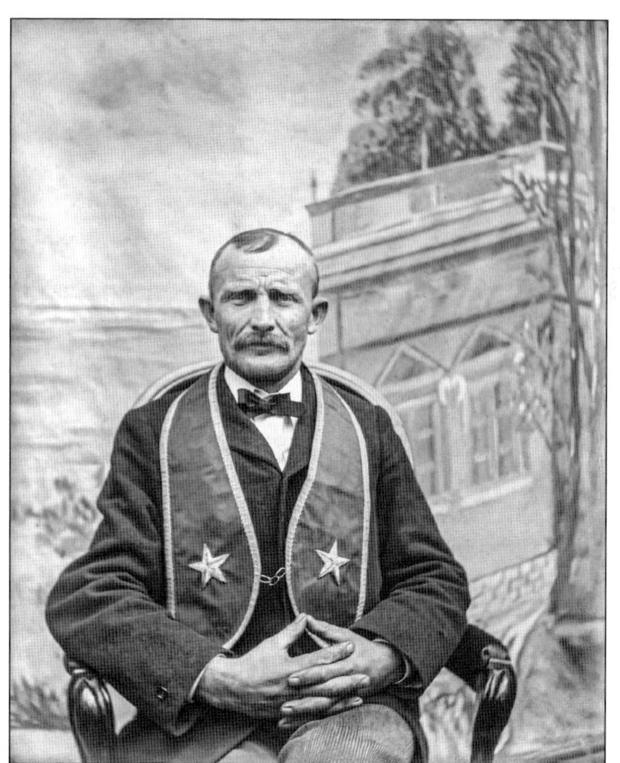

The Independent Order of Odd Fellows was founded in 1819 in Baltimore. It grew, and chapters opened across the United States. The last half of the 19th century has been referred to as the "golden age of fraternalism," and the IOOF became the largest fraternal organization at the time. It also became the first national fraternity to accept both men and women when it formed the Daughters of Rebekah. The purpose of the organization was to "Visit the sick, relieve the distressed, bury the dead, and educate the orphan." The stars on this unidentified member's vest indicate he had been a grand marshal.

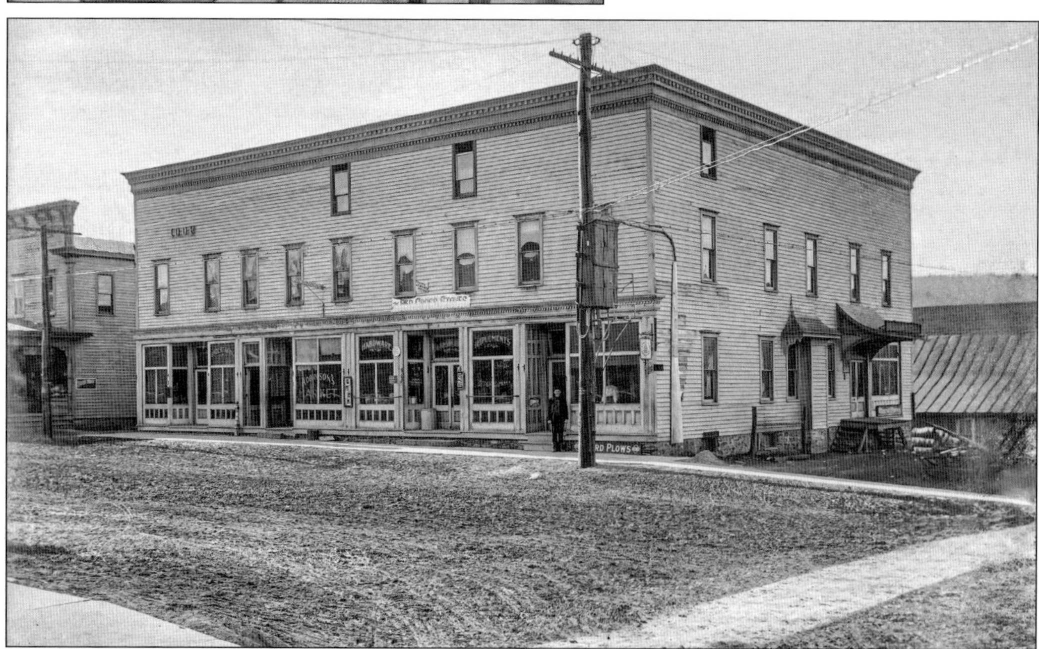

The Marvin Building on Main Street in Springwater held the meeting hall of the IOOF. The initials are high on the left side of the building, above the windows. The IOOF was assembled in Springwater as early as 1902 and provided security for its members in case of sickness or death at a time when insurance was not widely available. Floyd Ingraham and his father, Marchus, as well as his son Kenneth were all members.

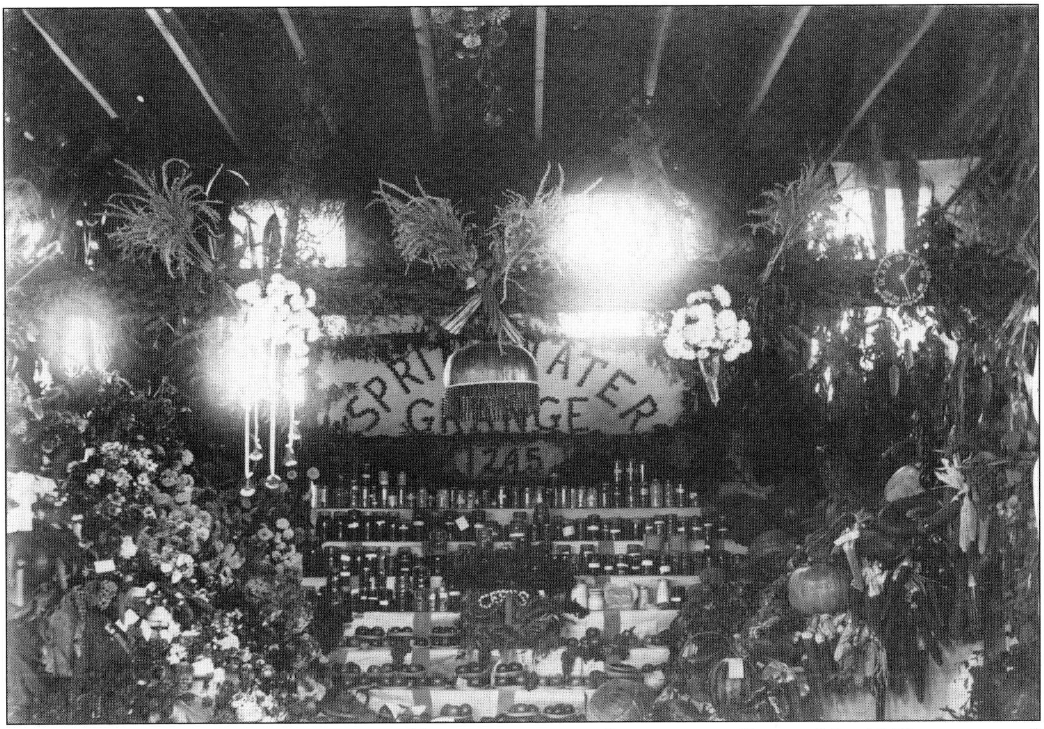

Floral displays like this one were part of fair competitions. Springwater Grange No. 1245 participated many times over the years. This display might be the one the Springwater Grange had at the Hemlock Fair in October 1916 that won the first prize of $60. Grange exhibits had grown in popularity, and many in the community were Grange members, including Floyd Ingraham.

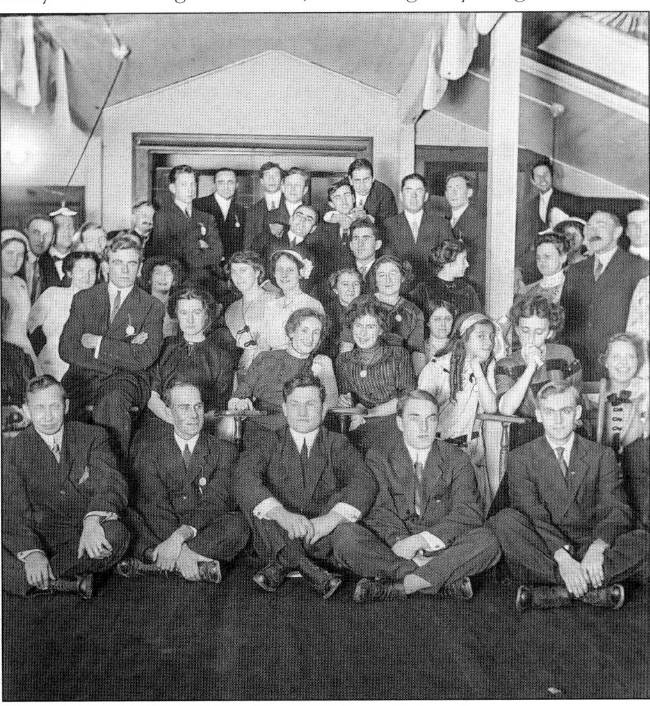

Springwater Grange No. 1245 was formed in 1911. By 1919, it had nearly 300 members. This photograph may have been a gathering of Grange members. The Springwater Grange held several events throughout the year and met in the town hall for a few years before it constructed a building of its own in 1925. The building is no longer standing.

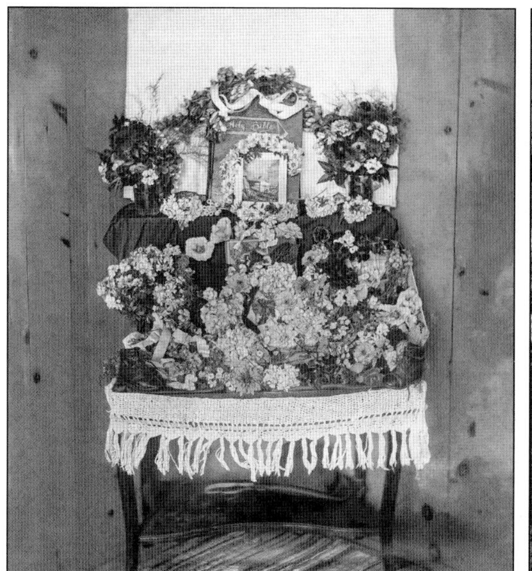

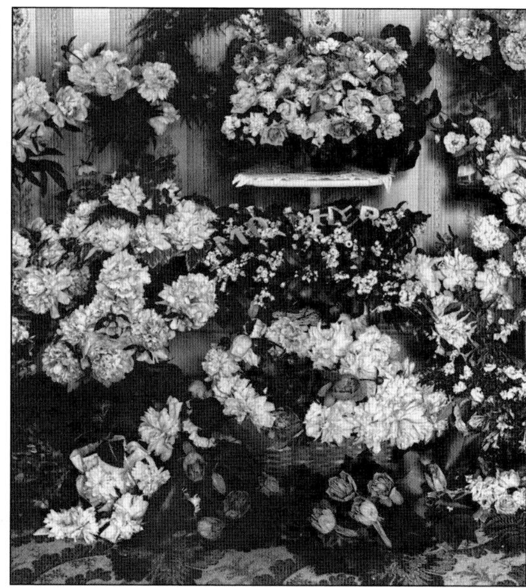

Due to rich soil and availability of water and irrigation, flowers thrived in the Finger Lakes region. Floral displays showed community pride at parades and fairs. They also served as memorials, as seen here. These floral arrangements were on display for a home viewing and a funeral. The one on the left was for a small child, whose identity and death date are unknown. The one on the right was displayed at the funeral of Luthera (Loveland) Cork, who died in 1913. She was the mother of Anna (Cork) Ingraham.

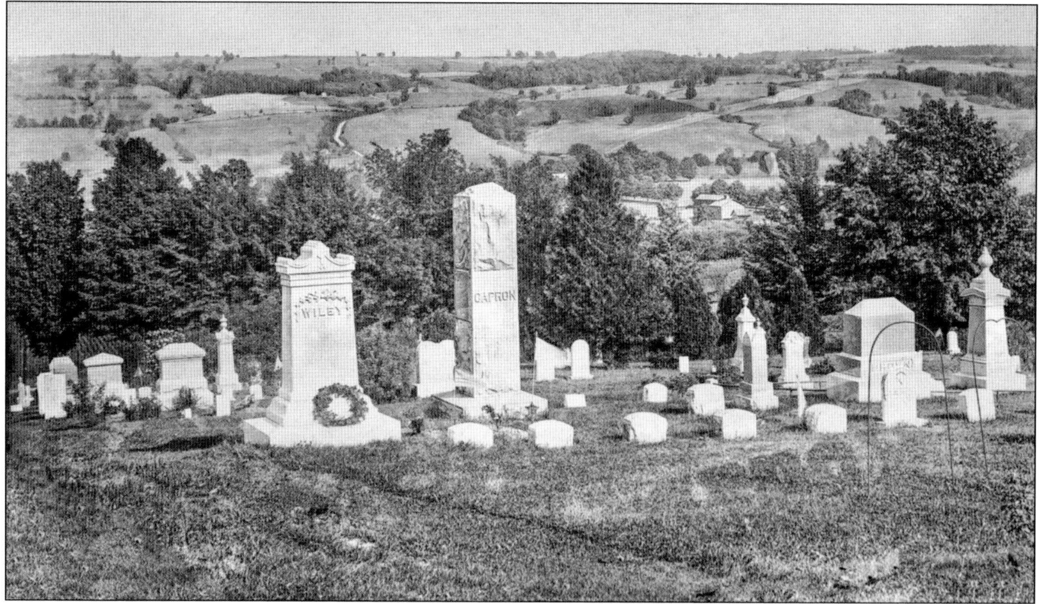

Although an undertaker might have been employed to care for the body of the deceased, the family still hosted the funeral, and a family's living room or parlor became the funeral home. This was common into the early 20th century. Friends and relatives came and brought food, sat with the family, and offered comfort. Numerous cemeteries dot the landscape of Livingston County. This one, Mount Vernon Evergreen Cemetery, not only holds the graves of members of the Wiley and Capron families seen here, but is also the final resting place for Floyd Ingraham.

Five

Lake Scenes

The Finger Lakes region encompasses 9,000 square miles. This region includes streams, waterfalls, rivers, ponds, and 11 lakes. This part of New York state got its name from the long, narrow lakes that run roughly north to south like fingers spread out across the northern Allegheny Plateau and south of the Ontario lowlands. The 11 major Finger Lakes empty north into the Genesee and Seneca Rivers, whose waters find their way to Lake Ontario.

Floyd Ingraham photographed the four westernmost lakes—Conesus, Hemlock, Canadice, and Honeoye—but many of his photographs feature the two lakes closest to his home of Springwater, Hemlock and Canadice.

The first European settlers came to Conesus Lake around 1792. Within 10 years, there were several small settlements in the area. As villages and towns were formed in the 19th century, cottages and homes around the beautiful lakes drew local residents and visitors from larger cities like Rochester. Lake-goers gathered at cottages or camped on the lakeshores. In Floyd Ingraham's day, fishing, boating, and swimming at the lakes were favorite pastimes.

In the late 1800s, the City of Rochester identified Hemlock and Canadice Lakes as a source for public drinking water and began acquiring properties around the lakes to protect the water. By 1951, all the lakeside cottages and buildings around Hemlock and Canadice Lakes were demolished, and the land was left to return to its natural state. Today, Hemlock and Canadice Lakes are the only lakes in the United States within 50 miles of a major metropolitan area that are undeveloped.

In the 1970s, the only known eagle's nest in the state of New York was at Hemlock Lake. Efforts were made to rebuild the bald eagle population in New York. As of 2019, over 300 nests exist. Many eagles make their home around New York's western Finger Lakes, specifically because it has become a desirable habitat for the protected species.

The western Finger Lakes continue to be a source of beauty and pride for area residents. Conservation efforts have further protected the shores and surrounding forests of Hemlock and Canadice. The establishment of hiking trails, water conservation efforts, and the protection of wildlife means that these lakes will be preserved for generations to come.

Though the lakeside cottages and boat launches seen in many of Floyd Ingraham's images are gone, the beauty of the lakes captured by Ingraham's camera 100 years ago remains.

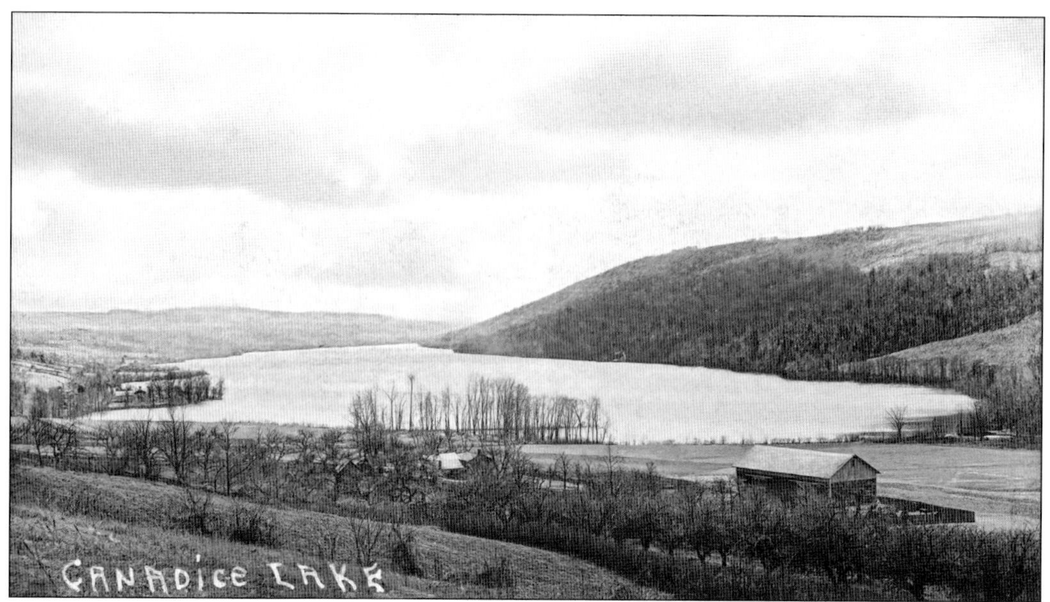

Canadice, named by Native Americans, means "long lake." Canadice Lake is in Ontario County 30 miles south of Rochester. At only three tenths of a mile wide and three miles long, it is the smallest of the Finger Lakes. Canadice Lake is one of two purchased by the City of Rochester whose shorelines are undeveloped. Canadice Lake has been owned by the New York Department of Environmental Conservation since 2010. (Courtesy of Ron and Sharon Ingraham.)

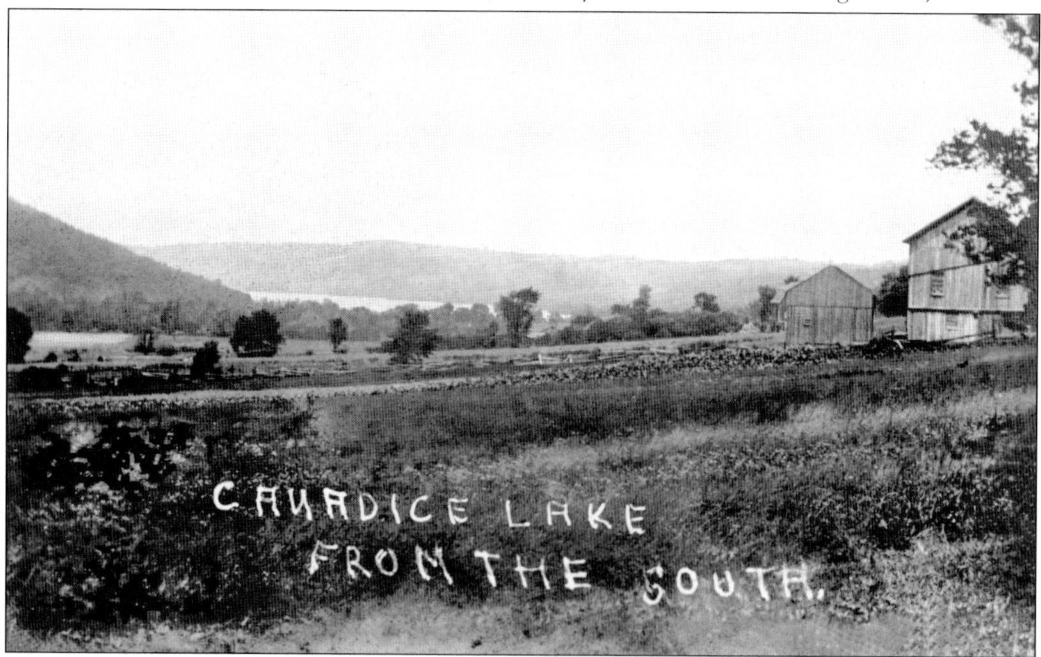

Canadice Lake may be the smallest of the major Finger Lakes, but it is the highest at 1,096 feet in elevation. It has beautiful scenery along its shores. Canadice and Hemlock Lakes were purchased in 2010 by the New York State Department of Environmental Conservation. Canadice Lake, although undeveloped and barren of the cottages and resorts that once dotted its shoreline, is now protected. (Courtesy of Ron and Sharon Ingraham.)

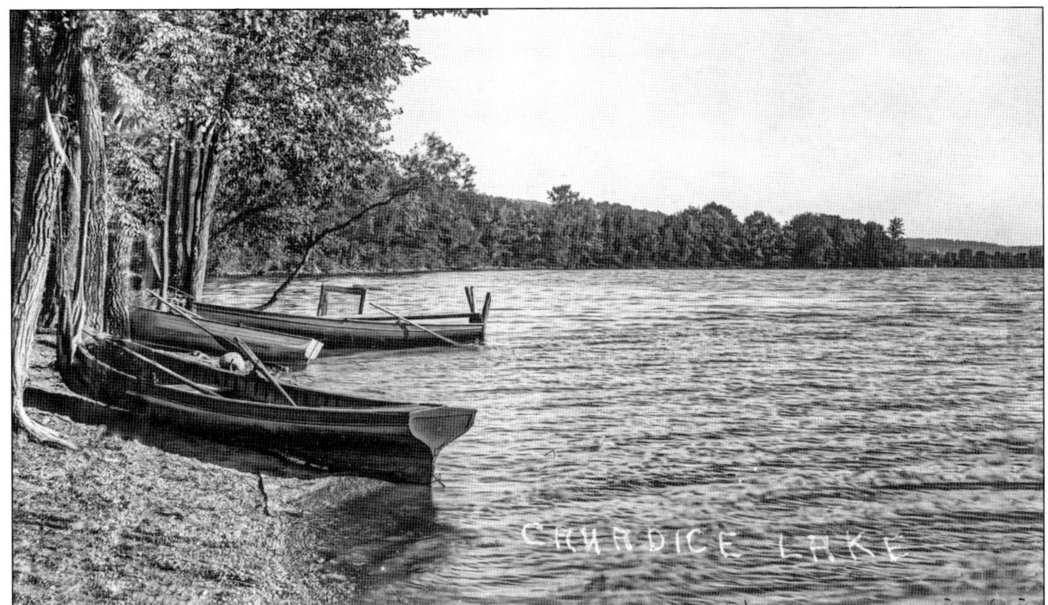

Canadice Lake offered several points and inlets. Families who owned land along the shoreline had boat liveries and could store rowboats and canoes until ready to use. To purchase a boat was to purchase what was then called "a launch." At what appears to be Barringer's Point on Canadice Lake, this scene shows boats pulled up onto shore, waiting to launch into the lake with their passengers. Today, only non-motorized watercraft or boats with outboard motors of 10 horsepower or less are permitted on Canadice Lake.

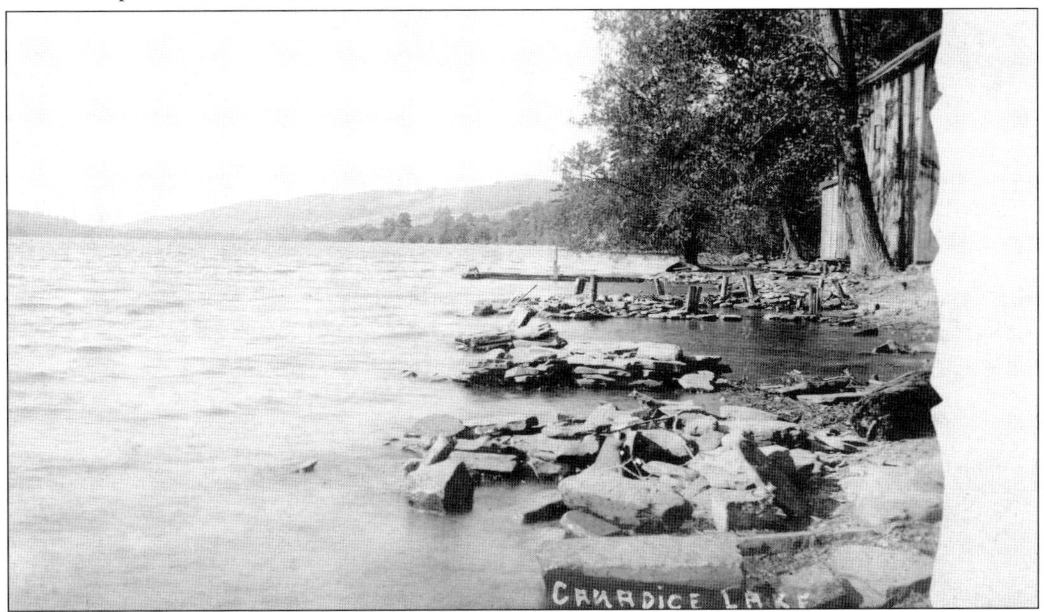

The location of the cottage in this postcard is believed to be Colegrove Point. Canadice Lake in the late 19th century and early 20th century was surrounded by cottages. Area residents would flock to the lakes in the summer for boating, fishing, and picnics on its banks. Floyd Ingraham took many pictures of Canadice Lake, and newspaper reports reveal he spent a lot of time there. (Courtesy of Ron and Sharon Ingraham.)

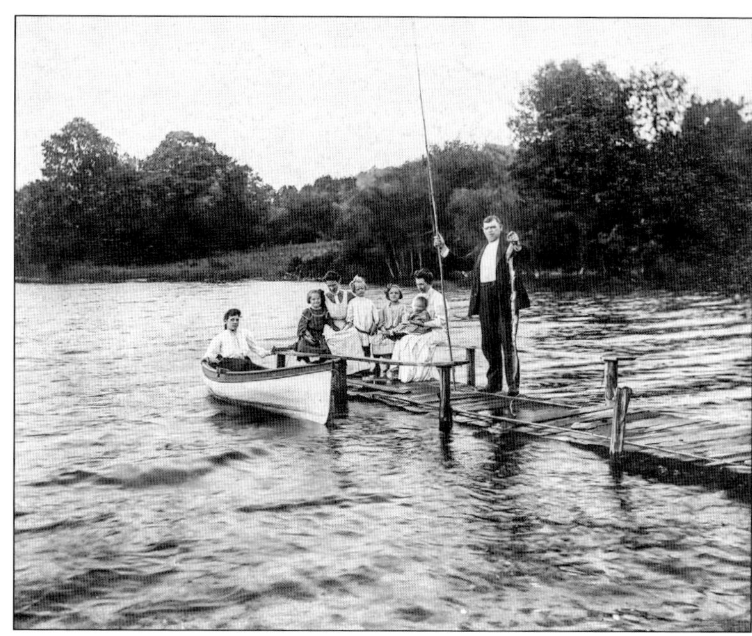

Fishing on the Finger Lakes was and still is a favorite pastime of area residents and visitors. This unidentified family on Hoppough Point at Canadice Lake has a string of fish to show for their efforts. The lake was stocked beginning in 1949, and now anglers can find trout, smallmouth bass, pickerel, brown bullhead, bluegill, black crappie, and yellow perch in the lake's waters. (Courtesy of Springwater–Webster Crossing Historical Society.)

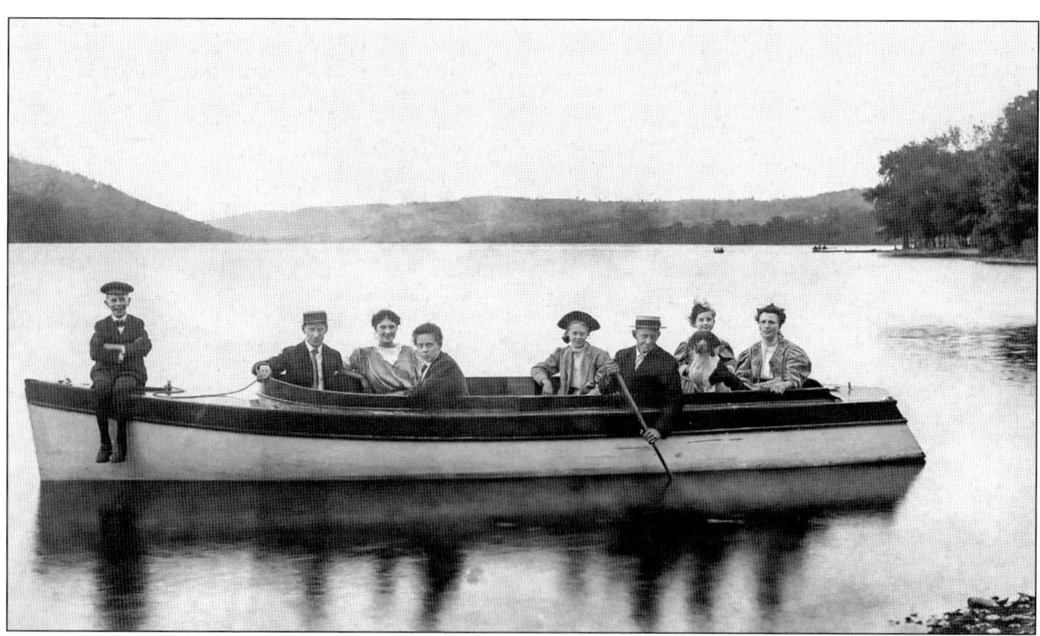

This family is enjoying a day at Canadice Lake in what appears to be a Johnson boat. Burdette Johnson was a boatbuilder in the area, and his boats were well-known and well-made. The family is unidentified, but the dog appears in several of Floyd Ingraham's images, including the one on page 147. In the background at right, Barringer's Point can be seen. (Courtesy of Ron and Sharon Ingraham.)

This unidentified family is at a cottage that once stood on the west side of Canadice Lake. Later, it was owned by Albert E. Ellinger. Ellinger was raised in Oneida County, New York, and moved to Buffalo, where he married Mary Hanner. The couple frequented the Finger Lakes, purchasing this cottage in the 1930s. In 1944, Ellinger refused to sell his lakefront land to the City of Rochester and fought the city's plan to raise the water level 3.5 feet, which would flood his land and wash out an access road. The Ellinger cottage was the last one sold to Rochester, in 1949. (Courtesy of Joyce O'Neil and Rick Osiecki.)

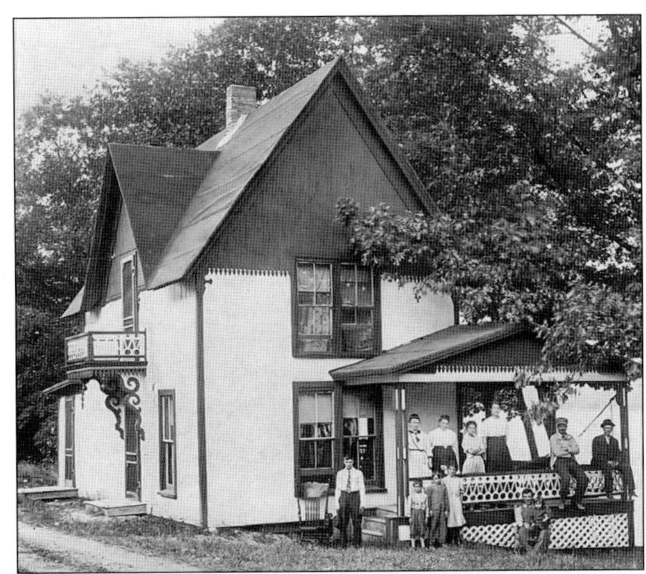

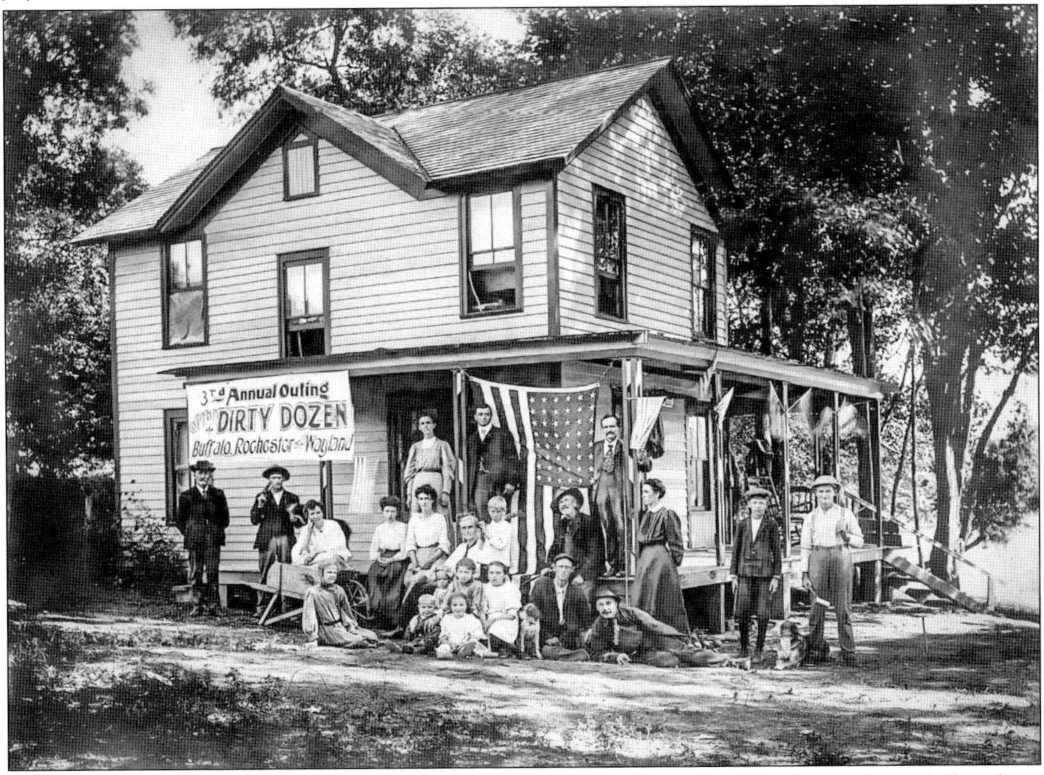

This cottage was owned by the Colegrove family on Canadice Lake. The descendants of brothers Orren, Charles, Elmer, and Jotham Colegrove gathered frequently at the lake in what became known as Colegrove Resort. The sign may indicate a reunion of the living grandchildren of Harlow Colegrove and Lydia Coykendall, parents of the brothers mentioned. Jotham Colegrove was a respected carpenter and builder. He built many of the Colegrove cottages on the lake. His beautiful home on Bald Hill Road in Canadice still stands. (Courtesy of Springwater–Webster Crossing Historical Society.)

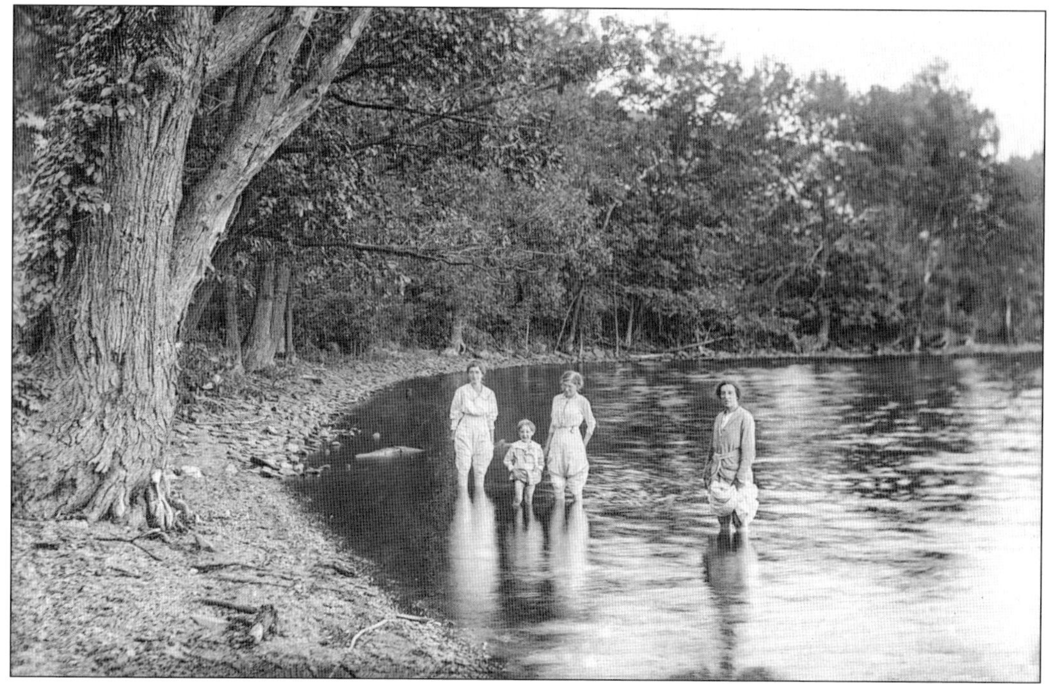

The Ingraham family spent a lot of time at Canadice Lake during the warmer months. Floyd Ingraham's picture is a scene from Canadice Lake's east side. From left to right, his wife, Anna; son Kenneth; aunt Carrie; and sister-in-law Louise enjoy wading in the water.

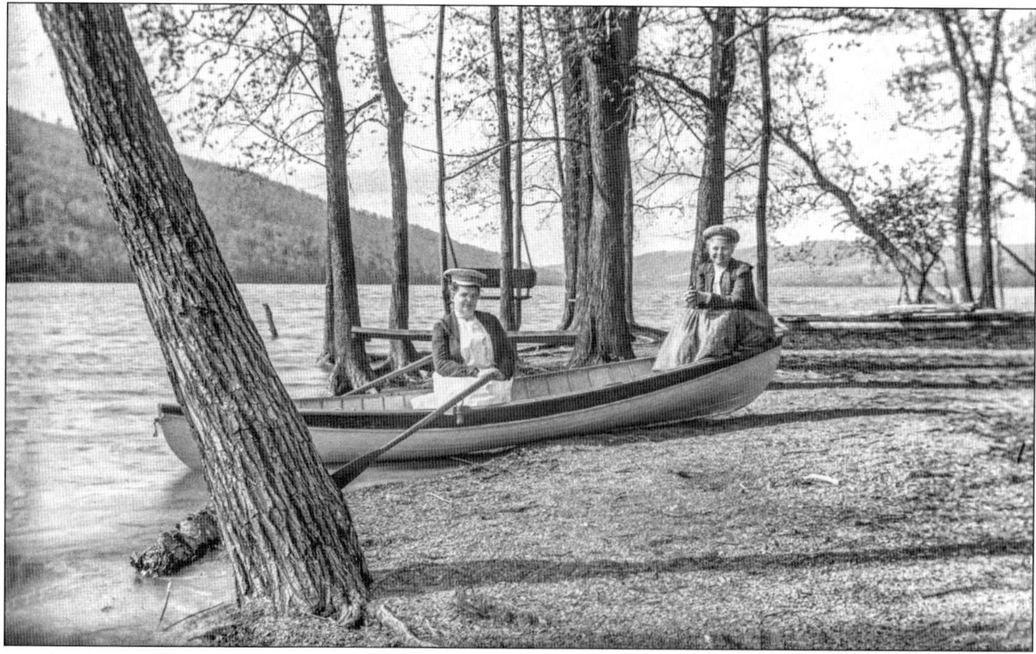

Pearl Johnson (left) and Carrie King are shown here in their nursing school uniforms ready to launch their boat onto Canadice Lake. This picture by Floyd Ingraham was taken in September 1906 near the King cottage, believed to have been on the east side of the lake. (Courtesy of Springwater–Webster Crossing Historical Society.)

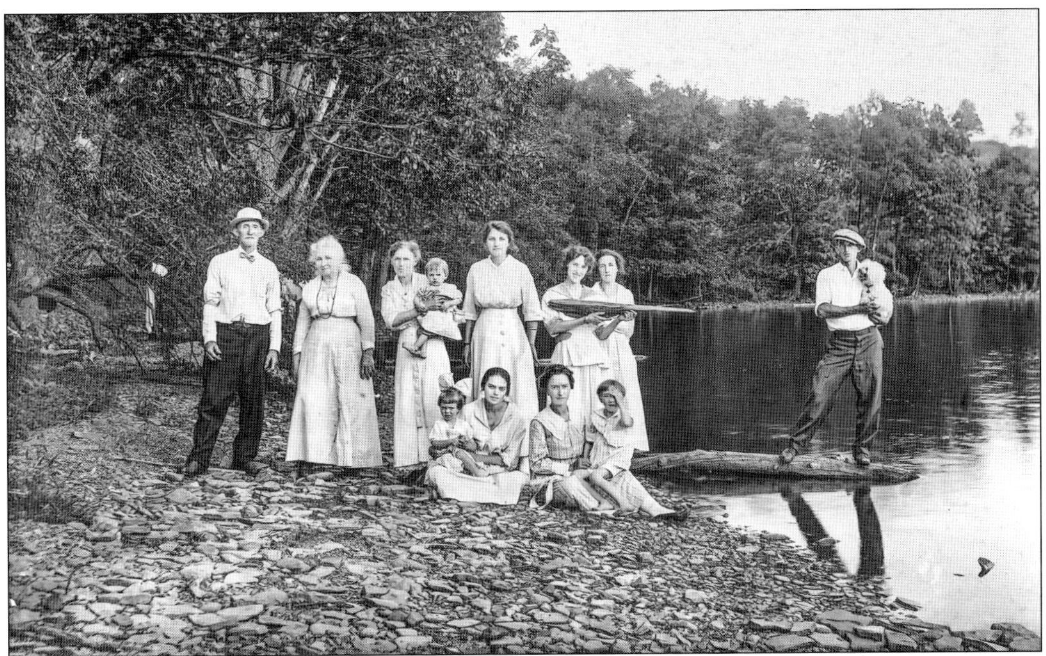

The Ingraham family is seen here enjoying a day together on the shore of Canadice Lake. From left to right are (seated) Mary Helen Ford and daughter Dorothy and Anna Ingraham and son Kenneth; (standing) Marchus and Nettie Ingraham, Carrie Ford holding Vivian, Eleanor Graves, Gertrude Ford, Louise Cork, and Leon Ford holding a dog.

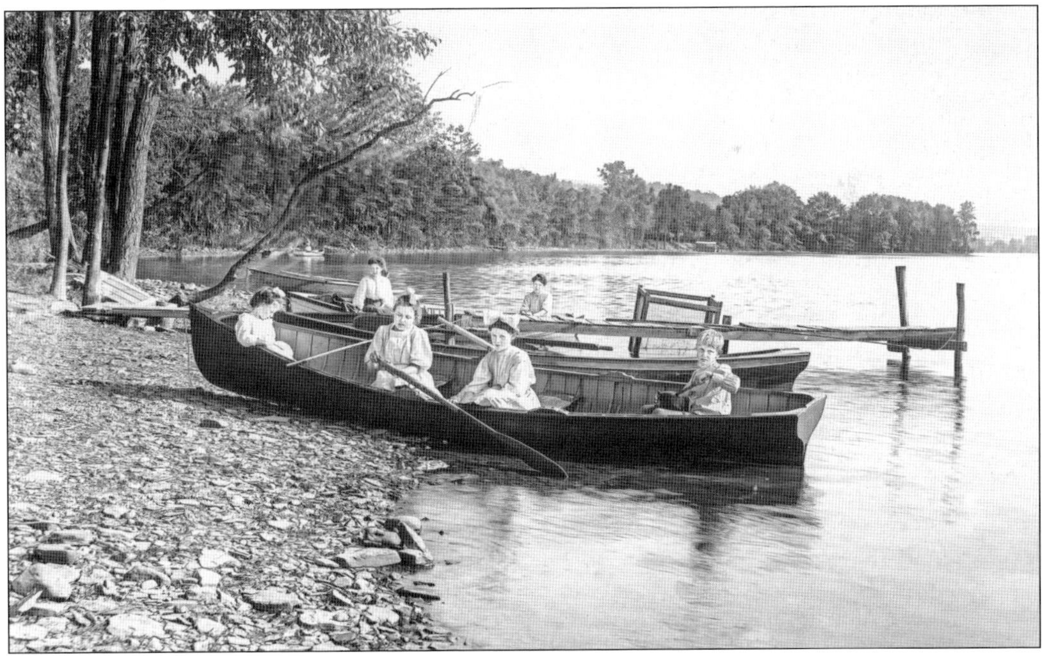

This boat dock on Canadice Lake is the launching point for the families seen here. Children sit in a boat under the watchful eye of women nearby. A young boy cuts a watermelon in preparation for a mid-lake snack, and just beyond them, a man may be fishing in the cool, shaded waters along the shoreline.

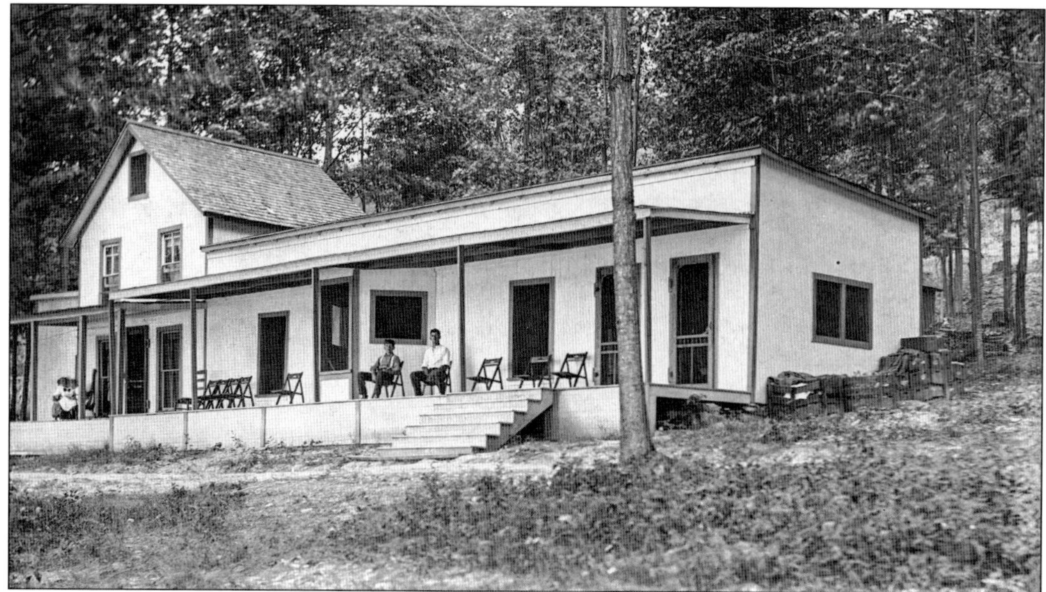

The Peabody store on Canadice Lake was owned by Frank Peabody. In 1913, he purchased a Victrola to entertain his guests and had a telephone installed. Parties and dances were held on the Peabody property. One lively gathering reportedly went until midnight, at which time Peabody began singing "Home Sweet Home" to signal it was time for guests to leave. Peabody rowed across to the east side of the lake to pick up his mail on November 7, 1926, when he had a heart attack and fell overboard. He clung to the boat but could not be resuscitated after help reached him.

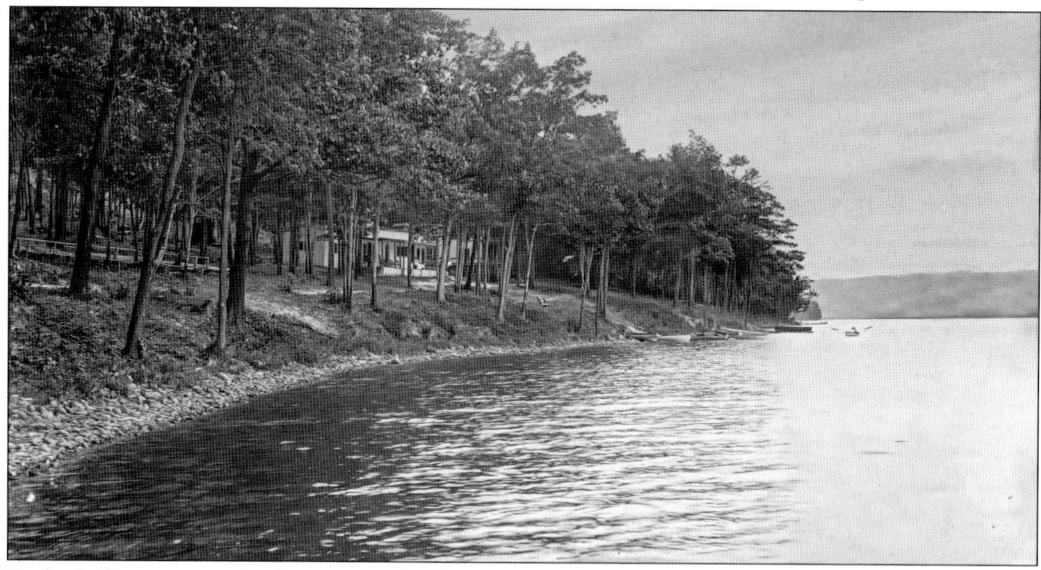

Peabody Point was a popular spot, visible here on the west shore of Canadice Lake. Frank Peabody purchased land on the lake sometime before 1903. In 1904, Barringer slid his engine across a frozen Candice Lake to provide power for a temporary sawmill that provided lumber for building on Peabody Point. In 1906, Frank Peabody, Dr. George Peabody, and John Sterner purchased 60 more acres of land, which was part of the Jonas Swarts estate. In 1907, they added another 96 acres. They built a store, cottages, boat livery, and hotel. The land was sold to the City of Rochester in 1937.

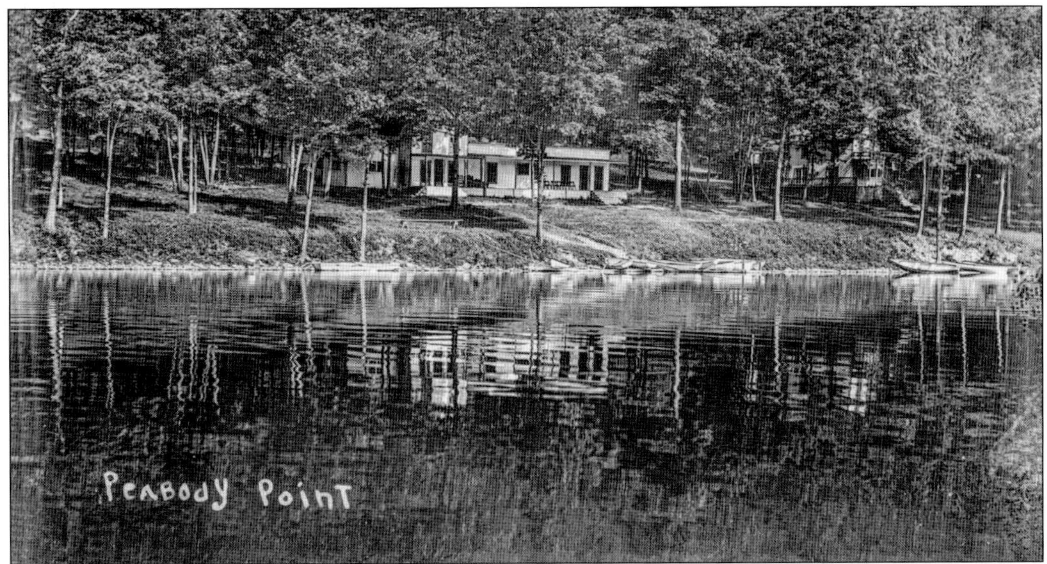

The last of the Peabody lakefront properties was sold to the City of Rochester in 1947. The Peabody cottages, hotel, and store were owned and built by the Peabody brothers, Dr. George and Frank Peabody. Dr. George Peabody was born in 1858. He studied medicine and chose Wayland as his home and the base for his practice. He made his last house call the morning of his death in 1928. The Peabody resort at Canadice Lake hosted reunions and gatherings of all kinds. In 1912, it hosted a dance with music provided by the Springwater Mandolin Club, which may have included Floyd Ingraham. Though the Peabody resort is gone now, remnants of the foundation of the store are still visible today.

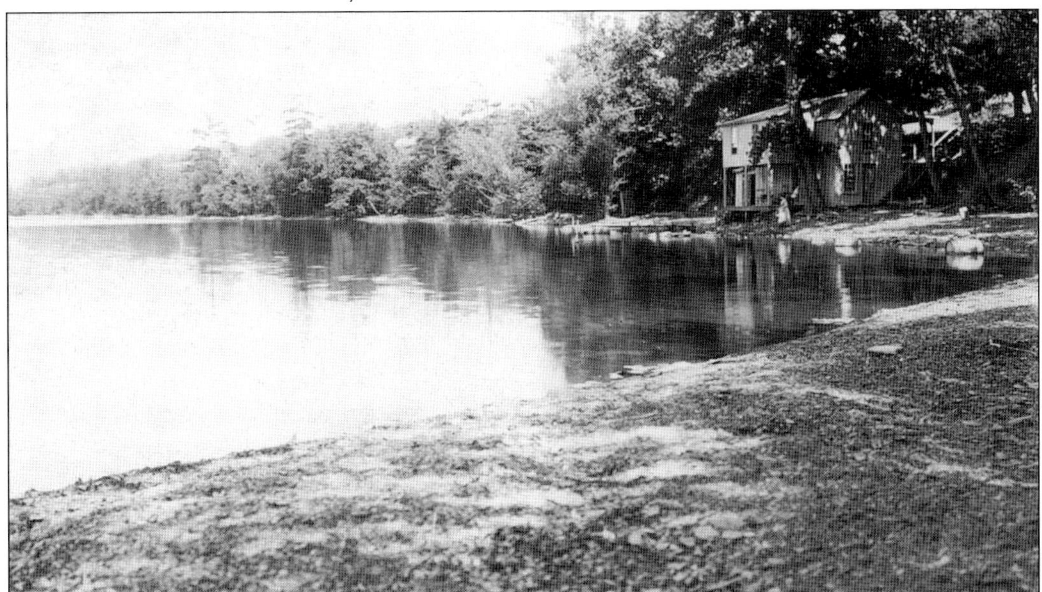

A collection of cottages on Canadice Lake, including a resort owned by E.E. Colegrove, one of Harlow and Lydia (Coykendall) Colegrove's sons, hosted reunions and parties for lakeside guests. It was the location for a large revival meeting in 1911 with Rev. J.W. Lawton. The Colegrove Resort also hosted the Springwater Strawberry Festival. The festival is still held today, hosted by Springwater Methodist Church. (Courtesy of Ron and Sharon Ingraham.)

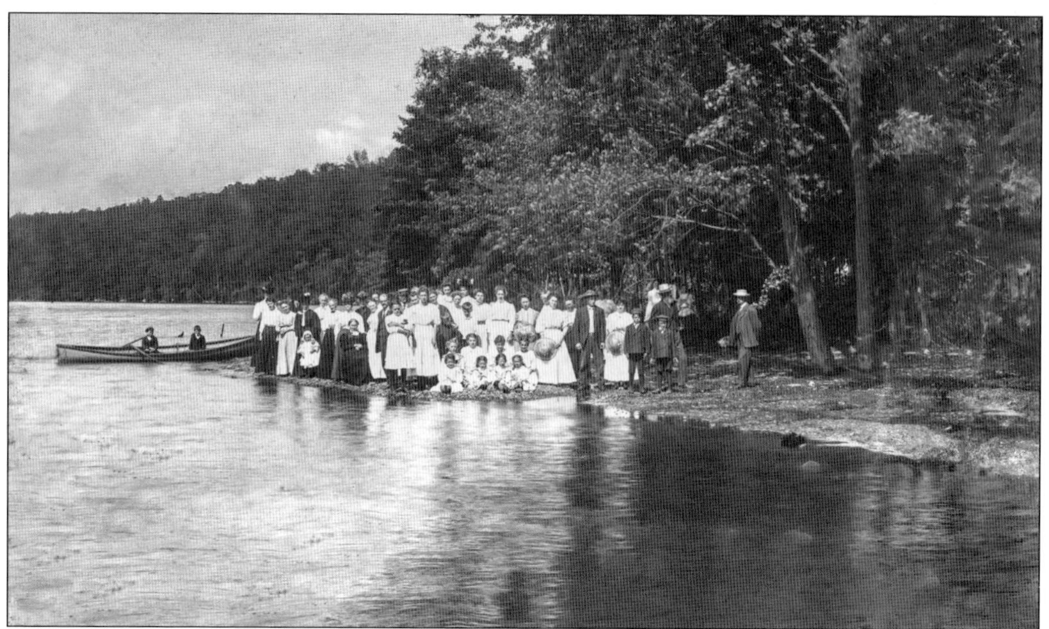

Barringer Point was the site for many gatherings and reunions. Larger properties on the lake offered a dock for boats, a lodge for gathering indoors, cottages, campsites, and picnic groves that were perfect for events such as family reunions, church picnics, or community gatherings. It was also a place of rest and refreshment for hardworking people from nearby rural communities. (Courtesy of Springwater–Webster Crossing Historical Society.)

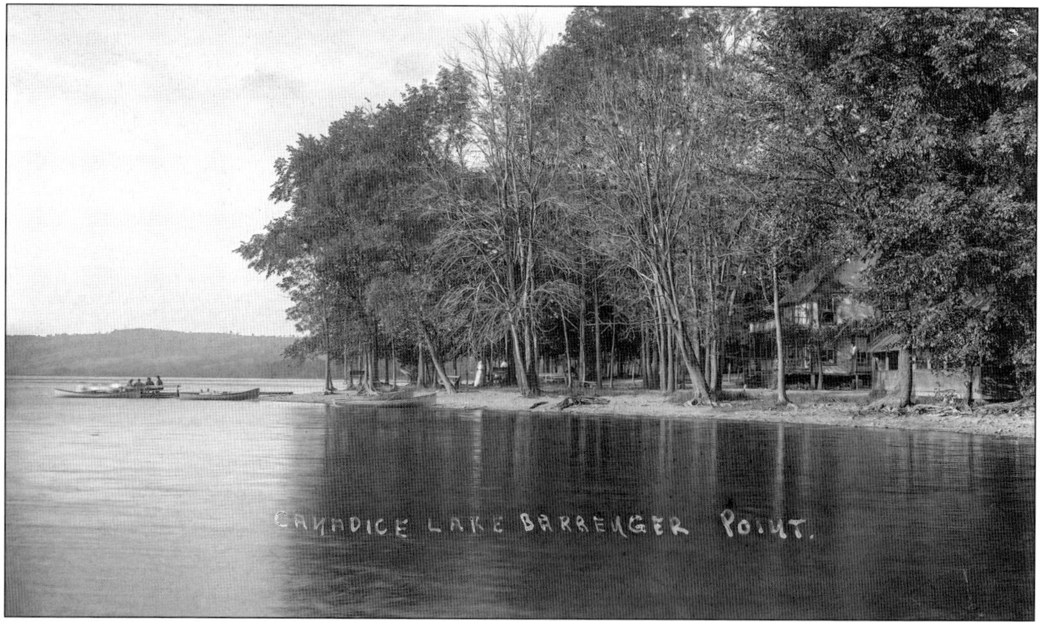

Barringer Point is noted for its trees and can be easily found today, although the structures are gone. Located on the north end of Canadice Lake, it held the Wyanoke resort cottages and some outbuildings. It is one of the most photographed spots on the lakes by Floyd Ingraham, who visited there often. A day trip to Barringer's could have included berry picking in the morning, a picnic lunch, and then the afternoon spent on the water before heading home by dark.

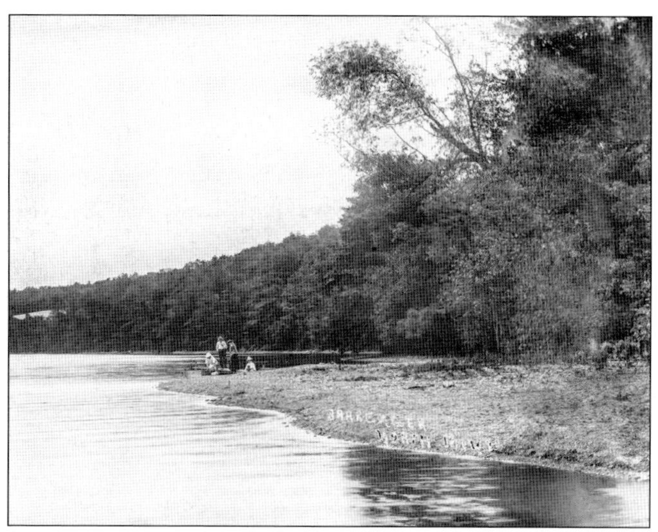

In 1905, Barringer Point's Wyanoke Resort held the annual Springwater Strawberry Festival, Ladies Aid Society picnics, church picnics, and family reunions. It was owned by E.H. Barringer of Springwater, son of William and Julia Barringer. E.H. Barringer was a farmer and carpenter. He owned property on Canadice Lake before 1903. In 1906, he purchased additional lakefront land that had been part of the Jonas Swartz estate and expanded his Wyanoke Resort. In 1911, he opened a feed mill and sawmill in Springwater.

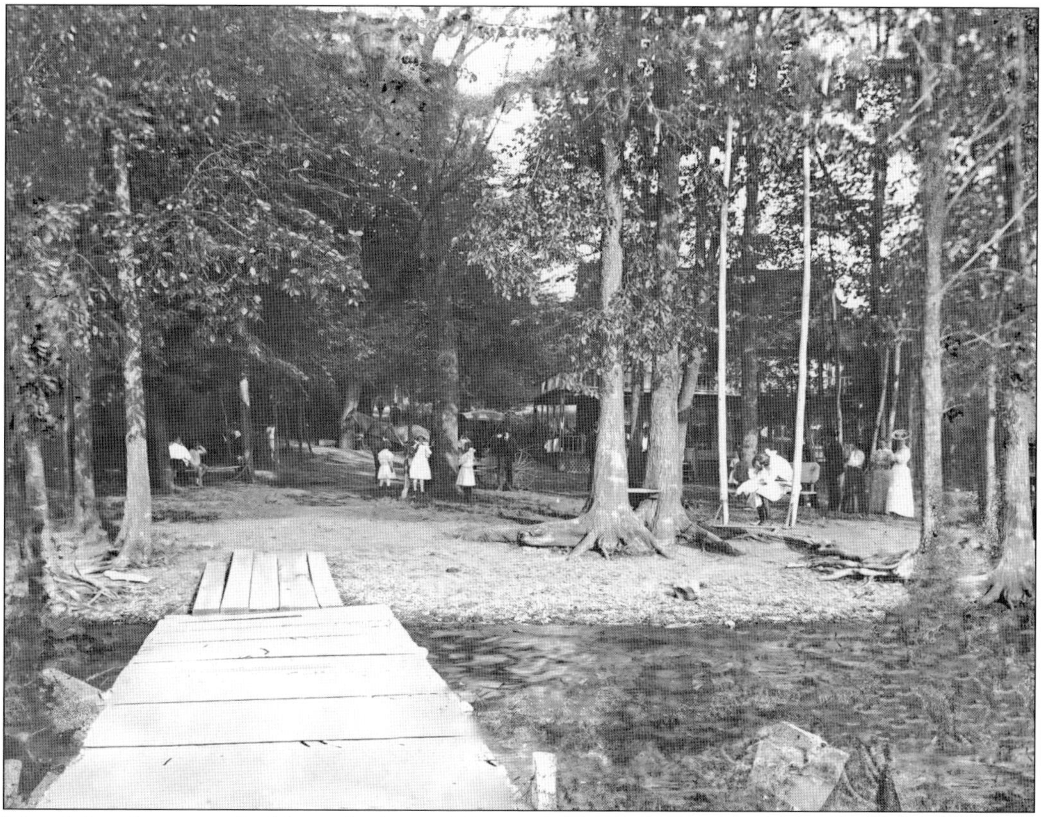

Most lakeside resorts had boat docks, and Barringer Point's Wyanoke Resort was easily spotted on the northern end along the western shoreline. It opened sometime in the late 1800s, and by 1898 was an active resort with cottages and a picnic grove. The *Cohocton Valley Times and Index* reported on July 25, 1900, that "The Wyanoke has become a very popular resort on account of its beautiful shade, its pleasant location, its large and commodious buildings and well-kept grounds. Boats are free to picnics and parties renting the grounds. Ice cream is served every Sunday."

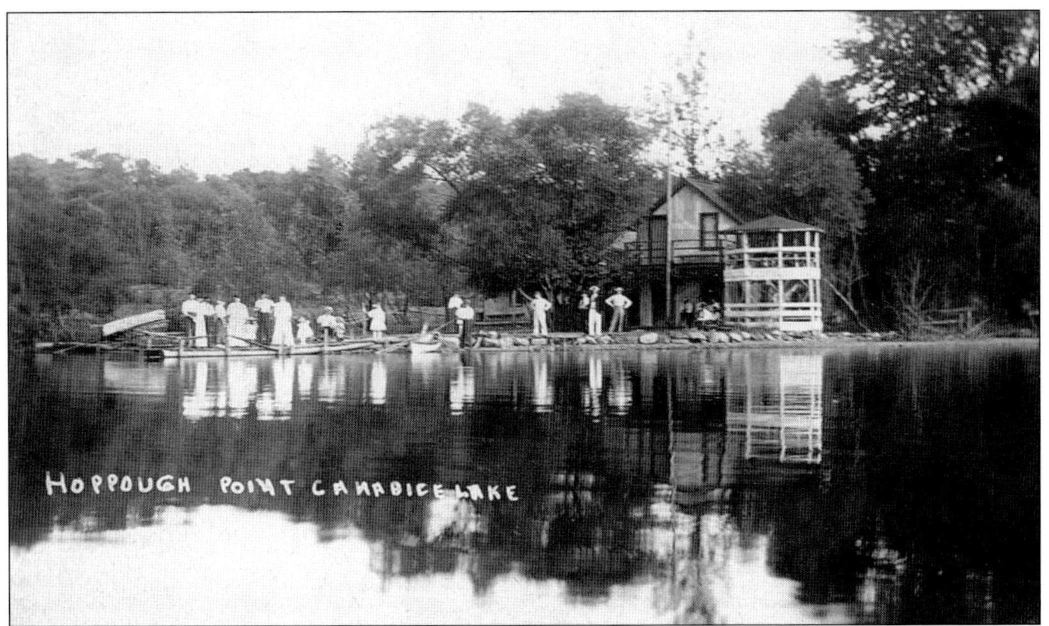

Many reunions and gatherings were held at Hoppough Point near the head of Canadice Lake in the early 20th century. Recognizable for its dock and two-tier gazebo, Hoppough Point had a boat livery and picnic grounds for large gatherings. Owned by Lewis F. Hoppough and later his son and daughter-in-law, Burdette and Ruth Hoppough, the Canadice Lake property was eventually purchased by the City of Rochester in 1937, and the cottages were removed or torn down.

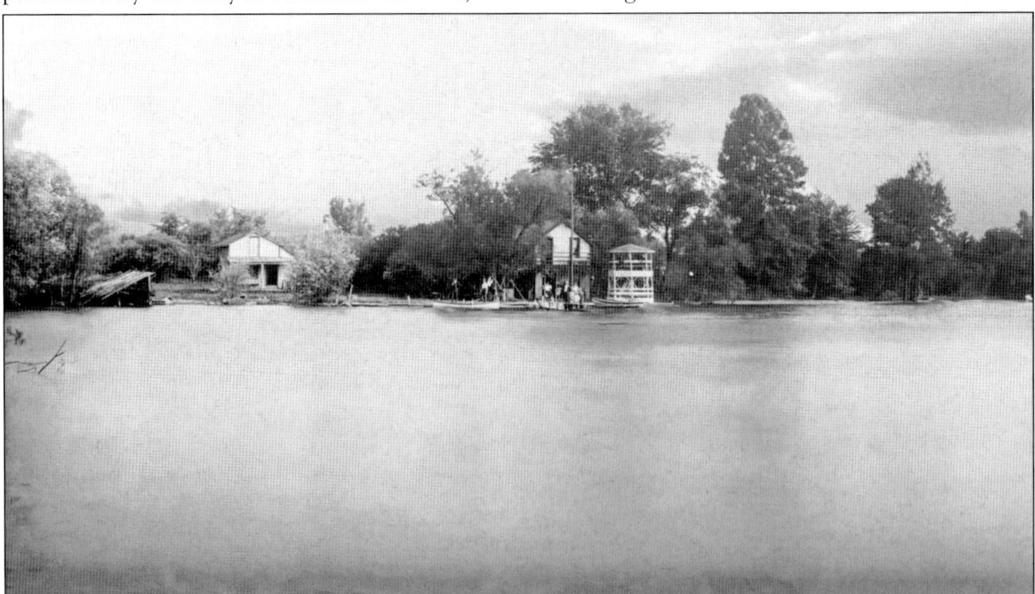

Lewis F. Hoppough owned land on Canadice Lake in Livonia that he operated as a farm. He built and ran the Hoppough resort for over 40 years. He was married to Adell Ingraham and had five children. The Hoppough family operated a mill in Hemlock in the late 1800s. Lewis Hoppough moved to Hemlock and owned a hardware store. He died in 1945. The annual reunion of the descendants of Lewis's parents, Frederick and Leah (Coykendall) Hoppough, was held at Hoppough Point.

Conrad Weinhart of Wayland owned the cottage at Elmhurst Point. The Weinhart family would fill their car with guests and drive to Canadice Lake for a weekend stay. In 1909, Conrad's son William arrived with a carload of friends and drove the automobile into the lake. He broke a wheel trying to get it out. A mechanic arrived in time to fix the Ford touring car so that the guests could return to Wayland.

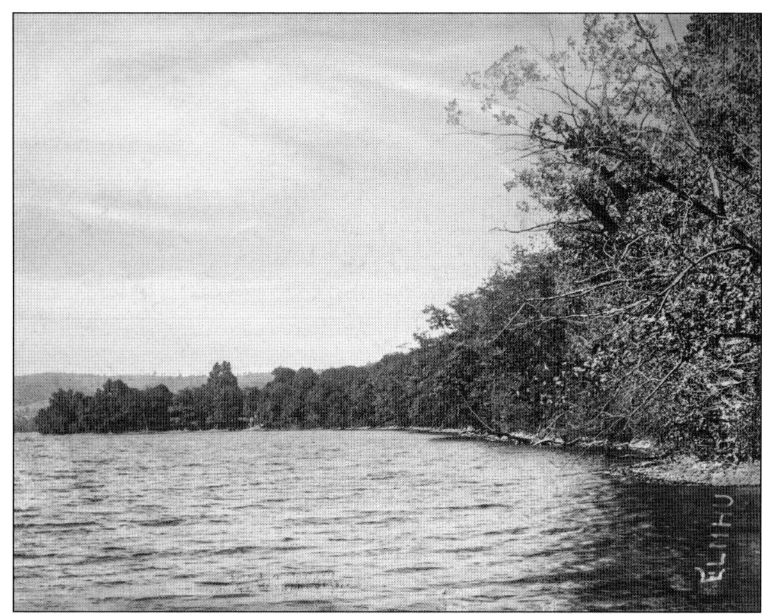

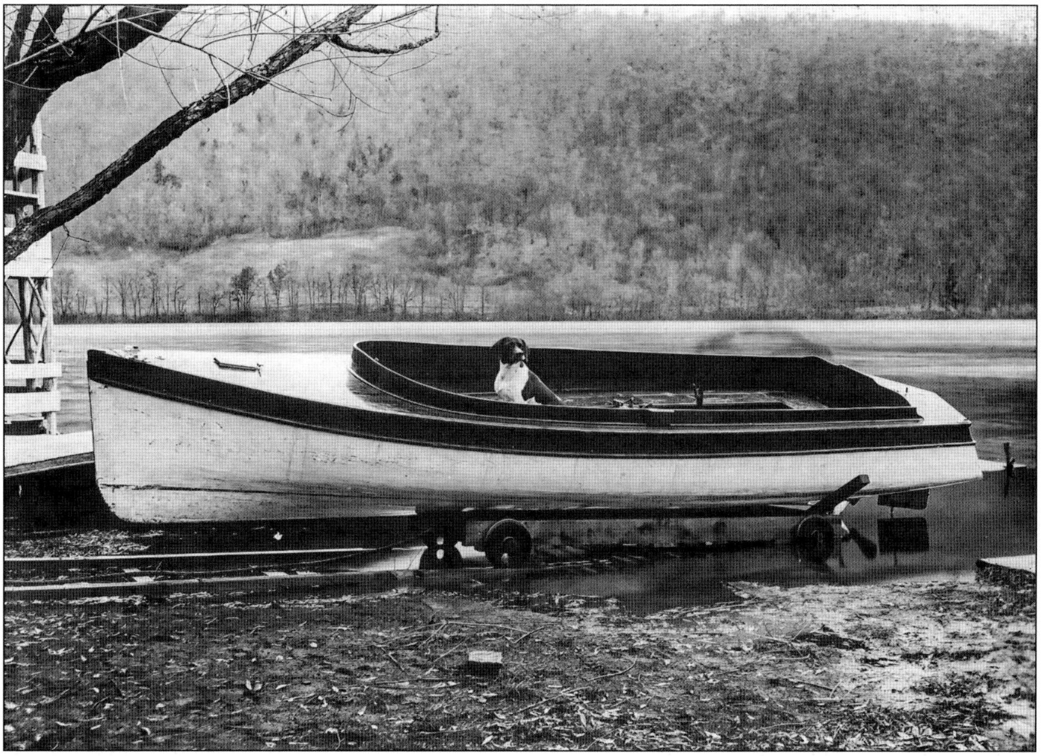

What appears to be a Johnson boat is pulled up to Hoppough Point on Canadice Lake. The dog is unidentified but has appeared in several of Ingraham's pictures. (Courtesy of Springwater–Webster Crossing Historical Society.)

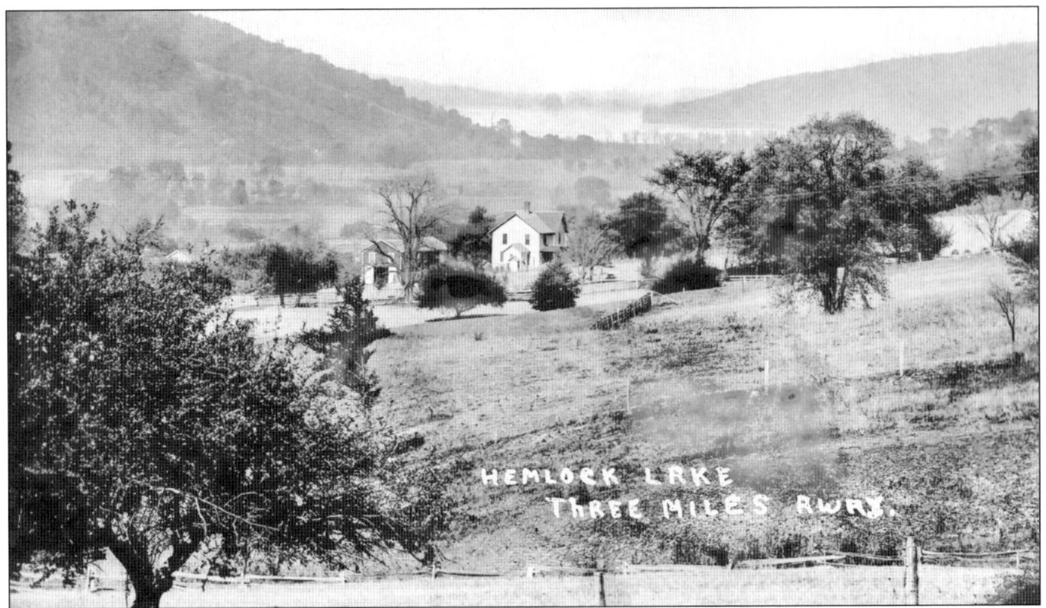

The first known settler near Hemlock Lake was Philip Short, who arrived in 1795. A man named Maloy, who was said to be a hermit, built a cabin on the lake around 1800. Others followed, and in Floyd Ingraham's day, many area residents had cabins and cottages at the lake. Logs were floated down Hemlock Lake or pulled over the ice. The first road was cleared along the shore in 1815. The home and farm seen here belonged to the Jackman family. It was later the home of the Cork family from 1902 to 1909. (Courtesy of Ron and Sharon Ingraham.)

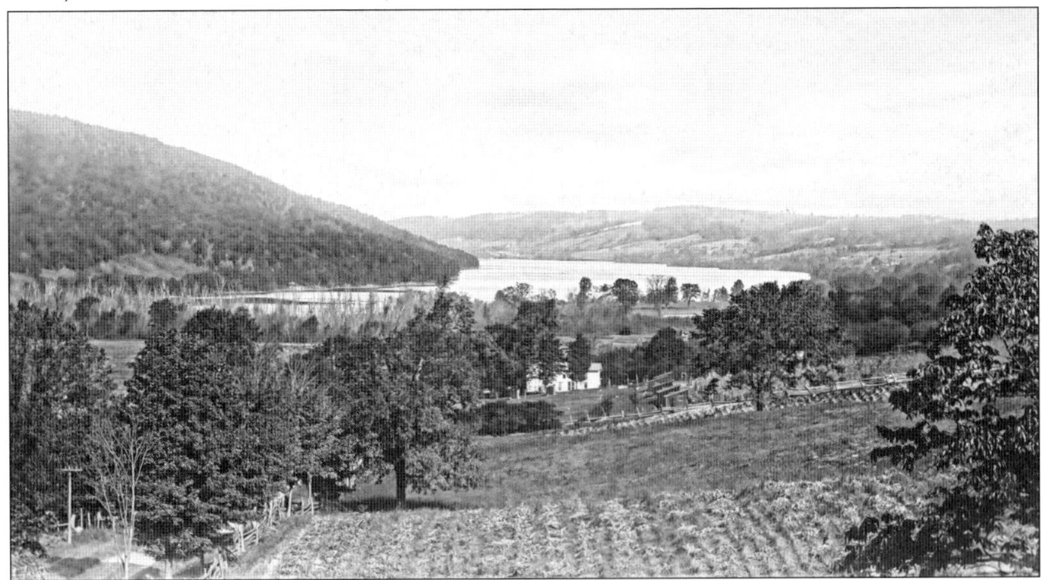

Hemlock Lake is in Livingston County, 25 miles south of Rochester. It is one of two Finger Lakes with undeveloped shorelines. By the mid-1900s, the City of Rochester had purchased Hemlock and Canadice Lakes and all the watershed property surrounding them as a way to protect water supply. Cottages were torn down or moved by their owners, and the banks of the lake grew over. Now, these lakes are enjoyed by nature lovers and anglers who appreciate the unspoiled environment and natural habitat that the lakes provide.

In 2010, the New York Department of Environmental Conservation purchased Hemlock Lake from the City of Rochester. Currently, the Hemlock Lake shoreline is undeveloped. It borders a 415-acre portion of the Hemlock-Canadice State Forest and includes old-growth trees, some of which are believed to be more than 500 years old.

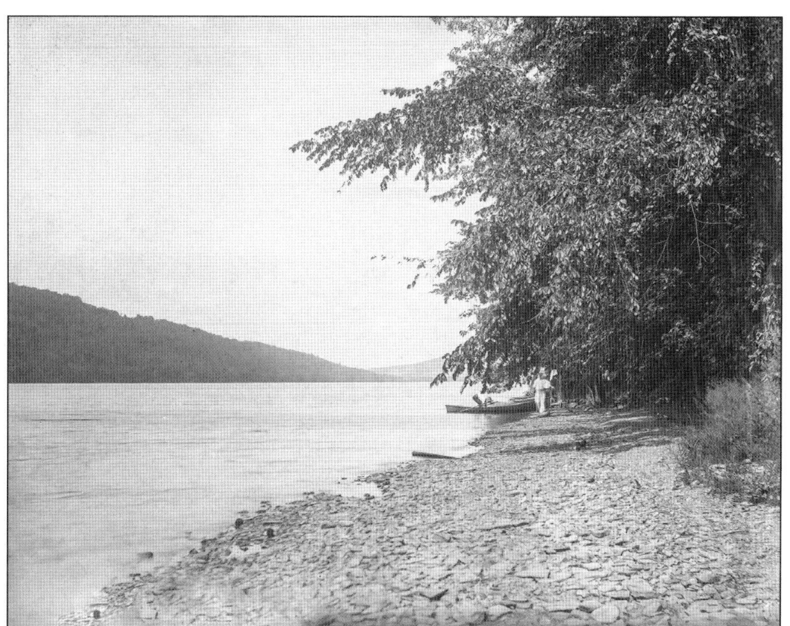

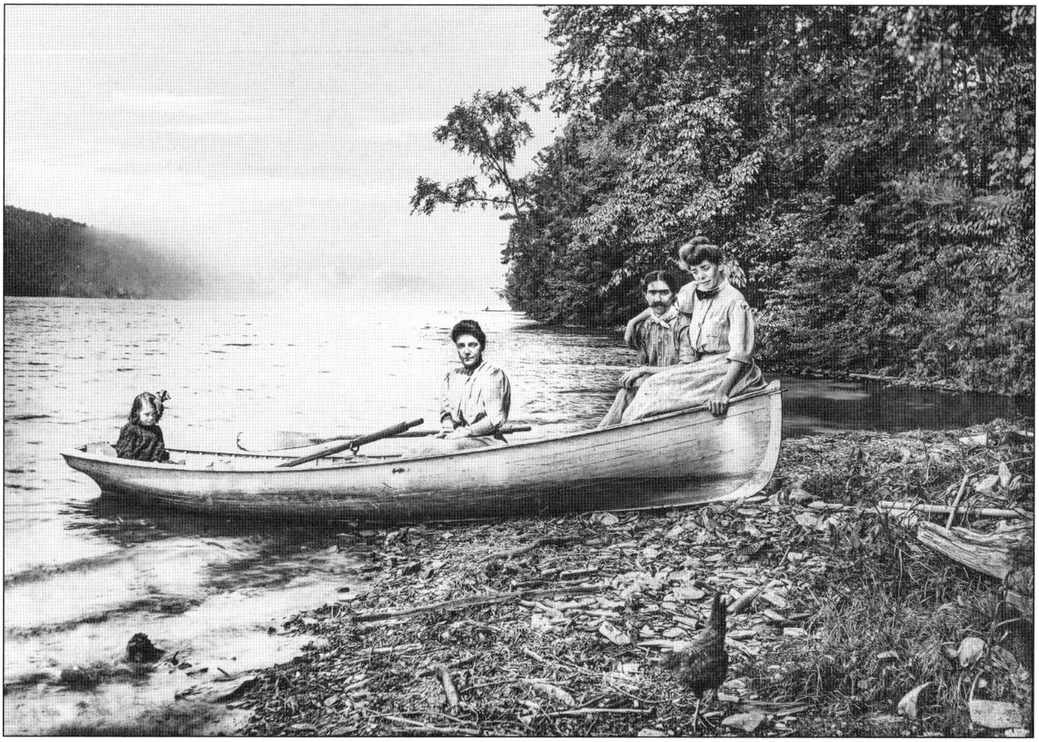

Portions of the lakes have narrow or steep shorelines, and others are easily accessible. This unidentified family gets ready to set out for a day on the water. This view is from Hemlock Lake's west side, looking south. Although at one time more than 100 cottages lined Hemlock Lake's shores, by the early 1930s, there were none. In 1930, the Scott family sold their 175-acre lakefront property on Hemlock Lake to the City of Rochester. They were the last family forced to sell their land, which included a cottage and vineyard.

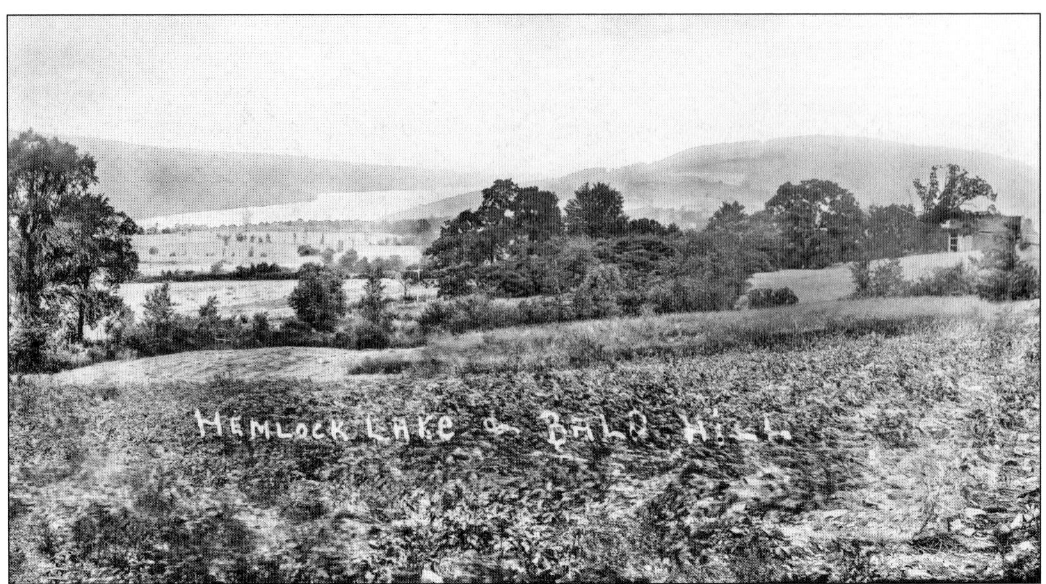

Bald Hill sits picturesquely on the east side of Hemlock Lake. On a long, hot day in the fields, farming families in Springwater could take a quick ride to Hemlock or Canadice Lake for a dip in the cool water. In 1914, James Barnes farmed on Bald Hill. Barnes was mentioned in the *Cohocton Valley Times and Index* as having caught an 18-pound pike that year from Hemlock Lake. Hemlock Lake is seen to the left of Bald Hill in this picture.

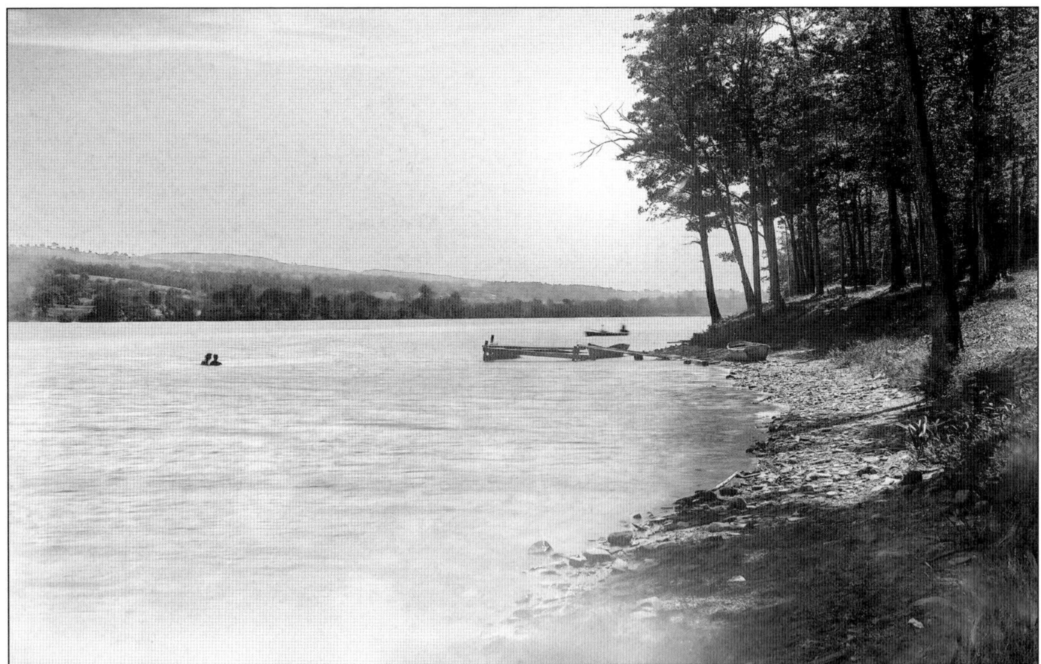

Swimmers are seen here just off a dock at Hemlock Lake. Hemlock Lake is seven miles long and only half a mile wide. In 1779, General Sullivan and his army crossed on the north end of Hemlock Lake, eliminating Native American settlements along the way. By the 1790s, Hemlock Lake was home to its first European settlers. They built their homes out of wooden slabs, and for a time, the place was known as "Slab City." By the 1900s, over 100 cottages lined the lake's shores.

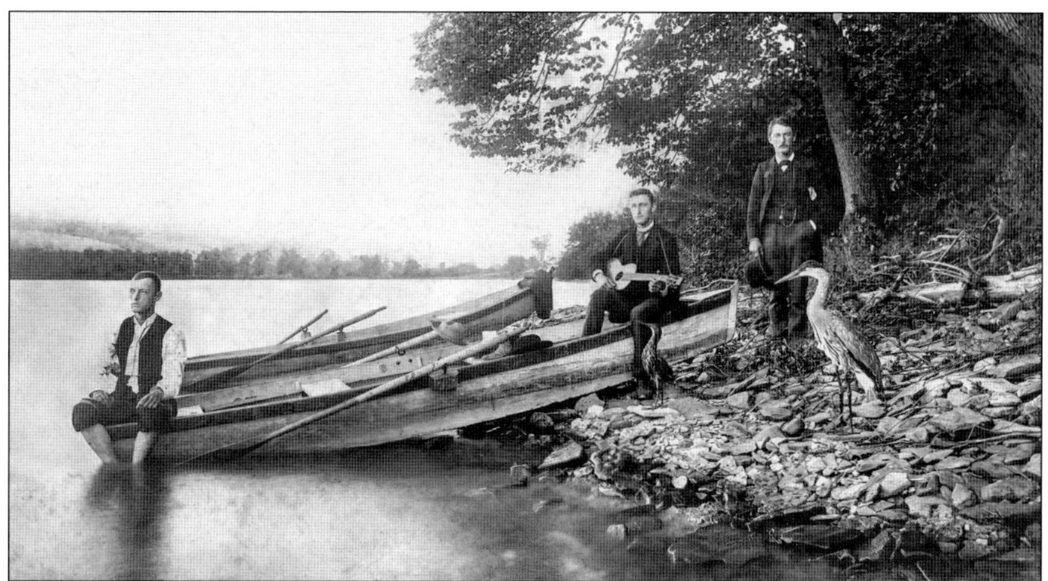

From left to right, Oscar, Edward, and Arthur Johnson pose at Johnson Point, near the head of Hemlock Lake on the west side. The brothers were three of the five sons of William and Angeline (Green) Johnson and cousins to famed boatbuilder Burdette "Bert" Johnson. Arthur married Malinda Robinson and was a farmer in Canadice. He was also a writer, a photographer with his brother Edward, and a loving grandfather to his daughter Florence's sons, Arthur and Havilah Toland. Havilah's memoir of his grandfather's tragic murder is described in the introduction to his book *Springwater and Surrounds: Last Quarter of the 20th Century*. (Courtesy of Springwater–Webster Crossing Historical Society.)

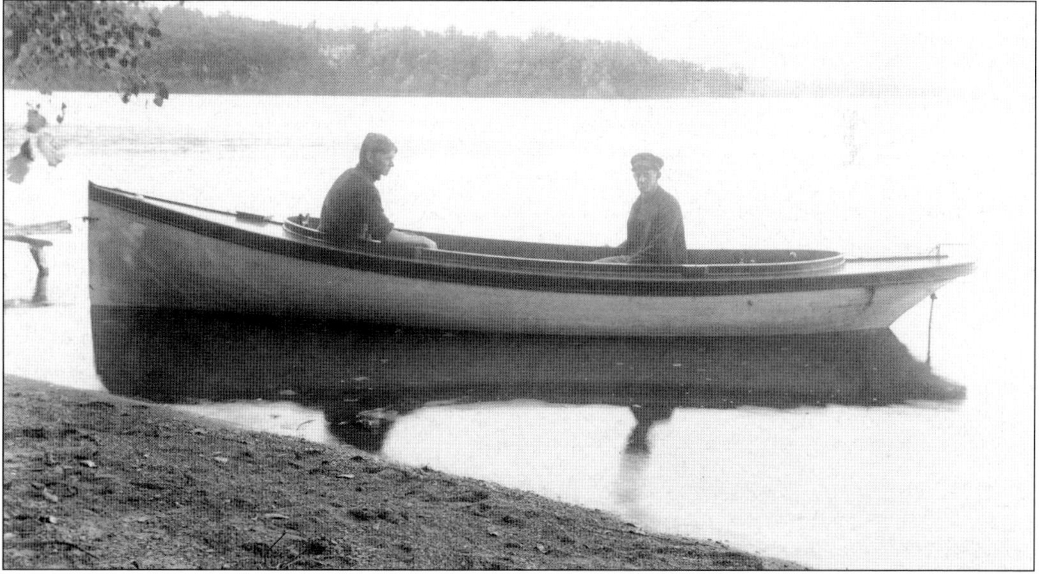

Bert Johnson and sons were famed boatbuilders, and one of their boats is pictured here. Bert Johnson was one of the first in the western Finger Lakes region to launch gasoline-powered boats. Today, boat motors must be no more than 10 horsepower, and watercraft must be less than 17 feet long. Canoes, kayaks, and rowboats still carve ripples on Hemlock Lake's surface. (Courtesy of Springwater–Webster Crossing Historical Society.)

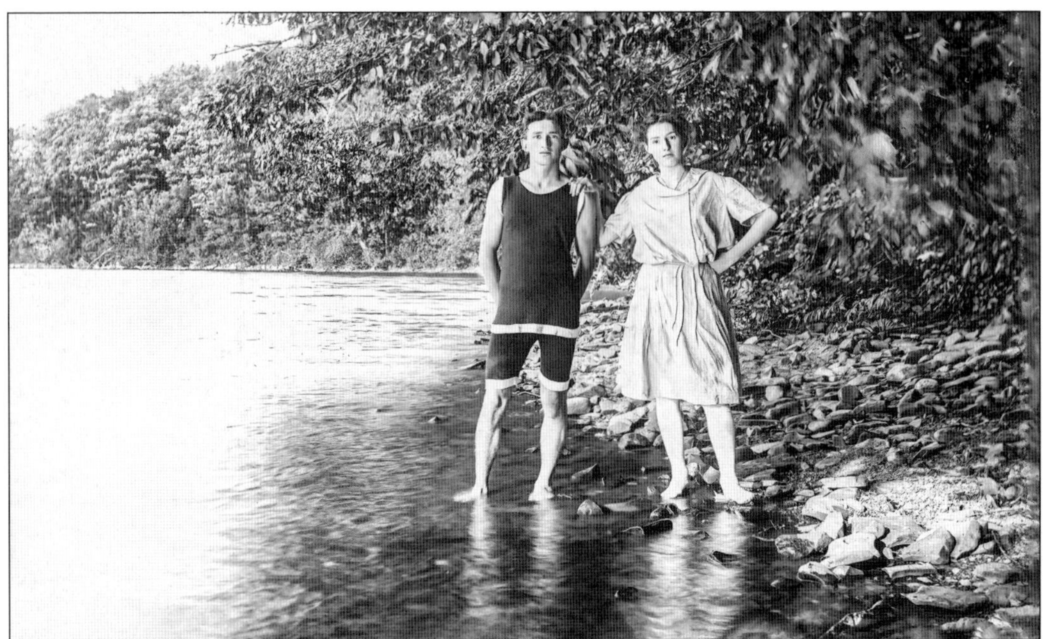

Leon and Gertrude Ford stand on the shore of Hemlock Lake, ready for a swim. The siblings were the children of Marvin and Carrie Ford and the cousins of photographer Floyd Ingraham. Swimsuits of the early 20th century were designed for modesty. Women wore loose tops that resembled a dress of today. Large bloomers were worn beneath. Early swimsuits were made from flannel fabric that was opaque when wet and sturdy enough to not rise with the water. Men wore long shorts and shirts.

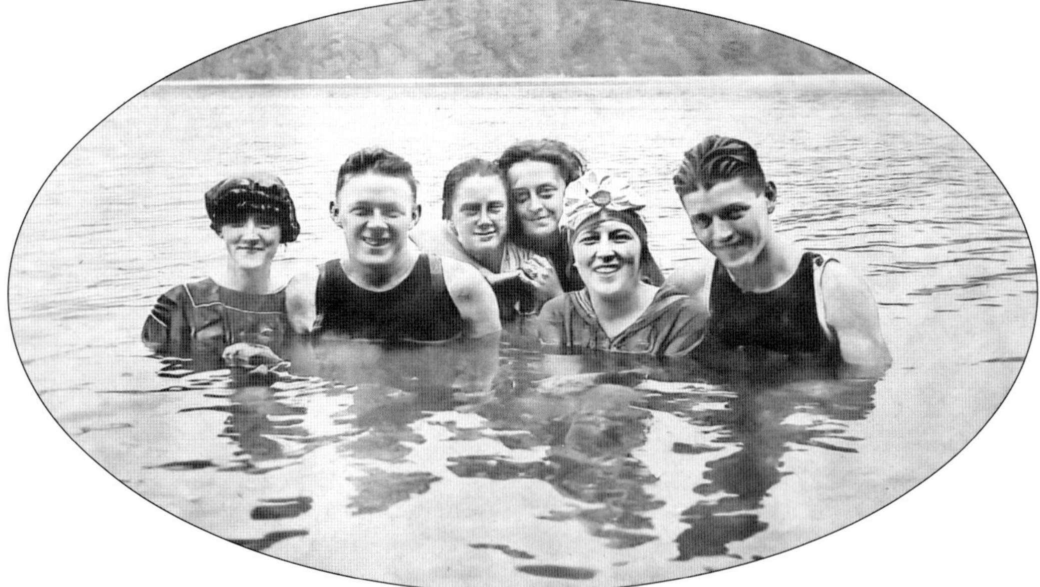

These swimmers enjoy a dip in the waters of Canadice Lake. Young people spent their leisure time outdoors at the lake in the warmer months. They not only enjoyed swimming, but boating, fishing, picnicking, and camping on the beautiful lakes near their home. (Courtesy of Springwater–Webster Crossing Historical Society.)

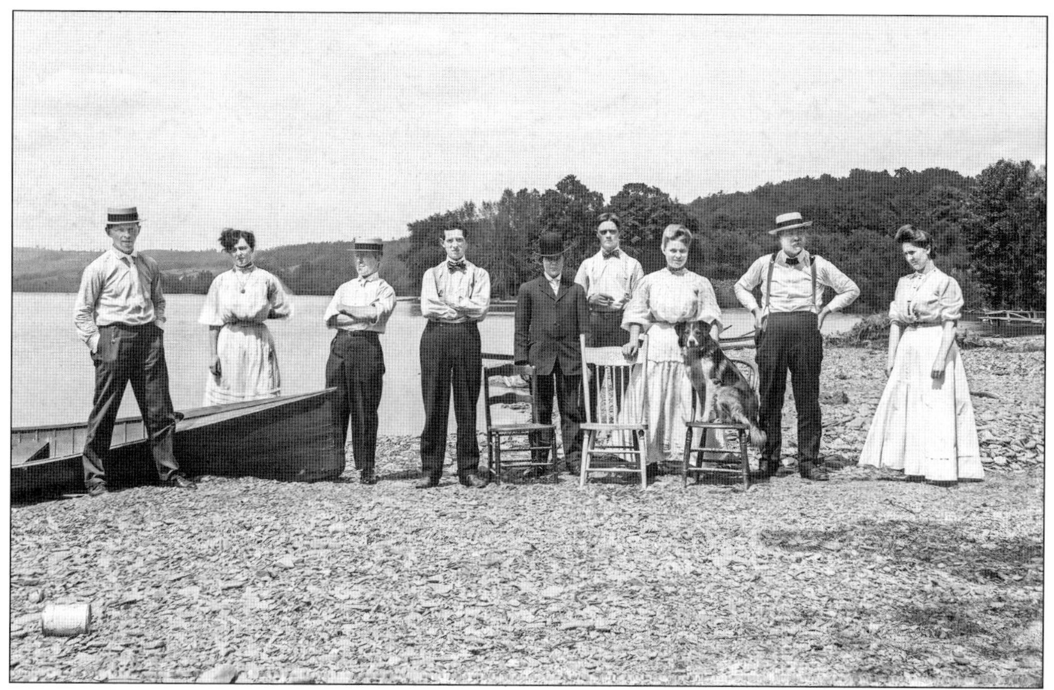

None of the individuals here have been identified. Believed to be on the shore of Canadice Lake, a cottage is assumed to be nearby as these chairs were pulled down to the shore. Ingraham enjoyed using props in his photographs, and that did not end outside of his home studio. Animals were often purposefully placed in the images. Chickens, horses, cats, and dogs, like the one seen here, all had their pictures taken by Ingraham.

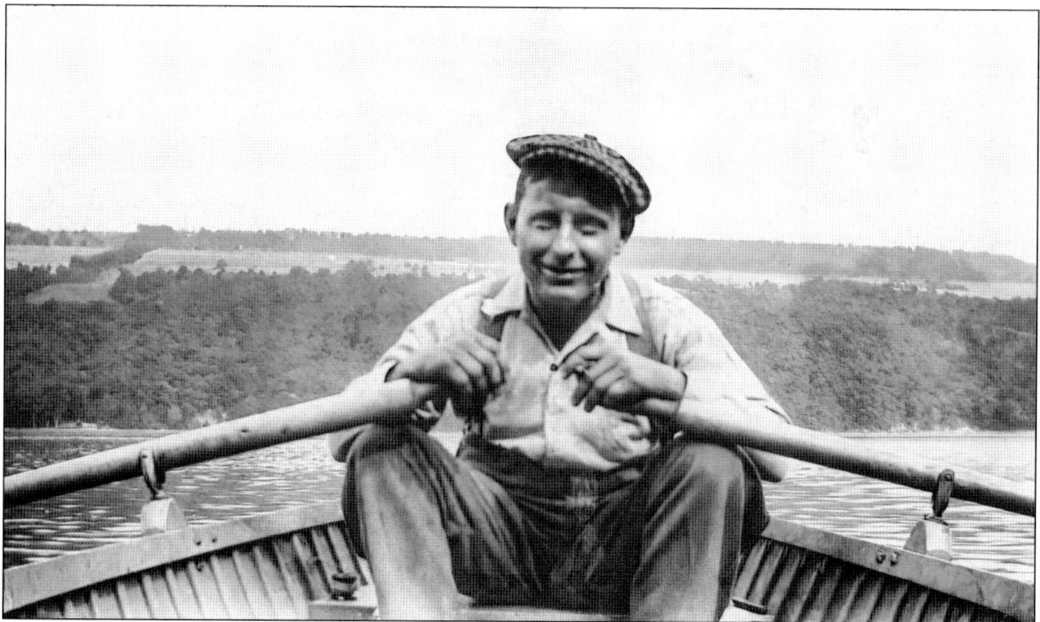

Frank Briggs West was born in Springwater. The son of James and Esther West, he never married. Like many other residents of the Finger Lakes region, when he was not working he could be found in his boat on the lakes. (Courtesy of Springwater–Webster Crossing Historical Society.)

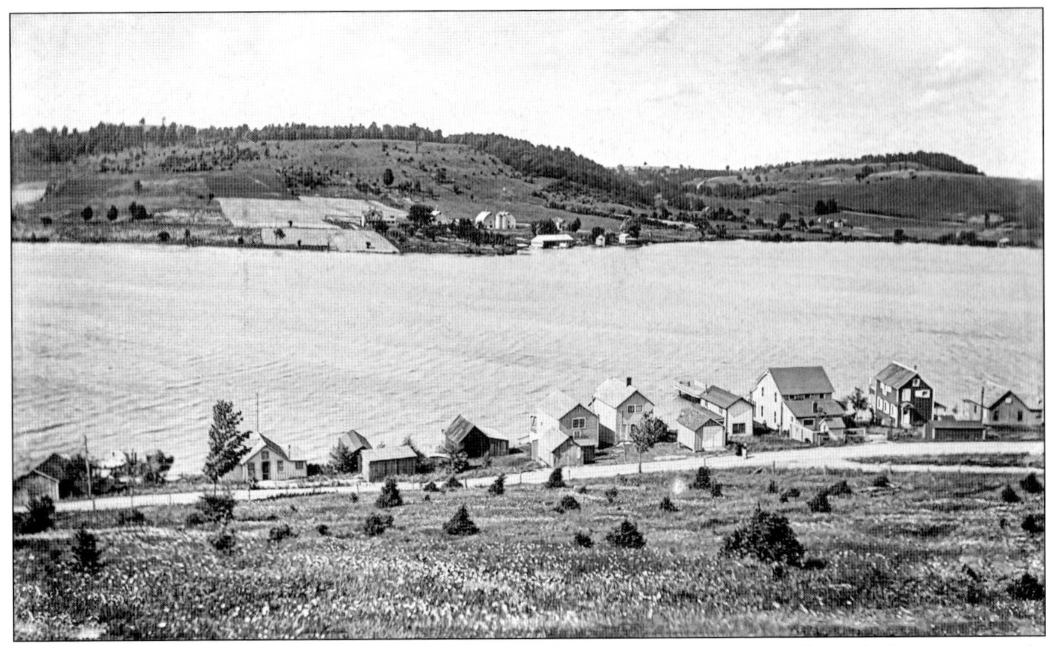

Located in Allegany County about 60 miles southwest of Springwater, Cuba Lake is primarily within the town of Cuba, New York. Although not considered one of the Finger Lakes, Cuba Lake has an area of 445 acres. Some of the cottages seen here are still standing on its shoreline.

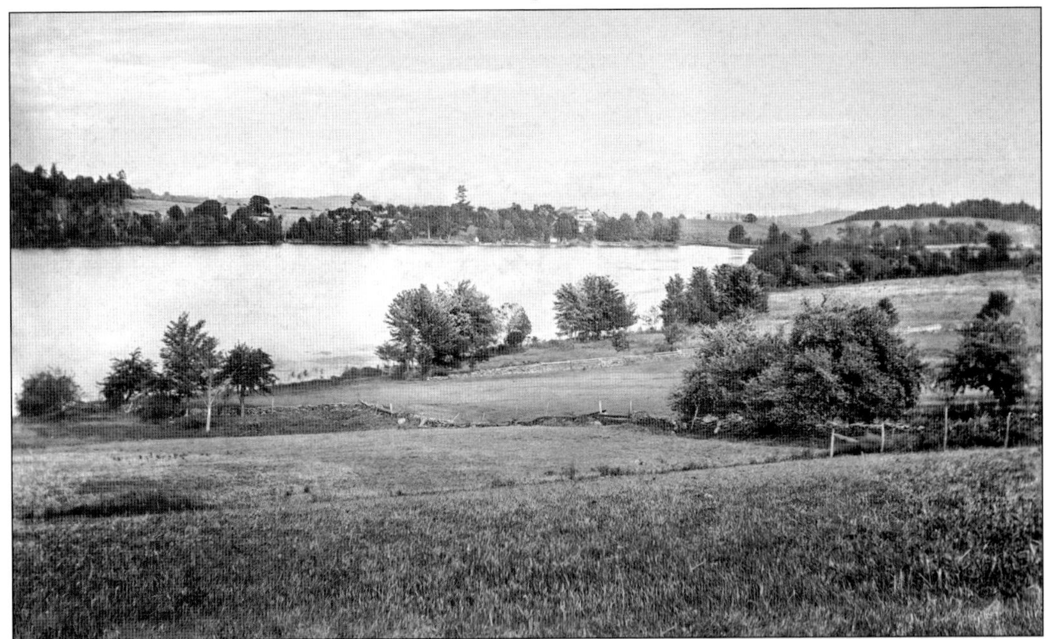

Though this lake has not been identified, many believe it to be Conesus, the westernmost Finger Lake. It is one of the smaller Finger Lakes, and at a depth of 66 feet, it is the second shallowest. It is about eight miles in length, and at its widest point is only one mile wide. Conesus Lake has a mysterious history with smooth turtle-like stones and a legend about a phantom some have claimed to see on the lake said to be Native American chief Big Tree, a leader in making treaties until his death in 1778. Conesus comes from the Native American word for "always beautiful."

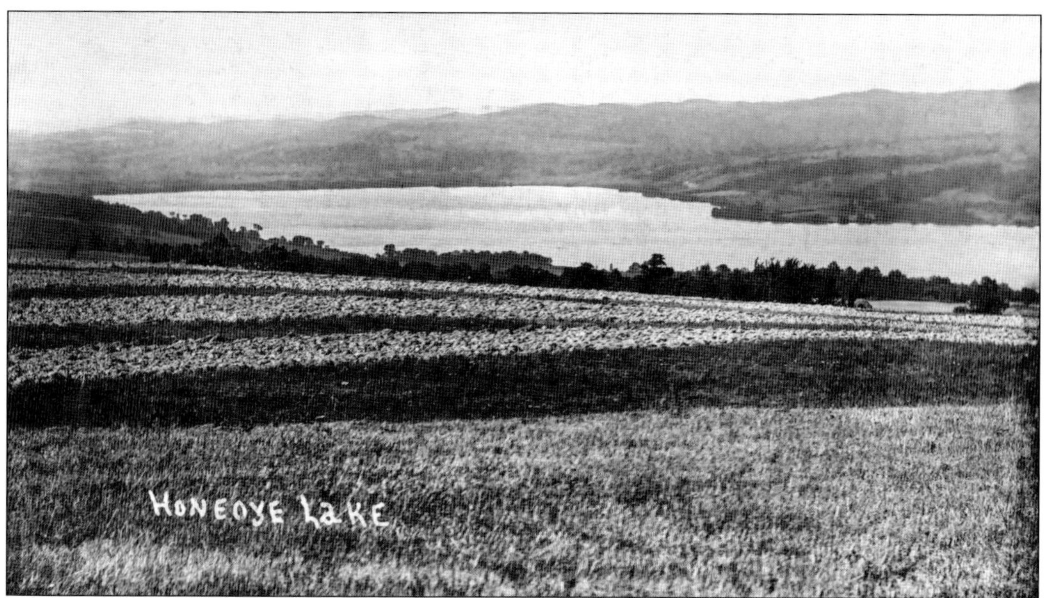

Honeoye retained its cottages, unlike neighboring Canadice and Hemlock Lakes. Numerous Native American settlements came and went from Honeoye's shores. Its name comes from the Seneca word *ha-ne-a-yah*, which means "lying finger" or "where the finger lies." Situated between Canadice and Canandaigua Lakes, Honeoye Lake is the 10th in size of 11 Finger Lakes, being only four and a half miles long and less than a mile wide. It is the shallowest of the lakes, with a maximum depth of only 30 feet.

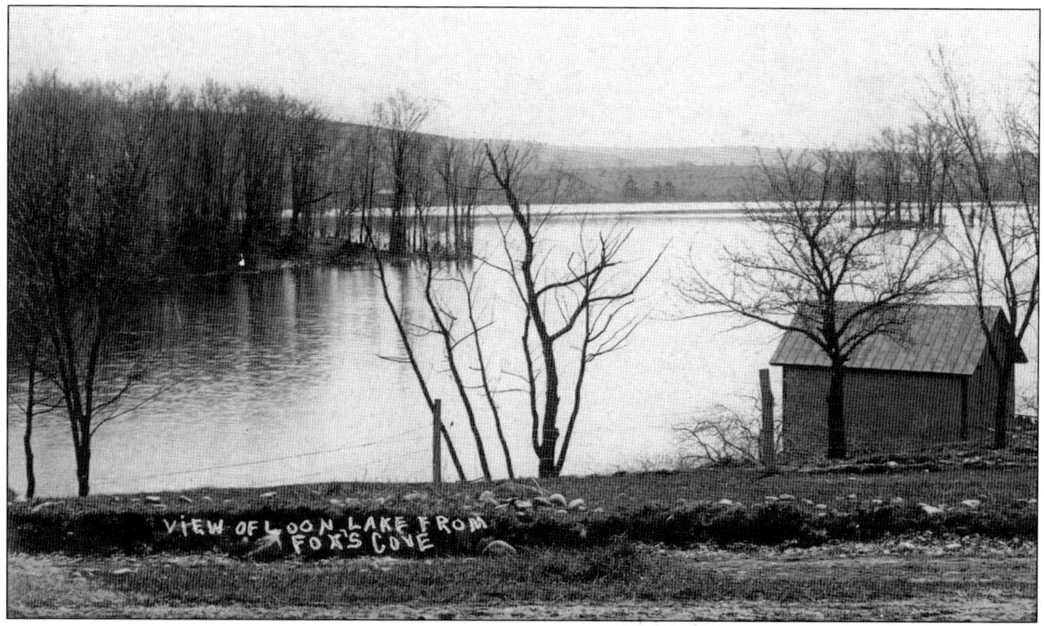

Loon Lake is in Steuben County, outside of Wayland. It is just over three miles long and covers 141 acres. Although not one of the major Finger Lakes, it enjoys the same natural beauty. Four US presidents visited Loon Lake: Benjamin Harrison, Grover Cleveland, William McKinley, and Theodore Roosevelt. Today, most of Loon lake is privately owned, with limited public access. (Courtesy of Ron and Sharon Ingraham.)

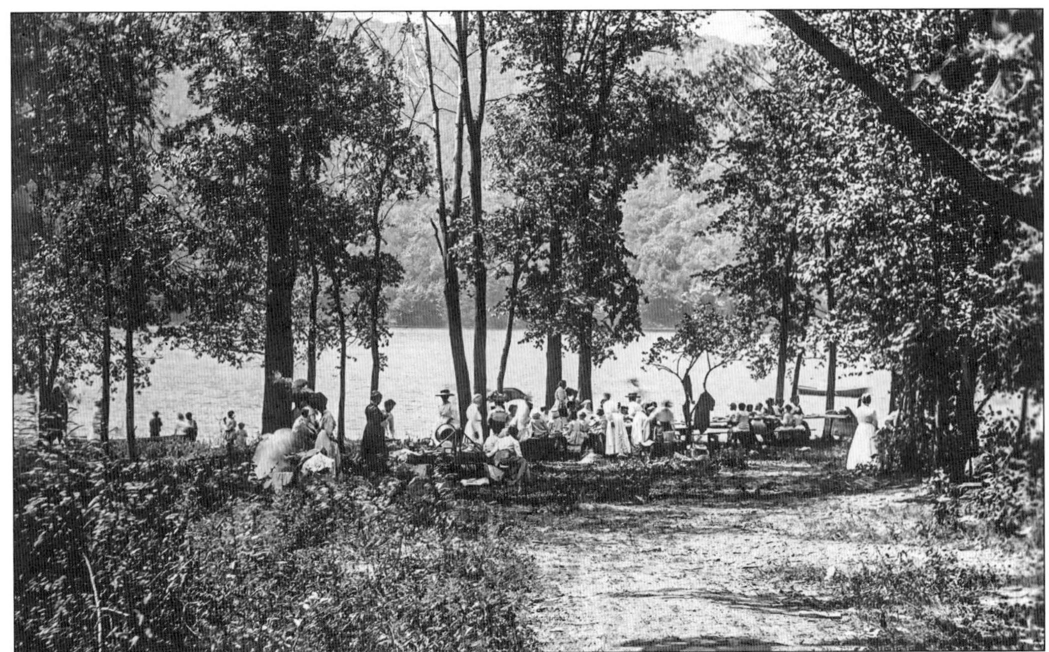

Springwater's Advent church congregation is seen here picnicking at Barringer Point on Canadice Lake. The Advent church was one that Floyd Ingraham and his parents attended. It held a picnic annually and also participated in Union Picnics with the Presbyterian and Methodist churches. (Courtesy of Springwater–Webster Crossing Historical Society.)

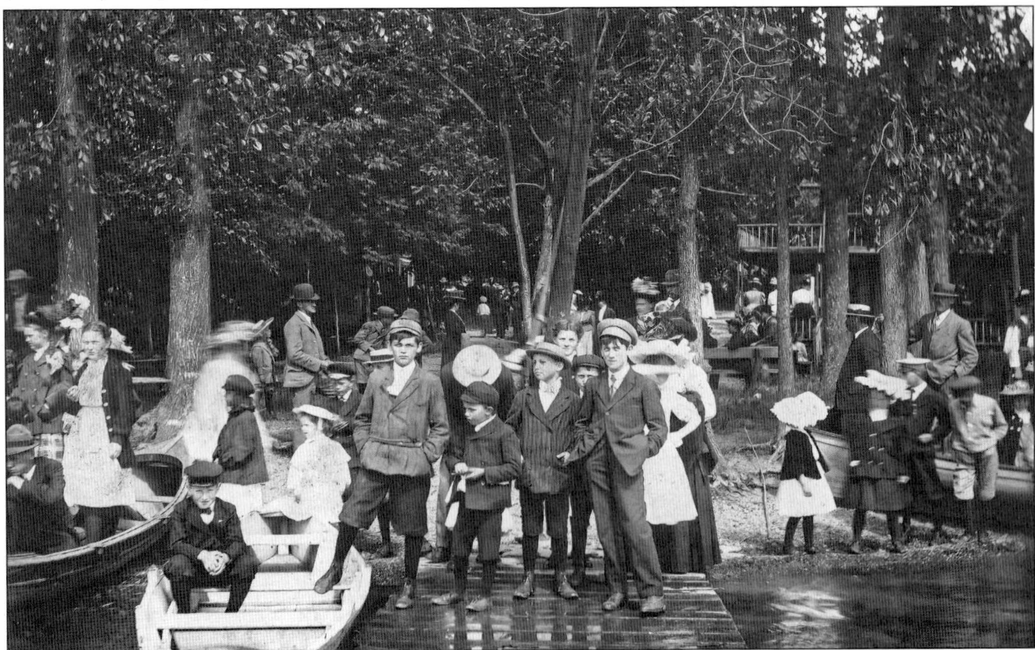

Another picture of the Advent church picnic on Barringer Point shows young boys ready to sail off in boats. In summer months, church meetings were often held outside, and food and fellowship followed. Weekly, the local newspapers were filled with announcements of picnics and gatherings at the lakes in the summer months. (Courtesy of Springwater–Webster Crossing Historical Society.)

A prank was underway with 17-year-old Anna Cork, who was camping with friends, at the center of it. They are, from left to right, Gertrude Ford, Anna, Veda McClellan, and Leon Ford. A scene from this same 1908 camping trip at Canadice Lake is pictured on the cover.

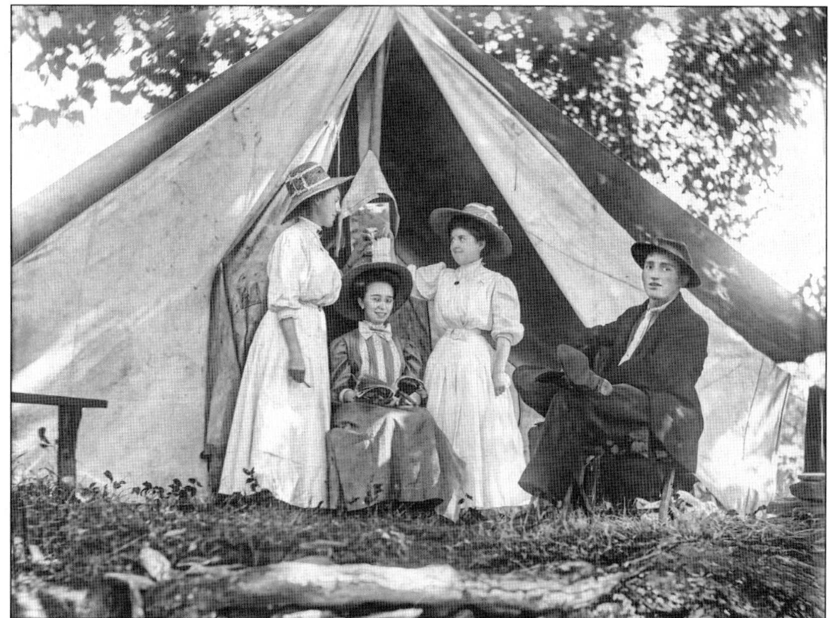

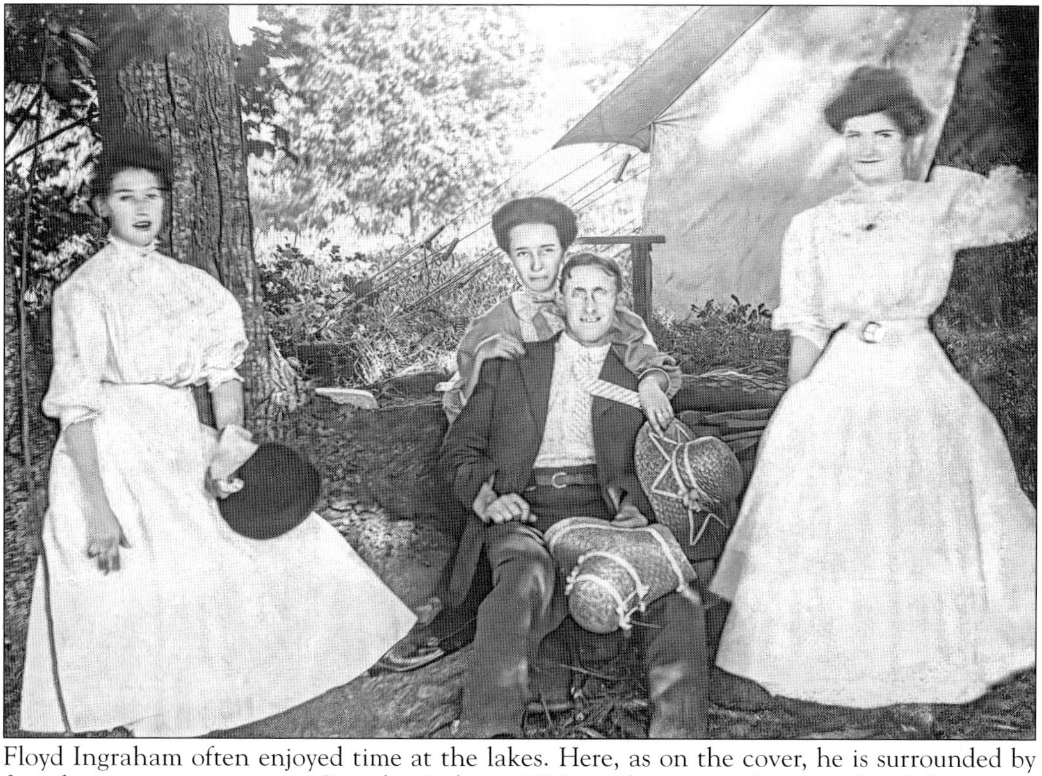

Floyd Ingraham often enjoyed time at the lakes. Here, as on the cover, he is surrounded by friends on a camping trip at Canadice Lake in 1908. In this image, Anna Cork is behind him. She would become his wife a year later. Standing to their left is Gertrude Ford, Floyd's cousin, and to their right, Veda McClellan, a friend. Although Ingraham would die just over a decade later, the photographic legacy he left behind captured more than just personal memories of a life well lived. It preserved forever a time in history and a place he loved.

Bibliography

Cohocton Valley Times and Index. Cohocton, NY.
Conover, George S. *History of Ontario County, New York*. Syracuse, NY: D. Mason & Co., 1893.
Dansville Express. Dansville, NY.
Democrat and Chronicle. Rochester, NY.
Fultonhistory.com or Old Fulton NY Post Cards. Compiled and published by Thomas Triniski, 1999.
Genesee Country Express. Dansville, NY.
Ingraham, Ron. Personal interviews. 2019–2021.
Livonia Gazette. Livonia, NY.
Mack, Clara. *Thoughts by a Country Woman*. Springwater, NY: Self-published, 1950.
Naples Record. Naples, NY.
New York State Archives. New York State Birth Index 1881–1942. New York County Marriage Records 1847–1849, 1907–1936. Lehi, UT: Ancestry.com Operations, 2016–2018.
New York State Archives. New York State Census 1905–1925. Provo, UT: Ancestry.com Operations, 2012.
Robinson, J. Reid. A *History: The Township of Springwater*. Springwater, NY: The Town of Springwater, 1997.
Smith, James H. *History of Livingston County, New York with Illustrations and Biographical Sketches*. Syracuse, NY: D. Mason & Co., 1881.
Social Security Administration. US Social Security Death Index, 1935–2014. Provo, UT: Ancestry.com Operations, 2014.
Springwater Enterprise. Springwater, NY.
Springwater Review. Springwater, NY.
Springwater Star. Springwater, NY.
Steuben Courier. Bath, NY.
Toland, Havilah, with contributions by Judy Tripp-Neu. *Springwater and Surrounds*. Springwater, NY: Livingston County Historian's Office, 2018.
US Bureau of the Census. 1850–1940 United States Federal Census. Provo, UT: Ancestry.com Operations, 2012.
US City Directories, 1822–1995. Provo, UT: Ancestry.com Operations, 2011.
Valley News. Springwater, NY.
Walbridge, Orson D. *Early History of the Town of Springwater, Livingston County, N.Y.* Springwater, NY: H.J. Niles, 1887.
Wayland Register (1897–1970). Wayland, NY.

About the Organizations

I am deeply grateful to the following historical societies and organizations for their support and research assistance. Their contributions to the preservation of history in the western Finger Lakes region is to be commended.

Springwater–Webster Crossing Historical Society
8130 Route 15, Springwater, New York
www.springwaterny.org/springwater-webster-crossing-histor

Livingston County Historian's Office
5 Murray Hill Drive, Mt. Morris, New York
www.livingstoncounty.us/162/County-Historian

Little Lakes Community Center and History Room
4705 South Main Street, Hemlock, New York
littlelakesny.org
www.hemlockandcanadicelakes.com